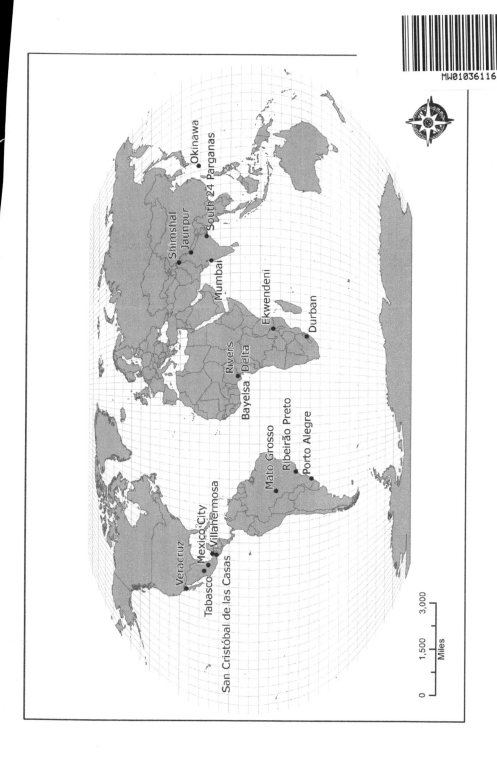

Okinawa

South 24 Parganas

Shimshal

Jaunpur

Mumbai

Ekwendeni

Durban

Rivers

Bayelsa Delta

Mato Grosso

Ribeirão Preto

Porto Alegre

Veracruz

Mexico City

Villahermosa

Tabasco

San Cristóbal de las Casas

0   1,500   3,000

Miles

CONTESTING DEVELOPMENT

At a time when the development promise is increasingly in question, with dwindling social gains, the vision of modernity is losing its legitimacy and coherence. This moment is observable through the lens of critical struggles of those who experience disempowerment, displacement, and development contradictions.

In this book, *case studies,* globally situated, serve as an effective means of teaching key concepts and theories in the sociology of development. This collection of cases, all original and never previously published and with framing essays by Philip McMichael, has been written with this purpose in mind.

An important additional feature is that the book as a whole reveals the limiting assumptions of development and suggests alternate conditions of possibility for social existence in the world today. In that sense, the book pushes the boundaries of "thinking about development" and makes an important theoretical contribution to the literature.

Philip McMichael is Professor of Development Sociology at Cornell University. His research focuses on the politics of globalization, agrarian struggles, and climate change. Author of *Development and Social Change*, he recently prepared a report for UNRISD on the food crisis, and works with La Vía Campesina and the food sovereignty movement.

ROUTLEDGE TITLES OF RELATED INTEREST

The Social Issues Collection: A Routledge / University Readers Custom Library for Teaching www.socialissuescollection.com

The Transnational Studies Reader by Peggy Leavitt and Sanjeev Khagram

The Global Architect by Donald McNeill

The Philippines: Mobilities, Identities, Globalization by James A. Tyner

China and Globalization, Second Edition by Doug Guthrie

Iberian Worlds by Gary McDonogh

Military Legacies by James A. Tyner

Global Gender Research, edited by Christine Bose and Minjeong Kim

Making Transnational Feminism by Millie Thayer

City Life from Jakarta to Dakar by Abdoumaliq Simone

Operation Gatekeeper And Beyond by Joe Nevins

Disrupted Cities: When Infrastructure Fails, edited by Stephen Graham

The Internet and Social Inequalities by James Witte and Susan Mannon

CONTESTING DEVELOPMENT

CRITICAL STRUGGLES
FOR SOCIAL CHANGE

Edited by

PHILIP McMICHAEL

Cornell University

Taylor & Francis Group

NEW YORK AND LONDON

First published 2010
by Routledge
270 Madison Avenue, New York, NY 10016

Simultaneously published in the UK
by Routledge
2 Park Square, Milton Park, Abingdon, Oxon OX14 4RN

Routledge is an imprint of the Taylor & Francis Group, an informa business

© 2010 Taylor & Francis

Typeset in Minion by EvS Communication Networx, Inc.

Library of Congress Cataloging in Publication Data
Contesting development : critical struggles for social change / edited by Philip McMichael.
p. cm. — (Contemporary sociological perspectives)
Includes bibliographical references and index.
[etc.]
1. Economic development—Sociological aspects—Case studies. 2. Social change—Case studies.
I. McMichael, Philip.
HD75.C662 2010
306.3—dc22
2009030857

ISBN 10: 0-415-87331-2 (hbk)
ISBN 10: 0-415-87332-0 (pbk)
ISBN 10: 0-203-86092-6 (ebk)

ISBN 13: 978-0-415-87331-4 (hbk)
ISBN 13: 978-0-415-87332-1 (pbk)
ISBN 13: 978-0-203-86092-2 (ebk)

CONTENTS

of shackdweller communities, as cities without citizens, who have theorized and reframed the meaning of (a community-based) citizenship, politicizing our understanding of what democratic development might mean.

Brings into question our commonsense association of education with development. Rural villagers in northern India experience and evaluate modern education in contradictory and ambiguous ways. While education is viewed as a solution to the "problem" of agrarian decline, educated youth fail to gain employment, yet have difficulty returning to rural livelihoods, thus devaluing the moral economy of village community. This essay questions the foreclosure of sustainable rural livelihoods by the neo-liberal development model, given the failure of this model to provide jobs for educated citizens (and urban-industrial incapacity to absorb those expelled from rural areas), despite narratives of social mobility through educated market participation.

In the context of the debate over nature protection and sustainability, the chapter examines development for whom? International conservation agencies in northern Pakistan have pushed for converting village pastures into national parks and trophy hunting reserves, and tried to compel local communities to abandon the practice of livestock grazing. This model of conservation and development has been successfully resisted by Shimshali villagers, who argue that it reflects a Western tendency to divorce nature from society, reinforces state control and abuse of resources, and undermines local livelihoods as well as ecologies by prioritizing the desires of elite tourists.

Examines the experience of "democratic transition" in Nigeria and Mexico, whose globally valued extractive resources (oil in particular) overshadow national politics. This essay shows how global market considerations influence (and undermine) electoral processes in these petro-states, through financial risk assessments that affect currency values and create the potential for political crisis. At the same time elections serve to legitimate export-oriented regimes. As a consequence, the manipulation of electoral processes in the context of popular resistance to repressive "resource-extractive" states highlights the ongoing struggles to realize real, substantive democracy and social justice.

Struggles of the disempowered offer perspective on development claims, and new ways of thinking about social change—approaches that question the development narrative and the market episteme, advocating for the right to represent and realize different ways of living in this world, and transcending the development impasse.

PREFACE

This book is about development from an unusual angle—from that of its misfits, or market casualties. It appears that development is now at a crossroads because of the combined effect of financial, energy, food, and climate crises. While these crises have shaken confidence in the future, faith in the market as ensuring the best means of social reproduction and enabling human aspirations remains unshaken. The world is grasping for solutions, but more often than not from the market-centric perspective that has produced these problems in the first place. Part of the problem is the difficulty in thinking outside of this market-centric box, simply because its assumptions seem like common sense—even if the benefits of a market culture are shared unequally. Protagonists in this book contest these assumptions.

Development prescriptions advocate market solutions to all manner of social and ecological problems. And yet there is substantial evidence that these are not optimal solutions by any means, and that there are other, emergent, solutions. We know this from observing the critical struggles of people disempowered in the process of development.

These are the excluded, the displaced, and the dispossessed—understood as "capitalism's externalities." They are, however, part of development, but not the visible part for whom development represents opportunity or freedom in one form or another. Their invisibility or marginality tends to confirm them as leftovers, or obsolete, or maladjusted. It also means their ways of being in the world are disregarded or discounted, even as a product of development itself. And yet investigation of their ways of being pierces the shroud of ignorance stemming from casual observation or unexamined assumptions.

Our investigation of these experiences of "externality," or human redundancy, reveals their capacity to mirror the dominant market culture, illuminating its flaws and limitations. The act of mirroring is accomplished through critical struggles—the real subjects of this book. The struggles depicted here range across the world, and, while each struggle has its particular spatial and social geography, together they represent and reinforce a critique of the core assumptions by which market-driven development organizes the world.

The value of this book is this—paying attention to those excluded and impoverished by development, and the particular quality of their struggles for survival and justice, provides ways to unsettle the common sense assumptions of development as well as resources to challenge them. As such, this collection also provides an important complement or corrective to existing accounts of development, grounded in a diverse array of "critical struggles" in quite different parts of the world—with substantive and unusual angles on how development is experienced, reformulated, and/or reclaimed.

These are "critical struggles" in a double sense: first, they struggle against disempowerment; and second, they contest the way social reality is represented as natural and inevitable in the current development narrative. They not only express the underside of development, but they also offer insight into how people displaced and excluded engage with the forces and assumptions ranged against them. Such struggle for material and meaningful security is epistemic: revealing, and contesting, what development takes for granted. That is, the people concerned call its assumptions into question, interjecting their own view of the social world and/or the meanings that derive from their experiences of survival and struggles for social justice. At once contesting and re-imagining development, these struggles contribute to the emerging sensibility that another world is possible.

In 2001, the authors of this book began a research working group on Social Movements in Cornell University's Department of Development Sociology under the auspices of the Polson Institute for Global Development. At that time, we aimed to revise the approach to social movement analysis by examining movements not as vehicles of social theory about popular mobilization, but as lenses on the restructuring of the global order. Over years of debate, workshops, retreats, writing and rewriting (from dissertation and post-doctoral fieldwork), we fine-tuned this approach with the epistemic perspective that organizes this book. This has been a truly collective endeavor that has enriched us all, and, hopefully, our relationship with the various struggles with which we identify and/or work. We were helped along the way by a number of colleagues, especially Amita Baviskar, Gillian Hart, Jackie Smith, and Wendy Wolford, who commented on first drafts at a workshop in 2007. We are grateful for their critical appreciation of this project. We also wish to thank three anonymous reviewers for their helpful feedback. Mary Jordan kindly assisted with bibliographic consolidation. We also received financial support from Cornell University's Institute for Social Sciences. And finally, we owe thanks to the vision, enthusiasm, and guidance of Stephen Rutter and Leah Babb-Rosenfeld.

1.

CHANGING THE SUBJECT OF DEVELOPMENT*

Philip McMichael

At a time when the development promise is increasingly in question, with dwindling social gains, the vision of modernity is losing its certitude. This moment is observable through the lens of critical struggles of those who experience disempowerment, displacement, and development contradictions. Our project is twofold: to illuminate the silences in the development narrative registered in social struggles in distinct but related spaces of the global political economy; and to propose a different "social movement analytic," where we focus on the epistemic content of these struggles—how they particularize the meaning of social change through place-based engagements. Through the lens of these critical struggles we learn about the underbelly of the system, how its disempowered subordinates self-organize, and how they reveal the limiting assumptions of development and alternative conditions of possibility, through their struggles to become historical subjects.

Introduction

At a time when the promise of development is increasingly in question, with dwindling social gains, the vision of modernity is losing its certainty. Financial meltdown, arctic thaw, imploding states, diminishing resources, global migrations of economic and environmental refugees, and the resurgence of slavery are a few of the dramatic changes that are now part of the social and natural landscape. By and large, these represent particularly visible and broad reversals in the narrative of progress. What about the everyday and smaller-scale casualties of progress? This is the subject of this volume.

The casualties of progress include those whose class, gender, racial/ethnic, sexual, or disability identities have served as axes of exploitation, as well as those regarded as redundant and at odds with the values and history of capitalist modernity. Both are seen to be different, occupying a place, or history, outside of progress. To classify them as outsiders, laggards, or residuals reaffirms the narrative of progress.[1] The most obvious category is "traditional," coined as the opposite of "modernity," and designating cultures at odds with (or as a baseline for) the process of development, and its particular calculus of value. Popularized by W.W. Rostow in *The Stages of Economic Growth* (1960), the representation of human history as a linear journey through developmental stages (from traditional society to the consumer state), etched forest-dwellers, artisanal fisher-folk, nomad-pastoralists, and peasants deeply into the modern consciousness as hangovers from a world left behind.

From here it has been a simple matter to project the modern concept of poverty onto that world, lending Rostow's progressive stages the status of an historical truth: namely, that these cultural forms we call traditional are also poor and destined to disappear, whether they or we like it or not, in the wake of progress. It is this "truth," for example, that informs the baseline assumption underlying Jeffrey Sachs' *The End of Poverty*, where he claims:

> The move from universal poverty to varying degrees of prosperity has happened rapidly in the span of human history. Two hundred years ago the idea that we could potentially achieve the end of extreme poverty would have been unimaginable. Just about everybody was poor, with the exception of a very small minority of rulers and large landowners (2005, p. 26).

Without romanticizing Napoleonic era life, in and outside of Europe, it is well to remember that humanity was a good deal more complex, resourceful, and diverse than simply being poor, by our standard. And that is perhaps the real casualty of progress, the extent to which those who do not conform, or measure up, to a single standard of modern development are misrepresented and discounted in the process of normalizing a dominant vision of progress.

That standard is generally represented monetarily. It is institutionalized in the United Nations System of National Accounts, by which all member governments must maintain uniform measures of national output (Gross National Product; GNP). Because such measures are monetized, other forms of social and ecological wealth (e.g., homemaking, community work, livelihood networks, biodiversity) are formally discounted in measures of progress. This means development is governed by a "market calculus," focused on a singular metric of output—which devalues non-monetized contributions to social life and disregards discrimination and environmental degradation. Because the latter outcomes do not command a price in the market, they do not register on the balance sheet of development (Waring, 1988). Through these devices development is normalized in market terms.

What are the consequences of understanding and prescribing the market as the site and vehicle of development? For one thing, it reinforces the belief that well-being depends on increasing GNP—a correlation questioned by recent studies.[2] The UN Development Program's Human Poverty Index ranks the United States last among 17 industrial (OECD) countries with respect to indicators of poverty, illiteracy, longevity, and social inclusion (Gardner, Assadourian, and Sarin, 2004, p. 18). For another thing, it reinforces the association of nonmonetized subsistence activity ("tradition") with poverty. If what is productive, and therefore key to development, is only that which can be measured in monetary terms, then women's unpaid labor cannot be counted, nor can the myriad activities through which people share common resources and construct livelihood networks. Smallholders customarily experiment with seed-sharing and crop rotations as risk-averse activity in variable environments to sustain communities and ecologies—activities not valued in monetary terms. Within the development narrative, then, these practices are targets for displacement or commercialization.

The market calculus, as the subject of development, pervades contemporary neo-liberal policies.[3] Emphasizing deregulation of trade and finance and privatization of public and environmental goods, such policies purportedly expand the "free market" (the "invisible hand") and development opportunity. Under the neo-liberal development project, social services (such as education, health, water provision) are converted into forms of private consumption. Yet markets remain unequal in their structure (subsidies to already powerful firms), and outcome (access to income and resources)—resulting in an ever-receding goal of overcoming poverty and discrimination across the world.[4] It is this material casualty that underlies and informs the social struggles represented in this collection.

A second order casualty is the inability or unwillingness to imagine alternatives to development as we know it. The categorical violence[5] directed toward development "misfits" ultimately inhibits social imagination by marginalizing, or silencing, values and knowledges (social, cultural, ecological) critical to sustaining human communities, rights and perhaps humanity itself. A singular market calculus applied across a heterogeneous world gives the appearance of equality as it denies diversity.

These struggles, then, challenge the "epistemic privilege" of the market calculus—where the market has become the dominant lens through which development is viewed. An *episteme* is an approach to knowledge about the world, based on a core set of assumptions that seem like common sense. Thus the market, and its "invisible hand" assumptions (neutrality, efficiency, rationality) has come to represent the central episteme in the modern enterprise of development. Since these assumptions have commonsense appeal, they normalize the market calculus in the discourse and pursuit of development. As a consequence, other such epistemes (views of the world) are rendered unviable, invisible, or unthinkable. The well-known neo-liberal axiom of "bad state/good market" reminds us that the market episteme depends on discounting alternative sets of ideas or knowledges. Accordingly, in contesting the epistemic privilege of the market calculus, these critical struggles do not simply alter the world, they transform the way we can think about the world and possibilities for social change.

This collection of essays gives voice to those who struggle with various material and epistemic exclusions of development. Critical struggles articulate alternative values and knowledges—not as intrinsically different from those associated with modern development, but as counterparts to, or commentaries on, the process by which development redefines human possibility via the singular calculus of the market.[6] Of course the efficacy of this calculus depends on institutional force, which channels development successes and failures together. The expansion of slums, for example, is related to private property, whose superior institutional force depends on the relative power of markets to override public goods and protections. In Gayatri Menon's chapter 10, pavement-dweller struggles to claim a right to the city find ways to work the balance of power between private and public resources. They expose the link between private property and liberal notions of those rights that would afford the protections they need but which are denied, because in lacking property they lack the capacity for political recognition. Politicizing the market in this way, and tempering development's claims to progress, this struggle opens space for new understandings and practices of citizenship.

Through the device of a set of critical struggles, this book examines the shortcomings of development in both material and epistemic terms. Materially, it considers such fundamental issues as the link between education and employment, corruption of electoral institutions, forms of dispossession and displacement, military and neo-colonial occupation, conservation and food security, and citizenship struggles. Epistemically, these struggles reveal perspectives made invisible through disempowerment of the people concerned. With their survival and self-representation at stake, we identify processes and values through which the protagonists address, subvert, and reframe the assumptions of a market-based project of global development.[7]

By *politicizing* market culture, and its material consequences, these struggles reformulate the meaning and content of social change. Those deemed casualties of progress become agents or vehicles of critique of the normalizing claims of development. Their critique is not so much in development's terms (success or failure), but in terms that are infused with the particular values and meanings through which they engage in struggle for rights, access, and representation.

Parameters of Social Change

While the critical struggles depicted here revalue what development devalues, they are not always agents of enduring, or large-scale social change as such. Nevertheless, they are all significant: first, in their own sites, since they address immediate issues of survival and justice; and second, in problematizing the dominant (and to them, exclusionary) vision of social progress under capitalist modernity. By injecting their counter-claims these struggles claim relevance and underscore that those excluded by development can and do self-organize and construct alternatives. They embody solutions to problems generated by development practices that are incapable of self-correction.[8]

These struggles subvert both the terms of development and the terms by which social movements are normally analyzed, in two ways. First, we do not claim for them the conventional status of "social movements," avoiding the burden of "social change" proof—as noted in the *Handbook of Political Sociology*:

> Social movement researchers need to confront the issue of demonstrating social movement change. This requires going beyond the study of social movement outcomes to look at the broader societal context within which these outcomes occur. If movement scholars fail to respond to this call, they risk being accused of trivial pursuits.... [p]ursuing this research program risks conclusions that most social movements are marginal to social change, in the sense of actually "moving society" (Jenkins and Form, 2005, p. 349).

Our own view is that declaring what may be "marginal to social change" makes linear or cause-and-effect assumptions about "social change." Rather than invoke direction and efficacy as such, we focus on rights and justice, and the significance of epistemic challenges to social change.

While these struggles are localized, their micro-politics nevertheless articulate with the macro-politics and contradictions of the development project at large. They particularize the meaning of social change, through place-based struggle within broader political–economic relations. Struggles occur in, and challenge or reproduce, a variety of social milieus[9] without necessarily registering (immediately) as "societal transformation." Instead of a cause-and-effect approach,[10] we refocus on the epistemic implications of struggle over resources and representation.[11] These struggles challenge the *premature closure* of categories such as "economic rationality," "conservation," "citizenship," "security," and "rights," in the conventional development paradigm—interjecting alternative meanings and consequences of such terms. Hannah Wittman's chapter 11, for example, documents the Brazilian landless struggle to realize an "agrarian citizenship" that would revalue smallholders as food and environmental stewards in an urban market culture premised on marginalizing them.

Second, the approach to these struggles avoids a "methodological individualism" that would examine particular social movements according to standard criteria of process, goals, and outcomes. Viewing social movements as units of analysis, and comparing their attributes of coherence and efficacy, risks cultural and historical abstraction. We invert this procedure, viewing struggles as units of observation, not in comparative relation to one another, but in relation to a shared political–economic conjuncture.[12] We view them as expressing this historical moment, and their cognitive engagement is precisely with the terms or claims of this neo-liberal conjuncture. Together, they comprise elements of a global process of "combined casualty"[13] in the development project. Each struggle has its particular meaning, form, and dynamics, but each shares the exclusionary force of multi-faceted forms of neo-liberal development. While development is a global project, it operates across a diverse world but with recognizable effects of both "interdependence and disjunction":

> The feeling of disconnection and exclusion in relation to the transformations occurring in space and time has never been so profound. In other words, never have so many social groups been so connected with the rest of the world by virtue of the intensification of their isolation; never have so many been integrated by virtue of the way in which their exclusion is deepened (B. d. S. Santos, 2005a, p. xxi).

In these terms, social change is far more complex and contradictory than the narrative of capitalist modernity would have it. By examining these struggles as expressions of development exclusions in this historical conjuncture, it is possible to specify development limitations and to identify the diversity of future possibilities.

Development in Question

These struggles confront localized forms of exclusion justified by a pervasive market episteme—which embodies "the constant imperative to reformulate people's multiple desires into a universal propensity to recognize, act on, and reinforce their economic self-interest" (Da Costa and McMichael, 2007, p. 594). Whether indigenous Okinawans struggling for collective rights for a political identity in Japan against the liberal formula of individualizing citizenship (chapter 12); or popular insurgencies in Nigeria and Mexico challenging commercialized elections that are informed by each state's global position as an oil supplier (chapter 6); or peasants in Malawi protecting their culture against the commercialization of agricultural inputs and outputs promoted by state-supported agribusiness (chapter 7)—the common bond is that each struggle problematizes development's market calculus.

In addressing the limits of a market-centered view of the world, this collection builds on a long tradition of critique of the political economy of capitalist development: beginning with Karl Marx, refracted through Karl Polanyi, and reproduced in a host of more contemporary critical studies of development.[14] Both Marx and Polanyi identified the commodity as the principal means by which exchange and the market calculus transformed modern societies. But monetary exchange covers the commodity's tracks so that the social and ecological conditions under which it is produced are not immediately apparent. These conditions are invisible in a commodity price, regarded as an objective measure of economic value through which development is calibrated.

Marx and Polanyi recognized that markets are social constructs, but that by attributing independent power to markets we lose sight of their social origins, which include in particular the conversion of human labor into a commodity to be bought and sold in the marketplace. For each theorist the consequences were that unregulated markets (as today) mean human labor is treated like a commodity and vulnerable to exploitation through tenuous employments, workplace abuse, and less-than-living wages. Marx theorized a scenario of accumulating contradictions between the classes of capital and labor, culminating in revolution and the collectivization of property and wealth. Polanyi's scenario was governed similarly by social mobilization, but of a different kind—one where European counter-movements of laborers, agrarians, industrialists, and citizens across the late-nineteenth and early-twentieth centuries managed to protect society from wholesale commodification by regulating markets through construction of the modern welfare state.

Each theorist viewed the power of social mobilization to potentially unmask the natural appearance of the market, and reveal its political content. What Marx called "commodity fetishism" (market objectification), and what Polanyi viewed as the illusion of self-interest as a natural human motive, were different ways of identifying a market episteme: the belief that markets best serve society's needs. Polanyi in particular focused on the rise *and* regulation of the market, terming this process a "double movement" animated by a counter-movement politics. This dialectic informs much contemporary social movement analysis, given the centrality of market forces and their social counterparts in the making of the modern world.[15] However, this dialectic is founded in, and reproduces, a conventional set of coordinates centered on the modern state, and movements (e.g., labor, suffragette, civil rights, land reform) concerned with reshaping states through their inclusion in the liberal project as such. They are central to the liberal project of social regulation of modern economies, a project that perhaps reached its apogee in the mid-twentieth century with the New Deal and European social democracy. But market regulation is not the focus of this collection, as our struggles concern the limitations of a politics of markets.

In this sense, Polanyi's double movement of market adjustment was a product of its time—of nation-state building and the institutionalization of the government/ citizen social contract.[16] Development emerged out of this period, as the movement for decolonization led to the completion of the nation-state system across the post-colonial world. As newly independent states in Asia and Africa joined the family of nations, the UN System of National Accounts established a state-managed economic calculus as the development marker. In this world-historical moment, development became a universal measure of human progress, and an instrument of state power. As an instrument of rule, the development project superimposed monetized commerce as the stimulus and referent of modernization, and post-colonial states harnessed populations and natural resources to the task of economic growth as the guarantor of development (and their legitimacy).[17] Gilbert Rist observed of these new states: "Their right to self-determination had been acquired in exchange for the right to self-definition" (1997, p. 79).

Arguably, this historic initiative is understood via a conventional set of coordinates of the political economy of development—in particular the state, state-system, markets, division of labor, investment, trade, commodity chains, and so forth. Critics of the world order have focused on questions of dependency, unequal exchange, underdevelopment, accumulation and exploitation of labor, and recently, the environment.[18] That is, the principal concern has been with the uneven development of capitalism across time and space: the economic enrichment of some nations and regions at the expense of others, expressed in First/Third World, and North/South binaries. This has produced a critical structural perspective on capitalist development, nevertheless still within an economic discourse. Post-structural development theory contests the legitimacy of this discourse as a misrepresentation of non-European cultures and a discourse of control.[19] The result is an unhealthy standoff in polarized economic/material versus cultural/discursive understandings of development, where structural prescriptions are critiqued as partial or falsifying by post-structuralists.

Our own perspective is to collapse this binary, noting that economic relationships are practiced culturally. Despite the fetishism of the market calculus as the development frame, markets do matter, but they operate through material cultures. That is, development is anchored not just in institutions and structures, but also in the lives of its subjects (Pieterse, 1998). Understanding how subjects of development receive, legitimize, or contest development is indispensable to understanding how development is accomplished,[20] the terms through which it is challenged, and how new possibilities are reformulated. This is our goal. To this end our various struggles reveal the impoverishing and discriminating assumptions of the market culture in reducing development to a singular, partial value.

Development Exclusions: Unity in Diversity

The different struggles represented here reveal the many sides of a single global project of development. The variety of development exclusions gives these struggle sites the appearance of disparate cases, but they share critical engagement with common terms of subjection. When Shimshali pastoralists confront conversion of their grazing lands to big game nature preserves by the Pakistan government, they claim their own conservationism, challenging "market environmentalism" by asserting the value of local knowledge in managing territory (cf. Escobar, 2008).[21] Nosheen Ali's research in a remote mountainous region (chapter 5) shows how local mobilization that values ecological and cultural reproduction over (export) revenues reveals the limiting assumptions of subjecting sustainable development to the (general) market calculus.

This intensely globalized market system "aims, on the one hand, to desocialize capital, freeing it from the social and political bonds that in the past guaranteed some social distribution; on the other hand it works to subject society as a whole to the market law of value, under the presupposition that all social activity is better organized when organized under the aegis of the market" (Santos, 2005, p. viii).[22] States partner with the market to realize this global development project, through policies that privatize social services and access to resources, and appeal to individualist values. Across the world, multivalent struggles confront the development industry's attempts to apprehend "proliferating meanings, repackaging them into 'marketable' ideas and institutionally useful tools" (Da Costa and McMichael, 2007, p. 594). The global market culture precipitates struggles over questions of value, confirming the world's "epistemological diversity" and, therefore, an epistemic crisis of development (Santos, 2005).

This epistemic crisis is of universalism, more as a historical project than a principle. While questioning a uniform vision of development, in a diverse world, local struggles do engage with universal principles (rights, sovereignty, equality). But they do so reflexively, confirming Anna Tsing's point that "engaged universals travel across difference and are charged and changed by their travels" (2005, p. 8). Here, the charging and changing is the process whereby universals like citizenship, education, elections, gender, race, property are reclaimed in counter-hegemonic[23] ways to serve specific needs of those subject to development exclusions and redundancy.

The act of reclaiming challenges the exclusionary processes of development, contradicting its claims to universality. In this collection, we are particularly concerned to examine the ways in which neo-liberalism has refocused development's claims (and generated new counter-claims). While enlarging the reach of the market culture, development claims have been progressively narrowed to the point of certain exclusion for certain social groups. Deeming certain social groups and their values as obsolete, obstructions, or blemishes on the development landscape forgets that development itself creates redundancy and marginal life-worlds. Massive displacement of peasants from the land may confirm a "development truth" about the competitive superiority of industrial agriculture (holding constant its subsidies and overwhelming power equation),[24] but it is now recognized that industrial agriculture is unsustainable.[25] Over a billion slum-dwellers without formal employment prospects is hardly an advertisement for development. The social redundancy of the "mass production of slums"[26] via neo-liberal development and neo-liberal structural adjustment policies is a prime example of the material and categorical violence embedded in the market calculus.

The Methodology of Structuring

Insofar as many struggles challenge or subvert the categories through which they may be depicted, disciplined, or displaced (cf. Starr, 2005), it is important to try to avoid *a priori* conceptions of struggles that may misconstrue their meaning and import.[27] These struggles engage critically with commonsense claims within particular power relations. They reconstitute what it means to be historical subjects. Rather than simply *enact* a liberal genealogy that would realize the progressive promise of development, these subjects question liberalism's assumed universal (development) trajectory. For example, Hannah Wittman's and Alex Da Costa's protagonists expose the limiting assumption of "citizenship" in Brazil by opening the window on the subordination of the cultural and material condition of agrarian and Afro-Brazilian subjects, and how they struggle to realize "agrarian citizenship" and "multicultural citizenship," respectively.

Conceptually, we take our cue from Philip Abrams, who noted:

> action is shaped by the meanings people bring to their predicaments or can wring out of them. An adequate sociology of such predicaments surely has to offer an analysis not only of the observable relationships of power and powerlessness within them but equally of what is made of those relationships by those involved in them; an analysis of the complex of meaning within which relationships are enacted (1982, p. 73).

We invoke Abrams's concept of "structuring": meaning that the "shaping of action by structure and transforming of structure by action both occur as processes in time" (1982, pp. xv, 3). To give substance and meaning to "structuring" Abrams asks "why particular men and women make the particular choices they do and why they succeed or fail in their projects" (p. 3). Understanding how and why people choose to act, or struggle, raises the question of what does and does not count in animating their courses of action. It also addresses how people's interpretations of their circumstances and "choices" may be constrained by, or seek to redefine, the "commonsense" terms of the social order; that is, historical possibility. Why do certain options seem unthinkable or impossible, and to whom, in a given context? What are the consequences of struggling with categorical exclusion and misrepresentation? Abrams calls this methodology, of making the world historically concrete, the "problematic of structuring."[28]

Abrams's use of the term "problematic" is the methodological core of the concept of structuring. He suggests that a "problematic is the sense of significance and coherence one brings to the world in general in order to make sense of it in particular" (Abrams, 1982, p. xv). This is precisely the point of this collection. These struggles individually and together specify the contradictory dynamics of the neo-liberal or global development project. Here social change materializes in and through struggles to negotiate, consolidate, or transform power relations—whether it is Brazilian commercial soy farmers promoting free markets, South African shack-dwellers reformulating the civic meaning of the property relation, or Indian women challenging the licensing of liquor markets as the only means of creating public revenues and jobs under jobless neo-liberal growth. And, to the extent that the protagonists historicize the meaning of their struggles, they situate them in an increasingly problematic world-historical conjuncture.[29]

The structuring problematic involves a delicate relationship between subjects and the development environment, which Santos characterizes as "the dialectics of the local and the global." Of course this relationship is entirely at odds with universalizing categories which presume, and reproduce, hierarchy—where "the local is the subordinated counterpart of a reality or entity that has the capacity to designate itself as global" (B. d. S. Santos, 2005a, p. xxiii). A "global perspective" makes invisible not only actions on the ground, but also its own power source, contributing to normalization of the development establishment and its decision-making privilege.[30] In contrast, our perspective represents local actors as they engage critically with their relations of subjection, in order to transcend the terms of their subjection.[31] This involves a subtle "dance," as emphasized by Gayatri Menon's treatment of the "quiet encroachment" of Mumbai pavement dwellers on the register of urban citizenship (chapter 10). How to bring coherence to the world through particular struggles such as these, then, becomes not only a method of analysis, but also a method of political engagement, whereby strategic goals are forged by appropriating universals (like citizenship, democracy, development, rights, sovereignty, property) through place-based struggle.

The import of this method is to rework the meaning of "global development." As a discursive neo-liberal project, "globalization" portrays the world's future in singular, universalist, and abstracted terms—as progressively realizing a market culture enabled by Western science and technology, and promoting expanding freedoms of capacity and choice. As critics maintain, this is a particular vision of the world, which is presented as a universal (and yet is unequal in its impact).[32] The struggles here not only particularize the universal pretensions of "development" as a normative master concept, but also seek to de-center knowledge and power. De-centering uncouples *modernity* from its abstracted Eurocentric claims, reformulating it as an unfinished, differentiated, and contradictory project, open to new possibilities.

Accordingly, we do not view these struggles as simply "case studies" of local activism. Certainly they have their immediate integrity, but together they constitute a multivalent response to a singular project of global development. They share common ground in the inclusion/exclusion dialectics associated with state-sponsored elaborations of the market episteme—such as extension of schooling, land titling, promoting elections, rhetorics of citizenship, agrarian transformations in the name of productivity, and privatization of the social contract. While these initiatives may all be represented as inclusionary, as these struggles show, inclusion also has exclusionary consequences.

Conclusion

In this collection, these various struggles contest a set of universal claims through which development orders the world. Together, these struggles provide a lens on the contradictions of development in the early twenty-first century, registering a shared condition of disempowerment. While they can be examined individually, the thread that binds them is the rationalizing claim of the market episteme. This unrealizable claim has so intensified in recent history that development is experiencing a substantial legitimacy crisis, as social exclusion and displacement and ecological decline now stalk the landscape. While these struggles give textured expression to problems of the neo-liberal era, displacement and disempowerment stem from historic processes of capitalist development, captured in the concept of "accumulation by dispossession" (Harvey, 2003).[33] The struggles represented in this collection address this not only as material dispossession but also the dispossession of cultural knowledge and meaning. In so doing, they challenge the exclusionary consequences of both material inequality and the epistemic assumptions that order the contemporary world. To rephrase Abrams: by problematizing the coherence of contemporary development claims, these struggles particularize the world, disclosing history and uncovering "unthinkable" possibilities.

Notes

*Acknowledgments This chapter has evolved through the process, helpful suggestions, and thoughtful deliberations of an extraordinary collective of thoughtful and committed junior activist-scholars.
1. Within the development lexicon, classifications such as "poor," "undeveloped," or even "uncivilized" represent people/s in hierarchical and linear terms, which perform the double function of legitimizing those who produce such classifications (e.g., states, development agencies), and legitimizing the subjection of such populations to forms of development governance (cf. Li, 1999).
2. See, for example, Hamilton (2003), LaTouche (1993), and McMurtry (2002).
3. Arguably neo-liberalism as a form of political economy is now in question, although its normative legacy of "bad state, good market" will endure for some time.
4. The last half century or so has been littered with anti-poverty strategies: "development decades," new "basic needs" development, the Millennium Development Goals (MDGs) of 2000, now being recalibrated in the light of combined crises of finance, food, and climate.
5. Objectified meanings represented in policy, social scientific, or internalized as common sense, discourse.
6. For instance, Karuna Morarji (chapter 2) examines the value discrepancy between formal education in India and the sensibilities of rural villagers negotiating education for development/ opportunity in the urban marketplace.
7. Cf. McMichael (2008a).
8. This may be due to the inertia of resource commitment, underpinned with power relations, or because of myopia; that is, the inability to conceive of alternatives given the development industry's market episteme or its need to reproduce its legitimacy, reinventing solutions to misconstrued problems (cf. Da Costa and McMichael, 2007).
9. The conventional view of the state as the principal locus or target for collective action limits the "political arena" of contestation, foreclosing consideration of actions that implicate other power realms (e.g., Snow, 2004).

10. Requiring the test of time, and risking reduction to generalizing representations that de-historicize struggles.
11. As Santos puts it: "there will be no global social justice without global cognitive justice" (2005, p. xviii). Raj Patel's chapter 3 argues, for instance, that the Durban Shackdwellers Movement may not yet have brought material benefits from the government, but has brought a new sensibility into public discourse regarding its members' citizenship claims, and, in so doing, has transformed the terrain of debate, opening the minimal set of entitlements offered by the neoliberal state to critical scrutiny, and constructively problematizing the meaning of "citizenship" in South Africa, at this time, for researchers or anyone else.
12. Thus we investigate global contradictions through the lens of social struggle, rather than studying struggles as vehicles for general theories of how and why social movements occur, within a given liberal development narrative. This inverts conventional procedure which tends to de-historicize movements as cases to be compared for the purpose of theoretical generalization (cf. Hopkins, 1978).
13. Meaning the "normalized" (and interrelated) exclusions of indigenous peoples, minorities, women, smallholders, unskilled labor, refugees, and so on. Cf. David Held's work on cosmopolitanism and trans-boundary relations, creating "overlapping communities of fate," which emphasizes a relational, rather than linear, understanding, where "the fortunes and prospects of individual political communities are increasingly bound together" (2000, p. 400).
14. Marx (1967), Polanyi (1957). For representative samples of the lineage of development thought, see Roberts and Hite (2007).
15. See, for example, Tarrow (1998), Tilly (2004), and Bandy and Smith (2005).
16. This point is elaborated in McMichael (2005).
17. Sugata Bose observed of the Indian state: "Instead of the state being used as an instrument of development, development became an instrument of the state's legitimacy" (1997, p. 153).
18. For a representative sample, see Appelbaum and Robinson (2005).
19. Cf. Crush (1995), Escobar (1995), Sachs (1992), Said (1978).
20. Cf. Baviskar (2005), Gupta (1998), Klenk (2004), Li (1999), Mosse (2004).
21. Santos contextualizes this: "In the name of modern science, many alternative knowledges and sciences have been destroyed, and the social groups that used these systems to support their own autonomous paths of development have been humiliated. In short, in the name of science, epistemicide has been committed, and the imperial powers have resorted to it to disarm any resistance of the conquered peoples and social groups" (2005, p. xviii).
22. Harvey (2005) refers to this as the "seductive possessive individualism" of a historically specific class project.
23. As "counter-hegemonic" these struggles contest the normalization of the meaning or prescriptive import of hegemonic claims to universality (e.g., "self-interest" as a singular, innate human behavior).
24. For a comprehensive critique of industrial agriculture's unfair trade and market power, see Patel (2007).
25. For example, the UN-sponsored International Assessment of Agricultural Knowledge, Science and Technology for Development (IAASTD) questions the viability and utility of industrial agriculture in the twenty-first century (2008).
26. See Davis (2006, p. 17).
27. This is a central ethical concern for all authors, as scholar-activists.
28. Abrams provides the methodological tool, but we endeavor to substantiate it through examination of a diverse set of structuring initiatives as struggles over the terms of rule and models of social change within the neo/liberal project at large.
29. Santos (2005, p. xxvi) represents this process as: "we are entering an era in which the dialectics of the local and the global replaces the dichotomy between the local and the global. Accordingly, in our time, social emancipation involves a dual movement of de-globalization of the local (vis-à-vis hegemonic globalization) and its re-globalization (as part of counter-hegemonic globalization)."

30. In relation to this, the global development industry has responded to the charge of top-down representation and decision-making by embracing the rhetoric of participation and empowerment. For critiques of this response, see Elyachar (2005) and Da Costa and McMichael (2007).

31. Cf. Beverly (2004). This invokes, and critiques, Hopkins's (1978) camera metaphor of the figure/ground dialectic, whereby the analyst, in focusing and then refocusing, recognizes the mutually productive relationship between actors and their formative relations—the terms/meaning of which may then become problematic.

32. For example, B. d. S. Santos:

    it is now clearer than ever that the universalism of modern science is a Western particularism, which has the power to define all rival forms of knowledge as particular, local, contextual and situational. Thus, there have been and there still are other, non-Western sciences and forms of modernity, as well as many other forms of knowledge, that are validated by criteria other than those of modern Western science. The epistemological diversity of the world is thus potentially infinite. All forms of knowledge are contextual, and the more they claim not to be, the more they are" (2005a, pp. xviii–xix).

33. Brad Weiss argues: "the neoliberal moment is plainly a dimension of a long-standing encounter with modernity. We gain little analytical purchase on the present by rushing to embrace the novelty of these immediate conditions in their own terms" (2004, p. 4). That is, "in what sense does neo-liberalism reformulate the past in the present? And in so doing, to what extent does it decompose liberalism's construction of the public, reducing sociality and indeed development, to the "calculus of markets driven (putatively) by 'individuals' recognized mainly as consumers making choices?" (p. 7).

PART I

DEVELOPMENT FOR WHAT, AND FOR WHOM?

Development as ideal and practice has always included a power equation: to improve the lot of humankind, and to govern in the name of developing a nation, its institutions, its resources, technology, material wealth, individual opportunity, and so forth. As such, development is a tool for those in power and their legitimacy, so long as there is economic growth and expanding opportunity. But development also brings inequality. Wealth for some, for example, may depend on low-paid labor for others. While the golden rule is that those who have the gold make the rules, at times the subjects of rule (colonials, slaves, citizens, workers, peasants, indigenous people, minorities) exercise power themselves to contest the rules and even the rulers. Development is frequently contested, even when its enduring principle of human emancipation is packaged in seductive appeals to self-interest—a hallmark of the neoliberal era and its emphasis on market rewards.

Given the origins of "development" in the era of European colonial empires, it assumed a step-like progression led by European modernization. As non-European peoples achieved their independence from colonialism, they were incorporated into this process as "developing nations." Thus, in historical and global terms, development is perceived as a universal "ladder" requiring a big first step onto the bottom rung (Sachs, 2005)—despite recent claims that the ladder has been "kicked away" (for newcomers) or that it is non-existent (Chang, 2002; Davis, 2006). But as a metaphor, the "development ladder" is self-referential. It legitimates those (on high rungs) who construct it, depicting the people at its base as poor, or backward, and requiring development. But who really are these people? Is their challenge to develop, or *with* development? What does development mean to them, especially since the "ladder" is not of their own making? What misleading assumptions about powerless or marginal people comprise the development vision? These are the questions addressed here.

As a universal standard, the notion of development projects a single vision onto a diverse world, ordering it horizontally (some are more developed than others) and vertically (some are more equal than others in setting the terms of reference). It is always tempting to equate the development vision with the goal of equality, in "one world." But this raises the question of equality with what, or whom? For those to whom this goal is addressed, equality may well mean having the right to their own interpretation of their condition, as well as security and resources. We know this from experience, from these struggles that are not simply about gaining access to resources (land, territory, jobs, housing, civil rights, toilets, schools) and securing livelihoods, but also about the right to define the terms through which people's lives find meaning. It is at the level of micro-politics, depicted here, that the macro-political assumptions of development are laid bare.

Struggles over meaning or resources raise questions about "development"—questions that focus on three key assumptions: (1) that all people are equal, except some are more developed than others; (2) that equal worth in an otherwise diverse world can be standardized through universal market-based measures of development; and (3) accordingly, development is most effectively institutionalized through the market. The four chapters in this section address such questions.

Dia Da Costa's chapter 2 depicts a grassroots struggle against a decision by West Bengal political elites to license home production of liquor in the name of revenue and job creation, claiming greater risk to community health and questioning the assumption that the poor have no other choice. This essay suggests that a market orientation to development pursued by elites may undermine the social fabric in a poor community, and that contrary to elite assumptions, the poor (women in this case) are quite capable of mobilization in defense of community values and championing "human development."

Raj Patel's chapter 3 examines the question "development and democracy for whom?" Despite the fact that the African National Congress drew its support from the poorest South Africans in the struggle against apartheid, the ANC government has betrayed this constituency by prioritizing middle class propertied interests, failing to fulfill promises to provide housing to shack dwellers. The consequence is a sprawl of shack dweller communities, as cities without citizens, who have theorized and reframed the meaning of (a community-based) citizenship, politicizing our understanding of what democratic development might mean.

Karuna Morarji's chapter 4 brings into question our commonsense association of education with development. Rural villagers in northern India experience and evaluate modern education in contradictory and ambiguous ways. While education is viewed as a solution to the "problem" of agrarian decline, educated youth fail to gain employment, yet have difficulty returning to rural livelihoods, thus devaluing the moral economy of village community. This essay questions the foreclosure of sustainable rural livelihoods by the neo-liberal development model, given the failure of this model to provide jobs for educated citizens (and urban-industrial incapacity to absorb those expelled from rural areas), despite narratives of social mobility through educated market participation.

In the context of the debate over nature protection and sustainability, Nosheen Ali's chapter 5 examines development for whom. International conservation agencies in northern Pakistan have pushed for converting village pastures into national parks and trophy hunting reserves, and tried to compel local communities to abandon the practice of livestock grazing. This model of conservation and development has been successfully resisted by Shimshali villagers, who argue that it reflects a Western tendency of divorcing nature from society, reinforces state control and abuse of resources, and undermines local livelihoods as well as ecologies by prioritizing the desires of elite tourists.

2.

CONTESTING LIQUOR PRODUCTION AND MATERIAL DISTRESS IN RURAL INDIA*

Dia Da Costa

Shows how distress rationalizes liquor production, as the chosen source of employment and public revenues by the West Bengal communist government, in a neo-liberal context of jobless growth. The liquor "choice" is mediated through a complex alliance of high-caste sellers, politicians, school teachers, panchayat leaders, and police, with overlapping interests in this "race to the bottom" program. There is opposition to the disabling effects on citizens, families and workers centers, on poor women, as primary caretakers of *sansar* (healthy private and public households), and frontline victims of broken homes, income loss, and abuse.

Introduction

Since 1985, Jana Sanskriti, a cultural organization composed of peasants and agricultural workers, has built village theater teams in the Indian state of West Bengal as sources of political theater and political activism. Much of their work on and offstage dramatizes and demands the right to work in their villages rather than depend on migration for rural viability. Yet, in the summer of 2005, Jana Sanskriti (JS) did something seemingly counter-intuitive to their ongoing demand for rural livelihoods. They mobilized a roadblock along the highway, halted the traffic of goods and people along the main artery of the local economy, and demanded an end to a lucrative and widely prevalent means of rural livelihood—liquor production. From JS's perspective this anti-liquor struggle articulates, rather than contradicts, their ongoing refusal to accept a world of shrinking possibilities. Liquor production, in their view, is an unacceptable source of local revenues given its destructive community impact. While development might be represented as entrepreneurial opportunity, the choice and nature of new business is not a neutral matter. To the extent that a market episteme of development forecloses debates on nature and choices of new business by privileging employment and revenue-generation alone, such an episteme affords minimal regard for community destruction as a result of development. Further, other ways of thinking, such as those of JS and its constituency of women who envision development as a process of constructing a healthy rural community, are excluded from view thus re-inscribing existing gender and class inequalities.

On the day of the roadblock, six men who were setting up posters and microphones for the protest were taken to the nearest police station even before the protest had officially begun. The microphone battery and glue were confiscated, posters and banners torn off trees. But protestors found a second battery and microphone, and the protest raged on until the six young men returned several hours later. One of the men, Prasad Sardar, told his audience about his interaction with the angry police escort which reprimanded them for illegal disruption of public life. Prasad had responded: "You are spineless policemen. You find our work illegal, and you don't notice the illegal production of liquor because it is in your self-interest. You think we are not intelligent enough to understand what makes certain things legal and others illegal?" Prasad challenged his audience, "Have they disabled us?" (*Amader pongu kore rekheche, na ki?*).

In Bengali, *pongu* means to become physically disabled. Colloquially the word describes drunks recognizable by their unsteady walk. In asking "have they disabled us," Prasad was recalling the physical effects of alcohol intoxication and asking if liquor was paralyzing critical thinking about the meaning of development as well.

Rural Bengalis like Prasad have unfailingly voted the Left Front Government (LFG) of West Bengal back into power since 1977. The LFG is made up of a coalition of parties led by the Communist Party of India (Marxist) or CPM. Going against the grain of post-colonial India's planned industrialization and the expansion of modernized agriculture as a solution to unemployment and under-development, the LFG implemented land reform and political decentralization in the late 1970s. Not surprisingly, Bengal's progressive policies for the rural sector and militant trade unionism and lockouts in the industrial sector increased capital flight and unemployment, while decreasing the industrial working class vote by the late-1980s (Pedersen, 2001, p. 656). The CPM counteracted political attrition and shrinking material investment with policies that were intended to regenerate industrialization, employment, and revenue.

Exhibit 2.1 "Have they disabled us?"

Apart from agricultural land acquisition and attractive policies for domestic and foreign capital investment, one recent employment- and revenue-generation measure is the liberalization of liquor licenses.

Considering the electoral popularity of this government, its responsiveness to rural employment and urban labor issues, and its enabling policies for generating rural livelihoods and state revenue, why ask "Have they disabled us?" Does Prasad not understand that liquor production is one mode, now increasingly legal, of rural livelihood and revenue generation in a place marginalized from such opportunities? In fact, the anti-liquor agitation is a struggle that highlights the divisive, destructive, indeed poverty-inducing effects of liquor production as source of employment and revenue generation. Jana Sanskriti's opposition to liquor production and blockage of commerce in an already depressed economy is not so much a shift from previous mobilizations for employment in villages as it is an epistemic challenge, a public rethinking, and a critical dramatization of what counts as development, poverty, and illegality within government policy and everyday practice.

In this essay, I contextualize various actors at the roadblock—anti-liquor agitators, police, local government officials, liquor producers, and liquor consumers' wives—to understand the politics around liquor production and consumption in West Bengal as it sheds light on competing claims about what produces poverty and what forms of political action can alleviate material distress. As a keyword of development discourse, poverty has been characterized both as the real world, material problem of survival, hunger, and life chances and as a discursive construct that classifies inequality (Elson & Pearson, 1981; Escobar, 1995; Sachs, 1992). Rather than retain this distinction between the reality of poverty and its representation, the JS anti-liquor movement goes to the heart of poverty in its communities by addressing all of its dimensions, and not simply that classified by the market episteme.

In questioning liquor production as a "solution" to rural unemployment, JS draws attention to the processes and mechanisms that render some experiences of material distress as poverty while denying others a similar definition. For example, while the material distress of people without livelihood counts as poverty, the materiality of household incomes drained by liquor consumption does not. What counts as poverty or illegality is constructed by mechanisms, processes, and people who enjoy social and epistemic privilege (T. Mitchell, 2002, p. 6). In other words, privilege prefigures the construct of "poverty" itself. Thus the epistemic struggle by JS is an effort to publicly question how we know poverty when we see it, and, by extension, to question what we mean by development. Jana Sanskriti understands that its role is to disrupt the normalized exclusions of certain forms of material distress from dominant definitions of poverty, and to construct political action that challenges the very mechanisms, people, and processes that set up the separations between well-being, material distress, and poverty.

Ruling Choice

Today, the West Bengal government finds itself constrained by massive capital flight, industrial decay, and inordinate rural unemployment. In West Bengal, as elsewhere, reconciling a shrinking tax base, the need for capital, the mandate of welfare for citizens, and the constitutional commitment to private property rights render state officials hard-pressed to deny the moral claim of people trying to survive even if by illegal means. To keep their vote (for the ruling coalition of Left Front parties) or to win votes (for the weak and divided opposition) the high ground of official politics faces little choice but to liberalize illegal liquor production and use this lucrative business as a means to generate revenue and employment.

In other words, the government's decision to liberalize rural liquor production as a solution to unemployment and revenue is legitimized on two interlocking bases. First, rural West Bengal is a marginalized destination for capital which means the government needs to innovate on revenue-generation in order to fulfill the moral claim to governmental care. Second, the condition of the rural poor justifies the management of poverty through the rationale that the poor have no choice but to accept illegal, precarious, or exploitative livelihoods. Here, the poor are seen as a population with particular characteristics rather than as citizens; and development becomes a process of managing poverty rather than politicizing and eliminating it. Simultaneously, against and within this process of legitimizing development as a mode of governing poverty, JS asks, "Is issuing of liquor licenses the only way for the government to generate revenue?" In asking this, rural Bengalis in the anti-liquor struggle are refusing closure on the question of their "choices"—highlighting the delimitation of choice as reproducing and explaining their poverty.

Viewed in a global context, the idea that the poor have no choice but to take on precarious and illegal work is a political rhetoric that reinforces the economic reality of neo-liberal globalization and its "race to the bottom." Global production systems and capital mobility across borders are premised on conceptions of the poor as having no choice but to "race to the bottom"; to do precarious and exploitative work for low wages. Seeing precarious, unjust, exploitative work as opportunity privileges notions of value that sustain powerful legacies of colonial history, modernization, and neo-liberal globalization reliant upon assumptions of racial, gender, and place-based inferiority. Rather than politicizing poverty by recognizing how livelihood choice is delimited, these ideas normalize measurement of people's worth as solely a function of an unequal market.

Against this calculus, JS dramatizes that "choice" is not strictly calibrated with political economic condition, in the sense that not all choices made directly flow from a "low" or "high" place in society. In theory, some wives of liquor consumers who are "low" on the political economic spectrum, juggling multiple forms of work, and desperate managers of meager household funds, should willingly accept liquor production as opportunity, but they don't. They actively refuse liquor production and its structure of enabled "choice." Here, despite their poverty, women refuse liquor production as form of poverty alleviation which they argue exacerbates their material experience of poverty.

On the other end of the political economic spectrum, the "high" place of the influential rich does not compel them to choose liquor production as livelihood, but they do. Thus, they actively make livelihood choices that are not the only available opportunities for them, while normalizing a destructive and divisive livelihood in the public sphere, and making the moral claim that the poor engage in liquor production all the more undeniable. Their political economic status allows them to corrupt choice and delimit opportunity in order to manage electoral votes, adjust the rural poor to a neo-liberal transition, and present the transition as an opportunity to alleviate rural unemployment. The politicians and police who turn a blind eye to illegal liquor production, and the effects of liquor production on social lives, could use their official power to distribute welfare, but instead they defer, deny, and corrupt welfare, and in so doing help construct the material distress that rules "choice." In so doing, they help construct consent for and generate closure on the matter of destructive livelihoods as both solution to and expression of poverty.

In the next section, I combine accounts of political–economic developments in Bengal with liquor protestors' voices—Prasad and Bibek—to sketch the social life of liquor. In the second substantive section, I consider liquor-sellers' voices—Baisakhi, Dilip, and Nimai—to show the rationale for their livelihood choices and their critique of anti-liquor agitation. Final sections show through narratives of liquor consumers' wives—Naina and Medha—how women perforate the comprehensive support for liquor production as solution to unemployment. These three sections show how rural Bengalis negotiate the intersecting political histories of capitalism, state-formation, and patriarchy. These competing accounts show that the distinctions between legal and illegal, well-being and poverty are not "fundamental oppositions" in the real world, but "uncertain forms of difference constituted, and at the same time undermined" (Mitchell, 2002, p. 15). The anti-liquor struggle reminds us that poverty is subject to change because people question and change the subject of poverty.

The Social Life of Liquor

Prasad Sardar[1] negated my fears that the dramatic increase in liquor production in recent years was a perception nurtured and exaggerated by a local moral police. He claimed that "Alcohol has a special tie with politics today." Politics today have to be understood in the context of the significant opportunity presented to West Bengal by India's formal political–economic liberalization process (1991), which transformed Bengal's position as a disreputable place for capital investment due to its "unruly" business climate and "sick" industry. Liberalization policies became Bengal's moment to start capital investment afresh because the discriminatory budgetary allocations and licenses of the central government came to an end. Chief Minister Bhattacharya recently invited ambitious capital investments to rejuvenate industry and address unemployment.[2]

Subsidizing these investment opportunities meant re-examining revenue-generation options. In 2002, the media criticized the government for losing revenue due to a faulty liquor policy. Reports argued that while the central government allowed potable alcohol to be made from "sugar beet, beet root, potatoes and coarse grain," West Bengal state policy disallowed production from any other substance but molasses ("Faulty Policies Hurt," 2002). Since West Bengal does not grow sugarcane, liquor producers had no option but to buy sugarcane from other states. Additionally, bottlers had to get at least 50 percent of their alcohol from domestic distilleries. All of this raised liquor prices, increased tax evasions, and decreased state revenues, while encouraging illicit liquor production. Responding to budget deficits and criticisms of its liquor policy, in March 2003, the West Bengal Finance Minister, Asim Dasgupta, liberalized liquor licensing policies in order to earn additional revenue of Rs. 100 crore or $1 billion ("Tax Reintroduced," 2003).

In 2006, Bibek Haldar[3] told me that "Even three years ago there were about 60,000 people to a license. Now there is a license for every 18,000 people." While the liberalization of liquor licensing policies was likely to address state revenue losses and pricing issues, it increased perceptions and reality of government support for the capillary insertion of liquor into daily village life. Liquor was now supplied through neighborhood grocery stores in residential areas. Despite increased licenses, most liquor production in areas I researched is done without licenses. This is because increased licenses showcased liquor production as lucrative business with cheap inputs available even for those with slim means of production. It is common local knowledge that molasses-based liquor concentrate is diluted with great quantities of water, multiplying liquor quantity and profits.

These indicators of increase coincide with narratives about changing social norms. Prasad contrasted norms from his childhood (fifteen years ago), when "there was not such a presence of alcohol.... At the very least, young children did not drink alcohol. Eighteen to twenty-year-olds never drank alcohol, didn't smoke *beedis* in front of people." Brazen, public drinking starkly contrasted with Prasad's memories of his own surreptitious transgressive consumption, riven with guilt, shame, and fear of being seen by an adult.

In this context Prasad challenged people to fortify critical and collective thinking against the accepted wisdom that a lack of income opportunities disabled people, compelling consent for liquor production. Roadblock mobilizers, including Prasad, concurred that roadblocks were illegal. But theirs was a desperate effort to call attention to liquor increase and government unwillingness to regulate it despite knowing the culprits. The collusions between party politicians and liquor producers were made public at the roadblock. Prasad recalled that when the police vans arrived, the liquor businessmen directed the police to the main culprits among the protestors who were then taken away to the police station. To Prasad, this indicated pre-planning and clear support for the liquor businessmen. I asked Prasad what was wrong with that considering the liquor businessmen are citizens too. He said,

> But they are conducting an illegal liquor business...instead they [the police] are angry at us for conducting raids.... If liquor businessmen are identifying us and police are catching us, when we identify liquor businessmen, why don't the police catch liquor businessmen? What should we conclude from this?

Bibek situated the collaboration in broader terms to argue that "If alcohol disappears, there is a problem in the market of votes." According to Bibek, the politician who has been corrupt and neglectful of welfare duties for all five years of his five-

Exhibit 2.2   Liquor businessmen and police physically and politically aligned at the JS anti-liquor agitation.

year term knows that alcohol disables thinking, which means that "what you cannot do with money alone, you can do with alcohol." When I asked Bibek if this was his impression, he said

> It is my experience. I live here. I have seen it…. Alcohol is a weapon for party politics. Meanwhile where do they get the money? Donations from the alcohol business. Here, take five thousand rupees. And then the party uses that to encourage voters to drink. Go drink at that liquor store. Is it not a good weapon?

Bibek said that "all parties are thieves" and he was certainly not the only one with this conviction.

Prasad and Bibek's analysis of political economic corruption in the management of rural employment and poverty indelibly shapes what might otherwise suggest an entirely moralistic view of alcohol. Politicians and police on the other hand normalized illegal and socially harmful liquor production as a lucrative opportunity within structures of neo-liberal choice. Liquor producers normalized their choice in terms of the moral right to a livelihood. Yet, they too affirmed the immorality of liquor.

Compelling Livelihood Choices

The notorious Khara neighborhood—known to be a CPM neighborhood—adjoins the bus stop where the roadblock was held. One resident calculated that twenty out of thirty-five households produced alcohol. Beyond numbers, people felt "Break the [liquor] pots there and it will stop everywhere else." However, according to Radha Das, a JS activist, policemen conducting raids and JS activists alike sought the company of women when entering the Khara neighborhood because "women in their [Khara] homes tear their blouses and shout rape if [men] go there." The Khara producers had entrenched support from party officials, *panchayats*,[4] and other powerful men such as school teachers. In turn, Bolai Master, a Khara resident, school teacher, and former *panchayat* leader entrenched liquor as social norm as he featured prominently in stories of neighborhood drunks.

Prasad's words about liquor disabling people were constantly with me as I conducted interviews. It seemed like an absurd coincidence when two of three liquor sellers (one man and one woman) turned out to be actually physically disabled. The woman was thirty-five years old, unmarried, with an obvious limp to her walk. She initially told me that she makes liquor, connecting pithy statements to explain why. "No one gives me food. I have not got married because my leg is broken, so I make liquor." Her mother spoke for her when I asked why she remained unmarried "She fell from a tree when she was young. And she asked not to get married because she felt that she could not do housework adequately. She was scared that her in-laws would get angry and beat her." No medical attention for a broken leg and patriarchal norms had left Baisakhi to fend for herself. As cultivators had harvest rights on the land she leased out, she effectively had no source of food. The government's special welfare programs for the disabled did not reach her. She said, "Disabled people get rice. They get unemployment money. They don't give me anything. What can I do?" She encountered this denial of welfare from two school teachers/politicians—Bimal Das, a Congress leader and a CPM leader, Bolai Master. "They tell me, keep doing what you're doing for now. We will give you a disability card. We will give you one. It is the Age of Will Give You (*debo* Raj) after all."

The significant role of school teachers (doubling as *panchayat* officials) in mediating illegality and material distress on behalf of liquor producers is not an isolated occurrence. In fact, school teachers have been instrumental in helping the CPM accomplish continuous electoral success since 1977 (Bhattacharyya, 2001). Bhattacharyya argues that the CPM built alliances with key sections of a segmented society in order to maintain popular support after its land tenancy reform program, Operation Barga. Rural school teachers were an ideal category as salaried people without vested interests or income from agricultural land, yet knowledgeable about rural society, and educated in leftist ideology. As such, they were perfect conduits to help form "socially extensive trust and reliance between communities and classes" and helped turn these relationships into "tangible support for the party" (Bhattacharyya, 2001, p. 677). Just as they helped make the government "local," they also subjected it to popular scrutiny. Over time, alliances between party, *panchayat*, and school teachers produced a nexus of corruption. When I began fieldwork, honest school teachers were still held in the highest esteem. Others, however, were seen as getting rich on permanently protected jobs, building massive brick houses, buying motor vehicles, and having too much time for politics. Teachers such as Bolai Master and Bimal Das have this kind of reputation. Bolai Master gave CPM ideology local reality, but in so doing he helped construct what Baisakhi refers to as a "*debo* Raj"—the paternalistic mechanisms of negotiating and binding the exchange of welfare for future votes.

Baisakhi, who bought liquor from the Khara neighborhood, said that protestors brought losses to liquor production. Highlighting the immorality of anti-liquor protest, she recounted telling protestors "If you can give me rice, then you can break them [liquor pots]. Otherwise, don't touch these." She argued that the business enabled her to eat. If she could find another type of business, she asked "why would I do such low work. Such dirty work?" She wished that a government institution would employ her as a cook so she could escape the contempt. Notwithstanding her anger at protestors she explained their rationale: "It is for the sake of peace around here. Otherwise, in homes there is beating, verbal abuse, people can't survive." While distress drove her to liquor production, she recognized that liquor caused other forms of material distress for families. In my interviews, I heard of three other women running liquor production units including a widow and another single woman with two sons. The material distress of women without income-generating male kin such as Baisakhi and the widows becomes poverty in public terms, because patriarchal vision views these women as belonging to a public rather than private household.

Nimai Mondol is a fifty-six-year-old liquor producer who invited us into his "dirty home." When we objected, pointing to the neat and tidy room, he said it might be neat, but the home was dirtied by his work. Each liquor seller made reference to the moral judgment they assumed hung in the air. With that out in the open, Nimai described the desperation behind his trade: his wife died of "some fever," he sold three *bighas*[5] of land to pay for his son's thalassemia treatment in Vellore; his son, who died despite these efforts, left him with no help for farm work, which pushed Nimai to resuscitate a trusty business. He earned an average of 50 rupees a day from producing about 60 to 70 (500 ml) bottles of liquor per month. When the *panchayat* leadership came to question him on his work, they left with the understanding that this man was alleviating his hunger.

Dilip Patra is a middle-aged liquor seller with a visibly bent leg, living with his wife, parents, and daughter in a small hut. His broken knee leaves him unable to do heavy labor. His son works in Kolkata city to supplement the household income. Dilip's father's land, received through government land redistribution, was divided among Dilip's four feuding brothers who now live in separate homes. Dilip inherited no land, but as the oldest son, has to look after his father. His monthly income from liquor varies depending on his monthly debt. His distress was expressed as the intimate duties of providing for his household and aging father against the odds of physical ability and opportunity. He asked "Look at my father's age. And if my father cannot eat, and I am not with my household, then am I a human being? What shall I do? There is nothing to be done. I don't even get [his] old age pension."

In another demonstration of welfare maldistribution, Dilip recounted how a pond-making loan opportunity available through the Sundarbans Development Board (local development agency) came to naught for him. He had even used a marital contact to place his name on the "lottery" for loan-receivers. Far from being a matter of bad luck, Mihir Nahiya's[6] understanding was that the corrupt *panchayat* leader had placed the names of jewelers on the "lottery" list meant to enable double cropping on farmland. This is how the corruption of the developmental state failed Dilip, and made it impossible for government officials to question his illegal work. After all, those who deny and corrupt welfare cannot but legitimize Dilip's material distress as poverty, recognizing his lack of choice, which forced him to choose liquor production. Rather than politicize poverty by recognizing the role of their own privilege in perpetuating mechanisms and processes of producing distress, such officials manage poverty by selectively characterizing some people's distress as compelling.

The desperation of disabled bodies, lack of healthcare facilities, financial need, and corruption in the distribution of welfare and livelihood opportunities in a patriarchal agrarian society had driven these three people into the liquor business. Their distress legalizes the work even if it does not take away its low status. While they recognize household distress caused by liquor as moral justification for the anti-liquor protest, Dilip and Baisakhi saw the JS roadblock and destruction of private property, as illegal, even merciless work. The backgrounds of liquor businessmen did however vary. Liquor businessmen typically belonged to Scheduled Castes[7] and roughly half the producers are known as landless or near landless. However, about 20 to 25 percent of named liquor sellers are influential politicians who are middle to high caste, and landowners. Further, since everyone in the Khara neighborhood had now become rich, initial landlessness was not at the forefront of people's imaginations.

School teachers, *panchayat* leaders, police, and liquor consumers help turn the distress and desperation of the liquor producers as a disparate population into a "community" that is justified in choosing liquor production as a livelihood and compelled to do so by their life circumstances. Witnessed drunkenness and visible negotiations with producers at roadblocks perform the social function of stretching the rules, normalizing illegal work in the public sphere. Politicians who questioned illegal producers also engaged in a public pedagogy of dissuading protest by suggesting that it is material distress that drives liquor production. Yet, by stalling disability cards and denying alternative livelihoods state officials materially reproduced distress. Together, they materially and discursively enabled liquor producers to form an, albeit uncoordinated "community" with common convictions about moral dilemmas and circumstantial compulsions. At the same time, the focus on the material compulsions of the poor hides from view the presence of landed and influential liquor producers, confirming that liquor production was not solely the livelihood of the desperate. These sellers made the most of a normalized opportunity, notwithstanding their position on the political–economic scales.

In response, JS activists challenge the selective management and construction of material distress that ignores governmental production of poverty and the ways in which liquor production normalizes a destructive livelihood that alleviates poverty as often as it reproduces it. Jana Sanskriti activists connect people's disparate experiences of a problematic livelihood to speak variously as householders, agricultural workers, landless, seasonal migrants, women abandoned by husbands, and victims of domestic violence. They unite people against a form of revenue generation that destroys families and communities rather than reinforcing a world of shrinking possibilities where *any* employment that generates economic value has to be accepted. Jana Sanskriti faces the massive challenge of constructing collectivity for healthy livelihoods in a context of unemployment and poverty. Against the assumption that epistemic struggles are for those who already have access to bread and land, JS focuses on the reality that those facing material distress do not recuse themselves from epistemic struggles in part because they cannot forfeit the terms of subjection to those who have an interest in reinforcing material distress and inequality.

Along with liquor consumers' wives, JS activists struggle against the mechanisms that delimit *opportunity* as destructive livelihood and *choice* of political action as submission to the paternalistic management of poverty. They thereby help reconstruct the social fabric. Their reconstruction of employment and poverty goes beyond normative political discourse by publicly articulating the value of ethical consumption and production, defining community and private well-being as constitutive of development, and taking multiple meanings of the materiality of poverty into account.

Material Distress in the Sansar

Family has been a historically significant vehicle to persuade women to work for neighborhood, community, or country (Sarkar, 1984; Chatterjee, 1993). Today, family structures help decentralize state responsibilities by invoking principles of reciprocity, obligation, and belonging within a Hindu *sansar* which means household in concrete terms and universe or larger household in abstract terms (Lamb, 2000). NGOs, for example, have used the rhetoric that selfless work for community (*sansar* in its abstract meaning) is the best route to alleviating poverty in the household (*sansar* in its privatized meaning) (Mohan, 2003, pp. 235–240).

Such invocation of *sansar* is significantly out of touch with contemporary anxieties expressed about growing disunity in families where sons are blamed for wasting expensive investment in education and leaving parents insecure and where brothers fight over inherited land (Da Costa, 2008). These anxieties around broken families have a political economic face captured in the Bengali Chief Minister's representation of the agrarian crisis: CPM-initiated land reform helped construct a stable social base, but rejuvenated landlessness has arisen from increasingly divided landholdings among children of land reform beneficiaries, neo-liberal policies worldwide, and increasingly costly agricultural inputs. Agricultural growth has reached a point of ever-diminishing returns for farmers (Bhattacharya, 2007).

The CPM rejuvenates revenue and rural livelihood by seeing liquor production as solution. Yet, fragmentation of land and family in rural Bengal is the very reason liquor production *as* solution is perceived as divisive, poverty-inducing, and harmful. For, along with land divisions within families, liquor production was an added factor dividing families and draining household incomes. While women informants were increasingly aware of their constant welfare and care work for the larger "public" household to alleviate the inequality generated by neo-liberalism, they found that the liquor-induced breakdown of the "private" household was ignored by the same leaders who sought electoral support or mobilized community development. Women are primary care-takers of household, community, and agricultural work, so amidst seasonal male migration, liquor production, and consumption they are not surprisingly at the forefront of anti-liquor protest.

In interviews, without exception, people cited domestic strife and violence as the main repercussions from liquor. Women and adolescent children bore the brunt of decreasing household incomes (for schooling) and increasing domestic violence. I remembered Naina Middha being unafraid of police, cameras, and the alcohol-producers anger at the roadblock in 2005. Naina is about forty years old and lives in the Khara neighborhood with her two sons and an alcoholic husband. To support her household she works on others' fields tying up ropes lining tomato plants and cutting the rice harvest, and growing rice on her ten *kathas* of land. Naina was seen as brave for speaking to me considering Bolai Master (school teacher and former *panchayat* official) is her neighbor from whom she borrows money in desperate times.

By borrowing money from Bolai Master, Naina reinforced paternalistic relations to secure her welfare as protection against her poverty. But, this did not stop her from politicizing her poverty. She said sometimes her husband drinks for three or four days till he is completely unconscious, although now her sons curb his drinking. Neighbors rarely intervene in household fights because there are too many fights, "Should neighbors help sort out all these fights?" Naina remembered asking the policemen at the roadblock, "If you don't do anything when people tell you of their difficulties and problems with liquor, then what interest do we have in telling you our problems? What interest, you tell me?! You tell me who should I complain to about conflicts in home after home?" Naina explained that officials remain unperturbed not only because household matters are private, but because "they take bribes behind the scenes. That

Exhibit 2.3   Naina at the forefront of efforts to gain an audience among unperturbed policemen at the anti-liquor agitation.

is why they cannot find a solution to our problems." Naina's point is that government representatives negotiating with liquor producers and consumers make her experience an unthinkable definition of material distress, too "domestic" to be grounds for policy decisions and party politics. Naina, who participated in the anti-liquor protest, also realizes that despite publicizing the connections of corruption, bodily harm, and impoverishment, she has no audience.

Her public protests generated further fighting at home because unlike Baisakhi and the widows engaged in liquor production subject to protections from a public household, Naina also has to contend with her husband's delimitations of "private" and "public" solutions to poverty. Her husband asked her why she was participating in "these women's organizations." She retorted, "Why shouldn't I go? They [liquor businesses] are making money from a poor household like ours. That does not hurt you? It does not touch your conscience? You go there and they buy land, they grow rice, buy cars, based on our pain, our difficulties. This is what you want. Is this the solution to our household's sorrows?" Responding to her husband's reluctance to go public with private problems, Naina questions him for worsening financial hardships and for having already made private problems public by using household money to enrich liquor producers.

I asked Naina whether liquor production in Khara neighborhood had in fact stopped as Baisakhi had claimed in her interview. Appalled at my question, she explained the challenge of ending liquor production, which goes right to the heart of divisive party politics.

> This is a CPM neighborhood. If you say anything about liquor production they shout at you.... We are divided. That's the other thing. The people in this neighborhood are partly in our camp, and another half in the Khara camp. The parties will not let us talk to each other and sort it out. The party wants to talk to both sides. But the parties say different things. They sing one song in our camp and another song in their camp. Now which song will you listen to?

While the dominant understanding of material distress counts on people racing to the bottom against each other, reaffirming beliefs in lack of choice and diminished sense of worth, Naina believes people can unite against a production process and political mechanisms that blatantly gain from divisions, desperation, grief, and poverty. Yet her faith in protest was wavering, "nothing has changed in fifty years.... In this life, I will not have happiness. We will only have burn and punishment, of a husband, burn of *sansar*, burn of children." And then back to resolve "we have to work together in a family, right? That's why I protest. I take blows from my husband, why not take blows from police?"

Here, Naina challenges patriarchal norms that foreclose the possibility of women giving meaning to "public" and "private." She questions patriarchal expectations of not bringing family dishonor and of working together for the *sansar* by revealing the continuities between her husband and the police in her private and public households. For her, to cause losses to the liquor business is essential work to strike a blow against the profit they make from addiction, impoverishment, and conflicts in poor homes.

For Naina, politicizing poverty requires: (1) representing multiple and differentiated forms of material distress, and, relatedly, (2) representing the burden of poverty in the public household as unequally borne by private households and citizens.

Medha Bairagi, a thirty-five-year-old woman who lives with her two teenage daughters and her alcoholic husband, also says that she participates in the anti-liquor agitation "so that *I* can get peace.... So that there isn't war at home day in and day out." As in Naina's home, where sons fight the father, Medha's daughters fight with their father, over money, marriage, and school. Medha had been to Congress Party leader Bimal Das "at least a hundred times." Her neighbors don't mobilize for change because they view liquor as inevitable: "Our lives will end, but liquor will not." Medha is convinced that she has to try. "It isn't always CPM rule or Trinamul rule. Things *do* change. Similarly, I don't accept that liquor is here to stay."

Naina and Medha's ongoing struggles to unite people mirror JS efforts to encourage a leap of faith against the political and economic common sense that the poor have no choice. On one liquor raid, villagers gathered in support of the producer who was a widow. They argued that she would have nothing to eat without the business. Jana Sanskriti activist Radha Das recalled her response to them:

Radha: She would not have anything to eat? How many families in your village? At least seventy, right? Now this one person's business is causing harm in hundreds of other homes and you are coming together to support her. But all of you in seventy homes have not found a way of coming together to say that we will all take turns to support this widow! That we will take turns—whether it is rice, or vegetables or whatever it is! Instead you are supporting an illegal business which is breaking up another twenty homes.... I said this to them.
Researcher: What did they say?
Radha: They all agreed that this is definitely bad work, but argued that government and the big fish should be attacked for giving licenses, not small fish. I said to them that in order to attack the government we need men and women from your homes. Where else am I supposed to find the strength to take on the government? We have to be together in this.

In light of a destructive but lucrative business, necessary in the vote market as it tames hunger while disabling conscience and collectives, JS activists hold up a mirror to people's consent for what does and does not count as poverty. They do so by highlighting the selective condemnation of illegality, demeaning choices, and divisive politics offered by a neo-liberal version of development. In the end, Naina, Medha, and JS activists believe that people can choose to act differently. In so doing, these protestors are combating the normalization of competition for scarce resources as the foundation for social relations, electoral politics, and community unity. They are reclaiming the possibility of defining the "social" in social relations as founded in material, emotional, and collective well-being of households. In short, they are reclaiming development.

Conclusions

I have recounted struggles for and against liquor production as a source of employment and alleviation of poverty, to reveal the competing, multiple, and differentiated meanings of poverty, livelihood, and legality in contemporary rural Bengal. Jana Sanskriti and protesting wives reveal the social processes and political mechanisms through which liquor becomes the only viable and valuable means of generating revenue and employment and the forms of material distress that are excluded from consideration in definitions of development.

From the point of view of JS activism, the undoubtedly real, but de-historicized, labeling of "having no choice," amounts to a foundational destruction of self-worth that perpetuates unjust forms of exploitation and rule. This syndrome reappears in debates about development, where, for example, it is routinely claimed that if not for sweatshop work, people would starve, prostitute themselves, or scour garbage dumps. Lack of income-generating opportunities combined with patriarchal constraints, physical disability, and death/absence of male farmhands push people in an agrarian economy toward distress and destructive livelihood options.

While cognizant of constraints that drive liquor production, JS activists publicize the mechanisms through which the influential rich embed a neo-liberal race to the bottom as a justified response to poverty today. Jana Sanskriti refuses to conceptually and politically reinforce this evaluation of people's worth and work. Studying the actions of liquor producers, state representatives, and protestors shows that within the terms of historically available options, particular and selective understandings of poverty are privileged and mobilized to structure "choice," delimiting possibilities and opportunities, and the very meanings of poverty and development. The political and economic processes of earning votes, livelihoods, and welfare distinguish liquor producers' poverty as part of constructing solutions while Naina and Medha's poverty is seen as a tragic, private story, too messy for development policy and its public program for managing material distress.

Jana Sanskriti presents this public construction of material distress and the mediating support of well-heeled politicians and the police for liquor producers as crucial reasons for constructing collective action. Jana Sanskriti organizes collective action against violent, divisive, and poverty-inducing results of liquor as an imperative and available choice for the poor. The members of JS struggle to represent and legitimize excluded realities and definitions of poverty to construct an alternative choice. Their alternative proposes poverty as an outcome of material and representational inequality within the multiple and intersecting political histories of capitalism, state formation, and patriarchy. Their struggle also reveals that marginal actors do not always consent to delimited possibilities and opportunities despite their marginal condition. Their struggles remind us that the question of who experiences and defines poverty is always subject to political choices by variously positioned actors simultaneously alienated from and embedded within power relations. For example, among the poor described in this essay, while Naina and Medha as much as Baisakhi, Dilip, and Nimai negotiate daily alienation and entrenched histories of class and gender inequality to meet survival needs, the liquor producers render the construction of poverty opaque while the women against liquor production expose and challenge the political choices which reinforce poverty and alienation.

While governments rely on a market episteme and a patriarchal public view of poverty, a grounded and politicized view of poverty would take multiple expressions of poverty—disabled bodies, domestic violence, increased workloads for poor women, bodies, and communities imploding with liquor consumption—into account as the concrete, competing realities that constitute a general problem. Without this attention to complexity, poverty (and development) is managed by reifying employment unconditionally as opportunity. Instead, as we have seen, employment conceived as a mode of governing poverty produces further divisions, exploitation, and competition. When the question "Have they disabled us?" is asked, it is at heart, a hope and conviction that private households have the "choice" to stop competing against each other (via impoverished experiences) and demand collective welfare. Without this, Naina, Medha, and JS argue, the poor consent to the dominant episteme that they, as the poor, have no choice.

Notes

* Acknowledgments: This paper could not have been written without the support of Jana Sanskriti leadership and activists. I am grateful to Amita Baviskar, Alexandre Da Costa, Ann Grodzins Gold, Andreas Hernandez, Aditya Nigam, Philip McMichael, Karuna Morarji, and Alicia Swords for their comments on previous versions of this paper. A version of chapter two and accompanying photos were previously published as Dia Da Costa, 2010. "Have They Disabled Us? Liquor Production and Grammars of Material Distress and Distribution" in *Development Dramas: Reimagining Rural Political Action in Eastern India* New Delhi: Routledge.
1. Prasad Sardar is one of twelve key actors/activists in Jana Sanskriti. He used to be a daily wage laborer before his JS work and lives with six others in a landless household in rural Bengal.
2. The land and infrastructural support promised to investors generated massive conflicts over the terms of development (Bhaduri, 2007; Da Costa, 2007).
3. Bibek Haldar is a thirty-nine-year-old male who has been a JS activist since 1999. Central to the anti-liquor agitation, he led other men in scripting the play *Hai Re Mod* (The Bane of Drink). He lives in a CPM household of ten that collectively owns twelve *bighas* of land.
4. Panchayats are local institutions of self-government that are conduits for development funds and projects.
5. 1 *bigha* = approximately 1/3rd acre.
6. Radha Das, Mihir Nahiya, and I collectively interviewed Dilip. Radha Das is a thirty-one-year-old woman and among the central activists of JS since 1994. Her landless parents supported four daughters. Mihir Nahiya is a thirty-five-year-old male, who has been a JS activist since 2002. He has one and a half *bighas* of land.
7. Scheduled Castes are designations in the Indian census which give special benefits, opportunities, and reservations in government programs and jobs to those historically low in the caste hierarchy.

3.

CITIES WITHOUT CITIZENS

A Perspective on the Struggle of Abahlali baseMjondolo,
the Durban Shackdweller Movement*

Raj Patel

Abahlali baseMjondolo problematizes "ownership" as means of production and self-improvement in the development narrative by investing it with the right to a place in the city—as a question of social reproduction and cultural entitlement (given the particular history of race and class in post-apartheid South Africa). In contesting betrayal of their urban land claims, in an electoral context, this movement brings a new sensibility into the public discourse of rights and responsibilities, challenging its members' impoverishment and demobilization as citizens of the anti-apartheid struggle.

While class struggle constitutes the motive force in history, it is not always clear and pure as *class* struggle and may take varied forms under different concrete situations. In non-revolutionary situations much of the class struggle is latent and even unidentifiable as such at any particular moment. To talk about class struggle at such times is really to register the fact of class struggle *ex-post facto*. The development of classes and class struggle can only be talked about tendentially in terms of historical trends. In fact, classes hardly become fully *class* conscious except in situations of intense political struggle. Class consciousness does not fully dawn upon individuals until they are locked in political battles. It is not surprising to find bourgeois critics of Marx always pointing to the proletariat's lack of class consciousness as an incontrovertible proof of the falsity of the theory...the conclusion is derived from a wrong premise through a wrong method (Shivji, 1975, p. 8).

Introduction

One of the oddest moments of my work in South Africa involved a visit by a distinguished American professor. A self-styled Marxist poet, he visited Durban in the early 2000s, graduate students in tow, to check out the struggle. I don't recall if he had a ponytail, but I imagine he did. A couple of us at the University of KwaZulu-Natal took him to some of the poorest settlements in the city, in which the failures of the African National Congress (ANC), to redistribute wealth and power after the end of apartheid had led to misery and, in some cases, rebellion. After hearing from some of the activists on the ground, hearing of the ways in which the ANC had become an impediment to the very goals it once espoused, the disappointed poet shook his head and said,

"Yeah, you know, this is hard. I'm not really sure people in America are ready to hear this." And, to those of us in the room who discussed it afterward, what it really seemed he meant was "I'm not ready to hear about this."

The myth of the ANC, particularly to activists and academics in the Global North who celebrated the release of Nelson Mandela in 1990 and the end of apartheid in 1994, was deeply cherished. From afar, the anti-apartheid struggle offered an example of progressive change at a time when the forces of market capitalism seemed ascendant—Francis Fukuyama's *End of History* was published in 1992 in the middle of negotiations over the end of apartheid. South Africa was, in the imagination of overseas activists at least, a place of cherished exception, where some sliver of progressive heaven might still fall to earth.

Those closer to the action had a different story. The transformation of the ANC into a party that advanced middle-class interests over those of the majority of the people could be read early on. Steve Biko anticipated it. In a 1972 interview, he argued:

> This is one country where it would be possible to create a capitalist black society, if whites were intelligent, if the nationalists were intelligent. And that capitalist black society, black middle class would be very effective.... South Africa could succeed in putting across to the world a pretty convincing, integrated picture, with still 70 percent of the population being underdogs (Mngxitama, Alexander, and Gibson, 2008).

Mandela himself, soon after his release, spoke of a program of nationalization, but after being given the party line, it was a program that he was never to mention again, even as he became President in 1994. Instead, the ANC rapidly launched into a program of neo-liberal economic development that was soon to earn it plaudits from the World Bank, even as its level of human development tumbled from 58th in 1995 in the United Nations Development Program's rankings to 121st in 2005. As the economy grew, and a few became very rich indeed, wealth was not shared equally, and the poor suffered.

It is possible to tell the story of the ANC's transformation into an elite party catering to the needs of the rich as a story about the structural necessities of the state being a committee for the elite, as Karl Marx argued (Marx & Bender, 1988). It would also be possible to tell the ANC's capture as the inevitable aftermath of the struggle for national liberation, as Franz Fanon predicted (1965). There's nothing inevitable about this process, though. Although the Third World state *appears* lost to the poor, it is never totally so, and it can certainly never appear to be an impregnable bastion of elite interests. The state needs legitimacy in order to govern and therefore needs to appear to be something that it is not. The way that modern states lay claim to legitimacy is through the practices and language of democracy.

In a sense, all social movement studies are examinations of struggles over democracy, because while democracy can be a tool of hegemony, the struggle for it is a demonstration that hegemony is always incomplete, and always a process. This explains why even "modern democracies" have social movements within them, making claims against the state for the right to politics (Rancière, 1998). In this chapter, I examine the fight for democracy by analyzing democracy's most conspicuous spectacle—the election. By examining the politics of elections (as distinct from electoral politics) I show how the ANC has become an organization with middle-class interests not through an elite history, but through ethnographic analysis of those betrayed by the party. The transformation of the state into a committee for the elite is never a generalized and theoretical exercise—it involves specific places and struggles, with fights over the meanings of citizenship, nation, state, and place.

The American academic was not the only person unprepared to hear this. The ANC itself has proved resistant to hearing the truth of its betrayal. Foucault's thoughts on the relation of power and knowledge are important guides here. Foucault argues that:

> There is a battle "for truth", or at least "around truth"—it being understood once again that by truth I do not mean "the ensemble of truths which are to be discovered and accepted", but rather "the ensemble of rules according to which the true and the false are separated and specific effects of power attached to the true", it being understood also that it's not a matter of a battle "on behalf" of the truth, but of a battle about the status of truth and the economic and political role it plays (1980, p. 132).

Truth, then, is itself the subject of contest. Knowledge production (by powers that be or their subjects) aims to configure truth in such a way as to address and (re) shape power relations.[1] The meaning of terms matters, for meaning is both an object of struggle, and the means to secure further victories. If consensus can be created through the limitation of the ambit of a question within certain parameters, a struggle is won before it is explicitly fought. This, perhaps, explains the reluctance of the American academic to accept the truth of the poor of the shack communities of Durban, clinging instead to his dated but dearly held notions of what the ANC was really about. The esteem in which he held the party was something the ANC was desperate to inculcate in its poorest citizens, but which it had done much, through its actions, to crush. To understand why the poorest people should break with a political party that seemingly held its interests dear, we need specifics.

Living Land Questions in Durban's Clare Estate

Exhibit 3.1 is a map of the Clare Estate area in Durban. In the center of it is the Bisasar Road[2] dump. The dump was located there by the apartheid-era Durban municipality at the beginning of the 1980s, in the middle of a residential area scheduled as Indian by the apartheid Group Areas Act.[3] After apartheid ended, the life of the dump was extended by the ANC-controlled municipality, despite objections from residents. Those objections pointed to the range of toxins and effluent that have been illegally dumped there, and poisoned the adjacent neighbourhood (Bond and Dada, 2005).

At its northeast rim, we see the Kennedy Road shack settlement, which has been there for over two decades. It was initially a small group of shacks, but it grew at the end of apartheid, with the rescinding in the 1980s of the Influx Control Laws.[4]

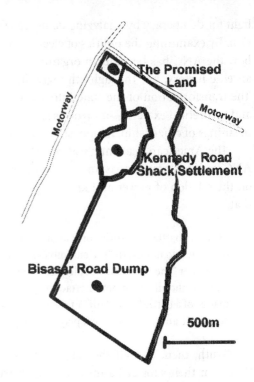

Exhibit 3.1   No Land, No Hope.

Africans from rural areas who had previously been prohibited from entering Durban were now free to look for work in the city, though they were invariably too poor to access formal housing. Today, the population of the settlement stands at between six and seven thousand people, who have access to six water pipes and rudimentary sanitation.

Three factors together meant that the state found it convenient to allow poor people to live in shacks around the edge of the rubbish dump in Kennedy Road: the undesirability of the land at the edge of a major solid waste facility; the need for low-cost/low-skill workers in the city; and the municipality's unwillingness to prioritize formal housing for Africans who were using their newfound freedom of movement to search for work. These general features of town planning, noted in *The Economist* (2007), were augmented by a further political consideration: the residents in formal housing in the electoral ward around Clare Estate were not historically members or supporters of the ANC, while shackdwellers strongly supported the ruling party.

Durban's 1999 poll results point to the strong presence of the Democratic Alliance, a party to the right of the ANC, with a constituency disproportionately white, coloured, Indian and middle class.[5] Within Durban, the ANC—a party that had fought the struggle against apartheid under the banner of standing up for the rights of the poor—fared considerably better in areas of the city with large shack settlements.[6] This is not a particularly South African phenomenon—poor people are used as vote banks throughout the world (Fernandes and Heller, 2006). The migration to these middle class areas of large numbers of Africans, who were organized *in situ* to support the ANC, secured consistently higher returns at the polls for the ruling party. This trend might have continued, with the ANC building its hegemony, with the Democratic Alliance struggling to maintain a falling electoral presence, and with shackdwellers as the faithful and local sirens of the ANC's national majority. But it was not to be.[7]

The positioning of the Bisasar Road dump had always been subject to objection and resistance from local residents (Bond and Dada, 2005), with recurrent action and activism around land in the area.[8] Among the recent opponents of land use and distribution was Sajida Khan, who had long fought for the closure of the Bisasar Road dump. She had led a group of concerned citizens and activists to reject the continued and illegal dumping of toxic waste near her home. She had also conducted an impromptu survey that found a "belt" of cancers near the dump, which could be traced to the dump's practice of burning solid waste, and the resultant production of carcinogenic compounds.[9]

Khan's ongoing activism focused on the cessation of polluting activities at the dump, the reimbursement of affected landowners at a fair market value rate, and the relocation of shackdwellers to other housing concomitant with the government's own housing plans.[10] Under these plans, shackdwellers from Kennedy Road were slated to be relocated from there to Verulam, a town a few dozen kilometers away from Clare Estate, which was widely perceived to lack adequate housing facilities, education, or healthcare. Most of all, the housing was far from the jobs and economic possibilities that had brought shackdwellers to Kennedy Road in the first place.

The view that the shackdwellers are dupes, fooled by the municipal authorities into believing that work and other benefits will be made available to them from the dump, and that shackdwellers are pawns in a bigger game of which they are unaware, is one shared both by Khan and by a range of other commentators (Bond and Dada, 2005). It may be the case that shackdwellers are manipulated—as a population in vote banks, they have indeed been used by the ANC. But, and this is a crucial distinction, in the process of this manipulation, shackdwellers were not impassive or foolish or even irrational. The ANC did, after all, bring social spending directed specifically at poor black people, through child grants and pensions. The ANC offered material and ideological goods that were important in the impoverished and multi-ethnic shack settlements, and were understood as such. And, more to the point, while Khan and other residents with formal housing and water are happy to consign shackdwellers to distant areas, shackdwellers themselves were, together, forming their own sophisticated views regarding both the opinions held about them across the class divide, and of the ANC itself.

In the words of Mnikelo Ndabankulu, a shackdweller from nearby Foreman Road:

> "(Mayor Obed) Mlaba wants to relocate us to Verulam. Why? Because of property prices. I thought the government slogan was Batho Pele (People First) and not property prices," he said. He points to an empty plot of land adjacent to the settlement, "They promised to build us housing on that side...we don't want to move to Verulam, we like it here in [electoral] ward 25" (Langanparsad, 2006).

Articulating the issues of land, nationhood, party, and citizenship, Ndabankulu invokes the memories of anti-apartheid struggle, the promises it brought, the slogans generated within it, and the disappointments in the wake of 1994. It is an analysis that demonstrates that shackdwellers need not have been cast as hapless and ignorant dupes, and it is a reminder that some civil society analysis, while offering progressive politics but ignoring class, can fall to forces of reaction.[11] Ndabankulu's words reward further analysis (below), but to be able to do them justice, we need yet more details, this time about the character of shackdweller analysis and organizing. The final detail in Exhibit 3.1 is an area of land less than a hectare in size. It is the land to which Ndabankulu was pointing in the above quotation. It is known to all as "the promised land," a moniker it earned as a result of its being promised repeatedly, over the course of a decade, to the residents of the Kennedy Road shack settlement.

Through the promises, the land achieved a mythic status similar to the original Promised Land, an embodiment of the post-apartheid dividend that was temporarily in limbo, but that when disbursed to the shack residents, would bring about the end of their poverty. It was with great hope, then, that in March 2005 residents of the shacks welcomed the arrival of bulldozers onto the Promised Land; but they were profoundly disillusioned when they learned that the local ANC councillor had given the land not to the residents, but to a local brick company. The residents organized a protest later that weekend, burning tires on a major arterial road at the bottom of their settlement. The police intervened, arresting fourteen people at random, including legal minors, and detaining them under charges of public violence (Patel and Pithouse, 2005).

The confrontation between the state and the shackdwellers escalated. Legal protests were organized to demand both clarity and action from the ANC representatives who had previously relied on the shackdwellers as a repository of votes and good faith.

First, a protest was launched against the incumbent Councillor, Yakoob Baig, a career politician who had switched his allegiance from the National Party—the architects of apartheid—to the Democratic Alliance to the ANC over the course of his career. When Councillor Baig failed to respond to demands, shackdwellers escalated their protests to the municipal level, demanding that Mayor Obed Mlaba, and city manager Mike Sutcliffe, respond to questions and issues relating to housing. One such protest was illegally and violently dispersed by the local Sydenham police force.[12] When the City Manager and Mayor failed to respond, the shackdwellers approached a higher level of government, petitioning Mike Mabuyakhulu, KwaZulu-Natal's Provincial Minister of Local Government Housing and Traditional Affairs. A march and rally at which a list of demands was scheduled to be handed to the Provincial Minister was illegally banned by the municipality. The shackdwellers obtained a high court injunction to proceed with their march.

The protests took place against the year-long run-up to the 2006 Municipal Elections, which were held on March 1. Throughout the escalating process, and increasingly at the marches, it became clear to the shackdwellers that their role in the state's plan was as patient recipients of development, rather than active participants in its conception. Despite the state's rhetoric of participatory development, the kind of participation expected reflected a more authoritarian vision. Reflecting on this five years earlier, Heller observed the trend:

> The ANC's drift toward centralized control and technocratic domination can only be explained by the demobilization of popular sectors and the state's disengagement from civil society (Heller, 2001, p. 158).

Many shackdwellers experienced this demobilization as symptomatic of a broader betrayal. The arts of citizenship, engagement, debate, and iconoclasm learned and practiced under the anti-apartheid struggles were systematically denigrated by the government. Instead, the state extolled the virtues of patience, and of faith in authority. While some residents of formal housing next to the dump shared with shackdwellers a disdain for the state, both the state and some middle-class residents seem to have shared a view of the poor as needing to do what they were told.

The dialectics of betrayal and disappointment, of protest and counter-maneuver, spawned a network of social organizations. Shackdwellers in different settlements, at weekly meetings, came to unite under the name of "Abahlali baseMjondolo"—Zulu for "those who stay in shacks." In response to the systematic denigration of their knowledge about their conditions, and the frequent use of knowledge in authority against them, the shackdwellers organized into a broad social movement, some members of the movement described it as "the University of Abahlali baseMjondolo" (see Pithouse, 2006; Patel, 2007). Shackdwellers came quickly to the realization that a great deal of their potential power lay precisely in their role as "vote banks," as deliverers of the ANC's mandate to rule on behalf of a racial and poor majority. The upcoming election offered a moment of "political opportunity."[13]

No Land No House No Vote

The slogan "No Land No House No Vote" is one that was circulated widely within the shack communities (see Exhibit 3.2). The slogan was an inspired piece of political propaganda, forged in widespread meetings across different settlements (at which the possibility of fielding their own candidate was discussed and then decided against). The slogan linked the popular mandate with a re-articulated question of land as a means to a place in the city. It resisted gentrification (Smith, 2002), demanding instead a right to live, move, work, and play in Durban. It was a demand with which the ANC was not pleased.

The rupture between the shackdwellers and the ANC happened at the same time that the party came under increasing attack in the media and on the streets for its failure to address growing inequality, and a widespread feeling that it had betrayed the poor. Although shackdwellers in Durban had organized into South Africa's largest social movement independent of the state,[14] the discontent to which it gave voice was being manifest nationwide. In 2005, over 6000 demonstrations, legal and illegal, were organized in South Africa.[15] In a bid to downplay these rebellions, the state referred

Exhibit 3.2   The No Land No House No Vote Movement in Action.

to them as "spontaneous service delivery protests" (Cape Argus, 2005). In fact, the protests were rarely spontaneous, nor were they about service delivery. As any community organizer knows, it takes forever to organize a spontaneous protest. Such was the case of the Kennedy Road protests, which were the culmination of over a decade of promise and betrayal. The description of "spontaneous protest," however, painted the participants in the protest as unthinking, and the government's failure as singularly a failure to provide, rather than as the broader demobilization and deskilling of its citizens in the arts of politics and citizenship. These rhetorical moves were augmented by a public spat in 2004 between President Thabo Mbeki and Desmond Tutu, ending with the Archbishop thanking Mbeki "for telling me what you think of me. That I am a liar with scant regard for the truth and a charlatan posing with his concern for the poor, the hungry, the oppressed and the voiceless."[16] Such attempts at delegitimization were the stock in trade of the apartheid regime, and it is ironic that it was Helen Zille, of the Democratic Alliance, the party to the right of the ANC, who observed that "It is a very poor reflection on the post-apartheid government that it is using exactly the same tactics [as under apartheid] in an attempt to silence him [Tutu]" (South African Press Association [SAPA], 2004).

Mbeki himself was at pains to address the discontent of poor people around his government's performance. In mid-2005, he appealed to the public saying that "We must stop this business of people going into the street to demonstrate about lack of delivery. These are the things that the youth used to do in the struggle against apartheid" (Mbeki 2005). The logic here, just to be clear, is that with the end of apartheid comes also the end of possibilities that the government's behavior is anything but legitimate, and therefore beyond reproach. Further ANC communications made it clear that any debate was a matter internal to the party.[17] It was, therefore, an extension of the discourse of unreason that "service delivery protesters" were seen as criminals.[18]

Attempts to criminalize the poor are, however, difficult to maintain when the numbers involved become as large as those involved in the Abahlali baseMjondolo movement (over 30,000 members today). When the official narrative has been unsuccessful in casting the majority of shackdwellers as wolves, it has tried to portray them as sheep. Responsibility for their deviant behavior has been placed almost everywhere but at the door of the poor themselves. Academics working with the poor have been accused of stirring up trouble—a repeat of the Third Force discourse under apartheid, when the ANC (correctly) accused the government of fomenting rebellion within black urban areas through paramilitary and covert operations.[19]

The language of a "third force" in the contemporary context suggests, more than anything else, that the poor themselves are not able to articulate their own grievances, much less organize to demand them. The third force is necessary because the poor are too stupid, incapable, or politically immature. In response, this language was appropriated and turned around in a widely circulated article, by the elected head of the Abahlali baseMjondolo, S'bu Zikode, entitled: "I am the Third Force," in which Zikode was able to flip the issue of power and representation on its head:

> We need to get things clear. There definitely is a Third Force. The question is what is it and who is part of the Third Force? Well, I am Third Force myself. The Third Force is all the pain and the suffering that the poor are subjected to every second in our lives. The shack dwellers have many things to say about the Third Force. It is time for us to speak out and to say this is who we are, this is where we are and this how we live. The life that we are living makes our communities the Third Force. Most of us are not working and have to spend all day struggling for small money. AIDS is worse in the shack settlements than anywhere else. Without proper houses, water, electricity, refuse removal and toilets all kinds of diseases breed. The causes are clearly visible…. Our bodies itch every day because of the insects. If it is raining everything is wet—blankets and floors. If it is hot the mosquitoes and flies are always there. There is no holiday in the shacks. When the evening comes—it is always a challenge. The night is supposed to be for relaxing and getting rest. But it doesn't happen like that in the jondolos. People stay awake worrying about their lives. You must see how big the rats are that will run across the small babies in the night. You must see how people have to sleep under the bridges when it rains because their floors are so wet. The rain comes right inside people's houses. Some people just stand up all night (2005).

The municipal authority met the counter-position of shackdwellers with its own moves in the run-up to the elections. It attempted to fracture the shack-based organizing with morsels of patronage, currying favor and fomenting dissent with promises for the future. As the elections drew closer, party representatives promised key community leaders in shack settlements that in exchange for guaranteeing ANC votes, the municipality would re-house them. The municipality also announced, prematurely it turns out,[20] that it was about to build between 15,000 and 20,000 houses for poor families in a R10 billion (approximately US$1 billion) development.[21] All that the municipality asked from the shackdwellers was a little patience, and that they refrain from embarrassing the government further by talking to the media. It was a request that was met with the response that "Democracy is not about us being loyal to Nkosi [traditional lord]. Democracy is about Nkosi being loyal to the citizens of this province."[22]

The political back-and-forth, between the shackdwellers, the local middle class, the municipality, and the government each had its own dimension, each with its own mobilization of concerns around land, and around the claims that would stabilize "ownership" of that land as an uncontested fact. At many protests, the South African flag has been a constant feature, linking the demands of the protest directly to claims on the nation, and the state. At the protest on March 27, 2006, the protest's memorandum began with the words:

> We the shackdwellers of Durban, democrats and loyal citizens of the Republic of South Africa, note that this country is rich because of the theft of our land and because of our work in the farms, mines, factories, kitchens and laundries of the rich. We cannot and will not continue to suffer the way that we do.[23]

The appeal to citizenship, and to loyalty, is also a feature of demands from other protests.[24] Mnikelo Ndabankulu's reference to house prices trumping people reveals the transformation of the state in its local government forms, as a class agent. And it is *house prices*, not housing, that Ndabankulu points to—the prices being the normalized institution of "ownership," rather than the politically charged notion of "people" that are summoned by citizenship. This range of tensions over land might be summarized in Table 3.1.

It was under these conditions that the 2006 municipal elections were held, with the shackdwellers pushing for a "no land no house no vote" position, with local home owners concerned about the value of their property, and with the government taking

Table 3.1 Constituencies and Concepts Mobilized Around Land in Kennedy Road

Constituency	Land value	Ways value might be increased	"Ownership" stabilized by claims to...
Local councillor	Source of patronage (alleged)	Trouble-free disposal of land to local business	Position as "elected official"
Shackdweller community	Means to access jobs, healthcare, education facilities Source of food (for a handful of families)	Security of tenure	Occupation, moral claim, political mobilization, citizenship
Local house-dwellers	Store of value Access to jobs, healthcare, education, facilities	Removal of shackdwellers (perceived reduced crime and increased house valuation)	harm already suffered by dump, history of occupation of land.
Property developers	Possibility of redevelopment	Removal of shackdwellers	Promise of "black economic empowerment"
Municipality	Sink for municipal refuse		Greater public good
Party	Vote bank (2000)	Site of trouble-markets—remove key organizers	Heritage of anti-apartheid struggle, guardians of nationhood, democracy and development

an increasingly and publicly hard line against the shackdwellers on whom they had relied for a vote. The meaning of the election was, at least as far as the government was concerned, a referendum on its post-apartheid policies, and an opportunity for citizens to participate in a process that would re-confer a mandate for its hegemony.

When the ANC won, it claimed precisely this vindication. As Thabo Mbeki put it:

> Once more the masses of our people have confirmed their confidence in our movement as the leading representative and repository of their hopes and aspirations. For our movement and indeed for all democrats, the days ahead of us must and will be days of celebration.
>
> There are many things that we must celebrate. We must celebrate the fact that we have further entrenched our position as the largest political formation in our country, freely chosen by our people as the leading party of government in all three spheres of government. We must celebrate the fact that the masses of our people continue to support the ANC perspective of progressive social transformation, and unreservedly acknowledge the positive changes we have brought about since 1994.[25]

A closer scrutiny of the election data suggests that while the ANC may have increased its majority, not least in Durban's electoral wards (23 and 25) in which shackdwellers organized, something else was afoot (see Table 3.2).

The two features to note in the election results are, first, a reduced turnout, and second, more revealing, a defection away from the Democratic Alliance greater than the increase of the ANC's vote. Indeed, had it not been for the shifting profile of the ANC's vote, it would have lost these two electoral wards. What happened, though, is that the Democratic Alliance, with its right-of-center agenda which appeals, in large part, to a middle-class constituency, saw its faithful voters draining into the ANC as the ANC marked out its willingness to cater to a new middle class, in the name of catering (as Mbeki fulsomely claimed) to every citizen.

It is important here to identify the election not as a final result, but as a further moment in the ongoing battle for hegemony. The election itself was part of the move and counter-move, in which the understanding of terms like "democracy," "citizenship," and nationhood inflect questions of land. Mbeki's claim to be acting for all is somewhat belied by the ballot data, and by the party and police actions which specifically targeted poor and "badly behaved" Africans living in the city, badly behaved because they dare to claim their rights before the ANC is ready to deliver them, years after they had been promised. Through these actions, the party and state displayed a particular, and important, attitude to shackdwellers, and their citizenship.

Citizens Without Citizenship

Giorgio Agamben offers an incisive analysis of citizenship. In his "Beyond Human Rights" (2003), he analyzes Hannah Arendt's (1943) essay "We Refugees." Agamben sees the refugee as the "only thinkable figure for the people of our time and the only category in which one may see today—at least until the process of dissolution of the nation-state and its sovereignty has achieved full completion—the forms and limits of a coming political community." He justifies this by reminding us that

Table 3.2 Election Data Wards 23 and 25

Party Name	2000		2006		% change
	Votes	%	Votes	%	
Ward 23					
Independent	656	15.0	41	1.0	−14.0
Democratic alliance	1007	23.0	639	15.6	−7.4
National United People's Organisation	36	0.8	16	0.4	−0.4
Pan Africanist Congress of Azania	15	0.3	5	0.1	−0.2
Vryheidsfront Plus			1	0.0	0.0
eThekwini Ecopeace	4	0.1	11	0.3	0.2
National Democratic Convention			10	0.2	0.2
United Democratic Movement			12	0.3	0.3
Scara Civic Party			14	0.3	0.3
Truly Alliance			45	1.1	1.1
African Christian Democratic Party			66	1.6	1.6
African National Congress	2024	46.3	1992	48.5	2.3
Inkatha Freedom Party	217	5.0	386	9.4	4.4
Minority Front	416	9.5	866	21.1	11.6
Total Valid Votes	4375	100	4104	100	
Registered Voters	13124		13297		
% Poll	33.4		30.9	-2.5	
Ward 25					
Democratic alliance	2043	39.2	1194	21.9	−17.3
eThekwini Ecopeace	27	0.5	28	0.5	0.0
Scara Civic Party			11	0.2	0.2
Vryheidsfront Plus			12	0.2	0.2
Azanian Peoples Organisation			15	0.3	0.3
National United People's Organisation			23	0.4	0.4
United Democratic Movement			28	0.5	0.5
Inkatha Freedom Party	266	5.1	373	6.8	1.7
Minority Front	372	7.1	484	8.9	1.7
Independent Democrat			104	1.9	1.9
African Christian Democratic Party	219	4.2	342	6.3	2.1
Truly Alliance			144	2.6	2.6
African National Congress	2292	43.9	2706	49.5	5.6
Total Valid Votes	5219	100	5464	100	
Registered Voters	14314		15919		
Voter turnout		36.5		34.3	−2.2

One of the few rules the Nazis constantly obeyed throughout the course of the "final solu-tion" was that Jews and Gypsies could be sent to extermination camps only after having been fully denationalized (that is, after they had been stripped of even that second-class citizenship to which they had been relegated after the Nuremberg Laws). When their rights are no longer the rights of the citizen, that is when human beings are truly *sacred*, in the sense that this term used to have in the Roman law of the archaic period: doomed to death (Agamben, 2003, p. 8).

Refugee camps can be thought of as cities without citizens. What we see in the blossoming shackdweller population in Durban, and indeed, elsewhere on the planet (Neuwirth, 2005), is a variation on this theme. Communities within the city whose residents provide cheap labor for the middle classes, and who reproduce their own labor in the city, but who can never be embraced as permanent members of that city in the places where they currently reside, those communities are formed of *citizens without citizenship*. The call of the shackdwellers is that they are 100 percent South African. The state is, nonetheless, unwilling to accommodate their demands, conso-nant though they might be with the letter of the constitution.

This points to an important difference between the resistance organized by Sajida Khan and other middle-class residents, and that of the shackdwellers. In the case of the former, citizenship rights are assumed, and their attempts to remove the dump from the city, and remove themselves from the vicinity of the dump, proceed on the basis of their assumption of citizenship. The rights of housed families affected by solid waste pollution are legible to the state, and acceptable to it. Notwithstanding the fact that the government has shown itself unwilling to accommodate them, Khan and her fellow residents do not live in fear of arrest. In the case of shackdwellers, whom both Khan and the state homogenize, organizing has time and again reasserted not merely their demands, but their right to have those demands heard. They have claimed equal-ity as humans, as South Africans, as families. They have needed to do this in order simply to claim the right to exist in the city. The language of citizenship is one that the state should, at least in principle, be able to hear—this is why it is claimed so force-fully. And it is why the state has reacted so forcefully in return, particularly around the shackdwellers' refusal to vote.

Alain Badiou argues that it is worthwhile to subject voting, and democracy as it is currently construed, to close scrutiny. In so doing, he offers an explanation of the state's behavior:

Today the word "democracy" is the principal organiser of consensus. It is a word that supposedly unites the collapse of the socialist States, the putative well-being enjoyed in our countries and the humanitarian crusades of the West. In fact, the word "democracy" concerns what I shall call *authoritarian opinion*. It is forbidden, as it were, not to be a democrat. More precisely, it stands to reason that humanity aspires to democracy, and any subjectivity suspected of not being democratic is regarded as pathological. At best it refers to a patient re-education, at worst to the right of military intervention by demo-cratic paratroopers.

Thus democracy necessarily elicits the philosopher's critical suspicion precisely insofar as it falls within the realm of public opinion and consensus. Since Plato, philosophy has stood for a rupture with opinion, and is meant to examine everything that is spontaneously considered as *normal*. If "democracy" names a supposedly normal state of collective organisation or political will, then the philosopher demands that we examine the norm of this normality (2005b, p. 78).

This, incidentally, implies a restatement of the theory developed by Andreasson (2003) and endorsed by Davis (2004), of "virtual democracy." Andreasson cites Joseph as defining virtual democracy as "having a formal basis in citizen rule but with key decision-making insulated from popular involvement and oversight." While this is certainly the case above, the idea of virtual democracy does not explain how the necessity of formal citizen-based rule also expresses electoral demands for class-oriented solutions. The ballot becomes at once the most disposable part of democracy, and the most vital symbol of acceptable tyranny. To put it another way, elections are more than simply window dressing of authoritarianism. They are a way of conscripting citizens to the authoritarian project, a way of creating class-based ownership of the rituals of democratic tyranny, and of legitimizing the exclusion of mass participation because the only opinions that matter have already been heard. And this process happens *through* the resistance to it, seemingly behind people's backs, but in their face at the same time. It would be hard to imagine that the ANC would have scored quite as substantial a draw from the Democratic Alliance had they not been so visibly and anxiously aligned in their economic policies with the interests of the middle classes they successfully drew to their side. And this would not have been made quite so manifest had there not been a year of long and visible confrontations with Durban's poorest residents.

Conclusion

One question, in conclusion, remains: Why, after all this, after the recent targeting of members of Kennedy Road in March 2007, which has, at the time of writing, led to five of them going on hunger strike in jail, has the movement never straightforwardly denounced the ANC? As de Souza notes, movement politics in which shackdwellers can find themselves acting as "urban planners" involves a suite of positions, "against, with and despite the state" (de Souza, 2006). But there is yet more to this. In some settlements, no party but the ANC is allowed—a break with the party would simply not be tolerated, and some shack residents live in fear of violence for expressing their disappointments with the ANC. Politics are forged with the tools at hand, and shackdwellers themselves were, in meetings on the subject, divided on the issue of the ANC, and the power of the president. Children wrote letters to Mbeki, from asking for his attention with pleas of "If you don't have the power to build us houses, please give us electricity at least," to analyses of rape, to numerous threats of withholding votes if nothing was done to address the situation, to personal indictments of the president's physique: "I know that you eat KFC and you have lots of money but you are so fat like a pig."[26] The ANC, however, continues to maintain a powerful historical connection to the anti-apartheid struggle. Although many within the shacks remember that other forces (the communists, Black Consciousness, etc.) were involved in the struggle to be free of white minority rule, the ANC has been successful in creating a "leadership cult."[27] It is one that is deployed subversively—the language of the ANC, referring primarily to the ranks of the middle class, is that "all races are welcome." Shackdwellers have tried to use the discourses of inclusivity to argue that the city should also include them, no matter what their allegiance or ethnicity—for they retain a (tactical) allegiance to the ANC.

Another way of understanding the attachment to the ANC is, however, to understand it as a fidelity to the principles of the anti-apartheid struggle (see Badiou, 2005a). Badiou's notion of fidelity is this: "To be faithful to an event is to move within the situation that this event has supplemented, but thinking (although all thought is a practice, a putting to the test) the situation *according to* the event" (Badiou, 2001, p. 41). The notion here is that the kinds of rupture with experience that produces militants, such as the struggle for freedom from apartheid, demands also that there be a constant positioning (and questioning of that positioning) vis-à-vis the anti-apartheid legacy as a result. Insofar as the ANC contains vestiges of the anti-apartheid event, it commands the fidelity of its militants. But, as it becomes increasingly clear that the party, from top to bottom, has betrayed the struggle against apartheid, the struggle for a deep kind of equality, then a fidelity with the ANC is misplaced—something that the shackdwellers are finding increasingly true of late. They have found, through their investigation into their citizenship and access to politics that they are "exiled without return," removed not only from the land, but from the possibility of citizenship through the party, and the nation.

Land is the stage on which this is carried out, the material condition of possibility. In other words, class struggles about land are *lived* through the dialectic, material and ideological. Precisely because it is a political experiment that has no safety net, that rejects patronage from the state, it is "exile without return."[28] This exile, increasingly, points to a politics beyond the party. Because of the bindings of party and state, it could even point towards a politics that bears a closer resemblance to Agamben's refugees.

Through this exile, and through the attempt to gain attention and recognition from the state, shackdwellers are forging new kinds of political community, which "citizenship" cannot explain, and which relate to territory and place in ways that "ownership" cannot comprehend. To understand this political community means being ready to lose faith with the hegemony of the ANC. It means being ready to understand that a cherished icon of liberation is trying to impose an agenda that betrays its rhetoric. But it also involves accepting that the definitions of citizenship and nation are not exhausted or defined by the laws of the state, or the dictates of a party. Citizenship is a call for a politics, a call that in this case has resulted in protest against the very institutions that once promised to provide a forum for citizenship. In protesting against the state, the members of Abahlali baseMjondolo are seizing the very citizenship that the ANC refuses to give them. What this means is that, for many shackdwellers, the struggle against apartheid remains alive, with all its hopes and contradictions. And although some American professors find that hard to accept, it does offer a beacon of hope that, while not reached in the 1990s, is itself a sign of the Promised Land.

Notes

* Acknowledgments This paper was funded in part by a generous grant from CODESRIA's Multinational Working Group on Land. It is much improved thanks to the help of the members of the Multinational Working Group, CODESRIA (with special thanks to Bruno Sonko), the University of Abahlali base Mjondolo, Richard Pithouse, Jun Borras, Dan Moshenberg, Shereen Essof, and Philip McMichael. It is dedicated to the memory of Archie Mafeje and Cosmos Chaz'muzi Bhengu.

1. The keenest observer of the process through which material and ideological clashes are fought daily, is Antonio Gramsci (Gramsci and Buttigieg, 1992). His understanding of hegemony might be paraphrased as the permanent politics of move and counter-move, fought not merely by classes but through subtler co-optations and blocs, reflecting the configuration of forces within classes that aims to secure and maintain domination through a mixture of coercion and consent.

2. Coordinates for dump: 29°48"51.76"S, 30°58"52.80"E.

3. See Jagarnath (2006) for a definitive history of race relations in nearby Sydenham.

4. As Pithouse and Butler note:

   In 1923 the state sought to stem the flow of people into the cities with the policy of Influx Control that aimed to prevent Africans from moving to cities, to force those (mostly men) with permits to inhabit segregated workers' quarters and those without permits to leave. It stayed, in different versions, on the statute books until 1986 and was replaced, in 1990-1, by a "non-racial urban policy framework designed largely by the think-tanks of big business" [2] with the Urban Foundation being the major player (2007, p. 5).

5. These areas correspond to Independent Electoral Commission districts 433900xx. See www.elections.org.za for more.

6. Compare the Pemary Ridge Primary school polling station results (station 43390054), in an area in which there are relatively low numbers of shackdwellers, and in which the ANC won 30 percent of the vote to the Democratic Party's 41 percent, to those of Hillview Primary School (station 43390032), in which the ANC secured 60 percent of the vote to the Democratic Party's 17 percent.

7. Richard Pithouse has detailed the story in a number of thoughtful articles, and the following summary should not be substituted for a reading of his work (Pithouse 2005, 2007). More information is available at the shackdweller's website, which I help to administer; there is an archive of academic work about the movement at http://www.abahlali.org.

8. For more, see (Lodge, 1983) and (Maylam and Edwards, 1996) passim, especially on the Cato Manor uprisings.

9. The dump is, however, the source of employment for some residents of the Kennedy Road settlement. Other work explores this tension further (Patel, forthcoming).

10. Which were only fully revealed to shackdwellers after an application under the Promotion of Access to Information Act. The full documents received, which still lack vital details, are available at http://www.abahlali.org/node/279.

11. See the special issue of *Critical Asian Studies*, December 2005, for development of this point.

12. See http://www.abahlali.org/node/20.

13. This is a not terribly helpful phrase, which is used by, among others, Tarrow (1998). To say that a political opportunity exists tells little about the precise dynamics, let alone dialectics, through which it becomes important.

14. This claim acknowledges that while movements like COSATU, the Confederation of South African Trade Unions, has more members, its claim to being independent of the state is null: COSATU is, with the Communist Party, a member of the ANC's tri-partite ruling alliance.

15. http://www.fxi.org.za/pages/Legal%20Unit/Gatherings%20Act/Taming%20the%20toyi%20toyi.html.

16. Tutu (2004) and http://news.bbc.co.uk/2/hi/africa/4052199.stm.

17. See ANC today passim.

18. The criminalization of poor people has recently reached new heights with a police sponsored publicity series, recalling the layout of a comic strip, in which local constabulary officials raided shacks, recovered stolen property, hunted "cop killers," and in which arrested "suspects... begin their long walk to freedom." http://www.sydenhamcpf.org.za/SAPS/SAPSRaid20050729. pdf.

19. http://www.abahlali.org/node/182.

20. Again, this has been discovered by the shackdwellers only through recourse to the Promotion of Access to Information Act, and the disclosures made by the government have been incomplete and partial at best.

21. http://www.themercury.co.za/index.php?fArticleId=3000079.

22. http://abahlali.bayareafood.org/node/72.

23. http://www.abahlali.org/node/100.

24. See, e.g., memoranda for protests on September 14, 2005 and October 4, 2005 at http://abahlali.bayareafood.org/node/138 and http://abahlali.bayareafood.org/node/211.

25. http://www.anc.org.za/ancdocs/anctoday/2006/text/at08.txt.

26. http://abahlali.bayareafood.org/files/Kennedy%20Road%20brochure.pdf.

27. It is part of what I have elsewhere termed "global fascism" (Patel and McMichael, 2004).

28. Pithouse (2006, p. 24) citing Hallward (2003, p. 77).

4.

WHERE DOES THE RURAL EDUCATED PERSON FIT?

*Development and Social Reproduction in Contemporary India**

Karuna Morarji

Examines how people in a rural mountain valley in northern India experience and evaluate modern education in contradictory and ambiguous ways. Education is a key development indicator, and, as a means to social mobility through employment, is cast as a "solution" to the "problem" of agrarian decline in contemporary India. While such assumptions resonate with people's aspirations, education is also recognized as a profoundly contradictory resource. Educated youth fail to gain employment, yet their educated status contributes to the foreclosure of agrarian livelihoods, and strains a moral economy valued as the foundation of village community. Such contradictions challenge seamless narratives of rural non-viability and social mobility through educated market participation.

Introduction

In a media interview, P. Chidambaram, India's Finance Minister at the time and a leading architect of the country's economic reforms since the early 1990s, was asked about the state's controversial acquisition of farmland for the creation of Special Economic Zones. He responded that "in India there is a sacred bond that binds the tiller with the land," yet added, "Should so many people depend on land? No country can afford to have 65 percent of its working population dependent on land.... *They are not there as a matter of choice,* they are there because they are not skilled to do anything else..." (*The Sunday Express,* 2007).

How does the Indian Finance Minister know that the majority of India's people living in rural areas are on the land not as a matter of choice? What does he see as more desirable choices, and how will they be enabled? These are questions which can be asked of dominant discourses about development in contemporary India, in which a lagging rural sector is seen as a key hindrance to the realization of a new "India Shining" of high economic growth rates and consumption by urban middle classes. In this chapter, I argue that such discourses often frame problems and solutions—and hence the parameters and meanings of choice—in terms of a *market calculus.* As the Finance Minister's comments suggest, this vision of development is one in which agriculture and rural life are inevitably residual, unfeasible and a compulsion rather than a rational choice. Other choices are presumed to be more realistic and profitable—such as urban residence, wage employment and consumption—and these rely on market participation.

Drawing on ethnographic research from a rural mountain region in North India, I argue that questions of choice around development and social reproduction are in fact far from clear-cut. I do so by analyzing people's ambiguous evaluations of education. Education is widely perceived as a way out of rural backwardness and into the modern economy. Yet my research indicates that not only do desirable choices often fail to materialize, but education reproduces rural decline by *closing off* cultural and material options for rural communities. People's responses are complex. They acknowledge the alienation associated with being educated but unemployed. But they also express alternative standards of value and choice associated with their village communities that fundamentally challenge the choices and values offered by the market calculus.

Education has long been a cornerstone of nation-state formation and development, and it continues to be taken for granted in both policy and popular discourses as a key enabler of expanded choice. For instance, Nobel Laureate economist Amartya Sen—one of the most vociferous advocates of the wide range of benefits associated with education in a developing society—has repeatedly stressed that education inherently enhances "...the freedoms that people actually enjoy to lead the kind of lives they have reason to value" (Dreze and Sen, 1995, p. 13). But as an article in a major daily newspaper titled "*Gaon* Goes Global," or "the village goes global," suggests, education is generally linked to market-inspired visions of values and choices. It tells the reader that "Everyone wants a good life, not just city people," presenting a "village farmer" and "shopper" browsing the aisles in India's first rural mall, and goes on to list the desires of India's rural consumers: processed foods, clothes, beauty products, technological gadgets, automated means of transport, and housing in the form of apartments (*Sunday Hinduastan Times*, 2007). Education and reduced dependence on agriculture are indicated as key means through which such acquisitive aspirations are realizable for the *aam aadmi*, the common man.

By framing social mobility for rural Indians in middle-class consumptive terms, the "village goes global" article presents a contemporary development discourse that weaves together modernization assumptions about individual choices and social trajectories with the market-centered frame of neo-liberal development. Media representations often promote such assumptions in contemporary India (Mazzarella, 2003).[1] But the newspaper story also highlights how this imaginary is a part of everyday experiences, quoting a rural shopper having just outfitted his children with jeans and Western clothes, and equipped his home with modern amenities: "I have girls to marry off, we shouldn't look like *dehatis* (villagers)" (*Sunday Hinduastan Times* 2007). As Liechty (2003) observes in his study of middle-class identity formation in Nepal, commercial compulsions therefore "exert their power less through their ability to somehow 'brainwash' consumers than through their proficiency in feeding off of, or capitalizing on, the *social imperatives* that people face in their daily lives" (p. 114).

In this chapter, I show how my research subjects in Jaunpur—a valley in the mountainous Tehri Garhwal district of the north Indian state of Uttarakhand—experience education as a "contradictory resource" (Jeffrey, Jeffery, and Jeffery, 2008, p. 210) at the center of changing imperatives and pressures of social reproduction. The first section locates education within the socio-economic context of Jaunpur, and demonstrates that parents in Jaunpur *do* want education for their children, and expect, or at least hope, that education will provide them with non-agrarian futures. Here, perceptions of the non-viability of small-scale agriculture and dreams of social mobility in middle-class terms are expressed as two sides of the same coin. Discourses around education in this rural mountain valley therefore seem to reproduce a "development subjectivity" (Gupta, 2003, p. 71) rooted in economically rational choices and dreams—such as inclusion in a market-oriented modernity through wage employment and consumption, and escape from the perceived drudgery of manual work and the limited returns of small-scale mountain agriculture.

The second section illustrates that education is equally linked to anxieties around exclusion, alienation, and individualization, as educated youth from this marginal region most often fail to gain a foothold in one of the world's most competitive labor markets, and express their educated status in terms which strain the economic and cultural fabric of village society. Parents and elders complain about the behaviors, attitudes and demands of educated youth. Educated youth feel pressured by expectations that they obtain jobs, and marginalized by their inability to meet them. These experiences address the fact that contradictory outcomes of education position it as "one of the most poignant illustrations of the polarizing structure of neoliberal policies" (Weiss, 2004, p.14). Policy and popular narratives equate education with employment and social opportunity, yet neo-liberal reform policies render this link extremely tenuous with the additional effect of destabilizing preexisting, often more localized, patterns of social reproduction in rural communities.[2]

Finally, I argue that the failures of education are not the "cause" of a crisis of social reproduction, but rather indicative of a deeper malaise. Many of my research subjects in rural Jaunpur continue to attach positive meaning and value to rural life and its moral economy, and feel that the compulsions associated with education are not only incompatible with, but directly *contribute to* the cultural and material foreclosure of rural livelihood choices and an overall sense of prosperity. Rather than assume that social mobility and empowerment are inherent in the experience of education—as Sen's framework, and most policy as well as popular thinking on education and development do—their experiences question the promise of education; that is, *what kinds of lives do people have reason to value?* Jaunpuri people's conflicting experiences of education critically challenge the neo-liberal developmental values of education and the market episteme on which such assumptions are based.

Something Should Change: The Necessity of Education in Today's World

The Aglar River valley of Jaunpur block, Tehri Garhwal, is a narrow valley in the new north Indian hill state of Uttarakhand. Apart from a couple of roadside administrative

Exhibit 4.1 School Girls in the Aglar River valley of Jaunpur Uttarakhand

qasbahs (between a village and town in classification), it is an entirely rural area with villages intermittently dotting both slopes of the valley. Villages are small, generally consisting of ten to twenty households, and are surrounded by steep terraced fields. The valley in many ways characterizes the mountainous, rural landscape of much of this newly formed hill state.[3] Eighty-eight percent of the landscape of Uttarakhand is defined as hilly, three-fourths of the population of eight and a half million live in rural areas, and more than 70 percent depend on agriculture for their livelihood. Although only 11 percent of land in the hills is cultivatable and the average size of landholdings is less than one hectare, agriculture and animal husbandry are the main source of livelihood for people living in the hill regions. About three-fourths of crops grown in the hills are food grains such as wheat, maize, millet and other cereals. Agriculture is largely rain-fed; in the mountainous Tehri Garhwal district less than 10 percent of land is irrigated (National Council of Applied Economic Research, 2006).

As a hill region that was formerly a marginalized corner of India's largest and most populous state, Uttar Pradesh, this area in the foothills of the Western Himalaya could historically have been characterized as a "development rain shadow" (Piggs, 1997, p. 266): it had been categorized as culturally and economically "backward," exploited as a source of labor and raw materials, and by-passed by state development projects such as roads, irrigation, healthcare, and educational facilities. Twenty years ago, there were therefore few primary schools in the scattered villages of Jaunpur, teacher absenteeism was common, and children had to trek long distances to get to a school. Basic education was therefore not a mass experience. However, the formation of Uttarakhand as a new federal state in 2000 has brought a massive increase in development funding and intervention in the region, including a significant improvement in government school facilities. Today, the educational landscape in the Aglar valley is defined largely by government schools, along with a few primary schools run by the Society for the Integrated Development of Himalayas (SIDH), a local NGO, and private institutions.[4] School-based education, at least up to class 5 and increasingly class

10 or 12, has become a part of daily life for communities in the Aglar valley since the late 1990s.

People routinely view education as a key indicator of change, and general associations with education are glowingly positive. Parents—many of whom are illiterate or have experienced only a few years of poor quality primary schooling—feel intense social pressure to educate their children. A father of several school-going children explained, "We cannot keep our children uneducated today. This has also become a source of embarrassment. We cannot keep them isolated. They need education to live today; before maybe 5% were educated, today 90% are." Many families are moving their children from villages to slum-like semi-urban settlements to provide them with private schooling or higher education, and express their readiness to sell land in their villages to educate their children. Education has become central to the organization of households as children spend most of their time in schools, and decisions about resources, residence and work are made around ensuring access to school-based education. As a middle-aged shopkeeper who has migrated from a village in the valley to the qasbah of Kempty to educate his children in non-governmental schools, categorically stated, "You are nothing without an education in today's world."

To "be nothing" without education practically equates education with being human—yet upon elaboration, it is a vision of humanness framed by the contours of "today's world." During a conversation with five or six young men in Nautha, a village in the valley located an hour's brisk walk from the closest road, a youth with a class 10 education told me that "Without education, thinking would be limited to the village, we would not see possibilities and opportunities outside." This cosmopolitan imaginary he called "the mentality of my generation," and it seemed to reference a lifestyle of more leisure and entertainment, variety, and consumption, as he went on to reflect that: "Educated people feel disappointed without things." Similarly, Rajan, a man in his early thirties, who has taught in a SIDH school in his village for over ten years, felt that

> People now see life as *"taat-baat"* (leisurely), they think "why are we working ourselves to death when we could live more easily…." From education people have gotten this sense that they want to preserve their bodies, take it easy, and not do such hard work, especially manual work. People feel that they will live better if they do less work. They also say that we did so much work, and we didn't get anything from it, there is no change. Now there is an expectation for change that wasn't there before, something should change.

Central to the expectation that "something should change" from being educated is therefore the ability to obtain more from less work, equated with employment, particularly in the form of non-manual labor. Almost every parent I have spoken to has said that their main hope from education of their children—at least for boys, at times for girls as well—is that they get good salaried service sector employment, mostly favorably defined as *sarkaari naukri*, government service, but increasingly also "*private*" employment. Young people almost always echo this aspiration. When I asked a group of boys and girls between the ages of seven and ten in Lagwalgao village government primary school why they go to school, they provided the "correct" answer in chorus, without hesitation: *naukri* (service sector job).

Aspirations of social mobility through employment via education in the villages of the Aglar valley are inseparable from perceptions of rural non-viability. There is a persistent discourse about how it is "no longer possible to live off farming" in the region, that "agriculture is not profitable compared to amount of time and effort put in," and that "wage labor or service sector jobs are much more profitable." As agrarian regions of India embrace forms of new rurality (Vasavi, 2006)—spaces geographically defined as rural, but economically and culturally urbanized—it seems reasonable that a key expectation from education should be to enable the "freedom of an individual to participate in labor markets" (Sen, 2000). Yet are education and labor market participation necessarily a solution to the problem of rural decline? In Rajan's view, the lack of interest in agriculture and the perceived benefits of employment mean that people place all their hopes on education, which in turn contributes to the further decline of agriculture:

> In the beginning when children went to school, they also did house work properly. Parents gave less attention to education. Now parents have started giving a lot of attention to education. They urge their children to study, and don't want them to do house work. So because of education, attention to farming and animals has decreased. As they get older, they have to study more, parents want them to do well, there is a lot of competition, so they don't want them to do much work. Their attention is on *naukri*, after all if they get a service sector job they are set for life. So parents want their children to enter into competition. This is happening in my family.… It used to happen in cities, now it is happening in villages. Ten years ago, my grandfather never said that we should compete.… My grandfather also did outside work but he also gave a lot of attention to house work.

Rajan's comments highlight how education is linked to the compulsion to compete and gain employment—and the seeming inadequacy of agriculture—in varying and complex ways. The impact of education on patterns of social reproduction includes changes in labor activities and relationships between and evaluations of different forms of labor. Children have traditionally played an important part in the household division of labor, contributing particularly to the care of livestock by collecting feed and grazing goats, cows and buffaloes. When children go to school every day, their farm labor is lost to the classroom. In anticipation of the deferred reward of government employment, parents are therefore choosing to withdraw their children from the household labor force, and they are generally unwilling to rejoin once they are out of school. Another community teacher felt that "even when kids have interest in farming, parents want them to study, to get a government job." Rajan's comments about his grandfather also doing wage labor but not valuing it more than agriculture also illustrate the changing relationships between household and wage employment. A colleague of Rajan's similarly recounted that his father had a high-school education and had obtained a service job but left to return to the village, "he did not value *naukri*." In the past, engaging in wage labor was not equated with competition and complete alienation from agricultural work, as it is today.

The displacement of locally based livelihood skills and options through education applies to traditional trades besides agriculture. For example, when a skilled artisan carpenter and carver was asked why none of his children were doing this work, even though it is a profitable trade, he responded initially by speaking of his own lack of focused engagement in carpentry as he is "doing ten other jobs." Had his children not learned this trade because it was devalued? He replied that no, this was not the case, yet no one in his family wants to learn. Did he try to teach them? He replied indirectly that "Well, I sent them to school...." The fact that schooling is seen as taking the place of the possibility of his children practicing carpentry, even though it is a direct source of cash income, illuminates how desirable education is, and how thoroughly the compulsions of development have transformed perceptions of viable options, choices and values. The stress on education for employment and the devaluation of agriculture and other local forms of manually based work are therefore closely connected. But framed by the assumptions of the market episteme, the relationship between education and agrarian decline is rarely recognized as one of potential negative reinforcement.

Illusory Freedoms: Employment Is a Pressure

The association of education with aspirations for wage employment echoes developmental assumptions about what kinds of choices and trajectories make rational sense for an educated rural person. But aspirations are interspersed with the anxieties induced by a shortage of desirable employment opportunities, rapidly increasing cash expenses, and unwillingness of youth with a high school or higher education to return to rural/household work. Parents convey intense disappointments, and even bitterness and anger, with the behavior of educated youth. A frequent refrain that I have heard is that "if they don't get work, in the end they get spoilt, become crooks."

> [Parents] see their kids as a problem these days. They feel that if they don't get a job at least they should do house work with responsibility, but if they even have an inter (high school) education, they refuse—for example if they are to take out the animals, they will wander around all day.

Parents feel pressured by young people's demands for consumer goods, based on what they see as an increasing rejection of all things local, and the economic costs of such changing tastes in a context where youth are not earning: "Now everyone wants good food, good clothes, good soap, good shoes.... Educated kids don't like the food that we produce here, like *mandua ka aata* (millet flour). If we make (these) *rotis* (breads) no one will eat them." Another elderly man went further, decrying the lack of concern about sources of income and a seemingly selfish focus on consumption among the youth. He asked "...where will this (the things that they want) come from? They don't think about this. Twenty-four hours they want money.... They put their hands in their back pant pockets and wander around, they just come home for food, and that too want special food."

The educated person's individualism, lack of responsibility and collective concern are often linked to particular dispositions, tastes and performances of identity. These are seen as further inhibiting the reproduction of local customs. A local government primary school teacher in the village of Ghed described educated youth as "*VIP*-like" (a very important person), reinforcing the notion that educated people become individualized as special. He went on to explain what he meant by this: "They don't want to listen to anyone, they look down on people, do everything on their own account.... They have their own system of behavior, dress, hair style.... They behave differently in weddings. And no matter how many times you say something, they don't respond."

Yet because the desirability of employment is equally shared by elders and youth, elders' sense of disappointment is often perceived as unfair by youth. Given the compulsions toward employment, one young man to whom I spoke strongly expressed his frustrations with the narrative of young people getting "ruined": "People say that young people have become ruined, but there is also a lot of pressure on them from parents and elders. If you are educated and want to stay in the house rather than leave the village, they say what is the point of education, why study if you are just going to do the same thing...."

In the village of Nautha, a group of young men with whom I spoke agreed with their parents on the desirability of employment in the face of agrarian decline, but also expressed the pressure and shame that the compulsion for particular kinds of employment exerts on them. In this village, not a single person has obtained permanent government employment within the last ten years. The youth I spoke to ranged in age from about sixteen to twenty-five and, apart from the oldest man who was illiterate, the rest had at least a class 10 education. They were engaged primarily in temporary wage employment of some kind; as cooks or tea-stall employees in nearby towns, and as daily wage laborers, including in construction work within the village. All of them also said that they contribute to household work. One of these men made a telling comparison between working for a wage and for self-sufficiency: "*naukri ek dabaav hei* (employment is a pressure), when people do farming for a living, they are self-sufficient, both the problems and successes are due to their own actions. But when people are not doing jobs, they feel useless." Similarly, another man in his early twenties expressed the perception that "If someone gets a job, they are a good person, if not they are bad. This is the feeling that comes from education. People also come to feel about themselves that if I get work I am OK, if not I am bad." Here, the sense of uselessness and inferiority is linked to the inability of youth to obtain the kinds of employment seen as financially and culturally worthwhile for an educated young man. For educated youth, desirable and appropriate work is not only evaluated in terms of wages: "If one asks people who have studied up to inter-college (high-school) to come for some daily labor work, they say no, they don't want to be seen picking up rocks, they are ashamed of this."

Many of these reflections by elders and youth in different ways express the sense of closure and alienation recognized by Marx in the process of proletarianization; the mixed feelings of desire for the seductions of modernity and despair in encountering the inherent discipline and exclusion of this system. The fact that experiences of bitter disillusionment and disappointment often co-exist with intense hope and aspiration is not recognized in development narratives of the value of education as a tool for participation in the market economy. For example, in linking education to employment to freedom, Amartya Sen (2000) suggests that even Marx saw the freedom to participate in labor markets as a benefit of the capitalist system—without recognizing that Marx's key point was to highlight the new, often more subtle, forms of alienation, exploitation and dispensability that the commodification of human labor entails. While Marx (1979) acknowledged the seductive side of inclusion via the formal equality of the market contract, he argued it is ultimately illusory since labor commodification brings relations of dependence and exploitation.

Experiences of alienation and disappointment around education illustrate how the dynamics of inclusion and exclusion of a market economy have meant that "becoming a part of the world has frequently entailed becoming marginal to the world" (Weiss, 2004, p. 8). In Jaunpur, these dynamics are amplified by the displacement of traditional cultures and production systems by first- and second-generation literacy. Developmentalist notions of self-improvement through market participation gloss over such uneven outcomes. They thereby ignore how compulsions experienced as aspirations stem from experiences of marginalization rather than representing "natural" values and choices.

Other Choices and Reasons to Value: A Parallel Moral Economy

Despite the increasing value of knowledge, skills and lifestyles associated with being educated and employed outside of the village and agriculture, I have shown how people in villages in the Aglar valley have countered the straightforward narrative of education and employment as the basis for social mobility and development, expressing anxieties and a sense of disappointment with their partial incorporation into a modern market economy. But they also do so by drawing on standards of value and meaning associated with an alternative moral economy. This became evident in the course of informal conversations that Shobhan—my research associate—and I had with elders in four villages in the valley about what kinds of socio-economic changes they have seen over the last twenty years. We repeatedly heard the perception that during this time education has increased, and income has decreased. To further probe the substantive meanings of these comments, we conducted a basic survey of one of the villages where such perceptions had been voiced. We asked both male and female representatives of each of the fourteen households in Dabla-Matela about current household economies, as well as perceptions about production, income and expenses twenty years ago.[5] The impression of economic decline was repeatedly reinforced by respondents of varying ages indicating that they felt that their household was worse off now than in the past.

Yet upon compiling the data, we found that contrary to popular perceptions, the overall village economy was running at a decent financial surplus, rather than at a loss. However, in terms of real production as well as its contribution to overall income, the role of agriculture has declined significantly. Agriculture can no longer be considered the economic mainstay of this village; real agricultural output has declined and at the same time village resources come increasingly from extra-agricultural sources. Currently, only about 30 percent of village income comes from agriculture and animal husbandry, while 70 percent is obtained from other employment (daily wage labor or private service employment, mostly in nearby tourist towns of Kempty Falls and Mussoorie). Twenty years ago, a rough estimate of 56 percent of income came from agriculture and animal husbandry, while 44 percent was obtained through other employment—hence there has been a 26 percent decline in the proportion of income from agriculture and animal husbandry, and an equivalent increase in the proportion of income from other sources of employment. Our survey indicated that for most households in Dabla-Matela, it is not cash income that is declining but a sense of worth and value obtained through agrarian production, and this is the loss that they had expressed. In their evaluation of their economy, people in this village had implicitly emphasized the value of agriculture and animal husbandry, as assets and wealth, and as the mainstay of a relatively secure, non-marketized economy.[6]

The sense of value and decline alluded to a meaning of economy defined not just monetarily, or even in terms of production, but equally held together by the rituals, norms and relationships of rural social reproduction—such as weddings, food, song and dance, architecture and families. Perhaps the most widely cited indication of weakening of social relations within villages is increasing tensions and fighting within families and subsequent break-up of extended families into nuclear families.[7] When asked about the causes of such fighting, I was told by a local SIDH school teacher who, as the eldest son, is the head of a large extended family that it is increasingly over money. He said that "Since most things have to be bought now, and one needs money, there is fighting as some family members earn more, others less." Others spoke of tensions in joint families between brothers/sons (and their wives) who are earning income and those who are doing household labor, as the latter are increasingly felt to be dependent on the former to meet market-based needs. The relative status of money compared to grain, given increasing dependency on the market, is therefore perceived as one cause of strain within families.

This sense of declining collective values and resources is therefore linked to increasingly market-dependent and modern lifestyles. For example, new ways of building houses in villages depend entirely on supplies from the market—mostly cement and tin—thereby increasing their financial cost. New designs of houses are in turn seen as connected to changing relationships within families. Traditional Jaunpuri houses are large but have only two rooms, and members of extended families spent most of their indoor time in one room together. The majority of households in the village of Dabla-Matela are extended families with ten to twenty members, but today most also live in new houses with many small rooms; people eat together and then disperse to their individual units. This is perceived as both a sign and a cause of the decline of families' sense of togetherness.

Similarly, I have repeatedly been told that people do not sing and dance together in the village square during festivals because they have TVs and CDs to watch in the comfort of their own homes, and "Educated people think that singing together is backward." This lack of collective feeling and behavior—or individualism and privatization of resources—is in turn seen as further producing an individual attitude toward joint resources. Whether in field work, building houses, marriages and festivals, making roads, protecting the local environment or taking care of sick neighbors, people—and educated youth in particular—are seen as giving minimal attention to these shared material and cultural resources today.

Elders commonly expressed the notion that education is linked to the cultivation of individualism, but it is also recognized by youth. In a written survey I conducted with about two hundred middle- and high-school aged children in villages in the valley asking them how they see the impact of education in their lives and communities, the majority linked education positively to all aspects of life except collective thinking and cooperation. Education and associated aspirations, tastes, desires and dispositions—including the compulsion toward employment—are therefore a part of the new cultural and material economy of production and consumption for private and individual ends. This is an economy fundamentally at odds with a collectivist ethic underlying a sustenance agrarian economy. For example, an elder felt that "Differences are definitely there (between educated and uneducated), their ways of doing work, talking, appearance—differences are definitely there. But in terms of the village perspective, the uneducated person's condition is better." Others differentiated not just between educated/uneducated and urban/rural, but also added the categories of educated people who get jobs and those who do not, or "are neither here nor there": "Educated people who get a good position do well, but for those who are neither here nor there, it is difficult. But those who are uneducated are more understanding, they are willing to do any work. Their economic condition is better than those in the in-between category."

The articulation of the feeling that from "the village perspective" an uneducated person is better off culturally and economically than an unemployed educated person confirms the significance of critically examining the social and economic values of education and the aspirations it engenders in particular contexts, rather than assume that education expands what people "have reason to value." The observations and comparisons that people make about the merits of traditional practices and systems are undoubtedly motivated partially by disappointments with education and the lack of jobs. But they also draw on competing values of a localized, sustenance-oriented agrarian moral economy. As a parallel—and at times intersecting—way of thinking about production and the organization of life, this moral economy does not merely signal a pre-modern tradition. Rather, it suggests that mutuality, cooperation and the quality of human relationships continue to orient people's (particularly elders') standards of value and action, thereby challenging narrow market-centric meanings of rationality, choice and freedom.

Conclusion

The aim in this chapter has been to highlight critical challenges to a market episteme in conflicting evaluations of education and its place in the social reproduction of village communities in the Aglar valley. I have illustrated that on the one hand, there is what one young man described as *"Naukri ka* craze," the craze for employment, that drives people's sense of the value of education in relation to agrarian decline and changing lifestyle expectations. Such aspirations seem to resonate with normative development models that assume a positive causal relationship between education and social mobility into a globalized world envisioned as urbanized, through participation in market relations of production and consumption—wage labor being the first step in this trajectory. Yet on the other hand, education is seen as breaking down a moral economy of agrarian production centered on collective value, which still serves as a compass for notions of security and well-being among old as well as young. The expressed sense of disappointment is therefore not just about educated youth not getting the desired jobs, but about lack of overall security, and the seeming collapse of norms of human behavior and relations. While people clearly value the cash income, facilities, consumer goods, and leisure associated with education and employment, they also express some ambiguity, feeling alienation and disappointment. *And* they articulate how they value security, hard work, cooperation, respect and honesty.[8] As such, contradictory sentiments expressed by Jaunpuris reflect not just the sense that education is never an automatic passport to social mobility, but that *the very meaning and desirability*—or the starting point and destination—of social mobility as it is defined in commonsense terms is questionable. It raises profound questions about what values development promotes.

My point is not to deny experiences of rural decline in contemporary India. Nor is it to reject the potential of education to encourage people's "capacity to aspire" (Appadurai, 2004). Instead, I seek to question the seamlessness of dominant narratives of rural decline on the one hand, and of aspirations and social mobility on the other. These narratives, framed by a market episteme, do not give space for recognizing how aspirations of rural communities reflect conflicting experiences and hopes for the future. As the experiences of people I have spoken to in the Aglar valley suggest, education *does* embody expectations for particular kinds of change, imagined in terms of a developmental vision of modernity and contrasted with a way of life seen as belonging to the past, as "backward." But while development visions therefore do seem to shape social trajectories and aspirations, the process is far from given, and cannot be taken for granted as historically given, or predetermined.

Here, I have therefore tried to reformulate questions of rural dispossession and social mobility and choice, to underline how both the problems and solutions have been formulated in terms of a market episteme. My ethnographic focus has been on the conflicting evaluations of education in relation to employment and agrarian social reproduction in a narrow mountain river valley in north India. But I also posit that this micro-context provides a lens through which to critically examine broader changes in rural India, and the decline of small-scale agrarian production more generally worldwide.

"De-peasantization" (Araghi, 1995) is an ongoing process through which sustenance farmers are incorporated into commoditized worlds on unequal terms. These processes are recognized as having structural roots—for instance the dominance of global agribusiness and export agriculture—as well as cultural dimensions such as the enticements of modern lifestyles (McMichael, 2007). I have argued that in contemporary India, the glamour of urbanized, middle-class forms of production and consumption, and the simultaneous erosion of the foundations of rural life, has meant that this process has come to be perceived as a kind of evolutionary common sense. By focusing on contradictory evaluations of education in Jaunpur, I have shifted the analytic focus of such processes to highlight *epistemic* challenges to such market-centered trajectories of change and development, and underlying questions about what constitutes desirable and realistic values and choices in the contemporary world at large.

Notes

* Acknowledgments I am grateful to Shobhan Singh Negi, for his invaluable research assistance and insights. I would also like to thank Philip McMichael, Dia Da Costa, Alex Da Costa, Nosheen Ali, Jason Cons, Amita Baviskar, Craig Jeffrey, Ann Gold, and Vinish Gupta for comments on earlier versions of this essay.

1. Academic discourses also contribute to the naturalization of particular terms of choice and change. For example, a prominent Indian sociologist has marked the Indian village as "a shrinking sociological reality" which is "no longer a site where futures can be planned" (Gupta, 2005, p. 752), while the ascendance of the "great Indian middle class" is often taken for granted (cf. Fernandes, 2006).

2. Such contradictions have served as a basis to question the optimism around education as a path to development. In particular, Sen's emphasis on the inherent value of education has been critiqued for neglecting to pay attention to "...how power and culture mediate people's access to the freedoms that education provides" (Jeffrey et al., 2008, p.3). But by seeing relations of power and culture as mediating unequal access rather than as constituting contested meanings of "freedom" and "choice," such critiques remain partial. Instead, I stress the importance of going beyond a delineation of the inclusionary and exclusionary dynamics of neoliberal development. These dynamics structure access—for example, to desirable forms of employment—but as negotiations over meanings and values, inclusion and exclusion do not merely reference a gap between development theory and practice.

3. Uttarakhand was formed as a new state in 2000 after a protracted struggle for separation from the largest Indian state of Uttar Pradesh. Demands for separation were based primarily on the economic and cultural marginalization of the hill region.

4. In this essay, I draw on conversations and interviews with community members, students and teachers associated with government schools and those run by SIDH. SIDH has been working in the Aglar valley since 1989, and began as a service-providing organization with the objective of setting up schools in remote rural villages lacking access to a government school. Over the years, SIDH team members—many of them local youth trained as teachers—have made substantive attempts to make education more relevant to people in this region. SIDH's critical engagements with education in the valley have had some impact on how some community members' view and talk about education. Yet an objective impact of SIDH schools has also been that it has contributed to making school-based education a mass experience in the valley for girls and boys in the last twenty years. I discuss the challenges and negotiations that this has entailed in the larger research project of which this is a part.

5. The village of Dabla-Matela is two small settlements with a total population of 166 people. The hamlets are separated by a perennial stream and a wide terrace of sloping fields. There is an unpaved road that skirts both settlements, and connects to a paved road leading to the larger qasbah of Kempty (3 km), the tourist day-trip site of Kempty Falls (3 km) and the hill-station town of Mussoorie (15 km). In Matela, there is a SIDH primary school, which has been operational for about fifteen years. Young children either attend this school or the government primary school in the nearby village of Lagwalgaon, which has existed for about twenty years.

After class 5, most children now attend at least a few years of junior high school and high school in Kempty.

6. As a recent development report on the region recognizes, sustenance agriculture brings low rates of return but is also linked to household food security and low levels of absolute poverty (National Council of Applied Economic Research, 2006). Such recognition of the productive benefits of small scale agriculture is increasingly being recognized in the face of the current global food crisis (McMichael, 2008c).

7. SIDH (2002) has published a detailed research monograph on the impact of family structure on children in Jaunpur.

8. While these negotiations over the value of education may not appear as a direct material challenge, they contain epistemic potential in that "moments of contradiction can be moments of possibility for the generation of new meanings, choices and trajectories of action" (Klenk, 2003, p. 119).

5.

RE-IMAGINING THE NATURE
OF DEVELOPMENT

Biodiversity Conservation and Pastoral Visions in the Northern Areas, Pakistan

Nosheen Ali

Examines how, in the mountainous village of Shimshal, national parks and "community-based" conservation projects such as trophy hunting are deeply problematic, promoting exploitive ideologies of nature and development while de-legitimizing the values and rights of pastoralists. The Shimshalis have creatively resisted the appropriations of their land by creating a Shimshal Nature Trust, implementing a model of ecological sovereignty instead of "community participation"—challenging the very logic of protected areas in international conservation.

Introduction

Over the last thirty years, almost 40 percent of the territory of the Northern Areas in Pakistan has been converted into government-owned protected areas, in the form of national parks, wildlife sanctuaries, game reserves, and hunting areas. Indeed, it is not unusual to hear that state authorities wish to transform the biodiversity-rich Northern Areas into a "living museum" for wildlife. This vision has been critically supported and shaped by international conservation NGOs, particularly the International Union for the Conservation of Nature (IUCN) and the World Wide Fund for Nature (WWF), both of which have a major presence in the region.

In this chapter, I explore the conflicts and contestations that such a vision of conservation has generated in lived practice. My focus is on the trajectory of the very first experiment embracing this vision—the Khunjerab National Park (KNP) that was founded in 1975—as well as more recent community-based conservation programs of international trophy hunting that have become popular in Northern Pakistan. I examine two key questions: First, what are the ideals and ideologies that underpin the projects of biodiversity conservation in the Northern Areas? And second, how and why do local communities in the region—specifically the pastoral villagers of Shimshal in the case of the KNP—critique and contest the practices of global conservation?

I argue that national parks in Northern Pakistan as well as more recent community-based conservation approaches are deeply problematic, as they are contingent on relinquishing the very land and livelihood on which pastoral communities are founded. Such projects often assume that practices of local societies pose a key threat to nature, instead of acknowledging that nature is embedded in social relations and cannot be protected without recognizing indigenous values, rights, and ownership. Further, conservation projects such as trophy hunting have introduced a market calculus in the management of nature, by commodifying it for elite, mostly Western tourists. These projects are framed as initiatives for "sustainable development," but in effect, they have served to entrench the power of the state and capital over local ecologies and communities.

Faced with displacement and distress as a result of conservation projects, villagers of Shimshal in Northern Pakistan have responded with courage and creativity, and hitherto managed to protect their homes and pastures from being seized in the name of global conservation. They have done this by creating a Shimshal Nature Trust (SNT)—which has established indigenous ownership and management of Shimshali ancestral land to counter its appropriation by the Khunjerab National Park. A biodiversity hotspot owned and managed entirely by a local community has long been considered unthinkable in global conservation practice, which mandates that the territory be owned by state authorities and managed primarily by national and international conservation agencies. The villagers of Shimshal have hence challenged the fundamental logic of international conservation.

While the Shimshalis have struggled against the KNP in order to protect their land and livelihood, their struggle is especially significant for it contests the epistemic exclusion of pastoral visions from the very definition of development. It challenges the dominant meanings of "nature" and "conservation" in global environmental practice, questions whose knowledge counts as "expertise," and recasts the very process through which "global" development ideals and projects are framed and terms of "community participation" defined. By creating a Shimshal Nature Trust which proposes indigenous ownership of local land and ecology—as opposed to a national park or revenue-sharing conservation schemes—Shimshalis engage in what Jean Franco has called the "struggle for interpretive power" (1999). This involves active appropriation and new repertoires of representation through which marginalized communities carve a space of maneuver within dominant paradigms (Pratt, 1999; Cornwall, Harrison, & Whitehead, 2007). Shimshalis have to strategically represent and position themselves in relation to conservation, in order to claim voice and value, and simply to survive. Simultaneously, they puncture the epistemic privilege through which state and international institutions construct particular visions of the world as natural, and particular interests as the right, universal, and inevitable path of progress.

From Natural Areas to Neo-Liberal Resources

The idea of a "natural protected area" such as a national park for biodiversity conservation emerged from an ahistorical construction of nature, in which nature was viewed as a pristine, peopleless wilderness instead of a lived social landscape (Cronon, 1995). Inspired by Enlightenment and Romantic values, this imagined wilderness had to be created, scientifically managed, preserved, and toured—primarily by urbanites for their own use and luxury. Such valuations of nature emerged in the context of an ongoing unfolding of liberal capitalist modernity, which produced the "natural" and the "social" as separate and distinct realms of existence. The social alienation and environmental degradation resulting from the process of capitalist development was partly the reason behind the conservationist impulse to find and preserve "untouched" and "endangered" nature—untouched by and endangered from capital.

The nature–society relation has undergone significant changes under recent conditions of neo-liberal capitalism. To begin with, nature has been transformed from a factor of production external to capital into a commodity that itself must be bought and sold according to the dictates of capital (O'Connor, 1994). In practice, this commodification of nature has been achieved through the institutionalization of tradable pollution permits, transferable fishing quotas, intellectual property rights over crop varieties, the privatization of public utilities, and other such market-based mechanisms for managing nature. Far from the claims of "efficient" and "sustainable" use, these practices in effect deepen the exploitation of natural resources and heighten the inequities characterizing their access. Countries in the Global South, and particularly their indigenous communities, which depend directly on natural resources, tend to lose out the most, as their rights and use values are delegitimized to make way for the interests and exchange values of global elites.

In the specific arena of biodiversity conservation, neo-liberal values have steadily encroached and become dominant over the last thirty years. In the 1970s, the protected area model and its conception of nature as divorced from society began to come under severe criticism for being exclusionary and ineffective, both from within the conservation community as well as from rural communities whose rights were being superseded by the imperatives of biodiversity preservation. By the early 90s, a series of conferences such as the 1982 and 1992 World Congress on National Parks and Protected Areas (WCNPPA) as well as the 1992 Earth Summit in Rio de Janeiro, had decisively transformed the discourse on biodiversity conservation against the "island mentality" (McNeely, 1993) that had hitherto guided the management of protected areas. The aim now was not strict preservation, but rather conservation combined with "sustainable development." International conservation organizations such as the Conservation International, WWF, and IUCN subsequently set about investigating how the goals of conservation could be achieved while simultaneously ensuring "community participation" and "benefit-sharing."

Part of the answer that they came up with was decidedly neo-liberal: the use of protected areas for the promotion of market ventures such as ecotourism, trophy hunting, and bioprospecting, which would commodify nature to serve mostly Western consumers, but also give local communities a share in the resulting revenue. This commodification of nature is presented as "conservation," employing the circular logic of selling nature in order to save it (McAfee, 1999) and saving nature in order to sell it (Breunig, 2006). It is also presented as a form of "community-based conservation" for "sustainable development," while simultaneously perpetuating a protected area model of conservation that is fundamentally anti-community: protected areas mostly convert commonly owned pastoral and agricultural land into state-owned territory in which subsistence-based uses of nature such as grazing and farming are severely curtailed. Frequently, indigenous communities are altogether evicted from their lands to create the imagined "natural" landscape, leading to an alarming number of "conservation refugees" around the world (Geisler, 2003). Indeed, subsistence uses have become delegitimized by the very definition of "biodiversity," which has come to be constructed as a national and global preserve that needs to be protected mostly from local "threats" such as "unsustainable grazing practices" (e.g., IUCN 1999, p. 31). Through such logics of protected areas as well as their neo-liberal uses, global biodiversity conservation has opened up a new frontier for the appropriation of local space by capital and state, thus embodying a form of what Harvey has called "accumulation by dispossession" (2003).[1]

The accomplishment of this neo-liberal conservation depends critically on the discourse of "sustainable development" and "community-based conservation." This discourse has served to re-legitimize the protected area model, leading to a vigorous expansion of protected areas, particularly in the developing world. Between 1986 and 1996, there was a 60 percent increase in the number of natural protected areas in Asia, Africa, the Middle East, and Latin America (Breunig, 2006). While critiques of neo-liberalism often target the policies promoted by organizations such as the World Bank and IMF, those of conservation organizations are rarely analyzed as linked to the realization of a neo-liberal agenda. This is partly due to the ways in which the aim of conserving biodiversity has become naturalized as "common sense"—an abstract, global value to be aspired toward by everyone for the sake of the earth as well as for future generations. Certainly, attention to the sustainability of the natural world and equitable access to it is of ultimate significance, and is made possible precisely by a language of environmental conservation that has the potential to offer a powerful counter to an ecologically and socially destructive consumerism driven by capitalist modernity. However, what this commonsense environmental ethic has come to embody in actual conservation practice deserves critical study, as the latter constitutes one of the modes through which rural livelihoods around the globe are being superseded by free market ideologies.

The Context of the Khunjerab National Park, Northern Areas

Historically known as Gilgit-Baltistan, the region today called the Northern Areas covers a vast terrain of some 72,496 square kilometers at the northern borders of Pakistan, India, China, and Afghanistan. It encompasses some of the world's highest mountain ranges, and is incredibly rich in plant and wildlife diversity, supporting several rare and endangered species such as the snow leopard (*Uncia uncia*), markhor (*Capra falconeri*), and Himalayan ibex (*Capra ibex siberica*). This ecologically fragile region also has a tenuous political status. It is claimed by both India and Pakistan as part of the disputed territory of Kashmir, but it is effectively ruled by Pakistan, and constitutes 86 percent of the territory of Kashmir under its control.

In 1975, the Northern Areas Wildlife Preservation Act was passed, under which the Northern Areas administration could declare any area in its domain as a national park, wildlife reserve, or wildlife sanctuary, and alter the boundaries of such areas as deemed necessary. Through a government notification in the same year, the Khunjerab National Park was subsequently established by the then Prime Minister, Zulfiqar Ali Bhutto, as the first national park in the Northern Areas. The KNP covers an area of 2270 sq. km, and comprises the grasslands of the Khunjerab, Ghujerab, and Shimshal valleys in the upper Hunza region of the Northern Areas. During the time of princely and colonial rule, the village communities which inhabited this area enjoyed grazing rights on its pastures and paid livestock and livestock products as tax to the Mir, the princely ruler of Hunza. Some pastures like that of Shimshal had been bought from the Mir and were directly owned by the local agro-pastoral communities.

The official rationale for the KNP was the protection of the endangered Marco Polo sheep, as well as the preservation of other Asian wildlife species such as the snow leopard, blue sheep, and Himalayan ibex. The park was recommended and delineated by the famous American field zoologist George B. Schaller, who was affiliated with the Wildlife Conservation Society and visited Pakistan several times between 1970 and 1975. It was designated as a Category II park; according to the guidelines provided by IUCN, this meant that human activity such as grazing and hunting would be banned and visitors would be allowed only for "inspirational, educational, cultural and recreational purposes at a level which will maintain the area in a natural or near natural state" (IUCN, 1994).

Contesting Conservation

While all the other villages that were going to be affected by the Khunjerab National Park eventually accepted its authority, the village of Shimshal still refuses to give up its land. This has been a major impediment in the implementation of the KNP, as two-thirds of it is comprised of Shimshali territory.

As the map in Figure 5.1 shows, Shimshal is located at the northeastern periphery of the Northern Areas, along the border of Pakistan with China. It comprises about 2700 sq. km of high altitude land in the Central Karakoram region, and is exclusively controlled by an agro-pastoral community of approximately 1700 people.[2] Within this area, Shimshalis maintain several village settlements, enough irrigated land to fulfill their food requirements, and over a dozen communal pastures for seasonal herding of their sizable livestock population.

Shimshalis offer a number of reasons to explain why they have been resisting the conversion of their territory into a national park. To begin with, Shimshalis argue that the Khunjerab National Park was created without any consultation with the affected communities regarding its boundaries, regulations, or management. They were simply informed that most of their pastures and even some of their village settlements were now part of a state-owned national park.

Beyond concerns about the arbitrary and undemocratic foundation of the KNP, the main apprehension of Shimshalis is the loss of their land and livelihood. The com-

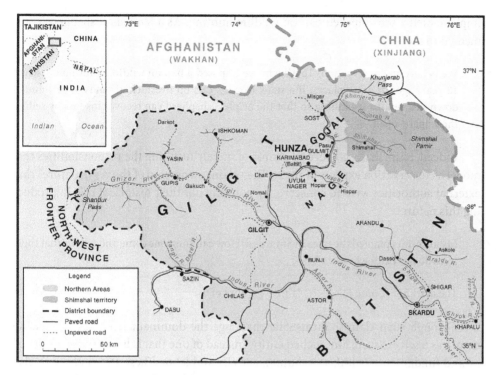

Exhibit 5.1 The Location of Shimshal in the Northern Areas (Gilgit-Baltistan), Pakistan (Source: Butz 1996).

munity of Shimshal stands to lose the most from the park due to its exceptionally high dependence on livestock herding as a source of livelihood. In 1995, Shimshalis owned a total of 4473 goats, 2547 sheep, 960 yaks, 399 cows, and 32 donkeys (Ali & Butz, 2003), and they continue to have the largest livestock holdings in the Hunza region. An enforcement of park regulations would entail a complete ban on grazing and hunting in most Shimshali pastures, so that wildlife species and their habitats can be preserved. This would directly threaten Shimshali livelihoods not only because of the loss of pastures, but also due to the prohibition on hunting certain wildlife predators of livestock. As Shimshali villagers said to me:

> We are supposed to protect the snow leopard, even though it eats up our goats and sheep and causes a huge economic loss for us. Who will compensate us for this loss? We have to pay the price for conservation. First our rights should be honored, then those of wildlife.

These statements challenge the modernist, universalizing agenda of biodiversity conservation that privileges the protection of wildlife for the "future of the earth" over the protection of pastoral livelihoods and futures. For Shimshalis, conservation—as promoted by international conservation organizations—is not of inherent value because it entails an appropriation of their territory, and because one of the rare species that needs to be protected is a deadly predator of livestock. Yet, to prevent their displacement by the Khunjerab National Park, Shimshalis have themselves implemented a self-imposed ban on wildlife hunting. As a Shimshali shepherd commented to me:

> We believe in conservation. That's why we imposed a ban on wildlife hunting ourselves 10 years ago. In other places, if a snow leopard eats up livestock, it tends to get hunted down in a retaliatory killing so that the helpless shepherd can recover his loss by selling the leopard's pelt.

Indeed, Shimshalis go beyond claims of merely fulfilling the responsibilities that modern conservation expects of them. They claim ownership of the very "nature" that external authorities wish to conserve, by pointing out their historical role in producing this nature:

> My ancestors planted the trees in Shimshal. How can someone come and tell me that these trees do not belong to me?

> The markhor (*Capra falconeri*) is alive because of us.

Through such claims, Shimshalis challenge the dominant tendency of viewing nature as a self-existing, untouched entity, instead of one that is historically produced by and fundamentally linked to human activity and labor. These statements can also be read as claims to a local form of ecological nationalism, in which the right to place is asserted through a discourse of lived landscape, nature intimacy, and stewardship (Cederlof & Sivaramakrishnan, 2006).

To support this assertion of local sovereignty based on a historically grounded, indigenous conservation, Shimshalis further point out the state's incompetence in conserving nature:

> We have inhabited and tended this difficult terrain for centuries. What does the DFO[3] or the consultant know about conservation? A while back, a park official came and told us that we need to sign a Memorandum of Understanding and give up the rights to our territory for the KNP so that wildlife habitats can be protected. I told him, "Come, I will show you the area where we have protected wildlife." And he responded, "I don't think I can trek that far." Then I politely asked him, "If you cannot walk to the area, how will you ever conserve it?"

> In areas where the KNP has been implemented, hunting by state officials has become more common and convenient. This is why the wildlife populations have decreased in these areas. And now the government is putting more pressure on us to accept the park so that wildlife in our areas can be exploited.[4]

Such statements assert a local aptitude for conservation that is presented as superior to that of state institutions and international organizations,[5] and also challenge the common portrayal of Shimshalis as incapable stewards of nature (Butz, 1998). This is significant, as the discourse of the state and conservation NGOs in the Northern Areas is centered precisely on problematizing the lack of local "capacity" in attaining conservation goals, which helps to justify an international organization's own role in creating, planning, and managing state-owned conservation zones. My point is not to romanticize the local community, and its interest and capability in conservation. Rather, I wish to point out that conservation agencies in the Northern Areas assume a priori that local communities lack credibility and experience with respect to conservation. They also do not research whether community practices might have a positive role in wildlife conservation in areas where there remain sizable numbers of rare species.

The tendency to undervalue the role of local communities in sustaining nature has indeed been a constitutive feature of global conservation discourse. It is assumed that natives lack ecological values that are supposedly the preserve only of Western elites (Gareau, 2007). The nature–society relation in communities across continents has come to be described through "degradation narratives" that perpetuate the stereotype of an essentialized, irresponsible native—often without the support of any scientific analysis—as they help to justify national and international interventions for protecting the "global commons" from its local users (Brockington & Homewood, 2001; Neumann, 2004). These narratives emerged from, and build upon a long-standing colonial discourse that helped to legitimize the appropriation of nature for varied interests including commercial exploitation, hunting pleasure, and strategic needs (Rangarajan, 2006). Today, they continue to thrive in conservation discourse, despite the rhetoric of including and valorizing the "local community."

Representation and Power: The Case of the Shimshal Nature Trust

Until the mid-90s, Shimshali villagers obstructed the implementation of the KNP through informal resistances such as the disruption of information-gathering

Exhibit 5.2   A Village Settlement in Central Shimshal.

mechanisms, refusal to follow administrative regulations, and the blocking of government and NGO officials from entering the community (Butz, 2002). However, the pressures on them to submit to park authorities kept increasing, as new programs and funds for conservation poured into the Northern Areas in the wake of a renewed global—and subsequently, national—concern for biodiversity preservation. In this context, the confrontational stance of Shimshalis that emphasized a complete rejection of the park was proving to be counterproductive, and served only to reinforce the stereotype of Shimshal as a backward and "wild" community. Realizing this, a group of men belonging mostly to Shimshal's first generation English-educated elite—and often employed in development NGOs based in Gilgit[6] or Islamabad—began to rally community members around a politics of appeasement and engagement, instead of one that endorsed confrontation.[7] They strongly felt—and feared—that a small, marginal border community like Shimshal could eventually suffer massive state action unless it was able to counter its negative image, and negotiate cordially with conservation organizations. As one of them said to me, they had to "fight with dialogue." After much deliberation, they came up with an answer: a community-based organization called the Shimshal Nature Trust (SNT) that would manage and showcase Shimshal's conservation efforts, and represent the community in dealings with external organizations.

Created in 1997, the key purpose of the SNT was to formally articulate, and give material force to the representational claims discussed in the previous section—claims to livelihood dependency, native authenticity and ownership, environmental responsibility, and a place-based conservation capability. As the "Fifteen Year Vision and Management Plan" of the SNT explains:

> Our largest challenge is not to develop a system of utilizing the natural surroundings sustainably, but rather to express our indigenous stewardship practices in language that will garner the financial, technical and political support of the international community, and that will persuade Pakistani authorities that we are indeed capable of protecting our own natural surroundings (SNT, 1999).

The SNT "management plan" is precisely a response to this representational challenge: how to counter the language, and hence, the power of a global conservation discourse that refuses to acknowledge indigenous values and rights? The plan describes the socio-economic context of the Shimshali community, the ways in which a conservation ethic has been historically practiced, and the community-initiated programs through which natural resource management is envisioned in the future.[8] Following the tropes of developmentalist writing, these programs are divided up into implementation phases, with various activities planned for each phase. The SNT management plan has been distributed to all the major government and non-governmental organizations working on conservation and development in the Northern Areas, and is also accessible through the Internet. Between 1999 and 2002, SNT members also conducted a series of "workshops" in Gilgit with different "stakeholders" to create awareness and legitimacy for their approach toward conservation.

The very language, format, and content of SNT practices reflect how communities have come to understand and reconfigure the nature of the power exercised by international conservation organizations. The global discourse of "community-based nature conservation" and "sustainable development" is appropriated by positing Shimshalis as the original and most suitable conservationists, who are equipped to ensure the sustainable future that international conservation NGOs are striving toward.[9] Moreover, the "participatory" approach adopted by NGOs in recent years—in part a response to the failure of and resistance to earlier development projects—is reconstituted to argue that effective participation must entail complete *ownership*. As the management plan explains:

> While we appreciate recent efforts by external agencies to develop [a] community-based nature conservation project…it is not enough that external initiatives be managed locally; rather, a culturally and contextually-sensitive nature stewardship programme should be developed and initiated, as well as managed, from within the community (SNT, 1997).

The existence and legitimacy of such a community-centered program is then established by describing how indigenous ways of environmental management have historically been based on ecologically sound practices such as land use zoning, as well as on culturally specific values such as the "Islamic religious ethic of nature stewardship" in which nature is respected as "God's ultimate creation" (SNT, 1997). The emphasis on such a moral ecology grounded in religion has an important discursive effect—it provides a way to unsettle the scientific authority of international conservation agencies by highlighting how the interpretation of nature and its conservation through ethical values is more locally appropriate and significant than one based on scientific principles.[10] However, this is not to suggest that religious and cultural practice does not have any real role in local systems of nature conservation. On the contrary, long-standing religious and cultural institutions have enabled Shimshalis—who follow the Ismaili sect of Islam—to collectively organize for conservation efforts ranging from hunting control to pasture management. The SNT itself is managed partly by local volunteer corps and boy scouts, who are affiliated with the *jamat khana* (religious center) in Ismaili-Muslim practice.

While the key purpose of SNT is a strategic celebration and vindication of an indigenous, ecological sovereignty, the role of external support is also valued. Indeed, as SNT members emphasize, foreign scholars from universities in Japan, Canada, and the United States have played a critical role in shaping local consciousness and enabling community initiatives.[11] The SNT also acknowledges that for activities such as a wildlife census and wildlife monitoring, the support of organizations like the WWF and IUCN is especially needed and welcomed.

Unfortunately, such collaborations have rarely materialized, as international conservation organizations continue to insist that any project of conservation in Shimshal must be linked to the conversion of community-owned land into the KNP. Even if it is now occasionally acknowledged—as the new rhetoric of respecting the "community" demands—that Shimshalis have responsibly taken care of the environment, it is argued matter-of-factly that their main livelihood practice of livestock grazing poses a fundamental threat to wildlife survival, and hence they cannot be trusted with the task of conservation.

Reorienting Livelihoods

The ban on livestock grazing in the Khunjerab National Park was marginally enforced until 1989, when the newly formed government organization—the National Council for Conservation of Wildlife (NCCW)—drafted a plan for a stricter enforcement of the Category II criteria. The affected villages nevertheless continued to practice their customary grazing rights, particularly since the government was not forthcoming with the promised compensation. Things came to a head in 1991, when the government used the paramilitary Khunjerab Security Force to evict herdsmen from the park's no-grazing zone and even killed some of their livestock. Eventually, in 1992, all the aggrieved communities except Shimshal signed an agreement with the KNP authorities that allowed them some concessions on their grazing rights as well a share in park-generated revenue in return for accepting the authority of the park (Knudsen, 1999).

While the ban on livestock grazing was somewhat relaxed, it soon gave way to a new emphasis on a reduction in livestock holdings. This reduction has in effect become a pre-condition for obtaining the community share in park-generated revenue such as entry fees. In fact, as a state wildlife official informed me, the very point of sharing the park revenue with the community is to enable them to engage in "conservation activities such as the reduction of their livestock over a period of time."

In recent years, this new logic of equating community conservation with livestock reduction has meant that park officials have withheld payment of the community share in KNP's entry fees for long periods on the grounds that the concerned communities are not reducing their livestock holdings.[12] Despite strong evidence of decreasing livestock ownership and grazing in the Northern Areas (Kreutzmann, 2006), KNP officials continue to claim otherwise. Such a claim about livestock holdings has thus become a tool in the hands of KNP officials to retain their hold over communities and their resources.

Conservation NGOs, on the other hand, concede that dependence on livestock herding is indeed decreasing in areas affecting the KNP. This, however, does not necessarily bring any credit for the community. As a manager at an international conservation NGO remarked:

> Communities are not reducing their livestock because they care about conservation. It is happening itself because people are increasingly seeking off-farm employment. It is only when they will consciously reduce livestock that we will achieve true community participation.

In other words, it is not just particular conservation outcomes that are desired; rather, a disciplining of community attitudes is being struggled for, and represented as the legitimate form of participation. Community participation is thus reconfigured as a measure of how well people in the Northern Areas have internalized the international conservation discourse, and sacrificed their own livelihoods for its sake.

Because it is believed that communities are not "participating" well, international conservation organizations have sought to go beyond the process of awareness-raising regarding the negative impact of livestock on wildlife conservation. They wish to actively steer people away from livestock herding by providing alternate sources of income (WWF, 1996). These alternate livelihoods must ideally be linked to the implementation of the park, so that people can realize that conservation can be a source of their "development" as opposed to pastoralism. Linking the global project of conservation to "income-generating opportunities" at the local level has become known as "community-based conservation" in the discourse of international conservation NGOs operating in the Northern Areas, and it is to its contested operations that I now turn my attention.

Community-Based Conservation

For international conservation NGOs in the Northern Areas, community-based conservation has become synonymous with projects of ecotourism and the international sport of trophy hunting. The latter has particularly come to dominate the conservation scene in the Northern Areas over the last ten years, during which twenty-two "Community Controlled Hunting Areas" (CCHAs) have been created in the region. These have been established primarily by IUCN, through the GEF/UNDP funded Mountain Areas Conservancy Project (MACP). The CCHAs have a strong appeal for communities, as 75 percent of the revenue generated through trophy hunting goes to the community that manages the relevant area.[13] Communities also earn income through the porters and guides that accompany the hunter. Moreover, hunters are also known to be generous, and might give up to $3000 as a donation for local development after a successful hunt.

International conservation organizations in the Northern Areas promote trophy hunting as a form of "sustainable community development" because of the cash it generates, which is either distributed evenly to all the households in a village, or saved with a recognized community-based organization that can utilize the funds for local development projects. It is also represented as a useful tool for conservation: the income that can be generated by occasionally catering to the needs of rich Pakistani and foreign hunters is deemed to be a significant disincentive for rampant local hunting which might be undertaken for subsistence, cultural significance, pleasure, or trade.

Conservation agencies perceive no contradiction between projects such as the KNP that seek to preserve landscapes in their "natural state" for the protection of wildlife, and projects such as the CCHAs that turn this wildlife into a commodity that can be killed for pleasure. In many cases, a CCHA is in fact located right along the boundaries of a national park, in what is called the "buffer zone." It is assumed that the hunting of treasured wildlife in these buffer zones does not disrupt their natural habitats, but the practice of livestock grazing and local hunting does. In effect, local use values of nature are delegitimized in order to secure its global exchange value.

This commodification of nature in the name of conservation is perfectly aligned with the interests of hunters. As trophy hunting faces increased resistance in North America and Europe, "hunters, like multinational industries, flee to grounds where they can escape those restrictive conditions" (MacDonald, 2005, p. 266). The continuation of their sport, however, is dependent on the protection of wildlife in these freer areas from local use and abuse. This link between local conservation and global hunting is captured tellingly in a Safari Club International (SFI) sticker which I saw at the head office of a prominent international conservation organization in the Northern Areas. It read: "Conserve Now, Hunt Later." No wonder that conservation agencies perceive no contradiction between saving nature and selling it: they want nature to be saved precisely so that it can be sold.

Community-based trophy hunting also serves the interests of the state, and particularly of the local forest bureaucracy that oversees the management of protected areas. It provides an important source of revenue, and also reinforces the power of the state to distribute patronage through the granting of hunting quotas to particular communities. This serves as an indirect means for regulating community behavior. Indeed, the KNP management has used trophy hunting as a lure to put pressure on Shimshalis for giving ownership of their land to the KNP. As a KNP official explained:

> In 2006, we gave a permit to an American hunter to hunt in Shimshal. The community got its due share for the trophy as well. We then allowed the creation of a Community Controlled Hunting Area as an additional incentive. Since then, we have given more permits, but we will not release the money till Shimshalis sign an MoU in which they accept the KNP and its regulations. We have to bring these communities in line. They think they can extract the benefits of the park, without obeying the writ of the government.

Hence, community-based conservation schemes that provide a community share in trophy hunting and in park entry fees, have come to perpetuate a state–community relation in which the very terms of participation are based on exclusion and dispossession, as they require communities to surrender ownership of their land on the one hand and abandon their livelihoods on the other. These projects have become forms of political and social control that help to entrench the power of the state over rural spaces and communities. This control is often asserted through sinister tactics. For example, in 2006, the Directorate of the Khunjerab National Park lodged a court case against a number of Shimshali youth for assaulting park rangers who had been sent to Shimshal. Members of the SNT, however, contend that there was only a verbal argument between the rangers and local youth, and that the case has been filed only to malign Shimshalis and further coerce them into accepting the authority of the KNP.

Analyses of community-based conservation initiatives elsewhere have likewise demonstrated how environmental agendas framed in participatory terms have served to intensify state power, often diminishing the political and economic security of rural communities instead of enhancing it (Neumann, 2001; Agrawal, 2001a; Li, 2002; Breunig, 2006). These agendas are defined by a dense network of national and transnational actors that cut across the traditional divides of state, non-governmental organization, and corporation (Igoe & Brockington, 2007). What is truly baffling and dangerous about the global conservation agenda is its insistence on promoting activities such as tourism and trophy hunting—which commodify nature primarily for the leisure of rich, Western consumers—as sustainable alternatives to local subsistence-based livelihoods. In this neo-liberal logic, the "sustainable development" of a community becomes equated with the ability to raise cash incomes through the market, and the development of "nature" is presumed to be achieved by turning it into a commodity that is subject to market forces of production and exchange. Such logics cannot be implemented without the necessary cultivation and appropriation of local subjectivities. Through promises of "benefit-sharing," already marginal, local communities are first expected to compromise their own livelihood concerns and take on the burden of conserving "nature," and then led to treat nature as a resource from which they can and must profit from.

The appeal and importance of such market-driven approaches to nature management for local communities should not be underestimated. In a context where the state is pushing for park development but shows very little interest in social development, communities like Shimshal tremendously value the revenue that they may get from projects like trophy hunting, as it can be directed for self-help initiatives ranging from water channels to health care provision. What they find problematic, however, is the contingency of "community-based conservation" schemes on relinquishing the very land and livelihood on which communities are founded.

The discourse of "alternative livelihoods" is also problematic because it assumes that a pastoral community's relationship with nature is merely about economic need, and hence alternative sources of incomes would, and should automatically translate into a reduced dependence on nature—ideally, a total surrender of it so that it becomes a "protected area" for state and capital. What is erased in such a discourse is the central role of nature and pastoral activity in defining a community's identity and its forms of belonging. In Shimshal, for example, pastures are considered key sites for historical events, spiritual renewal, and cultural celebrations (Butz, 1996). They are also particularly cherished by Shimshali women as places that provide respite from the constraints and anxieties of village life, by offering a meaningful experience of independence, female solidarity, and peace. Hence, what is considered a "natural" terrain of pristine wildlife is of tremendous material and symbolic value for Shimshalis (Moore, 1993), encompassing identity, history, and livelihood. Utlimately, it is the very source and meaning of life, which is why both its commodification and compensation is considered unthinkable.

Conclusion

Ten years after the establishment of the Shimshal Nature Trust, a number of SNT members expressed to me a sense of disillusionment about their initiative. As one of them commented:

> We created the SNT to engage with outside interests, and make them understand our concerns. Instead, we have become perceived as more of a threat, and portrayed as anti-state. This is completely false. We are eager to work with the state, and with international NGOs. We know that conservation is important. All we are saying is, don't make a park that will prevent us from owning our lands and living our lives.

These were the last impressions with which I left Shimshal in June 2007. By March 2008, however, the tide had changed. Shimshalis had managed to sign a Memorandum of Understanding with the Northern Areas Wildlife and Parks Department, which clearly acknowledged and guaranteed the land use rights and settlements of Shimshal, in return for cooperation in transnational and national conservation efforts—something Shimshalis were always prepared to do, but on their own terms. Subsequently, the Khunjerab National Park authorities have also withdrawn their criminal charges against Shimshali youth. Shimshal Nature Trust members now speak with a sense of relief and hope, instead of frustration and fear. It can thus be argued that the epistemic "struggle for interpretive power" (Franco, 1989)—which Shimshalis engaged in through the Shimshal Nature Trust—was ultimately successful, though the future course of interactions between Shimshal, state actors, and international institutions remains to be seen.

The case of Shimshal embodies a critical struggle for social and ecological justice, contributing to peasant struggles elsewhere that have sought to reclaim rural agency in global development projects (McMichael, 2006). Such struggles create an opening for alternate visions of being and becoming. Indeed, Shimshalis hope to change the dominant "global" discourse on conservation itself, by arguing that they themselves are central makers of the development project instead of its beneficiaries, and that they are eager to imagine new social futures with "government participation" and "international participation." This challenges the existing framework whereby epistemic and material powers are concentrated in the hands of a transnational–national nexus of institutions, the agendas of which are scripted from above while allowing "community participation." In effect, like indigenous communities elsewhere, Shimshalis are working toward an ecological sovereignty in which their community governs itself and sustainably tends the resources on which it depends—as it has always done.

Despite the Shimshali achievement, however, the normative narrative of biodiversity conservation remains wedded to projects that act in the name of community, but are unwilling to listen to it. Indeed, what I have tried to point out in this chapter is not only the unwillingness, but the structural *inability* of the global conservation nexus to understand and value the interests of local communities. Embedded in the global discourse of biodiversity conservation and sustainable development are *assumptions*—for example, about nature as divorced from society, and livestock as an irredeemable threat to wildlife—and *interests* such as those of conservation organizations, their corporate financiers, and hunters, which make it *unthinkable* to acknowledge that a local community can own and manage a protected area. What gets authorized, instead, is the commodification of nature which

> abstracts nature from its spatial and social contexts…reinforces the claims of global elites to the greatest share of the earth's biomass and all it contains…and speeds the extension of market relations into diverse and complex eco-social systems, with material and cultural outcomes that do more to diminish than to conserve diversity and sustainability (McAfee, 1999, pp. 1–3).

This process of commodification has simultaneously enhanced the power of the state to territorialize nature and to regulate subjects through the control of nature. The end result of this process is that almost 40 percent of the Northern Areas' territory has been declared as some form of conservation enclosure, benefiting state and capital at the cost of local sovereignty and livelihood.

To be sure, my critique of community-based conservation is not aimed at dismissing the participatory turn in global development and biodiversity conservation. This turn is surely a necessary corrective to earlier approaches which were characterized by a top-down imposition of agendas and frequent use of violence. Indeed, it is precisely the rhetoric of "participation" and "community empowerment" that enables negotiation on the part of Shimshalis. At the same time, however, we need to recognize the ways in which such rhetoric facilitates and conceals the manipulation, violence, and displacement that is still widespread in conservation practice.

I also do not wish to suggest that the role of conservation organizations in the Northern Areas has been entirely negative. Both the WWF and IUCN are staffed with several local managers who are all too aware of the dilemmas that conservation poses for their region and people, and have pushed their supervisors to be more sensitive to local contexts. These organizations have also undertaken important initiatives that address local needs of conservation, such as training of communities in restoring pastures, in protecting livestock from predators, and in addressing concerns of deforestation and overhunting. Importantly, they have also attempted to go beyond the drafting of management plans for protected areas, to undertaking valuable research on topics such as local understandings of ecology and wildlife management.

Initiatives such as these have the potential to promote a more meaningful attention to the "local" in conservation practice. For example, a report by IUCN (2003) examines customary and statutory regimes of resource control in the Northern Areas, arguing that the former favors conservation and sustainability whereas the latter promotes exploitation. It further explores how communities in the Northern Areas have had a varying historical experience of nature–society relations, and how differently situated actors within communities offer diverse explanations for declining wildlife populations. People point out that road construction, urbanization, and less rainfall due to climate change have been key threats to wildlife survival in their regions. While acknowledging that local hunting has been a threat, they also highlight how it has increased only in the last two decades due to the availability of modern weapons as well as the pressures of new market-generated economic needs.

Importantly, not one person in this comprehensive study argues that livestock is a threat to wildlife. This reinforces the findings of my own fieldwork in Shimshal, which revealed how people perceive wildlife and livestock populations as part of a complex ecological process in which a complementary relationship between plant, animal, and human life has been historically developed and maintained by local communities. From their perspective, they have been conserving all along and cannot understand why they must discontinue their practices *for* the sake of conservation. A shepherd from southern France has poignantly echoed this sentiment: "shepherds…are trapped between the desire to do what they know and want to do and the requirement to act as a manager of space and biodiversity. The most difficult thing is perhaps to explain that, all told, this is one and the same approach" (Grellier, 2006, p. 163).

Such reflections on biodiversity invite and enable a deeper analysis of environmental issues than that permitted by the dominant conservation discourse that pits local irresponsibility against global concerns. One hopes that for the cause of environmental sustainability as well as of social justice, such local understandings, values, and aspirations are not only researched, but actually allowed a central place in framing the agenda of biodiversity conservation as well as in shaping the future of development.

Notes

* Acknowledgments I am especially grateful to David Butz, Amita Baviskar, Fouad Makki, John Mock, and Alex Da Costa for their critical feedback on an earlier version of this paper.
1. However, it entails the nationalization of community land instead of its privatization as Harvey posits.
2. "Exclusive" in the sense that only villagers of Shimshal own and manage this vast terrain. The administrative role of the local or the national state has historically been limited, largely due to the rugged, inaccessible terrain of Shimshal. Shimshalis used to pay grazing taxes during the Mir's reign, but after the abolition of the Hunza princely state in 1974, no income taxes have been paid to the Pakistan government.
3. Abbreviation for the District Forest Officer, the key government official responsible for implementing state policies of conservation in the Northern Areas.
4. The occurrence of illegal hunting by state officials in the KNP has even been acknowledged by the WWF, which is the main international organization that has been pushing for the formalization of the park (WWF, 1996). Moreover, a higher-up official at WWF also acknowledged to me in a personal interview that "wildlife in Shimshal is most likely being conserved well."
5. Research elsewhere in South Asia has also demonstrated that replacing local forms of control with state control is not always productive for conserving nature, because the state is generally unable to enforce its own conservation policies (Guha, 1989, Saberwal, 1999, Agrawal, 2001b).
6. A town of around 50,000 people that serves as the administrative center of the Northern Areas.
7. Their intervention was openly vilified at first, particularly by some notable village elders who accused them of being bought by the state and conservation NGOs.
8. These programs include a community-enforced ban on wildlife hunting which was discussed earlier in this article. Keeping local needs in mind, the ban does not apply to the small number of ibex that are hunted for meat by yak herders in the winter.
9. Indeed, due to the unequal power relations embedded in global conservation regimes, indigenous communities around the world have had to re-present themselves as environmentally responsible subjects to ensure their survival (Martinez-Alier, 2002). This suggests that a claim to traditional property rights and livelihood dependency has increasingly become insufficient for preventing the appropriation of their rights.
10. At the same time, a scientific approach is also drawn upon by asserting that nature conservation by the Shimshal community would be based, in the first place, on up-to-date statistical information collected by local youth.
11. The SNT management plan itself was compiled and edited by David Butz, a geographer who has been working in Shimshal since 1988.
12. These communities do not include Shimshal; they belong to the seven Upper Hunza villages that accepted the authority of the park, and are hence, entitled to a share in park revenue.
13. The cost of a hunting permit varies with different wildlife species: for an ibex it is $3000, for a blue sheep it is $6500, and shooting an Astore Markhor can cost up to $40,000.

PART II

GLOBAL MARKETS, LOCAL JUSTICE

The assumption that markets are both natural and neutral is challenged not only by their unequal effects, but also by alternative value claims. Human social capacities and aspirations are not limited to the marketplace, despite neoliberal prescriptions for market-led global development and the application of a market calculus to current forms of governance and social organization. This set of essays raise the questions: What interests do (global) markets serve, who is excluded, and on what grounds? With what mechanisms do neo-liberal policies privilege markets in decisions about development policy and social needs? And where does the market perspective fail to register distinct needs?

The struggles depicted here provide some answers, not only in targeting injustice, but also in the fact that they do not necessarily strive to realize the values of the development narrative. Marketplace participation—the now standard development package of micro-credit initiatives, market-led land reforms, structural adjustment programs, export industry—is not always the solution for those with other cultural terms of reference. Their first task may be to survive, which often involves negotiating, and protecting themselves from, erosion of their life-worlds. It also involves conducting an epistemic struggle over what counts as survival resources. Global markets place a financial value on material resources (such as forests, oil deposits, crop land) and seek to develop these through export industries. While the host state and perhaps the region (or its elites) may gain new technologies, capital, and revenues, local communities may lose access to their means of social reproduction, including their knowledge base, common lands, habitat, and food security—in short, their cultural identity. Whereas global markets assign "comparative advantage" to regional products created for global consumers, the comparative disadvantage of those who forfeit control over their local resources underlines the profound consequences of development.

As these essays suggest, not only may development bring material inequality and exclusion, but also inequality in terms of the power to decide what ways of life count in a globalizing era. Prioritizing export cultures concentrates power in the hands of global financiers whose interests transcend those of local communities in their own political destiny and sustainability. It is for these reasons that struggles arise with a double purpose: to protect autonomy against singular and powerful market interests, and to reassert social or cultural values at odds with the reductionism of the market culture.

Anna Zalik's chapter 6 examines the experience of "democratic transition" in Nigeria and Mexico, whose globally valued extractive resources (oil in particular) overshadow national politics. This essay shows how global market considerations influence (and undermine) electoral processes in these petro-states, through financial risk assessments that affect currency values and create the potential for political crisis. At the same time elections serve to legitimate export-oriented regimes. As a consequence, the manipulation of electoral processes in the context of popular resistance to repressive "resource-extractive" states highlights the ongoing struggles to realize real, substantive democracy and social justice.

Rachel Bezner-Kerr's chapter 7 examines the alternative to export agriculture in Malawi, where agribusiness deepens monoculture, environmental degradation, and dependence on costly inputs (seeds, fertilizers). A countermovement of Soils, Food and Healthy Communities Project in over a hundred villages, dedicated to agro-ecology and supporting inter-generational and gender relations on the land, demonstrates that smallholder peasant agriculture, supported by government policies (excluded by the neoliberal development model), may be more productive and successful as a development strategy for food security and sustaining local economies.

Alicia Swords's chapter 8 explores the way military occupation serves neo-liberal policies opening up Mexico's rebellious Chiapas state to resource exploitation. In particular, militarization heightens the vulnerability of indigenous women and undermines the masculinity of indigenous men, deploying a discourse of *indigenismo* that justifies development intervention. This essay shows how political education and community organizing enable the development of cooperatives that reframe gender relations, bridge class and ethnic divides, and promote community-based resistance to divisive neo-liberal policies.

Emelie Peine's chapter 9 addresses a paradox: why Brazilian soy farmers misplace their struggle within a power structure that enables agribusinesses to promote and profit from neo-liberal development, while the risks of producing for global markets are borne by the farmers themselves. This essay documents how, in the name of the free market, soy farmers target the government when the market fails rather than the grain traders to whom they are deeply in debt, and who shape government policy anyway. While the global soy market structure is uncovered, the soy farmers remain steadfast in their neo-liberal belief that the state, rather than agribusiness, is the source of their distress.

6.

MARKETING AND MILITARIZING ELECTIONS?

Social Protest, Extractive Security, and the De/Legitimation of Civilian Transition in Nigeria and Mexico*

Anna Zalik

Electoral processes in Nigeria and Mexico, are juxtaposed against a backdrop of popular resistance to state authority and violence in deeply unequal petroleum extractive settings. The trappings of "democratic transition" in these states spotlight neo-liberal forms of development, which commercialize elections and generate opposition—challenging the lack of substantive democracy in monopolizing resource wealth, repression, and electoral posturing to financial interests to sustain foreign investment.

Introduction

As moments in democratic transition, the 2006 Mexican and 2007 Nigerian elections were historic. The Nigerian elections of 2007 were the first post-military era transition, while Mexico's 2006 elections were the first transition between two elected governments under the new electoral regime. But both were characterized by serious electoral irregularities, including outright violence against opposition groups in the period preceding the elections and during the polls themselves. In both, results proved highly controversial and ensuing protest and demands for a recount seriously undermined their legitimacy as an expression of popular sovereignty. Complicating these "democratic transitions" were global financial interests in electoral processes and outcomes.

In the lead-up to the 2006 polls, Mexico saw heavy police and military repression against groups supporting the Zapatistas' *Other Campaign*, which toured the country questioning the premise of party politics as an expression of popular interests. Following the July election night, extremely close results led to both Andres Manuel Lopez Obrador of the PRD left (Party of the Democratic Revolution) and Felipe Calderon of the PAN right (National Action Party) declaring themselves winner. While the Federal Electoral Institute eventually announced these for the PAN, support for the opposition led to huge protests in Mexico City and calls for a full recount. Indeed, into 2008 Mexican investigative journalists sought access to the 2006 election materials and requested intervention by the Inter-American Commission on Human Rights to prevent their destruction (Proceso, 2008). And since its inception, Calderon's presidency has been marked by intense violence between drug cartels and federal security, and impunity concerning human rights violations. In a climate of fear and insecurity, the Mexican state's function as policeman is legitimated (to protect the citizenry), even as its role as democratic representative has eroded.

In Nigeria, in both 2003 and 2007, national elections were marked by massive rigging, physical intimidation of voters, and the presence of armed groups seeking to control ballots, ballot boxes, and tally sheets. Young men were contracted to secure access to electoral materials and considerable violence broke out in struggles to appropriate them from competitors. Throughout the country the use of violence led many to stay home during the polls. Yet, the elections still served as pivotal moments in the installation of new regional representatives to the federal government. Later, election tribunals successfully overturned some controversial results—including certain highly charged gubernatorial races in the Niger Delta states. Nevertheless, recent by-election polls have been condemned as an ongoing expression of the interests of the ruling People's Democratic Party (PDP). But concurrently the Nigerian state's monopoly over means of violence is persistently challenged, in particular in the Niger Delta where physical attacks on oil installations by armed insurgents overlap with commercialized kidnappings and competition for control of the contraband oil trade. In protesting these conditions, the Niger Delta based organization Environmental Rights Action took out an ad entitled "Armed Struggle as Election" (ERA/Guardian, 2003) in a key Nigerian newspaper in 2003—which similarly applied in 2007. The descriptor could as well concern the context of popular unrest and state repression that typified the 2006 polls in Mexico.

Alongside violence, the polls in Mexico and Nigeria saw a lack of autonomy on the part of electoral institutions—with the respective directors of the INEC (Independent National Election Commission, Nigeria) and IFE (Federal Electoral Institute, Mexico) bearing the brunt of opposition jokes when they were over. In Nigeria this arose from denial of serious electoral irregularities, and in Mexico from exposure of the close relationship between the IFE director and the now ruling President. After the elections, social responses seriously challenged governmental legitimacy and the idea of the rule of law. In Mexico, Lopez Obrador, the former mayor of Mexico City declared a parallel government with considerable support. Despite skepticism regarding the IFE's conduct, a full recount was not held—as demanded by the opposition. The Mexican elections were in fact declared "free and fair" by much of the international observer community. In Nigeria, the Nigerian Labour Congress and civil society groups declared various days of mass action and a national strike to protest the election, while the INEC became the butt of derision.

This chapter argues that the national polling exercises in Nigeria and Mexico reveal deep disenchantment with the implementation of elections as a practice of democracy. Mexico and Nigeria are particularly salient examples of such disenchantment as their electoral outcomes hold special geo-political weight. Taken together, their elections manifest the increasingly high-stake outcomes associated with political rule in two strategic "petro-states." Via political office, competing elites secure access to the profits arising from the oil industry, whose rents constitute a significant portion of national accounts. The electoral processes in each site are thus particularly tense sites of competition and repression: competition to own the procedures and materials, and episodes of violence to subdue mobilizations against outcomes that threaten powerful corporate interests. As the most important suppliers of oil to the United States in Latin America and Sub-Saharan Africa respectively, the amenability of Mexican and Nigerian governments to economic relations with the transnational oil industry is highly pertinent to global approval. Thus, in addition to the implications of these elections for competing domestic power-holders, their outcomes are salient to transnational financial interests. By juxtaposing these two cases, revealing their respective forms of commodification of electoral procedure, this essay raises questions about the ways in which such democratic transitions legitimize and normalize a neo-liberal form of development.

To proceed, I consider how physical struggles around these elections compromise faith in the notion of democratic legitimacy on at least two grounds. First, and visibly in both sites, their outcomes were heavily influenced by surrounding violence, the outright commodification of the election materials and processes (ballots, ballot boxes, counting procedures, and purchase of voting machines), the collusion of electoral monitoring bodies, and the interests of bilateral institutions. This undermines the meaning of procedural democracy—through electoral polls—for the realization of representative and *substantive* democracy.

Second, and alongside this context of disenfranchisement, currently or formerly armed movements in both sites pose a profound challenge to the meaning of procedural democracy by forcefully asserting popular sovereignty from below. In Mexico, through the Other Campaign, the Zapatistas sought to reveal the inadequacies of electoral practice. In the Niger Delta insurgency, partially represented by MEND (the Movement for the Emancipation of the Niger Delta), criminalized struggles over contraband oil overlap with a local market in protection. In this market, armed militias secure (or plunder) industrial installations and provide physical services to competing politicians. Insurgents also compete with Nigerian state forces as providers of industrial security, threatening local populations with military incursions.

In addition, I examine how the highly contested and corrupted transition to neo-liberal market rule in each site reveals the illusory nature of liberal democratic procedure, even as these procedures are invested with the technologies of global electoral expertise. The elections serve conjuncturally as moments to reassert the financial imperatives of global market institutions, yet the absence of transparent practice undermines faith in the value of liberal, free market democracy.

The chapter begins by discussing the implications of electoral outcomes for domestic financial ratings in the global South. This section shows how market-insider perceptions concerning leading political candidates influence their ratings of incoming regime (and thus, national) credit-worthiness. It also considers the role of the international observer community in approving or rejecting polling legitimacy. Following this, I outline varying positions between resistance movements and liberal and conservative policy-makers regarding the role of the democratic electoral process in democratic transition. These discussions serve as a backdrop to an overview of the polls in Nigeria and Mexico, and how the violent context surrounding them revealed their commodification. In both countries electoral disillusionment may be understood as discursively constituting what is now being referred to as "post-neo-liberalism," a condition in which the promise of the free market has been revealed as illusory: That is, in the context of an ongoing financial crisis, the consequences of free market reforms are seen to undermine, rather than buttress, substantive democratic change.

Electoral Process and the Commercialization of the State

The era of neo-liberalism is marked by the "competition state," premised on the decline of social protections, the shrinking of public capacity as states sell public assets, and the opening of national economies to international trade and investment. With international exposure, elections become means by which the international community evaluates national policy and political authority in the competition state. Specifically, corporate investors and financial traders assess the relative "competitiveness" of a particular state in their daily transactions, in what some refer to as the daily referendum on a particular country's economic strength (Atvater & Mahnkopf, 1997; Eatwell, 1999) through continuous currency trading activity. This "referendum" however, is magnified at moments of presidential elections when attention from media, policy makers, and "opinion-leaders" is centered on possible outcomes in a given country. According to a recent analysis of economic ratings during elections, the perceived openness of the most popular candidate to market-liberal reforms shapes that country's financial ratings. The likelihood of election of a left-wing government in fact contributed to rating downgrades for the country in question (Vaaler, Schragge, and Block, 2006).

The ideology of a government contender may thus directly shape perceptions of its economic "competitiveness," underlining how the political categories associated with "right" and "left" influence market assessment of regime viability. This could, consequently, pre-determine the likelihood that "left-leaning" governments will be forced to execute decidedly neo-liberal policies upon taking office—so as to prevent an economic downturn. That said, the regular and timely process of a national/federal election is essential to the social performance and construction of procedural democracy.

Supplementing the above discussion about the influence of candidate policies on financial ratings, the act of voting serves a legitimacy function for the political system. In her ethnography of voting in rural India, Bannerjee (2007) highlights the "sacred" nature of popular participation, with voting numbers rising in recent elections. In the case of West Bengal, she suggests, elections may carry the possibility for popular empowerment since political representatives are confronted directly by their constituents, an argument also made by a colleague who directs an electoral-monitoring NGO in Nigeria. But her analysis ultimately underscores the ritual nature of elections:

> democracy is really an untrue but vitally important myth in support of social cohesion, with elections as its central and regular ritual enactment that help maintain and restore

equilibrium. The ability to vote is thus seen as a necessary safety valve which allows for the airing of popular disaffection and opinion, but which nevertheless ultimately restores status quo. In such a reading, elections require the complicity of all participants in a deliberate mis-recognition of the emptiness of its procedures and of the lack of any significant changes which this ritual brings about, but are yet a necessary charade to mollify a restless electorate (Bannerjee, 2007, p. 1556).

A key distinction between the Mexican and Nigerian elections and those of West Bengal is that the latter serve to legitimate *because* the majority in fact *do* vote and do so for the ruling Communists. Nevertheless, Bannerjee's point applies to contemporary democratization processes in Africa, described by critics as the "democratization of disempowerment" (Ake, 1994). In analyzing the relationship between formal democratization and the recently formed regional organization, New Partnership for African Development (in an article aptly titled "Charity Begins Abroad"), Ukiwo (2003) writes:

> A critical consequence of the external intervention in Africa's democratization was the simultaneous alienation of popular groups and social movements that championed the democratic movements in the first place...the transition programmes were hijacked by civilianizing military dictators, recycled politicians and returnee Bretton Woods African employees.... It is hardly surprising therefore that without exception, the new inheritance elite...have unabashedly implemented structural adjustment programmes against the wishes of their peoples. Consequently, for Africa, it does appear that democracy has been ritualized and trivialized to begin and end with conduct of elections. (Ukiwo, 2003, p. 114)

This ritualization includes the role of foreign observers in asserting norms for electoral performance. Observer groups, monitoring agencies, institutions that analyze political conflict, foreign policy elite-tied academics, constitute an epistemic community of experts on registration, polling processes, the conduct of voting, and the tallying of results (Brown, 2001).[1] Here the significance of each country's oil economy becomes relevant. In Mexico international interests have sought privatization and denationalization of that country's nationalized oil industry, a position implicitly endorsed by the PAN and rejected by the opposition PRD (Lopez Obrador, 2008). In Nigeria, a combination of international financial institutions, monetary policy and transnational oil industry calls for a crackdown on the lucrative contraband oil trade—partially prosecuted by insurgents in the Delta region—are salient.

Northern institutions associated with democratic procedures legitimized these two elections. While the 2003 Nigerian elections were endorsed by international observers, the 2007 elections were heavily critiqued with reverberations for the new Yar'Adua regime. In Mexico the 2006 elections were ultimately approved by bilateral and multilateral election monitoring bodies. Although commentators questioned the impartiality of the European Union's (2006) Mexico electoral mission (Almond, 2006), various U.S. based academics approved the polls in published writing.

The position of electoral observation missions in these two elections highlights how definitions of formal versus substantive democracy influence both global and local approval of electoral processes. Indeed, critical social movements question the existence of substantive justice under liberal democracy, viewing electoral practice as a technical form of democracy. Neo-conservatives similarly question whether democratic polls are meaningful in the absence of Westernized political culture, a position they refer to as "sequentialist," endorsing a sensationalized view of African "failed states" as verging on anarchy (Kaplan, 1994). But it is the liberals who call for greater aid to democratization in the Global South and continued Western support for democratic processes, promoting what is known as a "gradualist" approach to democratic change (Zakaria, 1997; Carothers, 2007; Castaneda & Morales, 2007). Liberals view electoral democracy as a constitutive force ("free and fair elections are the foundation of democracy")—which over time should help shape subjects of a free market. This contrasts markedly with conservative sequentialists who adopt the position that various societies of the Global South and East are not yet "ready" for liberal rule, given insufficiently consolidated nation-states (Fukuyama, 2007). Accordingly, in critiquing a Washington, DC security institution report on the lead-up to the 2007 elections, wherein the possibility of a military clique returning to power is referenced, Okonta (2007) writes:

> underpinning this...analysis is a nostalgia for a return to military rule in Nigeria. This nostalgia is to be found mainly in neo-conservative political and business circles in Europe and the United States whose favourite business model in Africa is using corrupt dictators to repress the ordinary people, thus paving the way for them to pillage the continent's natural resources undisturbed (Okonta, 2007).

For conservatives, ongoing autocracy may be required to guarantee security in mass-uprising prone, "insufficiently" developed states. Yet this is quite different from the critique of the elections posed by popular resistance movements, as detailed in the following sections.

Nigeria

The meaning of democracy across post-colonial Africa emerges as problematic in the debate over "multi-partyism." A critique of multi-partyism argues that political parties often represent ethnic and regional identity groups, shaping conditions for political violence. In Nigeria, such divisions emerged through regional associations deriving from colonial indirect rule. These became major political parties upon independence. A series of military dictatorships, as well as the civil war of the late 1960s pitting the Eastern Igbos against the Federal government of the West and North, fractured the new state.

For many Nigerians the annulment of the presidential election of June 1993, in which a highly popular candidate was the presumed winner, served as a critical turning point.[2] Since 1999, the end of military rule indeed allowed greater public debate over state institutions and legislation, but it has been equally associated with a dispersion of political violence, referred to as the "democratization of violence" (Peterside,

2007). Physical violence for control over democratic procedures, voting, and periodic elections becomes one arena in which political power may be asserted through dispersed physical force (Osuoka, 2007; Ibeanu, 2006; Peterside & Zalik, 2008)—the hijacking of the voting materials by armed groups. Such force, however, requires the purchase of localized security by rival politicians, made possible through the proliferation of small arms. As claimed by various key players in the Niger Deltan context, the exaggerated and fabricated results achieved during these elections *do* reflect some real power over the competitive exercise of violence (as democratization).

Concurrently, the deepening involvement of electoral technical expertise meant that the 2007 Nigerian elections were partially funded by a "joint donor basket" of $30 million dollars,[3] including support to the Nigerian Independent National Election Commission, with the usual flurry of international observation teams—including various recent college graduates—partaking in what has been described as "political tourism" running into the millions of dollars. Both domestic and international observers condemned the blatant disregard for democratic procedures, with strong statements issued by the European Union (2007) and by human rights monitors (Human Rights Watch, 2007).

Following the polls, a range of NGOs and human rights advocacy groups demanded reform of the electoral system and substantive democratic practices, calling for a new constitution—reflecting the broader goals of liberal gradualists. To cite from the Niger Delta Civil Society Coalition statement:

> No matter how many loopholes were plugged, no matter how many irregularities were exposed, it is plain fact that nothing is ever going to change, unless there is a fundamental constitutional transformation in the land. WE NEED A CONSTITUTION FOR NIGERIA, that has the command of the people....
>
> This call for action is aimed at peacefully attacking the very heart of the political structure of the State through a peaceful mass campaign for the right to participate in the government of our country and vote.
>
> ...(The) parasitic elitist class must be challenged, if we must not live another eight years of a future without hope in the region. The Judiciary through all the Election Tribunals must redeem what has been lost in the system: OUR COLLECTIVE CONSCIENCE AND CONFIDENCE IN THE SYSTEM.... (Nsirimovu and the Niger Delta Civil Society Coalition, 2007)

This condemnation buttressed calls for reelections at the state level as well as the presidency. While new polls were not to be held for the presidency certain gubernatorial contests were overturned including that of Rivers State, the site of Nigeria's oil capital Port Harcourt. At the state level, the most egregious case was that of Edo State, where the popular head of the Nigerian Labour Congress, Adams Oshiomole, was rigged out in the Governorship race. Initial mass protest led to the arrest of Oshiomole (later released), but ultimately mobilization served to demonstrate greater power to the electorate than foreign observers imagined: In March 2008 the Edo State Government electoral tribunal declared Oshiomole Governor.[4]

International critique of the elections did undermine presidential legitimacy.

President Obasanjo's chosen successor, Umar Yar'Adua is arguably no more worthy of condemnation than those who preceded him, were it not for his coming to power at this "historic" transitional moment from civilian-to-civilian rule. From the North, a former chemistry professor, he is the first university educated president of Nigeria in decades—in a country full of exceptional academics. He is a former state governor known for his distance from corruption—the Nigerian Union of Journalists in fact presented him with an award for such in 2002—and a one-time member of a radical socialist party, a fact that did not go unnoticed by the international media. On the eve of Yar'Adua's inauguration Reuters reported:

> International observers said the poll that brought the 56-year-old former state governor to power was "not credible" because of widespread vote-rigging and violence. In his inaugural address at a military parade ground in the capital Abuja, Yar'Adua began by saying there were "lapses and shortcomings" in the poll.... The handover was billed as a democratic landmark in Nigeria because it is the first transfer from one civilian leader to another in a nation scarred by decades of army misrule. But the flawed election wiped the gloss off the occasion. Washington and former colonial ruler Britain sent relatively junior envoys to the event, and only a handful of African heads of state showed up....
>
> Yar'Adua, a Muslim and former socialist, praised his predecessor, Olusegun Obasanjo, for laying the foundations for economic take-off. He promised to reduce inflation and interest rates and keep the exchange rate stable (Ashby, 2007).

The widespread and justified disillusionment with the electoral reform process in Nigeria by civil society groups, alongside the newfound capacity of the observer community to profoundly question the 2007 polls, warrants reflection.

A group of U.S. East Coast academics and think-tank analysts tied to the Council on Foreign Relations (including co-authors of the Council on Foreign Relations report *More than Humanitarianism: A Strategic US Approach to Africa*) emphasized the 2007 election's flaws, among them analysts who had approved those of 2003 and 1999.

> President-elect Yar'Adua will assume power on May 29 with weak legitimacy and credibility.... From a U.S. perspective, there is grave concern that Nigeria's failed elections will compromise the U.S.–Nigeria bilateral relationship and place at-risk rising U.S. interests in Nigeria and in Africa at-large....
>
> During the upcoming transition, Washington should expand its engagement with Nigeria's civic actors and the institutions of the judiciary and the National Assembly, the latter with special emphasis on fulfilling constitutional responsibilities for national finances. If the Yar'Adua government systematically improves its legitimacy and credibility within Nigeria, Washington should consider a new program of international support for Nigeria, including assistance to the Delta, introduction of Millennium Challenge Corporation transition assistance, and support of expanded Nigerian power generation and other infrastructure. Washington should make clear that the U.S. looks to Nigeria to effect major reforms so as to reinvigorate its democracy and leadership (Joseph et al., 2007).

As allies of the Nigerian pro-democracy movement, liberals in the U.S. foreign policy establishment thus embrace the gradualist position. Improvements in governmental legitimacy are here seen as cementing the road toward electoral democracy.

At first Yar'Adua did not seem so compliant. In Obasanjo's last week in office, the head of the Nigerian Central Bank, widely lauded by neo-liberals for his reforms to the bank system, announced that the Nigerian currency—the Naira—would be re-valued and tied to the U.S. dollar, making it fully convertible. In the last week in August, however, Yar'Adua reversed this decision, stating the power of the Central Bank of Nigeria to re-denominate the currency was unproven, nor was this move financially advisable. But by 2008, he was more amenable to international imperatives. Yar'Adua in fact endorsed the oil industry's own campaign to "fingerprint" oil, as a means to reduce the circulation on the global market of oil siphoned by the Delta's armed insurgency.

The Environmental Rights Action (ERA) ad claiming "armed struggle as election" indicates how a burgeoning armed insurgency among marginalized youth in the Niger Delta had gained sway (Peterside, 2007; Courson, 2007). Indeed, the ERA advertisement hints at an ongoing debate among Deltan youth leaders: This concerns whether or not force of arms should be used in the struggle for greater control over extractive revenues and environmental justice after years of socio-ecological degradation resulting from the oil industry. Here the emergence of MEND in 2006 is notable.

The constitution of MEND, "an idea rather than an organization" (Okonta, 2007), distinguished a sovereigntist armed insurgency from commercially motivated violence in the Delta. But rising cases of kidnappings for ransom and forced shutdowns of facilities to garner payments affect MEND's self-representation as freedom-movement. While MEND's electronic spokespeople have sought to maintain the position of regional freedom-fighters, the balaclava-clad Deltan youth projected via *Vanity Fair* and *National Geographic* offer menacing images. This contrasts markedly with the balaclava-clad indigenous women of the Chiapan highlands of Mexico. To be sure, this variation in global reception of the two movements is due not only to their tactics, but also to the racialized and gendered representation of their adherents, used strategically by the Zapatistas (see Swords, this volume) and used against MEND.

During the 2007 April elections, the Delta saw *relatively* little violence over the electoral materials although such activities were widespread elsewhere in the country. Here Deltan armed youth gangs seemed to have bowed to pressure or payment. A highly organized call by civil society and election monitoring groups for Deltan youth to desist from election violence was assisted by a number of factors: (1) there was essentially no contest for the presidency in the Ijaw areas due to the appointment of Bayelsa State's Ijaw governor as vice presidential candidate, and (2) where serious rivalry was possible—at the local and state levels—elections were in many places canceled.

Nevertheless Port Harcourt suffered pronounced cult and gang violence after the elections, prompting a curfew in late 2007. This violence was the work of armed youth dissatisfied with compensation from politicians for whom they had acted as "security" during the elections. Consequently, in 2007 just as in 2003—violent crime *increased* in the *post*-election period,[5] layered over ongoing political tensions within the ruling party itself. In an interview, a Niger Delta elder stressed that MEND was not behind post-2007 election violence, but described criminality in Port Harcourt with terminology that might be used by the "sequentialists" (conservatives)—conditions of rampant criminality and lawlessness. However, ensuing random violence—including against civilians—has furthered the militarization agenda of foreign powers, notably via military bombardment of villages said to be harboring MEND militants in the spring of 2009.

By making evident the commodification of election materials and payment to excluded youth as "protectors" of these materials, the emphasis on Nigeria's *failed* democratic performance actually promotes the interests of conservatives—who now describe the violence in the Niger Delta as "increasingly decentralized" (thus requiring militarization). Nigeria's democratizing, or liberal, state is thus illegitimate not only due to its inability to deliver some sort of "free and fair" electoral system. In addition, in the Niger Delta setting, the state does not maintain broad territorial physical authority, with armed insurgencies competing with it for power around oil installations (Watts, 2004). Popular fears concerning rising violence in Port Harcourt helped validate the formation of the U.S. Africa Command (Volman, 2008). But the UK's commitment of military aid to secure the Delta was harshly rebuked by MEND in July 2008. The 2009 Nigerian military attacks on MEND seek to crush the threat the insurgency poses to federal sovereignty, not simply in terms of MEND's ability to threaten installations, but also in its prosecution of an illicit trade. In that contraband trade, which siphons from oil reserves owned in a joint venture between private oil multinationals and the federal state, state security forces are also participants. Yet in the midst of a lucrative contraband trade the enduring violenceconfirms the high investment risk associated with oil extraction in the Delta, even as the region continued to offer record profits to transnationals.[6]

Mexico

In Mexico Lopez Obrador and factions of the "party-political" left challenged the legitimacy of the 2006 polls and opposed the project of energy sector reform that rightist Calderon promoted. But liberal democracy was even more profoundly undermined by the call for "substantive" democracy made by the Zapatista movement—rebuking the notion of elections—as well as a full-blown popular uprising on the part of the APPO (Popular Assembly of the Peoples of Oaxaca) against the Oaxacan state government, which preceded, and continued after, the national elections (Roman & Velasco Arregui, 2007). The rupture in federal authority is visible in the rise of violence by drug cartels who threaten state control even as their activities legitimate the need for a security state in the eyes of ordinary Mexicans.

The seventy years of PRI (Institutional Revolutionary Party) rule that followed the Mexican Revolution has been labeled the "perfect dictatorship." The protections—or partial decommodification—of land and labor through the 1917 constitution created space for popular claims on state development funds. Pacts between industrial, labor, and rural elites and state-affiliated labor unions, and the use of the pre-Colombian indigenous heritage to build national identity were complemented by state repression of agrarian resistance. The democratization process in Mexico in the last twenty years has partially disabled this regime. As in much of the Global South, this democratic transition was constituted alongside structural adjustment policies and neoliberalism.

Political–economic liberalization in Mexico created some space for greater political representation. As a result of the electoral openings of the 1980s, the PRD (Revolutionary Democratic Party, originally PRI dissidents) won governorship and municipal elections in various parts of the country. As the PRD leader in this period, Cuauhtémoc Cardenas apparently won the 1988 Presidency, but was pressured to allow a reversal (Klesner, 1994). In the 1994 gubernatorial election in Tabasco a similar fate befell Lopez Obrador. He lost to Roberto Madrazo of the PRI with whom he would later compete for the presidency in tri-party polls. Following the Tabasco elections Lopez Obrador led a protest march to Mexico City—one of various marches under his leadership that were known as "exoduses for democracy" (Lopez Obrador, 1995). Participants included campesinos demanding ecological compensation from the Mexican oil industry and oil industry workers from the Gulf states protesting industrial layoffs that were the result of neo-liberal restructuring. In the same period, a wholesale rejection of the neo-liberal project was expressed forcefully in the Zapatista uprising against NAFTA. Reflecting the legacy of a century of guerilla movements for substantive social justice, the Zapatistas became a clarion call both in Mexico and globally.

The gulf between Lopez Obrador and Subcomandante Marcos of the Zapatistas may be understood as that between the "political" and "social" left (Otero, 2007). As the "political left," the PRD employed in various local governments the same practices of paternalism and corruption common to the PRI and the PAN. In Southern Veracruz and parts of Tabasco, PRD mayors have distanced themselves from grassroots social movements. Outright clashes between PRD municipal governments and Zapatista autonomist communities in Chiapas widened the breach between popular movements and the political left. This disaffection was expressed through the Zapatista Other Campaign in the 2006 elections. Other Campaign sympathizers noted that Lopez Obrador was hardly free from elite influence in the run-up to the elections. Not only did Lopez Obrador receive support from multi-millionaire telecom magnate Carlos Slim, as the Mayor of Mexico City he supported the clearing of informal vendors from the historic center, a classic neo-liberal move. That said, Lopez Obrador's charisma and popularity was only furthered by the blatant attempt to exclude him from the presidential race by the Fox government in 2005 through what was known as the *desafuero*.

Following an incredibly close vote, which the IFE was unable to call on election night, critical statistical analyses indicated various irregularities. These concerned the non-randomness of the reporting of results, showing Calderon consistently ahead of Lopez Obrador from the beginning of the count. Analysts argued that this would be statistically impossible in sites where final results were only marginally different (Icaza-Herrera, 2006; Portillo Bobadilla, 2006; Sagardoa 2006) and prompted calls for a full recount (a position supported by at least one American University faculty member in contrast to his colleagues) (Pastor, 2006). These irregularities were discussed in the left paper *La Jornada* and were circulated widely over the Internet. Given the contentious federal outcomes, PRD supporters occupied IFE offices in Tabasco to prevent fraud in that state's gubernatorial race.

The Mexican IFE had been lauded as an example of electoral transparency in 2000, but was held accountable for the poorly managed contest in 2006. High-level cronyism between the ruling PAN and the IFE was reminiscent of the U.S. elections of 2000 and 2004. Doubts concerning IFE's non-partisanship were worsened by reports of the close relationship between Calderon and the IFE's director. These magnified concerns that IFE's non-partisanship had been compromised as early as 2003 when the PRD was shut out of its advisory board.

In the uncertainty following the polls, Calderon's legitimacy was heavily endorsed by a set of academics at DC-based institutions and at conservative Mexican think-tanks. When critical, this group argued that the electoral system needed to improve its *image*. They largely ignored, and discounted, the critiques of IFE referenced above (Eisenstadt & Poire, 2007; see also Schedler, 2007). Their central message was that Calderon legitimately won the election and that Lopez Obrador and his followers were embittered (or paranoid) and must "learn to lose." The weakness they identified in IFE and the electoral apparatus was the *appearance* of undue influence, breeding suspicion but not a reflection of actual dishonesty. When queried, a high level foreign observer *in Nigeria* stressed to me that the Mexican elections were closely fought but otherwise free. He pointed out, however, that the image of the EU's observation mission had been tarnished as its leader was a well-known Spanish conservative.[7]

In the conflict over the results, Subcomandante Marcos stated that Lopez Obrador had been the victim of fraud (Bellinghausen, 2006). But Marcos was still criticized by the left front, who argued that the Other Campaign contributed to AMLO's defeat by encouraging Zapatista supporters not to vote. In response, Marcos stressed that in most Mexican states visited by the Other Campaign, the PRD won a clear majority (including Mexico City)—especially in the states where the Campaign had spent the most time.

Despite the Other Campaign supporting the charge that the elections were fraudulent, the rift between the "political" PRD left and "social left" remains significant. The contestation over the results ultimately validates the Other Campaign's view: the political system is a sham, the interests of the organized parties are distant from the poor, in particular the indigenous population. Marcos articulated this view in a speech to indigenous communities in January 2006 in Veracruz. There he stated that he was not saying people should not vote:

> Vote for whomever you want, but remember to ask the candidates what they will do for the indigenous people. If you ask Lopez Obrador, he will tell you that he will carry out the San Andres Accords (reached in negotiation with the Mexican indigenous groups). But if this is so, ask him, why did you vote against the Ley Indigena? Why in some areas has your party persecuted indigenous communities simply because they were not in agreement with you?
>
> If you ask Madrazo (the PRI candidate) if he's honest he will say that we are going to make the indigenous people disappear. We will throw tons of chalk on them so that they become white.
>
> And if you ask Calderon (the PAN candidate) what he will do, he will just plug his nose because he doesn't like how we smell.... We are asking for another form of politics in which the people organize from below not with leaders but so that the politicians must do

what we, now organized, demand that they do. It is only in this way that we end the pain that we cannot change the system. The hour has arrived....[8]

The re-entry of the PAN with weakened legitimacy and a neo-liberal agenda thus broadened the breach between electoral process and constitutional liberalism by undermining the faith of many Mexicans in the former's *modus operandi*, further demystifying notions of liberal democracy, and, ideally, prompting the kind of social organization required for substantive change. But creeping liberalization of the energy sector has proceeded (Uribe Iniesta, 2008). Concurrently, a split between factions of the "political" left, Lopez Obrador, and other Democratic Front coalition members reflects ongoing disillusionment with the party system. This widens the gulf between the political and the social left expressed by Subcomandante Marcos.

Historian Lorenzo Meyer described these dynamics as a result of the (neo)-liberalization of the PRI state in which cronyism and economic influence were intertwined. Through a twenty-year process, says Meyer, weak individuals grew in power and private interests advanced in place of former mass-based institutions. "We see the passing of a State that was strong but authoritarian to one that is not really democratic but likely weak. Neither is what we need" (Meyer, 2007).

Disillusionment with electoral practice further undermines the promise of Western liberalism, demystifying notions of economic freedom. But while Mexican governmental legitimacy remains tenuous, 2007 and 2008 both destabilized and reinforced the PAN's security state, with increasing drug violence justifying further militarization. Conservative U.S. discourse suggested that Mexico's drug war was evidence of a failed state, deepening calls for a militarized border. Yet substantive democracy has been marginalized as a popular concern: In the face of the swine-flu alarm, Mexico demonstrated itself quite capable of securing public movement and national borders. Indeed the federal police went so far as to physically invade state legislatures governed by the opposition PRD in their quest to root out drug trafficking in May 2009. These actions were critiqued by the opposition as a violation of the sovereignty of sub-state governments, and misuse of the security crisis for electoral ends (Resendiz & Silva, 2009).

Conclusion

As we have seen, both Nigerian and Mexican electoral settings evidenced a crisis of political legitimacy and authority in the aftermath of the polls of 2006 and 2007. However, while in Mexico in 2006 the outcomes were seriously questioned domestically, in Nigeria they were also questioned internationally. The context that gave rise to these crises in both settings was in no small way connected to the extractive regime, raising the stakes for elites connected to the global oil industry. To be sure, these electoral processes are not only crucial to constructing notions of substantive citizenship or legitimacy. In addition, their representation to a global audience informs each country's currency values and financial risk assessments through the reaction of traders (Vaaler et al., 2006). Indeed, the Mexican elections are marked as legitimate, and oil production from the Gulf is exported at the rate of over 80 percent, of which 80 percent is destined for the United States. Ongoing volatility in the Delta, on the other hand, further compromises the economic authority/sovereignty of the ruling party—through democratic reforms whose relationship to substantive democracy Nigerian intellectuals have questioned for over a decade.

In the Delta region, the Nigerian ruling party provided in 2007 a slate that aimed to lessen popular alienation by including a vice presidential candidate from the Niger Delta states. Yet the actual conduct of the elections was broadly frowned upon in much of the country, including the Delta, seen as a disregard for electoral procedure more brazen than the 2003 elections. Likewise, Mexico's crisis of political legitimacy, following highly contested national elections, momentarily appeared to undermine state authority. Initial confrontation between popular movements and state governments increased while the opposition declared its own legitimate government. But popular movements in Mexico were, at least momentarily, effectively repressed through the state's tactics. Repression of a popular movement against the state government in Oaxaca (APPO), of PRD supporters in Tabasco, and, later, mobilizations in Southern Veracruz in support of the APPO involved arbitrary detentions, violence against protesters, and arrest of organizers and participants. The militarized climate has only deepened with rising drug violence.

The actions of Zapatista supporters and MEND each associated, previously or currently, with armed insurgency, partially undermine the physical authority of the state, expressing a civil resistance in favor of substantive democracy. Both movements offer visual images of armed struggle between agents of state security and popular groups contesting electoral results and governmental legitimacy. In Nigeria, the protagonist of the struggle is an insurgency, partially criminalized, that directly challenges the state's monopoly over the means of force. But the absence of a monopoly over force spurs more violence, with both the Mexican and Nigerian state engaged in an outright war with armed groups controlling lucrative markets in contraband resources. This buttresses the role of each government as a security state, while eroding the government's supposed position as democratically chosen representative. So in Nigeria insurgent groups demand legalization of the bunkering trade, or market in contraband oil, through which local youths/militias have increasingly wrested some control over oil profits from the central state and multinational companies.

Concurrently, relying on global media representations, currency traders who interpret and shape markets can destabilize governmental regulatory moves—perhaps prompting the socio-economic crises that may impel the more radical, transformative agenda espoused by portions of these movements. But MEND's portrayal as a criminal syndicate has so far precluded the wide embrace by the domestic and global social justice movement that is an important attribute of the Zapatistas.

When joined with the visible use of force, cash, and clientelism within a market for electoral outcomes, the activities of resistance movements clearly erode the legitimacy of liberal democratic practice.[9] This has two detrimental outcomes: first, to support claims for authoritarianism and the militarized security state; and second, to support claims for foreign intervention to secure markets (financial and resource-based).

Where the federal state as an expression of elite interests has been unable to consolidate deep national roots, as in Nigeria, the reproduction of the governing institutions is so disembedded from social foundations that the apparent tools of democratic practice are now partially subject to a "free" market. In Mexico, where corporatist integration has been relatively durable, the reproduction of formal/procedural democracy remains under the control of institutional and interest-group branches of a neo-liberal state—supported by the official legitimation of the elections by institutions of global governance. But ultimately, the ideal function of elections in Nigeria and Mexico, transitioning as market/competition states, is to project each as politically accommodating to financial markets in the broader global political economy.

Notes

* Dedication For comments on this chapter the author thanks Philip McMichael, Gillian Hart, Gayatri Menon, Dia Da Costa, and participants in the Neoliberalism in Contention workshop at Cornell University in the fall of 2007, as well as the Comparative Political Economy (Empire) Seminar at York University. For financial support for this research, thanks to York University, the Ciriacy Wantrup postdoc at the University of California at Berkeley, and Cornell University.
1. See for instance the *Electoral Knowledge Network:* http://aceproject.org/.
2. Chief Moshood Abiola, imprisoned by the Abacha dictatorship when he declared himself president a year following these elections, died suddenly of a heart attack in 1998 on the eve of "transition"—immediately following a meeting with the U.S. undersecretary. Obasanjo became first civilian head of state following Abacha's death, "winning" elections in 1999 and 2003. The lead-up to the 2007 elections was marked by various political controversies: see Mustapha (2007) and Okonta (2007).
3. Donors were Canada's Canadian International Development Agency (CIDA), UK's Department of International Development (DFID), the European Community, and the United Nations Development Programme (UNDP).
4. On the other hand, the success of the government endorsed gubernatorial candidate in the Ekiti state elections in May 2009 among numerous others, indicated that the success of some electoral tribunals did not mark a sea change.
5. In 2003, in attempt to curb post-election criminality, a government sponsored peace-building program *bought back* arms from youth gangs.
6. See http://globetrotter.berkeley.edu/EnvirPol/ColloqPapers/Zalik2006.pdf.
7. See M. Almond (2006, August 15). "People Power' Is a Global Brand Owned by America," *The Guardian.* http://www.guardian.co.uk/comment/story/0,,1844573,00.html
8. From author's fieldnotes and recorded speech, Sierra Marta, Veracruz, March 2006.
9. In recent closely fought elections

   voters made decisions of real importance concerning not only the alternation in office of professional politicians, but also the major issues of public policy. Voters responded not just as individual consumers—for whom the individually rational act might have been to stay home and "free ride" on the misplaced commitment of other voters—but as politically engaged citizens (Whitehead, 2007, 14).

7.

THE LAND IS CHANGING

*Contested Agricultural Narratives in Northern Malawi**

Rachel Bezner Kerr

Examines the mutual conditioning of alternative visions of agriculture in the Ekwendeni region, where agribusiness deepens colonial monoculture, degrading soils with inorganic fertilizers and hybrid seeds, and small-holder supports are removed under the assumption that peasant agriculture is unthinkable, or an obstacle to development and food security. Under pressure from agribusiness and structural adjustment policies, an alternative vision emerges in the Soils, Food and Healthy Communities projects (SFHC) across over a hundred villages, dedicated to agro-ecology and sustaining gender and inter-generational relations on the land.

Introduction

Since the late 1980s, many smallholder farmers in Malawi have struggled with chronic food shortages on an annual basis. Agricultural solutions to food insecurity are contested, however, through political and scientific debates that give insight into dimensions of power and knowledge in the current global order. This paper analyzes two agricultural complexes,[1] each of which privileges a certain set of practices, and provides a particular narrative, or story, about the problem and solution to agriculture and food security in Malawi.[2] These contrasting stories draw attention to the ways in which certain agricultural methods and approaches are seen to fall within or outside the realm of possibility. A dominant theme in the first agricultural complex is that increased food insecurity, land degradation and depeasantization is occurring on a rapid scale in Malawi and throughout Africa, with the proposed development solution to focus technological resources on smallholder farmers with access to more land, capital, and labor. The second agricultural complex posits that indigenous farming methods have been eroded by colonial and post-colonial policies and that the "freedom" of democracy and capitalism in the current neo-liberal era has not (and will not) result in freedom from hunger. Competing visions of agriculture and food security in Malawi then frame two contrasting agricultural complexes; competing narratives tell the story of each set of practices. While the dominant narrative assumes an inevitable disappearance of the peasantry, dissolved into a minority class of entrepreneurial farmers using commercial inputs, the alternative farmer narrative suggests that returning to indigenous farming practices, along with social relations, would improve food security. Since they are competing visions, each considers the other an obstacle to its full implementation, although these ideas are at times intertwined.

A case study of an alternative agricultural project in northern Malawi provides a vision of different possibilities, utilizing a mixture of practices and drawing on local farmer knowledge, which contests the "disappearance" of African peasant farming, and suggests that there are methods by which a dignified and sustainable livelihood can be maintained by farmers in Malawi. This possibility, as McMichael (2008b) argues, is one way that peasants are trying to make their own history by re-centering food and agriculture as a foundation for a real democratic and environmentally sound future. Ekwendeni farmers of the SFHC project utilize practices drawn from each complex, using some fertilizer while promoting the re-capture and enhancement of organic methods; selling some crops to trans-national traders while building community through enhanced farmer organization. By examining these different agricultural complexes and the experiences of farmers in Ekwendeni, we can also imagine different futures for peasant farmers in Malawi.

Setting

The stories told here are rooted in a specific place in Malawi, the region around the Ekwendeni region in northern Malawi (Exhibit 7.1). Ekwendeni is a town of about 20,000 people, with over 70,000 people living in the region considered the catchment area of Ekwendeni Hospital, established in 1889 by the Presbyterian Church of Central Africa. The Primary Health Care department began in the 1980s and includes

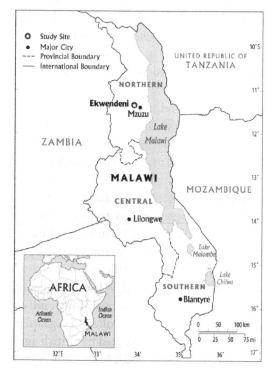

Exhibit 7.1 Map of Malawi indicating the town of Ekwendeni. Map created by the Cartography Section of the Department of Geography, University of Western Ontario.

mobile health clinics, malaria prevention, AIDS programs, and the agricultural project described in this paper.[3]

History of Agriculture In Malawi

Agriculture under Colonialism and Banda

> We are definitely of the opinion that if the natives of this country are left to their own devices they will *starve themselves* in a very few years (J. Kaye-Nicol, General Manager of the British Central Africa Company, 1933; emphasis in original).[4]

British control over Nyasaland (now Malawi) affected smallholder African agriculture in many ways. Sometimes called the Cinderella of the British colonies, Nyasaland had no major mineral resources for extraction, and the high level of malarial incidence made white settler agricultural production minimal (Palmer, 1985). While some white settlers established tea and tobacco plantations in the south, leading to highly inequitable land distribution (Vail, 1983), the low numbers of European settlers meant that, from a British colonial perspective, African Nyasalander farming had more potential compared to other British colonies in Africa (Kettlewell, 1965). The colonial administration looked to African Nyasalander smallholders as potential suppliers of food to prisons, mines, and plantations throughout southern Africa, in addition to being a source of migrant labor and tax revenue.

The hut tax was first imposed in Nyasaland in 1892, and as in all parts of British colonial Africa it served as a central component of colonial rule. Tax defaulters had their homes burned down, were arrested, and forced to do labor on public works (McCracken, 1986). In the northern region there were very few estates during the colonial period, and transporting cash crops to regions where European buyers lived was difficult. As a consequence many northern Malawian men could pay the hut tax only by migrating to southern Africa for work, while women took on the majority of agricultural tasks.

Initially Nyasaland was considered a fertile land, and there was considerable optimism about the potential for African production of maize.[5] Initially there was limited investment in smallholder African production practices, with the majority of agricultural research and funding channeled to plantation crops such as tea and tobacco.[6] African farming methods were generally viewed as inferior and backward compared to European methods. A survey was conducted in Nyasaland in the 1920s, which concluded that African production systems were going to destroy the land if left unchecked (Nyasaland Protectorate, 1927). The recommended solutions to this "problem" were increased use of synthetic fertilizer, better use of manures and legumes, and rotation. The focus of the British colonial concern was millet production, which involved burning trees and planting millet on the burned land. While scientists of the contemporary age continue to debate whether different forms of shifting cultivation are productive or more erosive (Metz, Wadley, Nielsen, Bruun, Colfer, Neergaard et al., 2008; Moore & Vaughan, 1993), at the time it was widely accepted by British agricultural scientists that this practice was destructive (Hodge, 2007; Moore and Vaughan,

1993). The story of African destructive farming practices and widespread perceptions of soil erosion grew throughout British colonial Africa and in Nyasaland focused on millet production, which was termed a "menace" in colonial agricultural reports (Beinhart, 1984; Bezner Kerr, 2006; Hodge, 2007; Moore and Vaughan, 1993). At the same time, colonial authorities were interested in encouraging more cash crops, and in the 1930s, African peasant farmers in northern Nyasaland were exhorted by the colonial regime to grow groundnuts as a means to increase hut tax payments and pay for railway expansion; it was hoped that increased groundnut production would also reduce millet production and enhance soil fertility (Bezner Kerr, 2006). The assumption of most colonial agricultural scientists, based on racist assumptions of European superiority rather than substantive experimentation, was that African farmers needed assistance to learn proper farming techniques to feed themselves and conserve the land. The Board of Agriculture report of 1933 went so far as to predict that: "...at the present rate of destruction the country would be a desert in a comparatively short period."[7] This decidedly modernist and pejorative perspective shaped the way colonial scientists viewed African agriculture. The lack of a scientific basis for these negative conceptions was assessed in studies of similar agricultural practices in nearby northern Zambia, which suggest that they are adaptive and environmentally sound tillage methods (Moore & Vaughan, 1993).

An extensive famine occurred throughout Nyasaland in 1949 that gave further fuel to the negative views of African farming practices held by colonial administrators. While colonial authorities blamed African agricultural practices for food shortages, Vaughan (1987) suggests that the hut tax, European takeover of the more favorable agricultural lands, and colonial restrictions on African trade were the primary causes of the famine. Colonial officials were spurred by the famine to take action on what they viewed as ineffective and destructive peasant agriculture. Coercive soil conservation policies and the nurturing of "progressive" farmers who adopted European farming methods became a common development theme in most British colonies in the 1940s and 1950s (Beinhart, 1984; Hodge, 2007). Agricultural officers began to monitor agricultural practices, and soil conservation legislation was enacted which enforced ridge-making, crop spacing and weeding, and cordoned off African land deemed unfit for production (Kalinga, 1993; Mulwafu, 2002). Fines and jail sentences were among the repercussions for those who did not follow the new agricultural practices. Hundreds of African farmers in the Ekwendeni region were fined, jailed, or even evicted from their land for violating these soil conservation regulations.[8]

In the 1950s, with increased nationalist movements, the "problem" in rural areas of Malawi from a British colonial perspective was both a lack of modern farming methods and increased nationalism (Hodge, 2007). British colonial agriculturalists attempted to gain control through elite African farmers by instituting the Master Farmer Scheme which aimed to create a special category of model farmer to carry out "modern" agricultural practices. The Master Farmers received agricultural extension services, loans, subsidized equipment, and cash bonuses. To qualify, farmers had to have a minimum of one block of ten acres, and had to carry out the prescribed farming requirements, including soil conservation measures. The vision of the Master Farmer

Scheme was to create a "yeoman" class of farmers who produced a surplus of food and cash crops, and provided an example for other farmers of "modern" farming methods. There was also an expectation that this agrarian transformation would produce a landless class as a labor pool. Most of the farmers who signed on to the plan had some capital and landholdings prior to joining, and thus the system increased disparities within an already differentiated peasantry. The scheme came to be associated with the colonial regime, and the associated resentment was an important part of the rising nationalist movement in the 1950s (Kalinga, 1993).

The nationalist movement in Nyasaland gained strength in the 1950s, and by 1964 the country had gained independence from Britain under Kamuzu Banda. While using the rhetoric of helping all farmers, the Banda regime encouraged dramatic expansion of tobacco estate production, to the detriment of smallholder production (Kydd and Christiansen, 1982). Similar to colonial scientists, Banda emphasized "modern" farming practices, including maize mono-cropping and the use of fertilizer, while actively discouraging the production of indigenous crops such as millet. As will be seen, the dominant modernist discourse about agriculture today builds on both this colonial and post-colonial national history.

Freedom, Chitukuko, and Democracy

Banda maintained a tight rein on power by jailing, executing, and expelling his political opponents and critics (Mapanje, 2002). During this period, Malawi was supported by many Western countries, which turned a blind eye to Banda's autocratic and repressive practices in order to have the support of a country next door to Soviet-supported Mozambique. Banda promoted national food security through maize production and increasingly suppressed information coming out of the Ministry of Health about high levels of malnutrition and food insecurity.[9] With the fall of the Soviet Union, many Western states became increasingly disinterested in supporting autocratic regimes in Africa, including Malawi. International development and human rights organizations began to support non-governmental organizations that advocated for political change. At the same time as external pressures changed, there was also increasing disenchantment with the Banda regime and calls for a democratic system coming from within Malawi. A referendum on whether the country should transition to a multi-party democracy was successful in 1993, and the first multi-party elections were held in 1994. The United Democratic Front (UDF) won, and the rhetoric of freedom and democracy solving problems of food security was widely hailed by politicians, donors, and human rights activists as a new era for Malawian citizens. The reality of democracy, which has involved instituting neo-liberal reforms and at the same time aligned a group of business elite with the political system, however, has largely reinforced and widened the gap between wealthy, educated Malawians and the majority of rural Malawian farmers. A system of patronage, often labeled *chitukuko* (development), expanded in the new democracy, with handouts given by a compassionate president in return for expected support for the UDF. Elitist, paternalistic attitudes toward the "poor" were perpetuated by this rhetoric while silencing dissent about inequalities in Malawi (Englund, 2006). The successor to Muluzi, Bingu wa Mutharika, has rein-stated fertilizer subsidies, which has been hailed as a new era for farming in Malawi. Bingu has drawn on the image of Banda and promoted himself as the defender of the farmer, but that farmer is very much one who uses fertilizer, hybrid seeds, and other external inputs.

Structural Adjustment, Neo-Liberalism, and Agriculture in Malawi

Democratization in Malawi, as in many parts of the Global South recovering from autocratic rule, has gone hand-in-hand with neo-liberal economic policies, ushered in initially through structural adjustment. The oil crisis, war in Mozambique, and the high debt load acquired by the Banda regime led to a debt crisis in the late 1970s. Beginning in the 1980s, as part of a structural adjustment program imposed by the World Bank and the IMF, Malawi removed fertilizer subsidies, devalued its currency, and scaled back agricultural support, including dismantling an agricultural market-ing board that distributed fertilizer and seeds and bought crops from smallholders (Devereux, 2002; Sahn and Arulpragasam, 1991). The National Seed Company of Malawi (NSCM), once a para-statal organization that produced seed bred by the Min-istry of Agriculture, which was then sold in rural depots, was sold to Cargill, a large U.S.-based transnational corporation (TNC). In 1996 Cargill sold the NSCM to Mon-santo, one of the largest agro-input TNCs in the world. Following the privatization of NSCM, all legumes and other self-pollinating plants were removed from production and sale and hybrid maize became the primary focus of the company. In addition, fertilizer prices tripled between 1994 and 1995, and continued to rise each year.

The Dominant Neo-Liberal Agricultural Complex

In concert with broader global trends, the neo-liberal project is the current dominant agricultural complex in Malawi. This corporate food regime includes elimination of public support for agriculture, private sector promotion of biotechnology, and export-oriented agriculture (McMichael 2008b). This agricultural complex, which has strong roots in the Green Revolution and a Western-driven concept of modernity and prog-ress, is guided by a notion that all agricultural production needs intensive use of mod-ern technology, including biotechnology, in order to produce adequate levels of food (Avery and Avery, 2003). Recent calls by the Gates and Rockefeller foundations for a "new Green Revolution for Africa"—focusing on fertilizer use, herbicide, and hybrid seed—posit, echoing colonial perceptions, that a technical "fix" needs to be found for the impoverished soils of Africa, which goes hand-in-hand with market reforms that largely benefit foreign companies. In this model, farmers must gain access to fertil-izer and hybrid seed through improved regional trade, reduced taxes, reduced import costs, and increased knowledge about fertilizer use (Adesina, 2006). Concurrent with this vision is an assumption that only better-off smallholder farmers, with access to capital, will be able to function in this context, while poorer smallholder farmers will either migrate to the city or else be shifted onto larger smallholder farms as wage laborers (Crawford, Jayne, and Kelley, 2006).

Exhibit 7.2 Esnai Ngwira standing in her field of mucuna pruriens, a nitrogen-fixing legume. Esnai has been a participating farmer since 2000. Photo credit: R. Bezner Kerr, March 2006.

In Malawi, the increased emphasis on fertilizers, hybrid seeds, and herbicides for better-off smallholders is coming from an array of fronts in addition to the agro-input TNCs, including bilateral donors (e.g., USAID), private philanthropic donors (e.g., the Gates Foundation), many NGOs (e.g., Sasakawa), Malawian Ministry of Agriculture officials, and the International Fertilizer Development Corporation (IFDC). The IFDC is closely associated with the fertilizer industry in the United States and Canada, and in Malawi works to support agro-input dealers to encourage high input sales. Another organization that strongly promotes this complex is Sasakawa Global 2000, a Japanese-funded NGO that promotes a package of technologies throughout Africa that they view as promising for "entrepreneurial smallholder farmers": one maize plant per planting station,[10] higher planting densities of single crop types, hybrid maize varieties, "micro-dosing" with fertilizers,[11] and herbicide use. Promoting higher maize planting densities discourages intercropping of legumes, squash, and other crops, which is the traditional planting system, and which is an important livelihood strategy for land-strapped farmers (Shaxson and Tauer 1992). The decision to grow the "Sasakawa way" is in direct conflict with intercropping legumes and adding organic material to improve soil fertility, as advocated by the Ekwendeni legume SFHC project discussed below.

Sasakawa has a strong ideological bent, viewing itself as bringing the "second Green Revolution" to Africa. They often work closely with agribusiness and government extension workers to promote their package, offering the inputs on credit to smallholder farmers.[12] Monsanto, for example, has worked closely with Sasakawa, providing herbicides and seeds for trials in Malawi (Keeley and Scoones, 2000; Puplampu & Tettey, 2000). The high cost of inputs, initially born by Sasakawa but over time transferred to farmers, has led to massive economic distress for those farmers who cannot pay back the loans.[13] Sasakawa's focus is smallholder commercial farmers, not the "average" smallholder farmer. This approach is evident in Ekwendeni, where wealthier farmers use Sasakawa technologies. Often younger, these farmers embrace the "modern" farming methods promoted by Monsanto and Sasakawa because they assume that these technologies are the best way to sustain a livelihood.

Roundup on HIV

The rising rates of HIV/AIDS in Malawi and elsewhere in Sub-Saharan Africa, beyond the high burdens borne by AIDS-affected families and communities, have also led to a new twist in the arguments made for increasingly capital-intensive technologies for agriculture. First, the rising HIV rates have strengthened scholarly assumptions that an inevitable process of depeasantization will occur (Bryceson and Fonseca, 2006). Second, agribusiness has promoted their technologies under the rubric of "conservation agriculture" as a means for AIDS-affected farmers in Malawi to save on agricultural labor costs. Conservation agriculture in soil science refers to a combination of practices to minimize soil erosion, including reduced or zero tillage, crop rotations and cover crops, and is often associated with an ecological approach (Haggblade and Tembo, 2003). The term has been adopted by Sasakawa Global 2000, Monsanto, and others for the use of herbicides with minimum tillage (Ito, Matsumoto, and Quinones, 2007). A Monsanto marketing manager indicated that their vision for Malawi in the long run was to have vastly increased herbicide use with "conservation agriculture," going so far as to describe this as their primary marketing strategy. They promote increased herbicide use as a means to reduce labor costs for large landholders and for HIV-affected families, an idea gaining currency among the government, the Consultive Group on International Agricultural Research (CGIAR), and NGOs in Malawi, including nation-wide trials using herbicides and legumes and a Conservation Agriculture Working Group in the Ministry of Agriculture as of 2009. The term "conservation agriculture" implies an ecological approach to what is essentially herbicide application, with some legumes thrown in. In other words, it is a slightly nuanced version of conventional agriculture in both a green and an ethical disguise. Most HIV-affected households, however, will not be able to afford herbicides, and the use of herbicides by better-off farmers will reduce the need to hire *ganyu* labor, a form of on-farm labor that is one of the most common means by which poor households access food, seed, and cash (Bezner Kerr, 2005b; Whiteside, 2000). As the dominant narrative, agribusiness proponents are framing the discourse about agriculture to exclude particular issues, such as economic inequalities, environmental concerns, and corporate benefits from herbicide sales. By raising the issue of HIV/AIDS, they are making an emotional appeal difficult to refute.

In sum, proponents of the dominant agricultural complex suggest that a package of technologies, including fertilizer, hybrid maize seeds, and herbicides, will improve food security and the plight of AIDS-affected farmers in Malawi (Table 7.1). They emphasize the important role of the private sector in fostering development, claim

Table 7.1 Key Concepts for Dominant Agricultural Complex

Topic	Key Concept or Quote	Narrative	Related Agricultural Practice
Soil fertility	"With the lowest use of fertilizers in the world, average grain yield in Africa is less than one ton per hectare, equivalent to just one quarter of the global average. We must, therefore, raise agricultural productivity and increase food production. This includes reforming outdated policies and investing in key inputs such as fertilizer, improved seeds... and new crop varieties, and linking farmers to markets via investments in basic infrastructure."[14]	Fertilizer is critical to increase food production.	Fertilizer subsidies
Tillage practices	"We are trying to shift people from doing manual work in the field that includes ridge making, frequent weedings etc.... This necessitates the introduction of conservation agriculture that requires minimum soil disturbances, use of herbicides for weed control..."[15]	Herbicides will reduce labor costs and improve food production for farmers, including HIV affected farmers.	Herbicide subsidies in input program (beginning 2009)
Seed varieties	"Our research efforts give us better and better hybrids. Our objective is to give the farmer high-yielding, disease tolerant cultivars, so that the smallholder farmer can have high yields."[16]	Democracy and the free market have increased the number of seed varieties on the market. Hybrid maize and biotechnology are key to future of farming in Malawi.	Hybrid seeds part of subsidized input distribution program
Seed access	"Another [fundamental prerequisite] is to give African products fair access to global markets."[17]	The private sector will improve access to many varieties of seeds. Access to global markets will improve food security in Africa.	Linkage of private sector through trials, input subsidy program.

that the demise of the majority of smallholder farmers is inevitable, and suggest that the small proportion of smallholder farmers with adequate land, capital, and technology should be supported to improve food security. In discursive terms, the net result is that oppositional discourses which have long criticized agribusiness for ecological and equity reasons have been appropriated and manipulated to represent their very targets.

Indigenous Elder Farmer Complex

A common phrase amongst farmers in Ekwendeni is that "the land is changing" and underpinning this is a very different complex of agrarian change than the one given by Monsanto, Sasakawa, and government bureaucrats. Choosing to grow hybrid maize and use fertilizer is part of a wider set of practices that are "changing the land" or "changing the world."[18] Older farmers talk about the ways in which, in the past, farming families were able to produce enough food using local maize seed varieties, intercropping legumes, and traditional tillage techniques.

The use of fertilizers was intimately tied with the idea of the "modern" nation of Malawi during the Banda regime, and more recently with the government of Bingu wa Mutharika. There are several historical and cultural reasons why older farmers are wary of fertilizer and other agricultural programs being promoted by the government. Successive governments pushed fertilizer and hybrid maize seed, which, according to this farmer narrative, have destroyed soil fertility, and made farmers reliant on weaker hybrid maize seed types and fertilizer. The narrative is rife with contradictions, since farmers are on one hand highly reliant on fertilizer to obtain adequate crop yields, while acknowledging that this same practice has led to a decline in soil fertility. It seems that farmers' realization of the effects of their heavy dependence on fertilizer occurred once soil quality had declined, and also after much local knowledge about how to improve soil fertility using indigenous techniques had diminished. As one elderly woman stated:

> In the past we farmed without fertilizer and we got high yields. During the leadership of Kamuzu [Banda] we started applying fertilizers.... He [Banda] was the first person who talked about fertilizer. He said that "wealth is in the soil, so you have to apply fertilizer...." In the past the soil was highly fertile. Now it has gone down (Interview with elderly woman, November 4, 2003, Ekwendeni region).

The shift to an increased reliance on fertilizer, rather than organic material, has led to a subsequent decline in soil quality, and uneven, unreliable yields. Previously, farmers relied on a combination of manure application, intercropping, and crop rotation to renew soil organic material (Vaughan, 1987). In this complex, fertilizers are intimately connected to declines in soil quality, as one middle-aged woman farmer stated, "we have destroyed the land with fertilizers."

While most soil scientists would contest the notion that fertilizer directly harms the soil, the combination of reduced organic matter incorporation, and increased fertilizer use can reduce soil quality over time, depending upon the type of soil and climate conditions (Mafongoya, Bationo, Kihara, and Waswa, 2006; Schlecht, Buerkert, Tielkes, and Bationo, 2006). Farmers, despite viewing fertilizer as "killing" the soil, feel that they have no choice but to apply it, due to the already diminished soil quality, leading to the feeling that they are destroying their way of life while producing food. Reduced soil fertility and lower yields mean that people are increasingly dependent on fertilizer use for food production. The recent efforts of Bingu wa Mutharika's government to increase food security and make Malawi "hunger-free" through fertilizer only reinforces this notion.

From the perspective of local farmers, the use of fertilizer is intimately connected to the use of hybrid maize. In the Ekwendeni region farmers talk about how the government agricultural extension workers, companies, and NGOs promoted hybrid maize, while noting that despite the higher yields obtained if adequate fertilizer is applied, hybrid maize stores poorly and is often infested with insect pests. Some farmers talk about hybrid maize getting 'tired' after two years of planting, with the cobs getting smaller and the yields going down.[19] In addition, hybrid maize is "weak" and produces less flour compared to local varieties. Nonetheless most farmers said that they liked to grow both hybrid (often recycled) and local maize, in order to have some maize for sale, and some for family consumption, because hybrid maize can be harvested earlier, yields more with fertilizer, and can be sold for cash needs early in the harvest season.

Not only do farmers suggest that soil fertility has gone down, but they also state that there is lower crop diversity, loss of local varieties, and increased child mortality. Growing hybrid maize with fertilizer, in the farmers' view, is part of a set of technologies promoted by the government and the "English" that is destroying the land and increasing hunger, as one elderly man summarizes it:

> Nowadays things have changed due to the coming of fertilizer.... Nowadays you cannot just plant your crops without fertilizer, that will mean that you won't harvest anything.... I wish that we continued growing our crops without fertilizer because fertilizer is killing us...it's not us but those who introduced fertilizer to us. They tell us to buy fertilizer. They have killed our seeds. We used to farm and the harvest was very good in the past without using fertilizer or any kind of chemical. We had high yield of maize. Now I am not doing well since I don't have fertilizer my yield is very small, so I have hunger (Interview with elderly man, November 6, 2003, translated from chiTumbuka).

Farmers link these changes in the land and agricultural practices to broader social changes, such as a decline in cooperative agricultural labor activities, seed exchanges, and HIV/AIDS. In the past they felt that they could rely on their extended kin and neighbors for labor, seed, and assistance in times of need. In general, they argue, respect for one another has declined, and there is an increase in theft, reliance on cash, and a focus on individual gain. Changes in farming practice, according to common farmer perceptions are emblematic of these broader societal changes.

Table 7.2 summarizes key aspects of the elder farmer complex. Freedom under neo-liberal economic policies has meant increasing input prices, declining crop prices, and fewer agricultural supports. The majority of smallholder farmers experience ongoing and severe hungry periods alongside chronic malnutrition and rising HIV/AIDS rates, compounded by a precipitous decline in the quality of health care and education. At the same time, a system of patronage has quickly developed in the new democracy. Political and civil freedoms are often used by the regime to mask increased economic hardships, particularly for smallholder farmers (Englund, 2006; Lwanda, 1996). Many older people feel that multi-party democracy has led to a general reduction in appropriate social behavior, particularly respect for elders. Thus the word "freedom" is often used in a disparaging or negative sense, that is, free from the propriety of custom and respect. People are "free" to choose in a nominal political sense of multi-party elections for an enfeebled state, but what has been termed democracy and freedom has had many negative effects on agricultural practices. The economy has declined, and although there are more things to buy in the shops, the prices are higher, and purchasing power has declined considerably. Although most farmers don't talk about structural adjustment, they name many of the changes that have occurred as a result: a declining currency, rising prices, a decline in the state marketing board, fewer agricultural extension officers, and less support for agricultural research.

Table 7.2   Key Concepts for Alternative Farmer Agricultural Complex

Topic	Key Concepts or Quotes	Implication for Farmer Practice
Soil fertility	"Fertilizer is killing us."[20] "You can be hard working, but if you don't have fertilizer, you can get nothing."[21]	Soil fertility has gone down with the use of fertilizer. People rely on fertilizer and do not use manure or plant residues. If they cannot afford fertilizer, they get poor yields and lack knowledge of alternatives.
Crop diversity	"In the past we used to grow a lot of crops like groundnuts, maize and millet. We were growing a lot so the seeds too were very much available."[22]	Reliance on fertilizer and maize has reduced crop diversity. People get low yields and cannot maintain as many crops as they did in the past.
Tillage practices	Mound-making was part of a set of practices that led to high food security.	In the past farmers added organic matter, had fallow periods, maintained soil fertility and crop yields were high.
Seed Varieties	English or government maize is weak. We have more varieties because of freedom.	There are more varieties, but they are all hybrid, and they cannot grow without fertilizer; they are "weak," they get "tired" and decline in yields over time. Knowledge about local varieties has gone down.
Seed access	Everyone is rushing to hybrids.	Lots of organizations are giving out seed for free but they are all *chizungu* varieties, and you cannot get seed as easily from the government.
Community relations	Everyone needs money now and they don't share work in each others' fields.	There is less seed sharing in the community, more theft and less labor sharing (*ulimizgo*). More people are doing piecework labor (*ganyu*).
Crop storage	"Nowadays thieves are many, thieves steal from the granaries. Had it been that the thieves were not there we would still be storing our maize in granaries as we used to do in the past."[23]	People now use chemicals and store crops in bags instead of in granaries, because there is more theft. The maize is prone to pest infestation and does not store well.
Social behavior	People do not show respect to one another anymore.	People are dying more because they are not respecting the old ways. The land has changed because of people's anti-social behaviors.

There are also many social changes which local older farmers emphasize. Many people mention that in the "old days" of the one-party state, there was little to no theft. Nowadays people have to store their maize indoors, rather than in traditional granaries, to avoid theft. They no longer share agricultural activities with their neighbors. Seed gift giving is less common. People do not follow traditional norms regarding sexual practices. Overall, the Ekwendeni farmer complex emphasizes nostalgia for the past and a reduction in living conditions and respect for tradition in many arenas (Table 7.2). There is a generational divide to this complex. Older farmers indicate that young people have "human rights" and lack respect for their elders' knowledge, both farming and otherwise.

SFHC: A Local Alternative Agricultural Complex

The Soils, Food and Healthy Communities (SFHC) project is described as a localized alternative complex which draws from both these two agricultural complexes. In 2000 a small pilot project began in seven villages around Ekwendeni, aiming to test different legume intercrop systems as a means to improve soil fertility, food security, and child nutrition. The project arose following research by the author and Ekwendeni Hospital staff which indicated that low maize yields, low crop diversity, and declining soil fertility were widespread and, according to local farmers, were a major cause of food insecurity (Bezner Kerr, 2005a). Funded by Canadian development organizations, the project has been managed by Malawian hospital staff, with input from Canadian researchers (including the author). A Farmer Research Team was selected by villagers to learn more about different legume intercrop systems and train others in promising options. This approach builds on a farmer participatory research model, which assumes that farmers have knowledge and skills to solve agricultural problems (Ashby, Gracia, Guerrero, Patino, Quiros, & Roa, 1997). Legume intercrop systems that were previously tested by the Ministry of Agriculture and the International Centre for Research in the Semi-Arid Tropics (ICRISAT) in central Malawi (Snapp, Mafongoya, & Waddington, 1998) were tested by farmers in small plots on their own fields.

The first year 183 farmers in the seven villages joined the project, receiving a small amount of legume seed to test, along with training from the FRT and SFHC staff on the legume intercrop systems. Each year more farmers asked to join, and by 2007 there were over 5000 farmers in over 100 villages who had received legume seed and training. An educational priority of the Farmer Research Team was to promote legume crop residue incorporation, through field visits and "crop residue promotion days." The Farmer Research Team and SFHC staff carried out research to assess whether these legumes are actively being used by farmers, and found an increase in the *size* of the legume fields as well as an increase in the *number* of farmers expanding legume production (Bezner Kerr, Snapp, Chirwa, Shumba, & Msachi, 2007). Farmers were using these residues to improve soil fertility, and experimented with the timing, pattern, and spacing. Farmers were also distributing legume seed in their communities, giving at least one-third of their legume seed to relatives, neighbors, and friends (Bezner Kerr, 2006). Recent surveys indicate that SFHC farmers continue to plant legume intercrops and bury residue significantly more than farmers not involved in the project. SFHC farmers also applied less than half the amount of fertilizer compared to non-SFHC farmers in the region, despite a national fertilizer subsidy program (SFHC unpublished report, 2008).

Farmer Perceptions of the SFHC Project

> I am not a doormat. I am clever. That is why I am using these legumes (Older woman farmer, Ekwendeni region, January 2007).

Farmers use the legume intercrops to improve their soils, their children's nutrition, and household income. Many of them express pride in being able to draw on their own resources to solve problems of food insecurity, as one woman farmer stated, "I also like that I don't need to go to the shop to buy my food. The resources are found right away from the field." The emphasis on local problem solving and farmers carry-

Exhibit 7.3 Participating SFHC farmer Enoch Chione, (group village headman of Chipetupetu), and his wife Lini Kawenjerere standing in front of their field of pigeonpea and soya. Photo credit: R. Bezner Kerr, April 2009.

ing out their own research has taken root in the minds of many farmers, who are testing different spacing methods, different legume combinations, and other agricultural practices. Many farmers talk about this project as having given them an alternative to costly fertilizer applications. When asked if they had applied fertilizer to their fields, many farmers indicated that they had, by burying legume residue. This change in the meaning of fertilizer—from an external input purchased or received as handout to a reusable organic material is in stark contrast to the dominant complex, which emphasizes a reliance on outside technology and "modern" fertilizer to solve food security. As one farmer noted:

> In the past [i.e., prior to the project] we were just waiting for fertilizer, which if you didn't have, you wouldn't grow [maize]. But now we have experience because we can plant and harvest with manure which we have after saving crop residues.... Sometimes by September we had no food. But since 2004, I am not having such problems.... All the maize that you are seeing on this plot was not applied with any type of fertilizer but I will harvest maize from the plot (Male farmer, Ekwendeni region, January 31, 2007).

Farmer pride was evident during annual field days, when hundreds of neighboring farmers, agricultural extension officers, hospital staff, sometimes even the media and foreign visitors went to farmers' fields to see their maize grown without fertilizer, and intercropped legumes. Many families have noted a significant improvement in food security on an annual basis, by increasing maize harvests and increasing crop diversity through different edible legumes. Many farmers also felt that the project approach valued their knowledge, rather than just promoting "modern" technology. Although many SFHC farmers still use some fertilizer if they are able to afford it, they have more autonomy and ability to produce adequate yields without it, and proudly note that their reliance on fertilizer has been reduced significantly through their efforts.

Discussion

The neo-liberal agricultural complex argues that increased reliance on the free market and technology will improve food security, amidst an inevitable process of agricultural stratification where commercially oriented smallholder farmers expand while the majority of smallholders are compelled to work for others or move out of agriculture altogether. This complex posits that the transition to democracy in Malawi and increased political freedoms, in contrast to the authoritarian regimes of the past, will lead to development and improvements in the quality of life for all. The elder agricultural complex of smallholder farmers in Ekwendeni challenges this dominant complex. In place of a natural, inevitable process, neo-liberal economic policies and previous regimes of power are viewed with skepticism by farmers. Rather than democracy and freedom viewed as having positively severed the link with colonialism and authoritarianism, most Ekwendeni farmers consider democracy a primarily negative experience, with no influence over government policies. Farmers note continuities between colonial, post-colonial, and neo-liberal projects, and reference these continuities in their language about seeds and agricultural development. While "freedom" allows them to choose the seeds they can buy, they cannot produce enough food to eat, their soils are impoverished, their seeds are weaker, there are more thieves, and children continue to die of malnutrition. At the same time, most farmers use some fertilizer and many grow hybrid maize (albeit often recycled over many years). These contradictory practices can be viewed as both pragmatic and a window into how helpless farmers feel about a lack of options in contemporary Malawi.

The hegemonic character of the dominant agricultural complex explains in part why the SFHC project, while not easily characterized as a grassroots movement, offers an alternative that is appealing to many farmers. Most farmers were extremely doubtful of the ability of legumes to replace fertilizer, and participating SFHC farmers were extraordinarily proud of their "fertilizer-free" maize fields. The dominant complex casts considerable doubt on any claim that maize can be grown and farmers can be food secure without fertilizer, while the elder farmer complex suggests that soil fertility has declined to such an extent that it cannot produce enough maize without fertilizer. In a sense the elder farmer complex is embedded within and responding to the dominant model, while the SFHC project provides an alternative that allows more choice and autonomy in achieving food security, including strategic rather than forced fertilizer use.

The two complexes are both intertwined and inextricably embedded in the particular historical circumstances of Malawi, while also linked with broader relations of agribusiness and peasant struggle. Several examples of the ways in which the complexes are intertwined illustrate this point. Soil fertility, for example, is depicted in both complexes as a primary cause of food insecurity. In the dominant complex, the solution is to grow closely spaced mono-cropped hybrid maize with fertilizer, which can only be afforded by better-off smallholders; in the elder farmer complex, this approach is the very problem that causes soil infertility, by excluding legumes and by making farming unaffordable for the majority.

The term "freedom" is another example of the ways in which the complexes are intertwined. The dominant agricultural complex has incorporated the term "freedom" into its discourse, championing freedom to choose different types of seeds and inputs, and freedom to sell. Farmers, in response, note the irony and problematic interpretations of "freedom" in a context of declining environmental, economic, and social conditions. Human rights discourse is rife and problematic in the new Malawi, promoted by elite, educated NGO workers while ignoring broad and growing social and economic inequalities (Englund, 2006). As Kalonde (2000: 42), a prominent Malawian author decries: "What should I eat with this new freedom?"

Though core funding comes from abroad, the SFHC project deviates from an authoritarian or colonial agricultural extension model in that the decision making and research is done by farmers themselves. Farmers participating in the Ekwendeni SFHC project take pride in their agricultural experiments, and the increased food availability within their households that is not dependent on outside assistance. They suggest that an alternative agricultural solution to the dominant complex is possible, that of dignified peasant agriculture with farmers as innovators, that integrates new scientific findings on legumes and treats organic material as the "new" fertilizer. The SFHC experience challenges us to think about new ways of being a "modern" smallholder farmer. Rather than viewing smallholder agriculture as back-breaking, backward, and requiring extensive outside inputs for survival, this approach offers a vision of a dignified farming livelihood which draws on agro-ecological research (Snapp, 2008; Weis, 2007). Farmers can draw on their own knowledge and observations from experiments done within their farming system. That is, the approach of farmers within SFHC, in keeping with other alternative agricultural efforts, is not to go back toward a more "traditional" agriculture, but to involve farmers as key participants and innovators, in a "process of learning" rather than "a simple model or package to be imposed" (Pretty, 1997: 249, cited in Weis 2007). SFHC can be viewed as a way that farmers negotiate between the two agricultural complexes, and create solutions to the problem of food created by the corporate food regime.

Conclusion

The paper began with the premise that there are competing complexes about agriculture, the solutions for food shortages, and the potential for peasant agriculture in Malawi. The dominant agricultural complex suggests that only the better-off smallholder farmers in Malawi will survive as farmers, using fertilizer, hybrid seeds, and planting practices advocated by external organizations. The majority of smallholder farmers will find other sources of livelihood, in part due to increasing HIV rates and a declining environment. This new agricultural approach should result in improved livelihoods for those smallholder farmers left behind. The farmer complex in Ekwendeni focuses on declining soils and yields, and links this decline with excessive reliance on and direction from outside inputs and "experts." This changing landscape is associated with a reduction in cooperative labor, sharing seed and food, and social respect. Increased rates of HIV and malnutrition and increasing criminality are also associated with this changing land, and these changes are linked to the transition to democracy, which has increased individualism in communities. Both complexes identify changes in agriculture being associated with the new democratic regime and freedom, but how that freedom is interpreted is the point of difference. Farmers experimenting with legumes suggest that another way is possible, which integrates legumes into a cropping system and provides an alternative vision for smallholder farmers. Rather than a disappearing peasantry, these Ekwendeni farmers are envisioning future possibilities, and are reformulating the "agrarian question" to question the key development issues of today (McMichael, 2008b, 213). The confrontation between these contradictory and intertwined complexes is an important starting point for seeing what possibilities are excluded from the dominant agricultural complex, and how freedoms could include freedom from hunger.

Notes

* Acknowledgments   Rodgers Msachi, Lizzie Shumba, Laifolo Dakishoni, the late Marko Chirwa, Stockard Nyirenda, and the farmers in the SFHC project have worked hard to make the lives of peasant farmers better. They are a source of inspiration and support. International Development Research Centre (IDRC) and the Social Sciences and Humanities Research Council provided grants to conduct this research, and IDRC in particular is gratefully acknowledged. Hannah Wittman, Phil McMichael, Tony Weis, Chuck Geisler, Wendy Wolford, and Alex Da Costa all provided helpful insights for improving this paper. The Social Movements Working Group has challenged my intellectual ideas and inspired me with stories of alternatives elsewhere. My husband Wayne and daughters Carmen and Miriam provide the love and unwavering support I need to do this work.
  1. The term "Complexes" is used in this paper to refer to a discourse and set of practices framed to solve a problem which is historically and spatially situated. I am grateful to Phil McMichael for the suggested use of this term.
  2. Narratives in this paper refer to compelling, plausible, cause-and-effect stories that frame our perceptions and actions, predict the future, as well as explain the past and present (Cameron and Palan, 2004; Foucault, 1980a; Roe, 1994). Limited narratives dominate in particular places and times, thereby framing what is excluded as well as what is included from analysis of a given issue (Cameron and Palan, 2004; Phimister, 1986)
  3. This paper arose from a broader study of social relations, practices, and narratives related to maize and groundnut seed and from ongoing participation in an agricultural project in northern Malawi. The findings from this paper are based on over 100 interviews and 20 focus group discussions.
  4. Report on Native Agriculture. 1933. Malawi National Archives (MNA).
  5. See, for example, Nyasaland Protectorate. (1910). *Annual report on the Agriculture and Forestry Department for the year ended March 31, 1909.* Zomba: Nyasaland Protectorate, 17.
  6. Until 1996, smallholder farmers with less than ten hectares of land were not permitted to grow the more lucrative burley tobacco. In 1996 there was full liberalization of this restriction.
  7. Board of Agriculture Minutes, 1933. MNA A 3/2/26, p.6.
  8. See, for example, MNA FE/1/2/4, Soil Erosion Branch, Control, 1937–1939, 1 DCMZ 1/2/1, Mzimba District: Prosecution cases for failing to construct bunds.

9. D. Pelletier, Associate Professor, Division of Nutritional Sciences, Cornell University, who worked for UNICEF Malawi during the Banda regime, personal communication.

10. Planting station refers to the planting hole. In Malawi the more common planting system is planting three maize plants per planting station with a lower plant density than is recommended by Sasakawa.

11. Micro-dosing involves putting a small amount of fertilizer in each hole.

12. Information on Sasakawa comes from an interview with Country Director of Malawi and the Africa Program Director, March 18, 2004.

13. Informal conversations with several international agricultural research scientists, 2003 to 2004.

14. Graca Machel, member of "Africa Progress Panel." http://www.africangreenrevolution.com/en/green_revolution/focus_stories/another_strong_call_for_an_agr.html

15. E-mail correspondence from Ministry of Agriculture employee to author, January 15, 2006.

16. Interview with Monsanto Malawi marketing manager, September 4, 2003, Lilongwe, Malawi.

17. Quotation from article on Yara International's website, one of the largest global fertilizer suppliers. See http://www.yara.com/en/sustaining_growth/societal_responsibility/green_rev_africa/green_feature_inter.html (accessed August 25, 2008).

18. The phrase used in many interviews was *charu chasintha* which can mean either "the land is changing" or "the world" or people's behavior is changing. The double meaning of the word is reflected in people's more general ideas about changes in agriculture being linked to broader changes in behavior and government.

19. Interview with food secure farmer, February 26, 2002.

20. Structured interview with elderly man, November 6, 2003, translated from chiTumbuka.

21. Interview with seed seller 4, March 3, 2004, translated from chiTumbuka.

22. Interview with elderly man, November 6, 2003, translated from chiTumbuka.

23. Interview with elderly man, November 6, 2003, translated from chiTumbuka.

8.

TEACHING AGAINST NEO-LIBERALISM IN CHIAPAS, MEXICO
Gendered Resistance via Neo-Zapatista Network Politics
Alicia Swords

In Chiapas, Mexico, grassroots organizations' political education workshops reveal that military occupation and debilitating neo-liberal development practices construct gendered experience, which in turn becomes the medium through which resistance builds. For many women in Chiapas, these policies represent a deepening denial of women's control over their own bodies, sexuality, and reproduction. The same policies deny men access to work and fatherhood, among the most common modes of expression of masculinity. Through community organizing, men and women shift gender relations to resist neo-liberal policies.

Introduction

At a workshop led by the Independent Women's Movement of Chiapas (MIM) in San Cristóbal, Chiapas, a team of facilitators enthusiastically introduced the agenda:

> Today we are going to talk about property—our land, our houses, our bodies, our animals...what is ours. Government plans for this region involve stealing our access to our natural resources, through plans for development and free trade, *maquiladoras*, the Plan Puebla Panama and the World Trade Organization. We reject the imposition of these government plans. Today we will learn about each other's experiences when what belongs to us is violated. What do we own as women? Do people respect our right to what is ours?

Participants, who unlike the facilitators were indigenous, from rural areas, and had little formal education, were divided into small groups. In our group, a young woman translated the question and the discussion began in Tseltal. One woman spoke up quietly. Then others began laughing and nodding. The translator smiled, "She says the property that they are angry about is their panties. They wash them and hang them on the clothesline to dry and men, maybe soldiers, steal them. But they are ours and we are ashamed and angry that our panties are stolen." The note taker wrote "panties." The workshop facilitators seemed not to have imagined that the conversation would focus on women's undergarments. I too was surprised, not only because talking about underwear transgressed conventional norms, but also because participants did not raise concerns about land (perhaps the primary source of identity in Mexico).

I arrived in Chiapas with questions crafted from my conversations with poor people's organizations in the United States,[1] and about how the Zapatistas built their movement and successfully projected their movement internationally. This workshop prompted me to begin asking how people in Chiapas experience neo-liberal development policy and military occupation. For example, how is this experience filtered through gender relations, and what gendered subjectivities emerge through resistance to neo-liberal versions of exploitation and oppression?

When thousands of indigenous men and women emerged from the mountains and the jungle in Chiapas on January 1, 1994, on the day the North American Free Trade Agreement (NAFTA) went into effect, the Ejército Zapatista de Liberación Nacional (EZLN or Zapatista Army of National Liberation) publicly challenged civil society, the Mexican government, and international institutions. The Zapatista army called for the creation of autonomous communities, which became their popular base of support. They denounced free trade policies, especially the removal of protections for corn and beans, which are staple foods and the basis of Mayan indigenous culture. The Zapatistas' demands reflected awareness that neo-liberal development policies fragment their communities across gender lines; they called on civil society to transform gender relations to resist such divisions. Building on prior efforts, they created the Revolutionary Women's Laws, included women in all levels of their military and political organization and made women's rights central. Many organizations in Chiapas have learned from the Zapatistas' discourse and practices and joined them in calling publicly for dignity, respect, and rights for all, including rights to gender equality. Most have developed political education programs, series of informal workshops to teach people to analyze their realities and to organize collective alternatives (see Exhibit 8.1).

Exhibit 8.1　Representatives of the Indigenous Women's Collective, the Coffee Initiative and other organizations were blindfolded at an educational workshop in San Cristóbal, Chiapas in March 2004. In this workshop series, participants learned communication, facilitation and organizing skills to bring back to their localities.

In Mexico, as the national development project yields to globalization, liberal ideology, with its dominant discourse of development and individual rights, is renewed and intensified in neo-liberalism. The emerging politics and ideology of neo-liberal development champion individual rights and choices, suggesting anyone can profit in the global economy. Yet with intensified commodification, nation-states protect the legal context for multi-national corporations and military contracts to force open markets in life forms, genetic codes, currency futures, and resources such as water and energy. Chiapas, in the national hinterland, was nearly forgotten under the development project, but with globalization, transnational capital has targeted its strategic resources, biodiversity, oil and natural gas, its indigenous cultures, and potentially its workers. Yet when the Zapatistas resist silent incorporation into multinational capitalist relations, they provoke a brutal military response.

In Chiapas, the military occupation that enforces exploitative and exclusionary economic policies is experienced in gendered ways and inspires resistances expressed in gendered terms. Local people create new norms and gendered subjectivities based on solidarity and cooperation, and thereby create possibilities for alternative modes of development.

This chapter examines how people experience neo-liberal development policies in Chiapas and how neo-Zapatista networks enact creative strategies and new gendered subjectivities in response. Through observation and participation in organizational and popular education settings, I identify ways that participants in three neo-Zapatista organizations re-order gender relations toward solidarity and cooperation. They do this by reworking gender roles, challenging leadership patterns, and subverting competitive relations used to divide impoverished farmers and workers in the face of military and sexual violence, economic crisis and displacement. By illuminating struggles by men and women to build solidarity across lines of division, these observations clarify possibilities for alternatives to exclusionary forms of development.

Research Process and Organizational Focus

Close contact allowed me to identify how experiences of neo-liberal policies and military occupation in Chiapas are gendered. With the welcome of several organizers interested in learning about the U.S. poor people's movement, I participated in 16 two- to three-day workshops, interviewed leaders and participants, and analyzed organizational documents. I focus on neo-Zapatista organizations in Chiapas, which are grassroots organizations and NGOs that support the demands of the Zapatista rebel army and autonomous communities, but are not part of them. These organizations go beyond advocacy to self-empowerment by confronting a variety of neo-liberal manifestations. They originate with the *campesino* (peasant), indigenous, liberation theology, and women's movements that emerged during the crisis of development in Chiapas, detailed below. Their access to resources varies. Some rely only on volunteers, while some receive national or international funding. They include participants from a range of ages, racial, ethnic, religious, class, and educational backgrounds, and use diverse political strategies.

The Independent Women's Movement of Chiapas (MIM) is a network of grass-roots women's organizations that was created by a circle of mestiza feminist social scientists and intellectuals who were committed to strengthening the organization of rural indigenous women. (Mestiza is a racial category implying a "mix" between the colonizers and indigenous people.) While the urban feminist intellectuals have more material and status privilege than the rural indigenous women with whom they work, they deeply respect indigenous women's knowledge. They have connected grassroots women's organizations—artisans' co-operatives, women's church organizations, and organizations of midwives, for example—and have built a network across the state based on relationships of caring support.

The Indigenous Women's Collective (IWC) is an independent, grassroots organi-zation made up of children of former indentured workers who now live in a rural vil-lage. Today, "being organized," running their corn mill and corner-store co-operative, and challenging violence in their community are matters of survival. Their poverty, history as indigenous people, and social connections give them a great deal in com-mon with the Zapatista support base.

The Coffee Initiative, a network of farmers' co-operatives, includes indigenous farmers of several ethnic groups (smallholders with less than two hectares), and mestizo university researchers and extension agents. Workshops promote organic fair-trade coffee production and strive to bridge social differences among the farm-ers. While researchers advance their studies and commitment to ecological farming, farmers earn a better price for their coffee so they can survive as rural producers. Some members of the Coffee Initiative belong to the Zapatista support base; others align themselves with other organizations, and still others oppose the movement.

I am interested in how ideas and experiences of gendered power relations develop in sites of popular political education and through grassroots organizing. Although many local organizations are dedicated to popular political education, few scholars have paid attention to the pedagogical practices of social movement organizations. I follow the lead of Chiapan organizers in studying community organizing and social movement activities as emancipatory and pedagogical practices. Transforming soci-ety is about re-ordering our consciousness and social relationships. I share the con-cern articulated by Paulo Freire in *The Pedagogy of the Oppressed* about how oppressed people can "participate in developing the pedagogy of their liberation" (1970, p. 33). He writes, "To surmount the situation of oppression, men must first critically recog-nize its causes, so that through transforming action, they can create a new situation, one which makes possible the pursuit of a fuller humanity" (1970, p. 32). Organizers in Chiapas draw on Freire's relational concept of oppression and his concern for build-ing a pedagogy of liberation in the sense that their work addresses multiple forms of oppression, including sexism and racism.

Women's Experiences of Neo-Liberalism in Chiapas: Military Occupation and the Violation of Intimate Property

When the facilitators heard the participants' concerns about their stolen panties, they did not trivialize their feelings. Instead, they checked their own assumptions—

that unequal gender relations are expressed in unequal property relations and are exacerbated by neo-liberal politics of removing protections for *ejido* lands, exploiting labor, assigning private land titles, and promoting free trade. They listened and began with the women's most strongly felt experiences. This workshop demonstrates how by listening to each other, women build solidarity and break down racial and class divisions lodged in a lack of awareness by wealthier mestizas of poor, indigenous people's experiences. This occurred when indigenous women began describing their experiences of threats to property and people.

At other points in the workshop, the conversation more directly addressed topics the facilitators had anticipated. At one point, the facilitators asked the group to share how they experienced the militarization of the state of Chiapas after the 1994 uprising. By inviting testimonies, they made the workshop a space for speaking publicly about events that the women had experienced alone:

> The women don't just sell food to the soldiers. They sell their bodies too.
>
> Married women go off with them, and then the soldiers take their land.... We were displaced from our village in 1995. The army threw us out and destroyed our houses. They raped lots of women and broke the law. We've been fighting since then with the government so they will return our houses (Anonymous testimonies at workshop, San Cristóbal, November 2003).

In this workshop, urban, mestiza, middle-class women (frequently "teachers" in workshop contexts) became learners as they listened to poor, indigenous women describe gender-based violence. While the facilitators described deepening inequality stemming from a neo-liberal project of privatizing land and furthering liberalization through *maquila* production, the indigenous women shared experiences of the gendered power relations of the military occupation. After affirming the women's experiences, the facilitators invited a local feminist lawyer who called the participants to unity and action:

> Impunity in the face of gender and sexual violence is a systematic problem. Part of the "cost" of the war is that the battle is fought on the battlegrounds of the women's bodies. Rape and forced pregnancies are used to subject the enemy, sometimes even by their own family members. This is the "collateral damage" of the war. We are fighting so that these will be recognized as crimes against humanity (Workshop, San Cristóbal, November 2003).

When indigenous people took over municipal governments, declared war on the Mexican government, and demanded an end to 500 years of oppression, the Mexican Armed Forces responded with war. They deployed thousands of troops, bombed indigenous communities, and established military checkpoints, bases, and blockades. When the dialogues between the Mexican government and the EZLN stalemated, the government instituted low intensity warfare. By the end of 1997, 50,000 soldiers, or 1/3 of the Mexican military forces were deployed in Chiapas and 10,000 people were displaced in the highlands (Centro de Derechos Humanos, 2005). As military bases were

Exhibit 8.2 The military base at Puerto Caté is located on a cliff at a key highway intersection in northern Chiapas. This location allows military officials to see for miles to monitor travel and trade in a region where the government seeks to assert control over strategic natural resources.

established outside Zapatista and indigenous communities, drug use and trafficking, alcoholism and prostitution increased dramatically. For many communities militarization meant constant surveillance, harassment, and restricted mobility (Harvey, 1998). The indigenous women's testimonies in this workshop confirm that soldiers used racial and sexual violence and harassment as weapons (see Exhibit 8.2).

The facilitators' respect for the women's concerns in their own terms prompted discussions about rape and sexual harassment as tools in the military occupation, labor rights violations in the *maquiladoras*, unequal land titling under the government titling program, and unequal inheritance laws. Participants' testimonies structured the discussion. The lawyer affirmed her respect for the women, and shed light on the broader context of power relations. At the end the facilitators suggested that participants themselves plan the next workshop.

Historically, indigenous women internalized messages of inferiority as mestizas, urban, middle class women systematically learned to disdain them. By not dismissing the participants' concern with their intimate property, and by affirming their testimonies about militarization, the facilitators demonstrated respect for indigenous women's knowledge in a way that was uncommon in Chiapas. How did the MIM feminists develop this respect for indigenous women's experience and knowledge?

Organizing as Women: Origins of Feminism in Chiapas

Early strands of a feminist movement emerged in Chiapas in the 1970s. In the 1980s, women began to develop a gender perspective within campesino and indigenous movements. Political and economic changes, such as the arrival of refugees from the Guatemalan civil war, displacements and expulsions due to religious conflicts, and new attention to ethnic questions evidenced that economic exploitation was not the only significant category of oppression. Women posed challenges within artisan, campesino, indigenous, refugee, anti-violence, and religious organizations (Masson, 2001). By the end of the 1980s, women's involvement was massive, among the teachers and campesino movements, in women's organizations, as artisans, and as Christians (Olivera, 1998).

Some feminists, or those whose organizing starts with an analysis of gender-based oppression, learned over time about how to respect and learn from indigenous women's experiences. Since the 1970s, the social terrain in Chiapas has been textured by development discourse and practice and by a strain of institutionalized racism known as *indigenismo*, a modernist ideology that prescribes development so that indigenous people can join Mexico's mestizo or mixed-race national identity. Mestizo state agents have worked to "develop" Indian subjects from "backwardness" into a mestizo national identity. Emphasis on building a national identity obscured the ideology that indigenous people would disappear as they conformed to the dominant national culture (Nash, 2001).

In the 1970s, feminist intellectual Mercedes Olivera created the state indigenous ministry's (INI) School for Regional Development and a rural theater that led indigenous youth in studying their own reality. These projects aimed to revalue indigenous cultures, recover languages, and train change agents dedicated to ending economic exploitation, but were shut down when Olivera was accused of building "Indian Power" (1999 interview in González Figueroa, 2002). Olivera also led research in northern Chiapas, about coffee production and campesino movements, writing about women serfs on plantations. Plantation owners remembered them as "the anthropologists that meddled on the plantations," hinting that they suspected the women were political agitators (Toledo Tello, 2002).

In challenging *indigenismo*, feminists have crossed ethnic, racial, and class divides between mestiza and indigenous women. One strand of feminism in Chiapas can be traced to Olivera's early work with a small circle of social scientists to revalue indigenous culture, recover languages, and train locally grounded change agents. Grounded in a critique of the development project, they have focused on organizing rural indigenous women. For the Women's Movement of Chiapas, respecting indigenous women's knowledge and ideas about development is fundamental. However, this is difficult because of enduring social and cultural norms about gender roles.

Gendered Roles and Neo-Liberalism in Chiapas

Interviews with participants in neo-Zapatista organizations show that the current economic, political, and military situation in Chiapas has put a strain on men's (stereotypical) roles as fathers and providers. Olivera notes, "the systemic violence of the neoliberal social structure...creates a social ecology in which men are driven to hypermasculinity, exaggerating the violent, authoritarian, aggressive aspects of male identity in an attempt to preserve that identity" (2006, p. 4). Economic development policies of the late 1980s and early 1990s removed agricultural credits and price supports for basic grains, devalued the peso, and raised prices of inputs. This meant food prices went up while farmers' incomes fell. When the Mexican government dismantled the coffee marketing board in 1989, world coffee prices fell by 50 percent (Stahler-Sholk, 2000). Small producers lost an average of 70 percent of their income (Harvey, 1998, p. 177). Thousands got caught in a cycle of debt and had to abandon production (p. 178). "We had to practically give away our coffee because there was no price for it," said a farmer from the Northern region of Chiapas (Interview, 2004). The coffee crisis threatened men's abilities to feed their families, keep their land, and maintain a campesino lifestyle and identity.

Neo-Liberal Development and Challenges to Fatherhood

Santiago, a member of the Coffee Initiative, described his family's experience after the Zapatista uprising: "I had four kids in 1994. We were really worried about them because they were little. It was very difficult to feed them. We had to be very brave" (Interview, San Cristóbal, 2004). The military surrounded the area around his community, so campesinos couldn't take agricultural products to market. For Coffee Initiative members, the desire to be "good fathers" and "take care of my family" was an important factor in men's narratives about why they formed farmers' co-operatives. "We are all fathers and we had to feed our families. So we formed a group of our own," described a co-op president. Many who had joined independent organizations during the 1970s returned to co-operatives as the best bet for feeding their families and keeping their land when economic conditions tightened. Co-op members described "standing up" with other men, "giving a hand," and being "in solidarity." They implied that these are values that "good men" should exercise. While women also develop solidarity relations, men's narratives about their co-operatives had a particular character. Men called each other "brothers" and described solidarity, loyalty, and fraternity in activities with other men. "My son and I gave our support when the army brought tons of soldiers to displace a Zapatista community. We always go when we are needed, because they help us too," explained a father who took part in the Coffee Initiative.

With militarization following the Zapatista uprising, gender and sexual stereotypes of indigenous men and women were used in military violence and torture (Stephen, 1992). Masculinity, and particularly fatherhood, became military targets, or objects of military control and manipulation in heavily militarized Chiapas. A majority of victims of torture, illegal detention, assassination, and disappearance in cases investigated by Human Rights Watch/Americas in 1997 (Stephen, 2000) in Chiapas, were men. In torture, men were feminized and symbolically subordinated to other men. A leader with the Coffee Initiative, Ramón, was kidnapped for several days by paramilitaries who blindfolded him, beat him, called him homosexual and "less than a man," and threatened him and his family. For Ramón, "The worst was I had to choose between telling others what happened and protecting my daughter. You cannot imagine how I felt when they said they might hurt my daughter." Ramón understood he was kidnapped by paramilitaries because coffee co-ops threatened local interests. But the kidnapping only strengthened his commitment to the Coffee Initiative's co-operatives:

The government uses political and religious differences to divide people, but if you talk with a pro-Zapatista community and a non-Zapatista community, their need, their common cause is "I want to feed my family." "I want to guarantee my family's well-being," right? And from whatever angle you look at it, it's a common problem and it means we need a collective solution (Interview, San Cristóbal de las Cásas, 2004).

These experiences suggest that the neo-liberal economic and military situation in Chiapas stimulates the creation and re-creation of subjectivities for men in Chiapas. Men are expected to provide for their families, but their possibilities are limited as individual producers, so they unite in co-operatives. When military and paramilitary attacks target men by challenging their masculinity, sexuality, and positions as fathers and heads of households, one successful response is to rely on co-operatives for support. Even so, within these forms of social organization, men frequently reinforce traditional norms about masculinity and gender roles.

Campesino Movements and the Growth of Co-operatives

Peasant movements have long included both men and women, although women's activities are often made invisible. In the 1970s and 80s, independent small farmer or campesino movements emerged in Chiapas and nation-wide calling for land reform, rural labor rights, and credit (Collier & Quaratiello, 1999). In 1977, organizers began working with indentured servants in northern Chiapas using federal labor laws to demand agrarian reform, back wages, and ranches from coffee estate owners. The Independent Union of Agricultural Workers and Campesinos (CIOAC), religious groups, political parties, and European development organizations began to form coffee co-operatives in Mexico. Some applied for government land and credit programs, invaded lands together, and marched to Mexico City. Campesino organizations established statewide and national communication, which the neo-Zapatista networks would re-activate.

Women's participation in Mexican popular movements in the 1980s did not necessarily change traditional gender roles or increase women's power in the household or in popular organizations (Stephen, 1992). Leaders of campesino organizations were predominantly men, and women faced sexism within these organizations. Even so, some women participated as organized groups within popular movements, sometimes facing opposition from men (Stephen, 1992).

Since the 1980s, Mexican farm policy declared its explicit intention to "drain" the rural population, or to remove some three million "unnecessary workers" and their families, around 15 million people, from the countryside (Barta, 2004, p. 23). From 1982 to 1988, guaranteed prices for staples were canceled and prices for agricultural inputs rose rapidly (Pickard, 2003) Economic restructuring tore apart indigenous cultures that centered on corn and beans and subsistence farming. Rural people were forcibly displaced to urban margins, or forced to risk undocumented migration. With the continuation of these policies during the last two decades, rural men and women struggle to feed their families, and experience additional stresses as more women are awaiting men who migrate to find work.

After 1989, co-operatives provided some collective protection for campesinos and their families in the face of the coffee crisis. More farmers (of staple and export crops like coffee) joined because "*no había precio*"—there wasn't an acceptable price for their products. Co-operatives allowed farmers to avoid intermediaries or *coyotes* and the transnational coffee corporations that paid pennies for their harvest.

The Coffee Network strives to sell their coffee over the market price in fair trade "solidarity markets." They organize workshops to educate themselves about such issues as how to improve their coffee for these markets, how to commercialize fair trade, and organic coffee. In public meetings they emphasize fair trade to challenge free trade. An initial grant from a U.S. foundation funded a Rural School with monthly workshops for coffee growers. The "school" combined traditional agricultural education, with appropriate technology, organics, and recently, participatory research. Today the network includes only men because although women play important roles in coffee planting, care, and harvest, and women were invited to participate, there have been no explicit practices to include them. Women I spoke with gave several reasons for not participating. They found it difficult to leave their families for weekend workshops. Sometimes they were accused of "looking for boyfriends" at workshops. In most cases, husbands were involved in the Rural School but did not want their wives to participate.

Like the Coffee Network, many campesino organizations do not address obstacles to women's participation because they maintain gender stereotypes that exclude women, undervalue their labor or make it invisible. At the same time, the history and the culture of brotherhood within co-operatives and campesino organizations create the possibility for solidarity and alliances among men. While excluding women reinforces historical gender dynamics, possibilities for solidarity among men gain new significance in the context of the individualizing politics of neo-liberal development. Gender roles are not only re-inscribed in practice, but in scholarship as well.

Beyond the "Great Man Theories"

In the workshops just described, examining social movement leadership with an awareness of gender and class dynamics reveals possibilities for gender and class solidarity that challenge social divisions fomented by neo-liberal policies. Yet the true character of social movement leadership often goes unrecognized in contemporary social movement analysis.

Scholars, the media, and our popular knowledge of social movements frequently describe the leadership of "great men," such as Rev. Dr. Martin Luther King, Jr. and Malcolm X (Theoharis and Woodard, 2005). In Chiapas, the mainstream media and many scholars contribute to "great man theories" of the Zapatista uprising when they focus on Subcomandante Marcos without revealing his history and social relationships. In some cases hero-centered explanations do focus on female heroines, but women who bridge class and ethnic divides are not the subjects of most analyses of the Zapatista movement. Most accounts emphasize activities that men are traditionally socialized to carry out, such as public speaking. Yet they make invisible the processes of relationship-building, political education, and leadership development.

Neither theories of "great men" nor "great men's clubs" which study male-led collectives such as campesino and indigenous movements (see Harvey 1998; Collier & Quaratiello, 1999), investigate gendered experiences nor do they comprehend women's participation or forms of leadership that are traditionally women's work. Researchers in Mexico (as elsewhere) even rely on male informants to represent all indigenous experiences, which demonstrates their lack of attention to gender differences (Hernandez Castillo, 1995). In Chiapas, some researchers pay attention to gender. Yet, as they include women, some narratives re-inscribe men as subjects and women as objects. For example, some scholars and human rights organizations consider the *impacts* of the Zapatista movement and the war on women, documenting "militarization and the situation of women" (Hidalgo, 2006).

As a growing network of feminist scholars write about women as revolutionary subjects in Chiapas, most not only consider how women can do what male leaders do, but rather reveal how women's activities re-define what is considered leadership.[2] Noticing leadership that breaks public–private binaries has pushed me to examine organizing in spaces outside the public view, workshops, organizational meetings, and conversations among leaders and participants, where leadership is less often observed. My observations revealed alliance-building across genders. What it seems most scholars miss is that gender roles are being re-worked and solidarity is happening across gender lines, which allows for stronger potential for class-based resistance.

In Chiapas, some organizations and scholars have developed a strong gender perspective, focusing mainly on impacts on women or on women's agency. More recently, some have adopted a gender relations approach.[3] For example, Mercedes Olivera's (2006) long-term academic and community work considers the gendered relations of violence against women resulting from neo-liberal policies that have caused social polarization and disintegration of the peasant economy. It is less common for scholars and community organizers to attend to masculinity or masculinities. Without ethnographic attention to male subjectivities, there is frequently a sharp contrast "between the tender attention to female subjectivities and the analytically crude cardboard cut-outs of pampered sons and patriarchs" (Jackson, 1999, p. 90). Understanding the whole complex of gender relations requires study of how men and women in particular social locations "make use of, comply with or subvert, hegemonic masculinities" (Jackson, 1999, p. 92). In the workshops I observed, I use a gender relations approach to examine the social construction of masculinities, and how these masculinities can resist neo-liberal development assumptions. The account to follow challenges and re-works conventional gendered views of social movement leadership.

Building Alliances: Brothers and Sisters

In this context, men are generally pressured to "provide" for their families. If they cannot provide by working in their own towns and villages, they face pressures to migrate. But the Indigenous Women's Collective shows that by re-arranging gender relations and concepts of masculinity in the face of economic pressures, an alliance between brothers and sisters could keep a family together and sustain their organizing efforts.

One of the leaders of the Indigenous Women's Collective, Francisca, described how the economic crisis of the late 1980s in the region affected her family. When her parents worked as indentured servants on a plantation, they were very poor, but when market conditions worsened, the plantation owner simply stopped paying them. With meager savings, her father bought a small piece of land and gradually built a house. With seven children, survival wasn't easy. By the time Francisca and her brothers were adults, it was difficult to find work in the region. Francisca explained,

> When I had been working for a while, I asked my dad to give me a piece of land. My brother disagreed. "You're a woman. You don't need that," he said. Once, my brother got mad and hit me, but I didn't stay quiet. I hit him too. But then I said, I don't want any more of this.... This was after 1994 when I had enemies from the PRI [former ruling party] in the community, who didn't want the women to organize.... When I decided to get the title to my land, we fought again because he didn't want me to have the title (Interview, Zona Fronteriza, 2004).

Francisca's borther Tomás explained that over the last ten years he found it increasingly difficult to find work. "Now there is no work for men here in our town." He was bored working in the coffee warehouse—he felt it was a job without dignity. "It was hard, because you had to receive 50 or 60 sacks of coffee from the truck and carry them to the warehouse. You spent the day carrying the sacks...running. They yelled at you to go faster. I couldn't stand it so I left." Tomás' reaction was not uncommon, as Chiapan feminist scholar Mercedes Olivera (2006) notes,

> For many men the stereotypical self-image of the macho makes it difficult to accept roles that are inferior either objectively or symbolically to those of their mates. It is not uncommon in this situation for men to direct their aggression against their wives and children. Men's insecurity under these circumstances is often the cause of abandonment, divorce, and murder.

In this case, Tomas's sister stopped his violent reactions by offering him an alternative that was masculine and not humiliating. Tomás explained:

> My sister and cousin started asking me if I wouldn't like to work with them as part of their Women's Collective, to run the mill. She said, "We need a man to help us with some jobs. We want to put down a floor in the patio. You could help us, and you could take care of the mill." So I said yes. In three days I learned, and the fourth day I could run the mill myself. I began to gather courage.

His sisters invited him to do work that they felt they could not do alone "as women." In some ways, the job he was invited to do reinforced hegemonic concepts of masculinity and femininity in Chiapas—he was invited to do the physical labor they could not do—to run the mechanized corn mill, a role he saw as desirable. But his role was clearly to serve the women and to learn from them. Francisca explained:

It hasn't been easy working with my brother, but little by little we've asked him to join our women's group and we've seen him gain awareness. He started working on his machismo.

Tomás began to realize he could share in work typically performed by women. They said, "We share the work of cleaning the store and the office.... " So I don't just hang around watching them clean. I'm a man but I can also work...." Beyond physical labor, his sisters invited him to learn from them. Tomás explained that they invited him to accompany them to workshops they gave in neighboring communities. "We went to a self-esteem workshop and when I saw my sister begin to give the workshop, I began to gather courage."

After giving up an alienating job, Tomás learned by joining the Women's Collective that he could do all kinds of work, including becoming an educator in his community. I ask if he faces any negative consequences in the community for his association with his sisters' organization:

Yes. Some people have criticized me... They say "he's too good for his pitchfork now because he's with the women...." I just listen and don't tell the women because those criticisms make them suffer. Now I am a conscious person. Now I don't have to listen to the men's gossip. I pray to God that we might continue to work just like I am working with the women now.

Tomás was not married or involved in partnership with any women, although our conversation never addressed this aspect of his life. I speculated about whether his experiences and people's perceptions of his position were shaped by norms about marriage or partnership, but could not be sure given the whole family's silence on this topic. Tomás not only defied traditional norms for masculinity, but also learned from his sisters' strength in the face of gossip against them. He was both protective, by refusing to relate the criticisms to his sisters, and deferred to their knowledge. Gossip, often a term used to discount a certain kind of conversations among women, was a term Tomás applied to men.

According to Francisca, Tomas's collaboration gave her hope that men can support women: "I thought my brother would be the hardest one to change, but now that he is working with us, I have faith that even the most stubborn men can think differently."

The IWC's experience is the exception rather than the rule in Chiapas, yet their story reveals a possibility. Under the alienating experience of neo-liberal labor relations, men do not always comply and accept their role as exploitable labor. The IWC case demonstrates that men may sometimes prefer to re-order gender norms rather than remain in an exploitative situation. The consequences might be terrible under military occupation in Chiapas, where men are often disciplined to conform to military culture through accusations about sexuality. Yet at least for one man, aligning himself with his sisters provided meaning that he did not find in agricultural work or physical labor.

As I got to know Tomás, I wondered if his case was completely unique or if there might be cultural precedents for men to join women's organizations and support their leadership. Liberation theology laid the cultural precedents for men to support women's organizing. I learned that the Indigenous Women's Collective (IWC) formed in the late 1990s among women who had all been indentured servants or children of indentured servants on plantations in the Frontier region. About thirty women began organizing as catechists with the Liberation Church. At the time, the Bishop encouraged indigenous men *and* women to develop their leadership as religious teachers in their community. For many women in the area, this was the first chance to "go out," to leave their rural communities or villages, to leave the supervision of their families. It was also a first time for women to take leadership, to have their voices and their *palabra*, or word, respected in public.

With a small loan from the church, the IWC formed when thirty women began a corn mill co-operative to contribute toward their families' survival. After the Zapatista uprising, they became involved as a Zapatista civil society support organization and began participating in workshops, forums, and marches outside their village. By the late 1990s, they received a small fund from an international NGO to begin a corner store co-operative and later to build a neighborhood shelter to care for domestic violence survivors. They also began offering workshops to rural communities' Liberation Church organizations, to teach them to organize, and to demand women's rights and human rights in general. Their co-operative provides significant support for their families and serves as a space for socialization and politicization. Today the organization includes women from 24 to 60 years of age. One woman is single; most have children, and a few are raising their children alone.

The IWC women explain that through organizing, they have learned that "we are worth as much as men are" and "we have rights as women." They identify two targets—men and the government:

> We discuss with the men, make them understand that we're not going to give in, that they must give us space. And with the government, well, it's about the same. We want the government to respect us. We don't want them to invade the co-operatives. It was in 1996–97 that the government ordered the army to check on the co-operatives and who worked there. They threatened several of us.... But we didn't stop. We want the men and the government to understand us; we want to work in our collective (Interview in Masson, 2001).

Masson (2001), an anthropologist who worked with the IWC for several years, confirms my observation that their organizing transgresses traditional gender roles through collective work, political participation, and popular education. They have a developing awareness about gender, ethnicity, and class; they describe experiencing triple oppression and their rights as poor, indigenous women. They explain that they have taken control of their destinies and they have their "heads raised." But their work to transform their triple oppression is not just inner work. By starting with self-esteem, they gain confidence to work with men, within and outside their organization. They challenge intra-family violence by supporting survivors and challenging perpetrators in their neighborhoods. Some report choosing when to have children and how many to have. Their organizing empowers them to re-shape their relationships with the men in their families, neighborhoods, and communities.

Revealed in this dynamic is a reworking of gender roles. The IWC women's experiences show that women exercise leadership that can build gender and class solidarity where there was neither. Sisters who offer opportunities to and challenge their brothers can help to shift relationships among women and men that allow them to challenge both the men in their homes and men in government. Their strength and confidence in so-called private spaces extends into their power in civil society. As a consequence, they transgress this artificial private/public boundary, offering new ways of ensuring gender is not used to divide and oppress. This is significant because we cannot comprehend how new social relations are possible if we cannot observe them. While the IWC women's experience is not happening everywhere, it does suggest that we must tune our sociological imaginations to recognize the social spaces where gender and race relations get re-worked, and from these, what social relations allow for class solidarity.

Discussion

Observations and interviews suggest that in Chiapas neo-liberal development policies, in their military and free market manifestations, exacerbate oppressive gender relations, along with relations of class and race. They impede men's abilities to successfully provide for their families and they treat women's bodies as the battleground for struggles over resource rights. Yet in the instances documented here, the resulting violence provokes some people to respond collectively and create new social relations—cooperation, alliances, and solidarity—to restructure relations of domination. Their collective responses combat neo-liberal policies and the military defense of such policies.

In all three instances, the organizations use popular education strategies and daily organizational activities to help participants recognize their situations, identify the causes of their conditions, and begin to transform basic social relationships in their lives. In the Independent Women's Movement workshop, indigenous women came to recognize that the military occupation violated their privacy, as well as causing displacement. The facilitators saw that the indigenous women's knowledge mattered. Men in the Coffee Initiative learned they were stronger if they acted together as part of a co-operative. Alone, they faced violence, discrimination, and poor prices, but together, they gained brotherhood and better prices for their coffee. The women in the Indigenous Women's Collective recognized that machismo and family violence limit collective well-being. One woman's brother saw he would survive better if he joined his sister's organization rather than fighting with her and her colleagues. In these ways, men and women have shifted gender relations to resist neo-liberal policies.

As they develop new alliances and social relations, participants in these organizations are forging new subjectivities. In the Independent Women's Movement workshop, feminist intellectuals proposed an ongoing, participatory process designed by the indigenous participants, thereby centering indigenous women's knowledge. The Indigenous Women's Collective demonstrated the power of a brother–sister alliance (indeed they re-structure the very meaning of brother–sister relationships, and "brother" "sister" as well), and of new relationships between men and women in which women can stand up for their rights, challenge men, and teach men. The Coffee Collective demonstrates the importance of co-operative work, based on solidarity, not competition, which opens the possibility of a solidarity-based economy for the whole community, and of transcending the liberal subject prescribed in development narratives.

These instances suggest that it is possible to create interpersonal relationships based on non-violence and solidarity and that these relationships can shape broader organizational politics. Further, the pedagogies and organizational practices that allow for shifts in gender relations are not complex, although they comprehend power's complexities. They involve listening and mutual respect. While there are precedents for particular kinds of alliances in the specific histories of feminism, liberation theology, and campesino movements in Chiapas, other communities may learn from the Chiapan experience to build alliances across lines of difference, challenge state violence, and to develop or sustain vibrant communities that draw on the strengths of our histories. If more respectful gender relations, inter-racial and cross-class solidarities are possible even under low-intensity warfare in Chiapas, where military force and state repression are used to divide and control the population, it may be that such changes are possible elsewhere as well.

Notes

1. I am involved in the Tompkins County Workers' Center (tcworkerscenter.org), which is part of the Poverty Initiative (povertyinitiative.org), a national network of poor people's organizations in the United States dedicated to building a movement to end poverty.
2. In *The Tradition that Has No Name*, Mary Belenky et al. identifies how civil rights leaders and other U.S. and European community organizers use a public leadership approach that "elaborates and extends women's traditional roles and relational styles" to "nurture the development of people, families and communities" (1997, pp. 11, 13). She reveals that activities that are often considered "private," such as mothering, nurturing, and homemaking, are critical elements of large-scale social changes.
3. These scholars demonstrate that the Zapatista movement and EZLN included Chiapan women's voices, organizing experiences, entry into civil society, and leadership (Rovira, 1997; Stephen, 1992; Nash, 2001). They show how women leaders have emerged through grassroots struggles (Speed and Forbis, 2005; Leyva-Solano, 2002). Their own experiences of violence catalyzed their demands for rights in the Revolutionary Laws of Zapatista Women (Rojas 1999; Olivera 2006; Nash 2001). Zapatista women create forms of personal autonomy as they participate in regional efforts to construct autonomy (Forbis, 2003). These and other writings contribute to making women's activities visible and show how women in the Zapatista movement do not entirely discard "traditional" gender roles but change gendered power relations.

9.

CORPORATE MOBILIZATION ON THE SOYBEAN FRONTIER OF MATO GROSSO, BRAZIL*

Emelie Kaye Peine

Addresses a paradox: why Brazilian soy farmers protest a power structure that enables agribusinesses to profit from neo-liberal development, while the farmers bear to risks of producing for global markets. This essay documents how, in the name of the free market, soy farmers target the state when the market fails rather than the grain traders to whom they are indebted, and who shape government policy anyway. While the global soy market structure is revealed, the soy farmers remain steadfast in their neoliberal beliefs that the state, rather than agribusiness, is the source of their distress.

Introduction: Protest and Paradox

In the spring of 2006, the smell of smoldering soybeans lingered in the air above Rondonópolis, an agroindustrial town in the state of Mato Grosso, Brazil—widely considered the "soybean capital of the world." Farmers had dumped thousands of tons of the beans in the streets and set them ablaze to protest market conditions that threatened their livelihoods. The trouble began in 2005 as soy prices dropped, oil prices rose (and therefore also the cost of agrochemicals and transportation), the dollar fell against the Brazilian *real*, and interest rates remained stubbornly high. In June of that year, a tractorcade (*tratoração*) descended upon the Brazilian capital city of Brasília as farmers from the central-west region—predominantly from the state of Mato Grosso—turned to the federal government to bail them out of an increasingly insurmountable financial crisis. During the soy boom of the mid-1990s, many farmers had taken out massive loans (some underwritten by the government, some not) for machinery, land, and production costs. While some of this debt was held by the federally financed Banco do Brasíl and some was subsidized under specific government programs,[1] the vast majority was and continues to be held by private companies. During the demonstration, farmers drove tractors down the capital's central promenade, prominently displaying signs proclaiming "*Financiado*," meaning "financed," to indicate that these were machines on which they were still making payments.

In April 2006, at the height of the soy harvest, a new wave of protests swept Mato Grosso, this time beginning with tractors, combines, and eventually piles of soybeans being set ablaze in the middle of federal highways. Soon, the National Truckers' Union—seeing the impact that the collapse of the soy market would have on their survival—joined in, completely blockading federal highways throughout the region, and eventually even in the southern states of São Paulo and Paraná. At this point the farmers' specific demands on the state included: reducing the *cost of production* (meaning, subsidizing the price of fertilizers and fungicides), adjusting macroeconomic policy to address the falling value of the dollar against the real, and reducing federal interest rates (*International Business Times*, April, 2006).

While these actions may look like traditional protests by an economically marginalized group, what they really represent is a paradox. By calling on the state to correct "market failures," the farmer protests mistake the source of their problem, which is the overwhelming power agribusiness corporations exert in the marketplace, especially over the farmers themselves (as explained below). State support merely props up that power structure, deepening the exploitative relationship between agribusiness and farmers. At the same time, the misdirected protest reinforces the neo-liberal idea that the market is a neutral arena.

In a sense then, farmer protests in Mato Grosso can be understood as a social movement in the interests of agribusiness, insofar as they mistake the location of power in the food system and help to obscure corporate monopoly. While it is not unusual in the history of agrarian relations to find tensions between farmers and commercial suppliers or grain merchants or processors, the tensions on this contemporary frontier focus on the government and not agribusiness. The question is why? This essay addresses this question by examining the rather unique configuration of social forces involved in developing the Mato Grosso soy frontier. I argue that the soy industry is a thoroughly market-based economy in which the public sector has participated in the construction of, and is now thoroughly integrated in, a private regime. As such, this is a farm economy in which farmers themselves are not only contractors working for the grain traders, but also perceive themselves in private terms, as independent market pioneers and heroes of a resurgent Brazilian export agriculture. They distinguish themselves from their U.S. and European counterparts who receive large public subsidies to grow soybeans for the global market. They are able to make this distinction because up until the time of the protest they were in fact not subsidized by the state, but through the market; that is, through the commercial relationship with agribusiness. But because the private regime itself is not a legitimate target for political intervention, they must target the state instead when market failures threaten their livelihoods. When they ask the state to prop up the market, these farmers become proxies for a mobilization by the agribusiness firms to consolidate their market power.[2] The farmers' participation in this mobilization confirms the power of the "market episteme" in shaping how social groups identify their interests—in this case with those who exploit them.

On the Brazilian soy frontier, therefore, we confront a paradox, where soy farmers mobilize to protest market conditions, but direct their dissatisfaction toward the state, rather than the transnational agribusinesses that dictate the terms of credit and production. The soy farmers' struggle is to secure their livelihood in a global market, but since agribusiness organizes that global market, the discourse with which farmers represent their struggle reinforces the agribusiness vision. Viewing agribusiness through a social movement lens thus allows us to see its power in mobilization, and, therefore, to recognize that even (subaltern) "popular protest" can sometimes work to harness state resources in support of corporate interests.

This investigation takes as its starting point the protests by Brazilian soybean farmers (mentioned above) that took place in Brasília in 2005 calling for government intervention in a faltering global soy industry that drastically reduced farmers' income and, given the enormous debt owed to transnational agribusiness, threatened to destabilize the economy of the entire central-west region of the country. Rather than focus on the farmers' struggle as such, I argue that the character, assumptions, and circumstances of these protests in fact assist the mobilization of agribusiness interests, insofar as farmers identify as free producers, and so advance a neo-liberal class project (cf., Harvey, 2005). The farmer protests represented a more fundamental issue governing the soy economy, namely its private origins and deeply held beliefs on the part of soy farmers that they constituted a free market economy in soy—but in effect act as surrogates for the agribusiness monopoly that controls this economy.

This chapter considers the motivating assumptions informing these protests, which assisted the mobilization of agribusiness power. Proceeding from this particular event, the chapter then examines corporate mobilization in the World Trade Organization (WTO). I argue that these farmer protests and corporate activism in the governance of global trade constitute complementary vectors of a larger movement. Rather than simply dichotomize opposing forces, it is important to examine ways in which transnational corporations strategically mobilize resources—both material and ideological/discursive—to co-opt any challenges via a "naturalized" conception of the market-based global food system.

Neo-Liberalism and the Making of a Hegemonic Worldview

Neo-liberal ideology views the market as a given, as a "natural" system (like an ecosystem) that, if left free of government meddling, will create socially optimal outcomes by distributing resources most efficiently. Since the early 1980s, this market rationality has assumed a commonsense quality, which is instrumental in the "construction of consent" legitimating markets over other forms of socio-political organization (Harvey, 2005, p. 39). There is a fundamental assumption that corporate-driven economic growth is good for society as a whole insofar as it increases the size of the pie, thereby rendering moot the question of distribution. In this sense, the neo-liberal project claims to realize the goals of development to incorporate ever more people into material security and eventual prosperity.

However, for rural communities, in both wealthy and poor countries throughout the world, the developmentalist promise has yet to materialize. Small farms are crushed under the weight of agricultural surpluses dumped on foreign markets by industrialized countries, rural populations are draining away to urban areas, and the countryside is increasingly dominated by larger and more concentrated agricultural operations, except in areas of marginal lands where remaining farmers struggle against intensifying weather conditions (drought/flood cycles) and degraded soils, depressed prices, lack of access to credit, and increasing input costs.

In order to explain the persistent ideological power of market rule despite the market's practical failures, Antonio Gramsci would encourage us to view a social movement like the soy farmers as co-opted by the dominant agribusiness interest. When the soy farmers of Mato Grosso—in the wake of a market crisis that threatened their economic survival—addressed their grievances to the federal government rather than to transnational agribusiness, they participated in an "illusory" conflict, one that targets small inconsistencies in the larger system rather than fundamentally challenging the exploitative relations embedded within it (Gramsci, 1971). Protest that wins marginal gains actually serves to strengthen the hegemonic system by eliminating points of conflict that weaken it (Femia, 1981).

What looked like a social protest movement *against* the vagaries of market rule, therefore, actually helped to reinforce it. The protest was essentially a demand by the private sector (farmers and, by extension, agribusiness) for the state to use public funds to bolster a failing market system. The farmers had the legitimacy of citizenship when making this request; these "soy citizens" had—in the popular imagination—raised the entire nation of Brazil from an "under-developed country" to an "emerging economy" (Steward, 2007). By asking the state to essentially bail the transnational corporations out of the fiscal mess that they had created by over-extending credit to already over-extended farmers, the farmers were affirming the basic ideological claims of neo-liberalism. In the end, the *tratorçáo* that took the form of a popular protest used conflict to re-inscribe the principles of neo-liberalism as "common sense": How exactly this was accomplished will be discussed later in the chapter.

Social movements are often conceptualized as movements *against* power. But power is not a zero-sum game, with some (states, corporations, upper classes, western societies) having it and others (peasants, poor countries, civil society) not. Rather, power is a relation operating through a "double movement" dialectic (Polanyi, 1957), and, as Gramsci suggests (1971), the accomplishment of power, or rule, is necessarily contested, partial, and ongoing. These farmer protests, in addition, show also the malleability of power, in that what appear to be protests *against* power actually consolidate it, since farmer claims against the state reinforce the power of agribusiness. In this sense these protests can be interpreted as the mobilization of agribusiness itself—with the cooperation of the state—to define and promote a neoliberal, corporate food system.

Key to this argument is the idea that the market is a political, not a neutral, construct. In particular, the soy market is constructed through the political mobilization of agribusiness. But because markets are universally represented and generally understood as neutral, blame for market crises facing soy farmers is easily attributed to the state, allowing agribusiness to present as "politically neutral" players in global markets rather than the politically *engaged* agents of market construction and governance that they really are. Mobilizations of farmers dependent on exploitative financial relationships with these corporations nearly always target the state in popular demonstrations, demanding government policies to support producers.

Farmer protests that target the state as the locus of responsibility for ameliorating market failures contradict neo-liberal ideology that governments should get *out* of markets. A deeper irony is that protesting Brazilian soy farmers call for *national* government intervention to ameliorate market failures *that are caused by government interventions elsewhere in the world* (namely agricultural subsidies in the United States and Europe). Soy farmers are very well acquainted with the American and EU subsidy systems, which hugely disadvantage non-subsidized Brazilian farmers in commodity markets.

So, while these protests call for short-term government bailouts, they also intensify the rhetorical pressure on foreign governments to "get out" of agricultural markets and allow them to function "naturally" at the global level. At the same time, they increase the necessity for public funding of the domestic farm sector year after year as agribusiness corporations continue to capture market gains, at farmer expense, through their political influence. When the state responds with concessions to the soy farmers, most of the credit, direct payments, and other fiscal bailouts are funneled eventually—via credit relationships, input markets, and production contracts—to the agribusinesses that hold a disproportionate share of farmer debt in Brazil, and especially in Mato Grosso.

In sum, the dynamics of corporate mobilization reveal how agribusiness works *in concert with the state* to not only protect profits but also to legitimize the construction of market interests *as* the social interest, thereby naturalizing the neo-liberal agenda.

Public/Private Cooperation in the Construction of the Mato Grosso Soy Machine

Between 1994 and 2004, Mato Grosso had a comparative advantage over the United States in producing soybeans. The crop was highly profitable for farmers and could be produced more cheaply than in the United States, largely due to lower land and labor costs (Warnken, 1999). This was the era of high soy prices, cheap oil, and a strong dollar. In 2005 and 2006, however, Mato Grosso experienced tremendous political and economic upheaval as soy prices plummeted to near record lows. While this volatility is not uncommon in agricultural markets, it is incredibly destructive for agriculture-dependent communities. In this case, the crisis was sparked by skyrocketing oil prices in 2004, which made agricultural chemicals and transportation much more expensive in the subsequent planting and harvest seasons. In addition, U.S. harvests rebounded at the same time that massive new tracts of land were being planted to soy in the central-west region of Brazil. This new source of global production served to depress prices quickly and dramatically. Many Brazilian government officials and farmers argue that subsidies give U.S. farmers an "artificial" advantage in global markets, insulating them from such devastating market down-turns. But under closer scrutiny, it becomes clear that the sheer existence of a soy economy in Mato Grosso is no more "organic"—is in fact just as *politically constructed*—as the heavily subsidized U.S. production.

In Brazil, a combination of government and private investment in research, a political project of internal colonization, and a renewed focus on creating a globally competitive economy brought the soybean to Mato Grosso and shifted the landscape of international agricultural markets forever (Zancopé, 2005). Mato Grosso's importance to the global soy market has experienced a dizzying rise since the late 1990s, shifting the country's economic profile, its political–economic agenda (embracing public–private partnerships[3] rather than the outright privatization that was instituted during structural adjustment), and transforming the physical landscape of a vast swath of the continent's remotest interior.

As much as neo-classical economics would argue that some countries or regions are intrinsically more competitive at producing a certain good than others, it is important to recognize the ways in which markets are constructed under specific historical circumstances by particular powerful players that stand to benefit from the political creation of that advantage. In Mato Grosso, the incentive to create a system of soybean production was manufactured in the laboratories of agronomists paid by both private seed companies *and* the Brazilian government. In order to produce soybeans in Mato Grosso, basic ecological barriers had to be overcome: tropically viable seed varieties had to be developed, soil fertility problems addressed, and funguses and insects unknown in temperate climates fought (Nasser, 1998).

Even with this research, soy in Mato Grosso would *never* have been a viable export, especially on the level that we see it today—without strategic investment by transnational corporations. And this investment has taken a very particular form. Throughout the central-west, transnational agribusinesses have tended to invest primarily in grain drying and storage facilities with relatively light involvement in processing, seeds, fertilizer manufacturing (though this may be changing), distribution, etc. This is largely because the remoteness of the region, great distance from consumer centers or ports of exit, and the lack of transportation infrastructure render such investments economically risky. This also reflects, however, a particular strategy on the part of a small handful of corporations to structure the value-added segment of the world soy market around the consumer centers of the East and policy-friendly (because of their lack of an ICMS-type tax[4] and incentives for exports) Argentina, relegating Brazil to the position of supplier of raw materials to the industrial protein machine.

Understanding the patterns of transnational investment in Brazilian soy cannot be disconnected from their strategic investments in other parts of the world. These are not regionally circumscribed economic relationships. Rather, the major buyers and brokers of Brazilian soy are also the major dealers, transporters, and processors of soy in every major producing *and* consuming country in the world. They are, in effect, not so different from any other manufacturing company looking to source its raw material from the cheapest possible supplier. However, these companies have been instrumental in *constructing* this competitiveness in multiple ways. First, they are often also suppliers *of* inputs *to* farmers, including fertilizers and other agrochemicals. Second, they are the largest suppliers of credit to the agricultural sector, thereby directly facilitating the expansion of soy production. Without credit from ADM, Cargill, Bunge, and Dreyfus it is questionable whether farmers could afford to plant a single soybean in the intensively chemical-dependent *cerrado* soils.

Government-subsidized credit in Brazil accounts for only a small fraction of yearly soybean production costs, and differs in this respect from both the United States and Europe. In 2004, each producer was allowed R$200,000 at a government subsidized interest rate, which at that time was enough to finance about 115 hectares. But the average farm size in Mato Grosso hovers around 2,000 hectares (about 5,000 acres). In the 2004 to 2005 harvest season, the resources available at this subsidized rate only accounted for around 6 percent of total production costs. The other 94 percent, at an interest rate of around 15 percent, came directly from agribusiness, almost entirely from the transnational corporations ADM, Bunge, Cargill, and the domestic conglomerate Groupo Maggi.[5] These are not banking institutions, they are soy processors; therefore, most of this farmer debt is held in soybeans, not in currency. According to one farmer, "agriculture has three currencies: soy, dollar, and real. When I'm insecure I guarantee all my loans in sacks of soy. This is the most stable currency" (Menegheti, 2005).

Not all farmers are satisfied with this, however, and many factors make this arrangement much more favorable to agribusiness than to farmers. First, farmers must sell their beans to their debtors first, which means these businesses can buy beans at harvest when prices are at rock-bottom. Second, in the event of crop failure, farmers have no other way to pay back their loans, and so they must promise a larger proportion of their harvest in the subsequent year. Eventually, most if not all of their product is owed in advance to one of these four major buyers. The president of the Mato Grosso farmers' association (FAMATO), Homero Pereira, expressed his discontent with this system:

> We don't have an alternative form today. As long as the government doesn't liberalize resources for rural credit, the producer doesn't have any other option than to be bound to the transnationals. We know that it is not the desire of all producers to be in these relationships. The desire of the producer is to get capital from a source of financial resources, and to owe in financial resources as well, rather than in produce. Because the biggest problem that we have with the system here today isn't so much the interest rates that you pay to the transnationals, but the market opportunities that you lose. Because when you get financing you tie yourself, you compromise so many tons of grain and so you lose sometimes a market much larger than your own interest rate. And so to be in debt to a financier and to remain in control of your own product is obviously much better.[6]

What Pereira is expressing here is something that recurred often in my conversations with farmers: frustration at the *lack* of independence they felt as producers, despite the equally widespread rhetoric that they were able to produce soybeans without government assistance. Clearly, although financially far less desirable a situation, debt peonage to agribusiness is more in concert with neo-liberal principles than reliance on government subsidies.

This heavy dependence on largely foreign capital of course calls into question the assumptions of comparative advantage. How "natural" is the competitiveness of *cerrado* soy when both the ecological and macroeconomic environments are hostile enough to require such intensive chemical and financial inputs? As long as farmers are making money, this question is rarely asked. The success of the regime that organizes relations of production masks the "implicit rules" that govern these relations, "such as which countries specialize in growing certain crops and which countries are importers" (Friedmann, 2005, p. 232). In other words, the constructed market is cast as a logical "evolutionary" outcome of economic development. Cutler (2002) calls this process the accomplishment of "private international regimes," while Ruggie (1982) talks of "embedded liberalism." These relationships are framed as efficient and competitive, even though by other metrics they appear to be neither of those things. Not only does Mato Grosso soy require heavy inputs, but it also must be dried in massive wood-burning furnaces (since it is harvested during the rainy season), trucked thousands of miles over sometimes unpaved roads (a journey that can take days or even weeks if the roads wash out), and aided in international markets by a weak real.[7] Neither ecologically efficient nor logistically competitive, soy production in Mato Grosso has continued to flourish because of the ability of dominant actors—soy traders, agricultural input companies, government—to frame these particular relations of production as advancing the broader economic and social "progress" of the "nation," insofar as that is defined by neo-liberal principles.

Here transnational agribusiness is constructing both the "reality" of the Mato Grosso soy economy, and the "frame" through which that reality is interpreted. This latter project is accomplished in two ways. First, it is a manifestation of the process by which this economy was created. Most of the towns of Mato Grosso were literally constructed by and for the soy economy. They appear strung out along federal highways as company towns, all physically configured in essentially the same way, with the visual and economic focal point being the row of grain storage and drying facilities along one side of the highway and the often large, new houses of the most successful soy farmers along the other. The downtowns rely on the economic activity generated by soy to also fuel the video stores, hair salons, supermarkets, Internet cafes, restaurants and bars. Everyone, even the teenager working behind the video counter, knows the bushel price of beans, and the anxiety when prices start to fall is palpable. Cost of living in

Exhibit 9.1 Soy trucks waiting to be pulled across a washed-out road one at a time by bulldozer south of Sapezal, Mato Grosso.

these towns is significantly higher than the national average since everything must be trucked in from hundreds or thousands of miles away (the other side of the coin that makes the cost of transportation of soy a difficult burden for farmers to bear).

This frame is again re-inscribed when prices fall, revealing the precariousness of the system for its least powerful members. Suddenly "the market" no longer provides for the community, and somehow the assumptions about competitiveness and efficiency must be reconciled with market failure. When soy prices plunge, the vulnerability of farmers is thrown into sharp relief, and the extent of their dependence on the availability of credit and capital from private sources—which have no particular allegiance to those farmers per se, as their only interest is in finding the world's cheapest and most convenient source of soybeans—becomes clear. Without access to public credit and without agricultural subsidies, farmers in Mato Grosso are dependent on the very entities, agribusiness, whose central interest is to exploit them as much as possible without driving them from the market altogether, or as one farmer put it, "to push our heads under the water, let us up just as we are about to suffocate, and then push us down again."[8]

Mobilization for Neo-Liberalism: Understanding Farmer Protest in Mato Grosso

When Mato Grosso's farmers took to the streets of the nation's capital and burned machinery to block the federal highways that bisect their hometowns, they clearly felt victimized by the market. One farmer profiled by the magazine *Produtor Rural*, Valcir Starasson, owes around $100,000[9] to the federally subsidized Banco do Brasil and an equal amount to "[chemical] input companies, and those that helped to plant the 2004/05 harvest" (Menegheti, 2005, p. 19). Valcir has no recourse to redress his debt to private companies, however, and so he drives his tractor up Brasília's central promenade.

In Mato Grosso, I heard over and over again about how Brazilian soy farmers are able to be competitive without government subsidies. This was a point of pride among both larger and smaller soy producers. Many farmers used this as evidence of the inherent logic of comparative advantage, and I heard many statements like this: we can do it without subsidies which means we are more competitive than you [meaning me, as representative of all American soy farmers], so let us grow the soy, and you guys grow the corn. In times of market crisis, however, the logic unravels. Rather than indicting the market itself for the failure to provide a selling price that reflects the cost of investment and production, farmers fault the state for failing to provide adequate insulation *from* "market forces" that threaten their viability. In other words, farmers direct their rancor at the state rather than at capital when demanding retribution, restitution, and rescue. They don't indict the corporations that have directly contributed to the construction of the system in such a way that makes such crises more and more likely and frequent. Clearly, the state guarantees the legitimacy of the system, and this is where citizens find their point of redress. According to the magazine story about Valcir, "He is in the following situation: if he pays one debt, he won't be able to pay the others" (Menegheti, 2005: 19).

What is interesting here is the way in which the farmer protests actually themselves uphold the ideal of the self-regulating market while at the same time directly challenge the assumption upon which it rests—that markets should, in principle, never require government assistance. This apparent contradiction is resolved, though, because of the assumption that market failure is caused by an *excess* of government involvement *in the United States and the European Union*, and since markets are now global they can blame their plight on foreign farm subsidies, the elimination of which could possibly depress prices even further, based on the economic principle of oligopsony (Ray, 2006a). This would not only deepen farmers' reliance on agribusiness and intensify land concentration throughout the world, but would increase corporate control over the structure of those markets. However, as long as the political blame remains remote, market rule will survive unindicted. This is already coming to fruition in the pressures that countries are exerting upon one another in WTO disputes over agricultural policy.

Mobilizing at the Global Level: Taking It to the WTO

As with the *tratoração*, much of the political impetus for cases brought against specific national agricultural policies in the WTO comes from organizations that supposedly represent the interests of farmers. This reflects and reinforces the assumption that WTO negotiation and dispute settlement are *political* processes in which governments represent the interests of their "citizens." When civil society groups weigh in on Brazil's negotiations or on the cases that Brazil brings against other countries in the Dispute Settlement Mechanism (DSM),[10] therefore, the process gains political legitimacy. Much as with domestic policy, however, these cases and negotiations work most often to deepen market structures that benefit *transnational* agribusiness at the expense of farmers (citizens) (Ray, 2006b).

However, because current agricultural market structure *and* policies create a path-dependency where highly capitalized farms rely on large-scale production for global markets, farmers often have no alternatives (in the form of supply control, price stabilization, or incentives for diversification or on-farm processing) to the exploitative economic system upon which they have become dependent. This is reflected in the credit relationships detailed above, where farmers become so indebted to agribusiness that they lose nearly all of their independence as producers while still assuming the majority of the risk inherent in agricultural production. Farmers producing for the global, industrial market, therefore, focus their political lobbying on "opening" markets for their produce in other countries, which usually means targeting national policies designed to protect domestic production via WTO dispute settlement.

A clear example of this is Brazil's 2002 case against U.S. cotton subsidies. Two years after a coalition of countries from the Global South (including Brazil) successfully blocked WTO negotiations in Seattle, Washington, Brazil mounted a challenge to specific provisions of the U.S. cotton program. By 2005, the DSM and successive appeals had all found against the U.S. program. While only governments can bring cases in the WTO against other governments' policies,[11] private actors are instrumental in the process. According to Pedro de Camargo Neto, former secretary of production and trade in Brazil's Ministry of Agriculture, Livestock and Food Supply and now director of the pork industry trade group ABIPECS, the Mato Grosso cotton producers' union (Associação Mato-grossense de Produtores de Algodão; AMPA) funded the legal team that brought the case and fought the appeals. According to Camargo, without pressure and resources coming from the farmers, neither the political will nor the finances would have existed to mount such a complex and expensive case.[12] The Mato Grosso soy producers' association—Aprosoja—is investigating the possibility of a similar case against U.S. soy programs.[13]

What is important here is that these cases nearly always work to *remove* government controls over agricultural markets. Farmers are indicting the protective agricultural policies of other countries in an attempt to enhance their own competitiveness in the market, essentially trying to level the playing field by forcing richer countries to subject their own economies to the neo-liberal principles they have been preaching (and imposing on the Global South) for decades. Because the WTO is a nation-state-based system of governance, however, private interests *need* the political legitimacy gained by operating through the channels of the state in order to dismantle the agricultural safety nets of their rivals.

All of this has an analog in the movement by the Southern coalition, the Group of 20 (G-20) to block WTO negotiations at the 2000 WTO summit in Seattle and the subsequent development of that group into an unlikely and surprising voice for expansion of neo-liberal policies, in both poor and rich nations. During and immediately after the breakdown of the 2000 talks, the G-20 was lauded by critics of free trade as "the voice of the Global South" finally standing up to the dominance of the United States, European Union, Canada, and Australia in the negotiating process. It soon became clear, however, as groups like Focus on the Global South have pointed out, that much of what the G-20 actually calls for more closely mirrors a recent "trade mission" launched by soy farmers from the United States and Brazil who joined forces in India to try and convince greater domestic use of the soy grown in that country (in an attempt to take Indian soy off the export market). While the stated goal of this trade mission was to enhance the competitiveness of U.S. and Brazilian soy through "reverse marketing," it also in effect deepens market penetration in India by tying Indian consumers more closely to global soy markets through the active creation of new consumer demand for soy products. Likewise, since 2000 the G-20 has focused much more closely on market access than on any measures protecting producers, sensitive products, or sovereignty in general. In fact, many now see their agenda as actually deepening and strengthening the entrenchment of neo-liberal policies in both rich and poor country markets by pushing market access above these other provisions.[14]

In addition to farmers, transnational agribusiness corporations also participate actively in the WTO process, and not just by proxy through producers' organizations. Often these threads of influence are difficult to trace because the companies have much at stake in appearing to remain "apolitical." It is common in the United States to see corporations sitting on presidential advisory boards and even drafting legislation at the national level, and while often criticized by citizen groups, this political participation is justified by the identification of a "national" company with the "national" interest. In the case of national policy-making, companies can be seen as important stakeholders in what Cutler describes as the "economic issue areas" governed by a combination of public policy and industry-based regulation (2002).

However, because markets are global, while TNCs have much at stake in the negotiation of trade rules, their interests often do not map onto the interests of their home governments (meaning those of the country where the company is incorporated and headquartered). Political participation, therefore, becomes tricky because these corporations do significant business in countries that often have conflicting trade positions in the WTO. In Brazil, perhaps the single most influential organization outside government in agricultural trade policy is the Institute for the Study of Trade and International Negotiations (ICONE). The majority of the research on which Brazil's agricultural trade policies are based comes from this institute. Researchers from the Institute advocate for heavy cuts of up to 90 percent in agricultural tariffs for developing countries. Brazil is a major player in WTO talks on agriculture, and ICONE's advice is reflected in its strategy for the negotiations. Funding received by ICONE comes indirectly from agribusiness corporations including Archer Daniels Midland (ADM), Cargill, and Bunge. It is also funded by various industry associations, including the Brazilian Oilseeds Association (ABIOVE), as well as sugar and livestock industry groups, and its board of directors is made up of representatives from these associations. In turn, ABIOVE is funded directly by the Brazilian affiliates of the agribusiness giants ADM, Bunge, Cargill, and Louis-Dreyfus. The Brazilian Agribusiness Association (ABAG) played a key role in creating ICONE, and it continues to provide institutional support. Cargill and ADM also fund ABAG along with many other corporations that include Bayer, Monsanto, and Pioneer Hi-Bred. Carlo Lovatelli, president of both ABIOVE and ABAG, is the director of Bunge in Brazil. Brazil's pro-agribusiness Ministry of Agriculture and Food Supply, as well as other university research groups dedicated to promoting agribusiness issues are also claimed by ICONE as its partners.

According to one ICONE researcher, agribusiness interests commission studies that are given to the Brazilian government only after receiving the companies' approval via their industry associations. The focus of ICONE's research program is on increasing agribusiness companies' access to markets and boosting the flow of farm exports around the world. Issues such as protecting food security and poor farmers' livelihoods are not on its agenda. Within the G-20, Brazil declines to lend technical support to work on issues related to protecting farmer livelihoods, sensitive products, etc. "There exists a certain division of labor in the G-20," says an ICONE researcher. "Brazil has done all the technical work about the issues of market access and domestic subsidies. And everything related to special and differential treatment, food security, livelihood needs, food sovereignty...the countries that are interested in this need to do the work."[15] Brazilian groups with an interest in these issues, including the landless laborers' movement, small farmers' organizations, and the Ministry of Agrarian Development, lack both the resources and the access to trade ministers and senior negotiators to push them up the Brazilian government's WTO agenda. According to one official at the Ministry of Foreign Relations, the Brazilian government recognizes that promoting market access could cause problems for the integrity of the G-20 coalition. But it also anticipates that "if there is a critical mass of agreement, the others will fall into line."[16] The G-20, therefore, has become a very effective platform for promoting the type of trade liberalization sought by transnational agribusiness interests while also lending international legitimacy to the project because of its broad representation of countries of the Global South.

Conclusion

It is clear from the example of the G-20 that resistance to the U.S. agenda does not necessarily constitute a substantive critique of neo-liberal trade policy, just as farmer protests in Brasília do not constitute a substantive critique of neo-liberal agricultural policy. Both of these instances can be understood as mobilizations *for* or *of* capital interests rather than against them. By seeing these as mobilizations, from a social movements' perspective, we reveal neo-liberalism as a political project rather than a natural outcome of "development." As a project, this set of organizing principles—privileging the market over other ways of organizing societies—frames progress in terms of market freedom, which for agriculture means the integration of large-scale industrial farming into global commodity markets. When market volatilities threaten the stability of that economic system, it is perfectly appropriate for farmers to call on the state to implement policies that will allow agribusiness to survive and ameliorate the worst effects of its monopoly power. This is, in effect, what the protesting Mato Grosso soy farmers participated in: a mobilization of state resources for the long-term stability of a corporate system of industrial agriculture.

Neo-liberal development co-opts rationality, as the market is not an instrument that necessarily serves social needs or ecological sustainability. Limited resources are exhausted at ever-increasing rates, an increasing percentage of the world's population lives in poverty, the wealth gap widens, and millions of people starve as corporations spend trillions of dollars trying to find new ways of processing and marketing the world's considerable, and undiminished, agricultural *surplus*.

The backward logic of the current system promises to become even more perverse as biofuels become the savior of a collapsing industrial agriculture regime. The Brazilian agriculture magazine, *Produtor Rural*, recently featured biodiesel on its cover with the caption, "Óleo da esperança"—Oil of hope. Food is a notoriously inelastic market, which means that, regardless of income, class, or culture, there are only so many calories a day that one person can consume. This is what has driven food corporations to continually invent and market new processed food products, in order to shift consumption *patterns* and continue increasing profits. With the new emphasis on biofuels sparked by mounting panic over global climate change, industrial agriculture is no longer shackled to the millstone of the limited capacity of people's stomachs. If the biofuel revolution succeeds in rescuing agricultural markets (albeit temporarily) from the slow but certain death by diminishing returns, neo-liberalism will triumph once again, proving that given a product and a need, the market will devise the most efficient solution (disregarding an ecological calculus).

Of course, there are powerful voices that demonstrate alternatives to the neo-liberal regime. Many peasant organizations such as Via Campesina and the Brazilian Landless-Workers Movement (MST) criticize the panacea of soy and biofuels as the savior of the *campo*. But neo-liberalism—because it claims to advance freedom of trade and capital as a desirable end in itself—renders all other systems regressive by its very logic. Any organizational system that privileges any social good over the right of property is deemed to be an enemy of progress. It is this *a priori* reasoning that requires the social movement analytic to get to the heart of neo-liberalism as a political project. Only through a social movement's lens of analysis, however, is it possible to see how this project—which is a mobilization using strategies and tactics to frame its interpretation of reality like any other—is accomplished.

Notes

* Acknowledgments The author would like to thank Wendy Wolford, Gillian Hart, Philip McMichael, and Nosheen Ali for valuable feedback on earlier drafts of this paper.
1. Such as the MODEFROTA program that subsidizes loans to buy machinery and equipment.
2. The point here is to extend analysis of social movements to the powerful forces that shape political–economic relations, traditionally seen as the context *in which* powerless actors seek to make political gains through mobilization.
3. As opposed to outright privatization, these partnerships (PPPs) usually involve some kind of cost sharing between private entities and the government. The first example was a plan to pave roads in Mato Grosso where, if soy farmers put up the money to prepare the roadbed, the state government would supply the asphalt.
4. This is a tax levied on products crossing state lines that are destined for export. In 1996 this tax was lifted for the first time on whole soybeans.
5. Ministério de Agricultura, Pecuária, e Abastacimento (Mapa).
6. Interview #51, May 2005.
7. Though this is changing, which compounds the crisis today, to be explained in greater detail below.
8. Interview #36 Sapezal, Brazil: March 2005.
9. At 2005 exchange rates.
10. The Dispute Settlement Mechanism adjudicates complaints brought to the WTO by countries that believe they are the victims of trade violations by other countries, providing for some form of redress or penalty.
11. Unlike in the investment title of NAFTA (chapter 11) where individual firms can bring cases against national, state, or municipal governments.
12. Interview #8, November 2004.
13. At the time of my research in Mato Grosso, soy prices were still too high to warrant a case, since producers have to be able to show that they are being harmed by U.S. subsidies, and counter-cyclical payments had not kicked in to cushion falling prices in some years.
14. It is important to note that the G-20 does indeed have particular provisions for special treatment for LDCs and sensitive products, but these have proven to be highly controversial within the group and have served to fracture consensus due to the overwhelming emphasis on market access.
15. Interview conducted at ICONE offices in São Paulo, Brazil, December 7, 2004.
16. Interview conducted at the Ministério de Relações Exteriores, Brasília, Brazil, June 22, 2005.

PART III

OVERCOMING EXCLUSION, RECLAIMING DEVELOPMENT

In reordering the social world, development inevitably excludes or marginalizes certain categories of people. This is not simply a linear process where "traditional" crafts give way to modernizing industries, where peasants and artisans are dispossessed to make way for development. It is also a cultural process whereby market deepening erodes the social and natural foundations of different life-worlds, where market relations attempt to "level" cultural difference and values (either by ignoring them or by commercial repackaging), and where authorities deploy cultural hierarchies (e.g., race) to secure power. Development is not just about clearing the old to make way for the new, it also produces and reproduces inequalities as part of the process of laying down the foundations for the accumulation of wealth and power.

This set of essays spotlights struggles over exclusion. These are not just struggles about being included in the process that causes exclusion in the first place. These are struggles about the process itself, and its exclusionary assumptions and consequences. A key mechanism here is the market calculus, which identifies singular aspirations (self-gain, self-improvement) as universal values and therefore equalizing. However, by definition this means alternative values or cultures are candidates for exclusion, and classified as residual, secondary, or simply "undeveloped." It also privileges an ideal of equality in the marketplace over the reality of prejudice and oppression that constitutes minorities (e.g., women, non-whites, indigenous people, peasants) in the first place. Disregard for the existential impact and power-laden relations of discrimination makes for a more subtle exclusionary process.

In these ways, development offers solutions in the name of equality that may reinforce injustice. Alternative solutions must come from practices and movements that engage critically with development and its assumptions. These struggles challenge the "epistemic privilege" through which powerful institutions and discourses naturalize a particular vision of the world as the universal and inevitable destiny of humanity. Over the last three decades in particular a "development partnership" of international financial institutions, global corporations, national governments, and some non-governmental organizations has extended the reach of the market culture and state-corporate power, often at the expense of empowering the poor and excluded—recognizing them as full citizens with rights, and capable of pursuing social change in democratic, just, and sustainable ways.

The struggles depicted here provide a glimpse into a world in which such conceptions and capacities are not only possible but sustaining, lending new definition to people who are regarded through the development lens as "leftovers" or destined to disappear. They also provide a new perspective on the assumptions that comprise the market calculus and its system of power. The people subjected to these terms do not necessarily live by such a calculus. Why should they be held to such an abstract standard—for what purpose, and in whose interest?

Gayatri Menon's chapter 10 offers a vivid account of Mumbai slum-dwellers contesting their exclusion through developing a unique capacity for self-organization and resistance to slum-clearance everyday violence. Squatting illegally on public space, the alliance of pavement dwellers creates a political space by directly addressing the methods through which they are rendered insecure and denied the rights of citizenship. Tactics of self-enumeration in a slum-census, savings networks, and federation among other slum-dwellers create a politics of accommodation through struggles to survive and obtain recognition in a revanchist global city, infiltrating categories of rule to claim civic rights.

Hannah Wittman's chapter 11 shows how Brazil's Movimento dos Trabalhadores Rurais Sem Terra (MST) mobilizes the landless to claim land and to develop an alternative development vision. As one of the largest social movements in the world, the MST challenges two key assumptions in the development narrative: first, that smallholder agriculture is a thing of the past; second, that a productive society depends on a culture of self-improving, market-oriented individuals. The MST's struggle is dedicated to forging a culture of mutual support and collective responsibility on the land, in the service of national food security and preserving ecology—in short, a new "agrarian citizenship."

Kelly Dietz's chapter 12 documents the struggle of the Okinawan people against American military occupation, and the complicity of the Japanese state in internal colonial basing, which compromises Okinawan citizenship and the struggle itself. This essay shows how, in developing a politics of self-determination mirroring other contemporary autonomist struggles to protect rights to territory, resources, and culture, the Okinawan anti-base movement redefines sovereignty and citizenship in collective terms beyond liberal conceptions of individual rights within a militarized space.

Alexandre Da Costa's chapter 13 examines how the contributions and cultural beliefs of Afro-Brazilians have been suppressed in Brazilian civic education through an ideology of whitening (*embranqueamento*). A recent cultural project to reclaim Afro-Brazilian heritage in Brazilian society draws on past and present struggles to revalue embodied learning and values produced in and through Afro-descendant communities. The Baobá Project challenges racial inequality through developing alternative understandings of history, cultural identity, and social progress. This essay shows how the Afro-Brazilian struggle practices a "critical multi-culturalism"—challenging neoliberal multi-culturalism that only acknowledges diversity without addressing its structural inequality.

Andreas Hernandez's chapter 14 describes how the World Social Forum, emerging in 2001 as an activist counterweight to the power of the World Economic Forum, established in 1971, provides a venue for a spiritual critique of market culture. The essay argues that an ecumenical vision of spirituality offers a more complex and ecological understanding of humanity, compared with the reductionism of neo-liberalism and fundamentalist religion. The World Social Forum brings a new religious subjectivity to social change movements, countering the identification of development with self-interest and advocating a new ethic of "global citizenship."

10.

RECOVERIES OF SPACE AND SUBJECTIVITY IN THE SHADOW OF VIOLENCE

The Clandestine Politics of Pavement Dwellers in Mumbai

Gayatri A. Menon

Less a movement and more a permanent mobilization, the Alliance of pavement dwellers asserts itself through encroachment on a public ontology that consigns dispossessed people to a condition of placelessness, reproduced through episodes of violent slum clearance. This, and the violence of everyday life as illegitimate squatters on public space, drives them to create a political space that trains a critical light on the exclusions through which the contemporary political subject is secured, and the poor made insecure. Tactics of self-enumeration, savings networks, and federation among groups contribute to a politics of accommodation, through struggles to survive and obtain recognition in a revanchist global city, infiltrating the very categories through which rule is accomplished.

Introduction

Land is the currency of power in Mumbai, and housing is the principal arena in which this power is expressed, experienced, contested, and transformed. The defining characteristic of its housing politics is that as Mumbai's elites vie with other urban elites to provide a home for global capital, its poor find it increasingly challenging to negotiate a home in the city. The urban poor find themselves cast as outsiders who threaten the neo-liberal re-visioning of the city through their presence and their trespasses. The "annihilation of space by time" that enables the globalization project, the geographer Don Mitchell (2003) points out, has precipitated an "annihilation of space by law" as city after city institutes measures to criminalize the homeless in a bid to provide an attractive, secure home for global capital. These measures, he argues, by denying the homeless the space to reproduce themselves, ultimately boil down to their physical annihilation: "We are creating a world," he contends, "in which a whole class of people cannot be—simply because they have no place to be" (p. 171).

What we find is that, rendered placeless, not only do the urban poor not have a place to *be*, but they are also denied a place to *become*; that is, to engage the world proactively, as historical subjects. Caught in the relentless dialectic of evictions and encroachments the urban poor are imperilled in both their social reproduction and their cultural reproduction as subjects, as experiences of marginalization and violence corrode their sense of self. In such a world, it is abjectivity[1] rather than subjectivity that captures the political status of Mumbai's pavement dwellers on the uneven terrain of citizenship (Appadurai, 2002). Given these alienating circumstances how do pavement dwellers secure a house and a sense of home for themselves? What prospects do they have for exercising what Lefebvre (1996) famously referred to as "the right to the city?" I explore these prospects in this chapter by focusing on how an alliance of three organizations—*Mahila Milan*, the National Slum Dwellers' Federation, and the Society for the Promotion of Area Resource Centres (SPARC)—have endeavored to restore historical subjectivity to those denied it in this revanchist city.

The former two organizations are comprised of people who live on the pavements and in the slums of India, respectively. The latter, SPARC, is a non-government organization lead by middle-class activists. They have worked in alliance with each other for over twenty years to transform the conditions of the urban poor. The proportions of the challenge they face in Mumbai are worth keeping in mind: 60 percent of the city's population are perceived to be squatters. The worst-off among them are the 10 percent or so who live on the pavements of the city. They cannot afford to live in a slum settlement and must carve out a space on the pavements of the city to house themselves. Despite their careful selection of sites, because they live on public thoroughfares, pavement dwellers are routinely subjected to violent evictions and demolitions of their homes.

To understand the political practice of the Alliance, therefore, it is necessary to recognize the role of violence in shaping the conditions and possibilities of pavement dwellers in Mumbai. Pavement dwellers face a constant threat of demolition, and the fear and anticipation of this violence haunts their lives and their struggles. It is a condition of alienation that is produced by systematically rendering them invisible, destroying any attempts that they make to produce a locality which might provide them with a sense of belonging, and erasing any spatial claims that they may make. The demolitions of their dwellings thus are routine practices by which the exclusionary cartography of citizenship is made manifest and the abject status of the urban poor is reproduced.

Not only are pavement dwellers rendered invisible by violence, but they must remain invisible in order to avoid being subjected to further violence. For, what is distinctive about the conditions under which pavement dwellers have to stake their right to the city is that they actually *live* in public. As a SPARC activist observed, the consequence of living in public is that public protests about the living conditions of the urban poor, rather than creating a space where they can register their protest, "produce[s] angst and fear for them as they have to deal with the long term wrath of the state and the police after that. Because soon after the event of the protest is over, the external people leave, life has to go on, and they have to deal with this aftermath by themselves." That is, the momentary space of protest and confrontation with the state is also the pavement dwellers' everyday living space, a space that is produced out of a welter of negotiations with the local police, municipality ward officers, and organized crime. This predicament complicates, in very significant ways, the kinds of challenges pavement dwellers can make to those who destroy their homes and deny their right to the city. Consequently, they must craft a politics of articulating themselves that does not jeopardize their ever so fragile negotiations of home on public thoroughfares (i.e., clandestinely). The creative ways in which pavement dwellers have recovered space and subjectivity, given their precarious political and physical location in the city, is the focus of my analysis.

The interpretive approach that I take to the Alliance's practice is a prospective one. It is an approach to the study of struggles for social justice where "traits of the struggles are amplified so as to render visible and credible the potential that lies implicit or remains embryonic in the experiences under examination" (Santos and Rodriguez-Garavito, 2005, p. 17). My approach emerges from the recognition that the categories through which we apprehend the social world are often complicit in rendering invisible and devaluing the people and activities of disenfranchised populations. It thus asks that we train the analytical and political lens beyond the horizons provided by extant epistemic conditions, seeking instead, to discern the critical possibilities that are anticipated in, and animate, the often "quiet" (Bayat, 2000), counter-hegemonic tactics forged in the fragile present of marginalized populations such as the pavement dwellers' of Mumbai.

I adopt this prospective approach in my investigation of how pavement dwellers organize to recover their subjectivity from the rubble left by the city's demolition squads, conditions meant to render them abject. The rituals of savings, of enumeration, and of federation that I discuss are practices by which the alliance has challenged the profound alienation and abjectivity of the urban poor, and provided a sense of home, a space where futures can be considered, of becoming. Given that citizenship, our political framework for claims making, is increasingly and violently determined by property relations, leaving growing numbers of people in a condition of abjectivity, the political practice of pavement dwellers of Mumbai to recover subjectivity (i.e., a sense of home) and ultimately a house, in the face of devastating material and discursive attrition, bears a prospective consideration.

What I find to be of particular significance about the Alliance's practice is that rather than expressing a nostalgic desire for the liberal subject (or the promise thereof, that, for example, fueled the development project), it suggests an alternate conception of constituting a democratic citizenship. It is a politics of recognition advanced through the fluidity of becoming (i.e., historical subjectivity), rather than one based in the fixities of belonging to a defined political community, for example, citizenship, which is inevitably exclusive (cf. Gotz and Simone, 2003). This alternative political imaginary is forged out of a visceral understanding of exclusion and emerges from the improvisations through which this group of the urban poor builds their homes on the pavements and mobilizes for change. That is, this politics of recognition, based on becoming rather than belonging, is one that is grounded in a critical and canny understanding of the epistemic roots of the urban poor's homelessness on the political and physical terrain of the city. It is a praxis of accommodation, of making place for those who would otherwise be left behind, through the fabrication of plural subjects and spaces in which even pavement dwellers can feel at home. It is a creative politics crafted in fragile and compromised circumstances marked by destruction. It not only spurs its constituents, but challenges its analysts "to identify emerging qualities and entities at a moment in which they can be easily discarded" and offer "a prospective account of what is possible' (Santos and Rodriguez-Garavito, 2005, p. 17).

Making Place

The predicament of placelessness faced by pavement dwellers illuminates the deterritorializing effects of neo-liberal flows of global capital, specifically its attrition of the historical configuration of power and place that we know as the nation-state, in which national sovereignty and national citizenship have operated as axes of governance. As is increasingly evident, the hyphen securing the nation to the state buckles as "Central banks and governments appear now to be increasingly concerned about pleasing the financial markets rather than setting goals for social and economic well-being" (Sassen, 1996, p.50). The effect, Sassen points out, is that national citizens become nominal participants in the practice of power and legitimacy that comprises "citizenship," while political power is aggregated by global corporations who become "economic citizens," who exercise substantive citizenship and wield the ability to demand accountability from the state. Enabling this reconfiguration of governance and of personhood is the redefinition of the meaning and the narrowing of the space and subject of the public, in terms of extending, validating, and ensuring global accumulation processes. The outcome of the increasing determination of the space and subject of the political by property is that the urban poor do not just physically, but also politically, have a place to be.

Analyzing how African cities have countered this unbundling of the spatial relations that held the nation-state together and the uncertainty and insecurity that issues as a consequence, Gotz and Simone (2003) provide a useful framework for reading the possibilities that emerge from this condition of placelessness. They identify two emerging trends of place making: belonging and becoming. The former refers to "increasingly zealous attempts to claim rights to exclusive geographic territories within which to profess highly parochial identities" (p. 124). In the case of Mumbai, the Shiv Sena provides an example of a belonging-based attempt to produce the context within which individuals perform as historical subjects. In their violent and revanchist *Mee Mumbaikar* campaign anti-migrant sentiment reigns supreme and identities are increasingly invigilated in order to provide a sense of security, belonging, and certainty in a deterritorialized, neo-liberal Mumbai. Such projects have little to offer pavement dwellers as is indicated by their predicament of placelessness and by the violence directed toward them by the state and by parochial movements such as the Shiv Sena.[2]

Becoming, Gotz and Simone (2003, p. 124) argue, is a more promising approach to "regrounding social relations." Here the disenfranchised respond to the unravelling of the place-making endeavor of the nation-state by creatively assembling pluralized, mobile, and contingent identities and affiliations that operate in and through the multiple geographies that course through their lives. While promising, the grassroots cosmopolitanism celebrated in the notion of becoming is hard work. This is particularly so for populations whose contingent associations and improvised homes are always under threat of destruction and dispersal and whose sense of self is jeopardized by this relentless violence. That is, their context for social and cultural production of self is constantly under threat of being reduced to rubble (cf. Appadurai, 1996). So while survival has spurred the improvisational skills of pavement dwellers, evictions inflect these affiliations with ephemerality, which prevents them from forming a reliable basis for cultural and social reproduction; that is, a sense of home, and a context in which to craft subjectivity. It is to this challenge that the Alliance addresses itself in its endeavor to transform the conditions of abjectivity that pavement dwellers find themselves in: to provide a place, a relatively enduring assemblage of meanings and relationships, for piecing together and reproducing historical subjects.

The Rhetoric of the Daily Savings Round

Critically informing my analysis of the recovery of subjectivity is bell hooks's notion of homeplace. By "homeplace" hooks is drawing attention to the everyday, unrecognized practices of care and of recognition through which black women constructed the home as a place of restoring subjectivity to those denied it outside the confines of the domestic space:

> Despite the brutal reality of racial apartheid, of domination, one's homeplace was the one site where one could freely confront the issue of humanization, where one could resist. Black women resisted by making homes where all black people could strive to be subjects, not objects.... This task of making homeplace was not simply a matter of black women providing service; it was about the construction of a safe place where black people could affirm one another and by doing so heal many of the wounds inflicted by racist domination (hooks, 1990, p. 42).

What I found as I explored the Alliance's political practice is a similar process of creating a space for the recovery and affirmation of self, a space for bodies exposed to dehumanizing violence and degradation on a daily basis. Tellingly, most of the pavement dwellers I met remarked that they did not know their neighbors before they began to engage in the mobilizational practices of the Alliance. Given that most poor migrants tend to gravitate to locations in the city where they might have some kin, regional, or language based associations that they can use to negotiate a stretch of pavement, it is clear that the claim to not "know" one's neighbor is an expression of abjectivity, where one is left bereft of the capacity to create a neighborhood, a space of certitude (cf. Appadurai, 1996, p. 184), and is resigned to perpetual uncertainty.

The daily savings round, an account of which I provide below, lies at the heart of the Alliance's struggle to recover space and subjectivity in the face of this violence. It is a practice by which impoverished communities pool meager financial resources, or "savings," to create a cooperatively managed fund from which they can take loans and thereby avoid having to go to a moneylender or go without. As I accompanied Kamala as she went on her daily savings round, just as she has done every morning for the past twenty years, I began to understand its significance, for what it does is to create a "homeplace" for those abandoned by the contemporary social order. It is a ritual that quietly redresses the alienation and abjectivity of the urban poor through its everyday acts of recognition. I provide a short account of my walk with Kamala as she made her daily savings round of her neighborhood in Nagpada, and discuss some of the discursive elements of the subversive politics of articulation in which it is located.

I alight from the bus in front of Nagpada Police Station a little bit bleary-eyed. Kamala had told me not to be late when I arranged to accompany her on her daily "savings round." She is the Mahila Milan leader of a street in Nagpada, and every day she visits every pavement dwelling on her street and collects the savings that each household deposits into their Mahila Milan savings account. She left at 7:30 a.m. and so here I was at 7:15 looking at the row of dwellings that occupied the pavement opposite the police station, trying to figure out which one was Kamala's house. All along the opposite pavement were people in various stages of getting ready for the day. Little children with their hair painfully scraped back, dressed in school uniforms and bearing huge satchels were being dispatched to school. Scooping mugs of water from disused chemical barrels, a few women squatted on the road washing clothes, some washing dishes. There is an intimacy to these scenes of ordinariness, of a household gearing up for the day that belies their public display. Because I am standing on the opposite side of the road, these images are chopped up by the fast-paced vehicular traffic—double-decker buses, cars, and vans racing through this narrow one-way street. There is no pavement on this side of the street and I was in danger of losing my toes as the vehicles passed within a hair's breadth. Where was Kamala? Luckily, I spot her son Shekhar who leads me to her house. A bright blue shack, less than 40 square feet, and like the others, it is built against the compound wall of a rather large multi-storied residential building. The shacks are all numbered and at the end of the row is an official looking board announcing them as Mahila Milan *zhopadpatties* (shacks), the name of the locality and the number of dwellings. Kamala gestures to me to enter. She had just finished her pooja and was ready to go. I take a quick glance at her altar and am rather bemused to find a picture of Jesus alongside those of Hindu deities. Catching my look, she laughs and tells me that a Kenyan federation member had given it to her last time she was in Nairobi,[3] and she had incorporated it into her worship. As we leave the house on her round, she tells me that before the compound wall was built, there was only a wrought-iron fence and the pavement dwellers would have to erect and dismantle their shelters every day, the shelter itself used to be only three or four feet high. She hands me the savings bag to carry and we turn left, toward the police station. As we walk from house to house she explains that some households make daily deposits while others make them weekly. It takes her half an hour, 7:30 to 8 a.m., to complete her collection round. Often she has to wake people up she tells me, and in the very next house she does exactly that and a woman, half-asleep pulls out Rs.20 from her clothes and soundlessly hands it to her. We double back and visit the shacks on the other side of Kamala's shack. The amount that is deposited varies quite widely, from Rs. 80 to nothing at all—there are also some are loan repayments being made in addition to the savings deposits. There is the occasional conversation. We stop for a while at Nasreen's; she has been very unwell for the past few months. It is almost 8 and we are almost done, the plastic bag is perceptibly heavier than when we set out. On the way back to her house, we run into a woman who rather bashfully gives Kamala a 10-rupee note, apparently she has not been making her deposits regularly. As she moves away, Kamala confides that the woman is a *bahar rehene vala* ("lives outside")—did she mean outsider, I asked a little perplexed? No, she doesn't have a shack, she sleeps where she can, and she makes deposits when she can. Apparently not everyone is thrilled with the prospect of making loans from their collective fund to such itinerant members and she has had to take some flak, but Kamala trusts her, and besides, she points out, who else would loan her the money?

Who indeed? The geography of the savings round, traced out by Kamala's steps and transactions, in its ability to accommodate the worst-off among the urban poor, stands in stark contrast to the violent exclusions that they face as pavement dwellers in a city that is striving to attract global finance. If squatting on the pavement signifies the abjectivity of pavement dwellers, then the pedestrian activity of the savings round tells quite another story. De Certeau's (1984, p. 97) formulation of walking as a "pedestrian speech act," where he draws attention to its enunciative property, is a useful way to begin to unpack the story narrated in Kamala's morning walk. He contends that:

> The act of walking is to the urban system what the speech act is to language or to the statements uttered. At the most elementary level, it has a triple "enunciative" function: it is a process of *appropriation* of the topographical system on the part of the pedestrian...it is a spatial acting-out of the place...and it implies *relations* among differentiated positions.... It thus seems possible to give a preliminary definition of walking as a space of enunciation (pp. 97–98).

And so in Nagpada, walking from house to house, relationships were renewed that would otherwise atrophy into a state of alienation as the attrition of countless evictions took their toll. Money, the very medium by which pavement dwellers are devalued and alienated, acquires a different valency as the transactions are informed by and accommodate the exigent circumstances of the households living on the edge of that busy one-way street in Nagpada (cf. Reddy, 1987). The pedestrian—in the sense of both ambulatory and quotidian—ritual of the savings round is thus a quiet process of crafting an alternative sociality for pavement dwellers.

What de Certeau's understanding of walking as a creative appropriation and re-composition of the spatial ordering of the city allows us to appreciate, is how the ritual of the savings round produces a neighborhood where there was close to none. That is, drawing on Appadurai's (1996, p. 181) discussion of phenomenological dimensions of locality, I understand neighborhood as an affective practice of recognition and basis for cultural reproduction. It is a practice that allows the experience of inhabitation to be apprehended as one of inclusion rather than that of exile. As Appadurai has argued, neighborhood is the context through which subjectivity is realized for it provides the social basis for cultural reproduction, and, as I argue, the basis for a politics of articulation. It provides the ground for political mobilization and action. The subversiveness of "homeplace," as hooks points out, is that by providing a refuge from which a sense of self could be recovered from the attritional processes of material and symbolic othering that African Americans are subjected to in public life, "homeplace" became the basis for building "a community of resistance" (hooks, 1990, p. 42). In the subsequent sections of the paper I provide a prospective reading of some of the organizing practices of the Alliance; I discuss how the neighborhoods crafted by the Alliance not only allow pavement dwellers to recover their historical subjectivity but also engage it in order to transform their living conditions.

Recovering Subjectivity

The foremost tactic in the Alliance's arsenal to counter the invisibility rendered by the multiple exclusions of the urban poor in Mumbai, is enumeration. While enumerative exercises have typically been the prerogative of the state, and are taxonomic exercises in subjectivity—seeking to establish the terms by which populations may be recognized—the Alliance has appropriated the practice. Recognizing that statistics and the making of them are fundamentally social processes, that is, practices of power, the Alliance has used enumeration as a mobilizational tool, collecting people and information with which to negotiate with the state, in short, to posit *their* terms of recognition.

Their first foray into enumeration, *We, the Invisible* contained the results of a census of pavement dwellers undertaken in the city's E Ward, generating data on 6000 households (27,000 individuals; Society for the Promotion of Area Resource Cewnters, SPARC,1985). They provided information on a segment of the city's population about whom no systematic information existed—a vacuum that allowed for the poor to be seen as Other and to be misrepresented. Crucially, this information was owned not by the state or by professionals, but was produced and owned by the poorest populations in the city. Consequently it challenged the epistemic privilege that states and experts requisition for themselves, especially with regard to the poor and "under-developed," which is to produce and interpret knowledge.

The enumerations produced the information that pavement dwellers would require to negotiate for and claim entitlements. As community enumerators fanned out across the city collecting information on pavement and slum settlements, houses were numbered, maps were drawn of each settlement, family sizes were recorded, as were the number of years that families had lived in Mumbai; employment statistics were gathered, migration histories were recounted, incomes were revealed, and identity cards were issued. They literally wrote themselves into existence, producing papers and representational forms that they were excluded from, countering the erasures effected by the state's demolitions and neglect. This practice, where pavement dwellers appropriated a tool of government and went from house to house collecting, tabulating, and correcting information about themselves, also served to create a shared interpretive framework that allowed previously isolated families to engage with each other by seeing the patterns and threads that drew their personal stories together. This is an outcome quite distinct from the state's production of statistics. For here a shared subject space was created; that is, the neighborhood that Appadurai has argued is the affective context of cultural reproduction through which "subjects of history become historical subjects" (1996, p. 185).

As communities of the urban poor mobilize information about themselves, and collectively work to define their localities, they begin to construct the epistemic contexts in and through which their subjectivity may be realized. There are no assumptions or requirements of *a priori* sameness; rather, the rituals craft a process of becoming by specifying and reproducing the terms of interconnection that link people with each other and produce locality.[4] An example is provided by the pavement dwellers of 14th

Street in Kamathipura, who are in various ways engaged with the sex trade. In the process of enumerating themselves they renamed their locality as Shantinagar (trans. peace town) as a way of constituting themselves and their relationships with each other on a different plane. By doing so they supplanted the identifications provided them by the trade that makes Kamathipura notorious, and that have contributed to their sense of abjectivity.

Building and maintaining these emergent relationships is no mean feat given that these populations are subjected to periodic evictions and demolitions that threaten to annihilate these precarious constructions of locality and scatter its subjects.[5] Their rituals, such as the daily savings round, have been crucial to developing the endurance of these precipitously located subjects to withstand these assaults and maintain their ground, politically and physically, by crafting a rhythm and a space that is informed by urban visions that are distinct from those expressed through demolitions and genocidal violence. Deploying Appadurai's (1996) dialectically conceived notion of locality, what we find is that the daily savings (and the promise of a future that these investments renew daily) interject into the unpredictable rhythm of locality-destroying demolitions a locality-reproducing regularity essential to the resilience of these interpretive frameworks and the subjects they constitute.

Given the neoliberal valorization of micro-credit, it is difficult to immediately discern how the Alliance's particular performance of this practice advances a politics of accommodation. It is only close inspection of the form of savings and credit in circulation that reveals that the Alliance does not make a virtue of disciplining defaulters or increasing the corpus through raising interest rates, practices of exclusion that arguably increase rather than decrease the vulnerability of the poor. Rather, the focus is on social inclusion; on the collection of daily savings of small, even miniscule amounts of money that represent very little in material terms (even to the urban poor) but convey much symbolic and organizational value that is communicated and replenished daily as community leaders like Kamala visit each pavement or slum dwelling on their street. As Gibson-Graham indicates:

> To join such a group is to engage in new practice of the self—setting aside savings from what is already too little to live on.... In the process, new senses of self are instituted— through self-development as citizens, house designers, investors, or entrepreneurs, through self-recognition of their survival capacities as poor women and migrants, through daily recommitment to the cultivation of solidarity(2006, p. xxv).

For what is exchanged in these visits is not just small change, but information, people, and trust, the sinews of the pavement dwellers' political formation.

Transforming Politics

The numbers and statistics generated by the Alliance's enumeration exercises have proved useful not only in the aftermath of demolitions as affected communities sought to get compensation for damages incurred to person and personal property, but also to create the basis for laying claim to welfare entitlements that had previously been denied to pavement dwellers because they were presumed to be transients. Over time, local government officials have been invited to accompany these community enumerators and conduct joint surveys, thereby "quietly" recalibrating the relationship between the urban poor and the state as these unofficial enumeration practices and previously ignored numbers were normalized and entered into the city's calculus of governance.

The use of enumeration as a tactic of encroachment on political space is a movement away from a politics of confrontation, which the pavement dwellers' imperilled circumstances of living cannot permit, to one of engagement with the very institutions and individuals that make their present homes perilous. For many observers the asymmetry of these emergent relationships is unsettling. That is, the specter of co-optation looms large in their interpretation of the potential of such relationships to advance the cause of social justice. For the constituents of this praxis, however, who are acutely aware of the power asymmetries that separate them and the state, opportunities to cultivate such relationships are nevertheless painstakingly nurtured and quickly seized upon as tactical openings to broaden and institutionalize the transformations that they have stealthily crafted (cf. de Certeau, 1984).

For, having been abandoned by the state, these openings provide opportunities for the urban poor to make the state accountable to the urban poor as well as to introduce norms of engagement where the poor are not infantilized (as is the case with most government development programs) but are seen as capable of participating in the solutions to the problems that they face. Government subsidies earmarked for the poor—for the construction of public toilets or housing for *beedi* workers, for example—that are lying unutilized have been identified and resurrected by the Alliance. The resurrection, effected through persistent lobbying and developing pilot programs, occurs on new terms however, where the beneficiaries, instead of the state and construction companies, design and produce the assets intended by these subsidies. Consequently instead of staging demonstrations, which is a risky proposition for those who live on the street, they would rather demonstrate new forms of engagement between the urban poor and the state. These are forms that do not incarcerate the poor into the subject-space of the under-developed "primitive" historically provided in projects of modernization, but provide them with opportunities to cast themselves as constituents of a democratic polity. So from the Alliance's perspective such opportunities offer the urban poor the chance to exercise what Lefebvre (1996) referred to as "a right to the city," which he understood to be maintained as not just the right of habitation but of *in*habitation; that is, of participation in the urban as a space of vibrant, creative, life-enhancing possibilities.

What their tactics indicate is what Gibson-Graham calls an "ontological reframing" (2006, p. xxx) of power that allows for a "politics of possibility" (p. xxxvii), a refusal to "see co-optation as a necessary condition of consorting with power" (p. xxvi). For pavement dwellers such engagements provide recognition that they have thus far been denied, and on terms that they themselves have created, and offer opportunities to infiltrate the categories and actions of power and inflect them with meanings that will accommodate these previously excluded populations. For them, co-optation only occurs when you stop encroaching, when you start policing boundaries instead of transgressing them. An overly punctilious attention to the rules imposed by the state and others, when seen to work to the detriment of the Alliance's constituents, usually invites a fierce reprimand, "Are we working for the World Bank? Municipality? Or are we working for the people?"

A Politics of Accommodation

The Alliance's politics of engagement, whereby they seek to transform the relationship between the state and the urban poor from one of abandonment to one of accountability, is advanced through a political formation they call federation. The federation is as much an organizational form as it is a political imaginary. As an organizational form it allows the urban poor to leverage the advantages of scale to address the state and advance their claims to *a home*. As a political imaginary it attempts to build a political space in which each of its constituents can feel *at home*.

There are several federations that constitute the National Slum Dwellers' Federation. Each federation brings together people based on the ownership of land upon which they have squatted, to collectively negotiate with the landowner for facilities (like toilets or water taps), tenancy possibilities or resettlement. The scale that the federation provides plays a particularly important role in its ability to engage the state. It is grounded in the particular, in the place-making struggles and experiences of the urban poor, and by articulating these efforts the federation expands the circuit of knowledge available to the urban poor. In doing so it challenges the discursive paradigm of development, of the "globally" informed professional and the "locally" situated poor. Additionally, the scalar reach of these federations allows for breakthroughs in negotiations and successful examples forged in one area to be adapted, reproduced, and refined across cities, states, and even countries.[6] For example, the successful resettlement of slums along the railway lines in Mumbai offered strategies and examples that were quickly adapted by federations of the urban poor in Nairobi. Further, the scale provided by the federations strengthens the Alliance's effort to negotiate for a transformation of existing institutional arrangements instead of being placated by token dispensations from the state.

While the scalar reach that is afforded by federation certainly plays an important role in its negotiations with the state, of greater political significance is the *kind* of political space that it provides the urban poor. Resonating the practice of social inclusion expressed in the Alliance's offbeat interpretation of credit exchanges, the federation model practiced by the Alliance allows its constituents to determine when and how they want to participate, creating a pluralistic polity rather than a membership cadre defined by strictly disciplined rituals of belonging. As the description of the daily savings round with Kamala illustrates, Mahila Milan's practice of savings and credit is quite distinctive, betraying little of the disciplinary intent that has made micro-credit such a popular development practice among policy-makers. Here, much to the consternation of visiting bankers and other representatives of financial institutions, loan defaulters are not penalized or "exiled." Their inability to repay a loan in time is not seen as a symptom of moral bankruptcy or profligacy, but of attenuated circumstances. It is a practice that recognizes the fluctuating circumstances of the majority of the urban poor, and whose practitioners know all too well, what can happen if one of their neighbors were deprived of the opportunity to borrow money that they needed, for each of their bodies bear the memory of such deprivation. The federation likewise is a political formation that reflects the contingent circumstances of its constituents' everyday lives.

While far from perfect, for like all political formations it is replete with tussles for leadership, betrayals, and hubris, what is significant is the kind of political space that the federation is attempting to create: one in which each constituent can feel at home. Unlike the singular subject space of populist politics, where the claim to unity is derived from a projection of a uniform community, the federation is grounded in the particular, the *paada* (neighborhood) and offers a way of imagining a political constituency pluralistically. To fully appreciate the distinctiveness of the kind of space produced in the federation it is useful to recall Young (1990) and Harvey's (1997) critiques of community. While they both recognize the progressive intent posited in notions of community leveraged by social justice activists, they argue that community based political formations ultimately founder as a vehicle for social justice, for they, like the imagined communities they oppose, are sodalities that are constituted by exclusions.

The pluralistic political space that the federation creates, on the other hand, is one that recognizes people's multiple affiliations and differences, and does not require that these be renounced or suppressed in order to be a federation member. Nor does it perceive these differences as anything other than contingent locations salvaged from the scrap heap of historical circumstance. Eschewing the relatively mono-tonal shared subject space offered by populist politics where members are bound to each other by virtue of some perceived essential sameness, the federation is a multi-hued political formation whose subjects are perceived to be works-in-progress rather than defined by essentialism. It helps that the federation itself is often referenced in terms of a process—as in "the pavement dwellers are 'federating'"—rather than as a product. Their constituency, consequently, is linked together through improvised and open-ended affiliations (cf. Caraway, 1991; Laclau and Mouffe, 1985). That is, this process of "federating" produces a political space for the cultural reproduction of subjects that is oriented toward becoming rather than belonging. The nebulous, permeable margins of different standpoints are the source of coalitions. For, recognizing the different claims to the category "federation member" necessitates moving beyond one's particular experience/standpoint (though not renouncing it) in the process of making a political "self."

In this alternative political imaginary it is not surprising therefore to find people affiliated to violently opposed political parties working together as members of the federation. When I enquired how such ideologically distinct and opposed politics were able to find a common ground I was met with rather puzzled looks, as if to ask why I thought there would be a problem. Given the ironies that structure the lives of the urban poor—where municipality demolition workers are often slum dwellers themselves, or water connections for a predominantly Muslim settlement of pavement dwellers are provided by a councillor from a Hindu fundamentalist party—my questions about their transgressions across party lines probably sounded incredibly naïve. Transgression and improvisation was their condition of living in the city. For, the associational life of the urban poor is one of *jugaad*, the creative and opportunistic piecing together of deals, exemplified by the practice of squatting (cf. Gotz and Simone, 2003). Their survival depended on such improvisations, and their politics reflected and affirmed this experience of negotiating battle lines and making deals through the creation of coalitional subjects and politics.

What we find is that, while seeking recognition as political subjects, the Alliance's praxis advances a politics of accommodation that is distinct from the abstract equalities and universalities of private citizens and public spaces, the very properties that have rendered the urban poor placeless. Through crafting a plural and permeable, that is, transformative political space and subject that is defined by becoming, they have appropriated as a critical location their displacement from the normative space of politics (one that is defined by belonging). It is a location from which to challenge the private determination of the space and subject of the public, to demand accountability from the state that has thus far abetted rather than "abated" (Marshall, 1964) this determination, and to call forth a vision of an inclusive, improvisational political subject.

Conclusion

Given the prevalence of increasingly exclusionary conceptions of citizenship that are produced as cities violently reconfigure the urban landscape to provide attractive nodes for global capital, the attempts of the Alliance to create a place for the urban poor that challenges this "politics of closure" (Hall and Held, 1990, p.175) become quite important to understand. They have sought to resolve their predicament of placelessness not by pursuing inclusion into extant spaces and subjectivities of citizenship, but by forging an alternative politics of recognition—one that is based on accommodation and becoming rather than on exclusion and belonging. They have advanced this politics by embracing the encroachment of the urban poor on the physical space of the city as a critical location, and making of this abject condition a politics of transgression that enables them to reclaim the historical subjectivity that is denied to them.

However the Alliance's particular practice of mobilization has often puzzled analysts, leading them to ask if it constitutes a social movement. Jockin, the President of the NSDF, typically lobs the question back, saying something along the lines of "Well, do *you* think we fit the definition? If we do, then I guess we are, but...," clearly indicating that he and the federation members are quite used to not being at home in the categories by which others engage the world. That is, in fact, what their politics of accommodation is about. It is a steadfast commitment to create spaces and subjectivities that those who have been expelled from the realm of the political can be *at home* in, for that constitutes their best chance of securing *a home*. If they paid heed to boundaries—physical or conceptual—their lives would be in jeopardy; their very survival depended on working the boundaries, quietly.

Their struggle is borne out of a profound sense of homelessness. By building their recoveries of subjectivity and space as *jugaad,* the creative piecing together of social relations, they reveal a canny understanding of the epistemic conditions underpinning their predicament of placelessness. It is an understanding that their lack of a home, a location from which to engage the world as historical subjects, is a relational outcome of the construction of contemporary categories of rule and terms of belonging. To pursue inclusion into this spatial order within extant terms of belonging would only serve to discipline the urban poor, not provide them with a home. To secure a home they must therefore unsettle these categories and the practices through which they derive their meaning and authority. It is thus a praxis that challenges its analysts to make of its unplaceability in contemporary formulations of social struggle a critical location, just as they have, from which to query representations of politics and their terms of recognition.

Notes

1. Cf. Ferguson's (1999) deployment of Kristeva's (1982) formulation of abjectivity. He uses it to interrogate the condition of abandonment experienced in urban Zambia as a result of contemporary economic policies, which he argues is not only a matter of exclusion, but also of being discarded.
2. Pavement dwellers know all too well that they cannot be accommodated in the sodalities of such belonging-based projects of place making. They are, after all, the sacrificial bodies of the nation, the quintessential modern project of place making, through whose displacement and dispossession the assimilative projects of "national development" and ethno-nationalism have been realized.
3. Mahila Milan and NSDF are founding members of Shack Dwellers' International, a transnational network of organizations of the urban poor. Kamala is one of many pavement and slum dwellers from Mumbai who has visited, organized, and hosted federations of the urban poor in countries across Asia and Africa.
4. The particular meaning of locality I deploy is a phenomenological one, drawing on Raymond Williams's (1977) assessment of it as a "structure of feeling" (cited in Appadurai, 1996).
5. There are also other violent political geographies of belonging that they have to contend with, such as those traced out by the Shiv Sena, a right-wing Hindu nationalist party. Hansen's (2001) account of the Shiv Sena details the way in which the *shakhas* or neighborhood branches of the party become the geographical and political grid in and through which identities take shape, the politics of belonging is negotiated, and the work of ethnic cleansing is carried out. Hansen points out that the public celebration of festivals organized by *shakha* members work to reproduce and provide interpretive frames for its political geography. Members of NSDF and *Mahila Milan,* some of whom may well have participated in the Shiv Sena's cartographic rituals, however offer another geography of the city, an inclusive one that is traced by daily savings collection routes, held in place by enumeration exercises, and fueled by the dreams of a secure home.
6. The federations are constantly engaged in peer learning exchanges where people from various informal settlements regularly visit each other within Mumbai, across the approximately eighty cities in India in which the Alliance operates, and across the fifteen countries represented in the Shack Dwellers' International.

11.

MOBILIZING AGRARIAN CITIZENSHIP
A New Rural Paradigm for Brazil

Hannah Wittman

The unthinkability of a modern peasantry stems from modernist visions of urban-centered industrial culture, and economistic visions of producers as individual maximizers in the marketplace. The Movimento dos Trabalhadores Rurais Sem Terra (MST) challenges both of these visions in asserting the rights, responsibility, and social-ecological rationality of a collectivist vision of "agrarian citizenship." This essay looks at how participation in the MST allows people to redraw historical relationships between land ownership and political power, and, by occupying unused private land and creating new spaces of social participation, the MST has revalorized agrarian steward-ship and redefined citizenship beyond a development narrative which views smallholders as obsolete.

Introduction

In traditional notions of political development and democratic change, the acquisition of civil, political, and social rights is a linear, cumulative process, as citizenship rights are awarded to members of society by virtue of their location in a particular territory. This conceptualization of citizenship is contested, with citizenship now viewed as a social process "through which individuals and social groups engage in claiming, expanding, or losing rights" (Isin, 2000, p. 5). Ideas about citizenship have thus expanded from explorations of civil and social citizenship emphasizing the relation between nationality, political rights, and social welfare (Marshall and Bottomore, 1992; Turner, 1993) to examinations of how differentiated "citizenships" are produced and transformed across space and time (Brysk and Shafir, 2004; Dietz, 1992; Isin and Turner, 2002; Yashar, 2005). For example, modernization theories predicting the disappearance of rural populations and the incorporation of labor into industrial development processes (Araghi, 1995; McMichael, 2008b; Otero, 1999; Wallerstein, 1974) have been supported by the rapid transformation of rural landscapes from subsistence to export economies. Associated changes in individual and community access to land have then influenced not only the organization of people, power, and resources, but also the social relations of identity and citizenship (Hallowell, 1943; Rose, 1994; Singer, 2000).

With almost half the world's population still living and working in rural areas, however, the resurgence of peasant organizations increasingly calls into question longstanding assumptions about the relationships between property, production practices, and political power. Rural movements reassert their physical and political relevance, demand new guarantees and political rights (Desmarais, 2002, 2007; Edelman, 1999), and call for the revaluation of agrarian culture as a "virtuous activity" (Mariola, 2005). One such group, Brazil's Movimento dos Trabalhadores Rurais Sem Terra (Landless Rural Workers Movement; MST), includes over one million members that conduct grassroots action demanding land, agrarian reform, and "a broader social transformation." The MST promotes family farm production and sustainable agriculture based on a well-developed discourse around rural rights and citizenship. Political change and rural survival are simultaneously pursued through political education and mobilization to broaden public conceptions of the responsibilities and rights associated with rural life.

The calls of rural social movements for new conceptualizations of citizenship has laid the groundwork for a new research agenda on the changing relationships between land, power, social organization, and citizenship in the countryside. For example Parker (2006) has explored the role of regulation in refining the structure of a "countryside" citizenship in the Britain, in which a rural governance regime defines how rural space is produced and consumed. Woods (2006, 2008) has called for research on how a new "critical politics of citizenship" reshapes relationships between rural citizenship norms, rural polities, and structures of power and governance. In this light, the actions of the MST are encompassed within the concept of agrarian citizenship, modeled not on the geographic location of rurality but rather on the changing political basis for agrarian social action, which includes diverse practices of production and political participation conducted within and beyond rural spaces.

This investigation of agrarian citizenship is based on ethnographic fieldwork conducted between 2003 and 2006 in Mato Grosso, Brazil, where land related policies have historically situated political and economic rights in the hands of an elite land-owning minority. This research exposes how relations between land, power, and citizenship are negotiated and reconfigured in the Brazilian countryside as a result of grassroots mobilizations around land access and political articulation by rural people. By contesting the traditional liberal links between property and citizenship, agrarian citizenship, as expressed and enacted by members of the MST, foregrounds new collective roles and rights for rural dwellers. Contemporary agrarian actors aim for the diversification of new forms of rural political and production-oriented practices when they decenter the role of land possession as the historical mediator of citizenship rights. These are designed to ensure not only the economic survival and political demarginalization of the rural poor but also a broader conception of land stewardship as a social relation that involves all members of society. In what follows, I first examine the historical development of the relationship between landholding, citizenship, and grassroots demands for reform in Brazil. I then explore how actors within the land reform movement negotiate the terms of citizenship in discursive and practical ways through alternative forms of political participation.

Land and Citizenship In Brazil

In Brazil, centuries of exclusion and discriminatory land administration laws have resulted in a contemporary system in which 3.5 percent of landowners control over half of Brazil's arable land (MDA, 2003), while the link between land possession and political power has been a formative part of society since the colonial period. Based on liberal notions of property as a principal organizer of both individual personhood and its relation to land, rights, and the state (Holston, 2008), land administration in Brazil has served a dual purpose: to ensure sovereignty over inland territory, and to ensure access to land and labor for elite sectors of society by excluding workers from direct political participation in the daily affairs of the nation. In colonial Brazil, land grants to elites with political ties to the Crown were a mark of social prestige, with the possession of property guaranteeing political voice and substantive citizenship rights. Eligibility requirements for voting established in 1822 limited suffrage to those with income from property and industry, explicitly excluding wage laborers, women, and the rural landless (Da Costa, 2000). Land possession was the basis of power and a clear territorial mechanism ensuring a "citizenship gap" (Brysk and Shafir, 2004) by limiting access to political participation.

Brazil's 1850 Land Law created a series of new obstacles to landownership for poor laborers by creating individual property rights and requiring payment for land titles (Da Costa, 2000; Silva, 1996). Civil rights were granted to landless populations not by the state, but by the *senhores da terra* (landed elite) through the social relation of *coronelismo,* or the hierarchical political relations between the rural elite and other rural people, especially those without land. *Coronelismo* used violence and patronage to control labor and votes and enforced widespread exclusion from land ownership and active political participation (Bruno, 2003; Leal, 1977 [1949]).

Reform via Colonization in Mato Grosso

The Center-West state of Mato Grosso, like much of Brazil, is characterized not only by the historical relations of *coronelismo*, but also by the ongoing displacement of indigenous peoples and migrant populations, violence around land, and extreme land concentration. Federal colonization programs transferred frontier land to national elites, in an attempt to attenuate political debate and social mobilization for land reform that accompanied the years approaching the 1964 military coup, at a time when land reform beyond anything known previously in the hemisphere had triumphed in Cuba. Through limited state investment in road-based infrastructure but little material support for agricultural settlements, state-led colonization established the illusion of governability and land distribution.

The resulting colonization projects distributed land to 60,000 families between 1940 and 1995 in Mato Grosso. Smallholder settlers at the frontier faced financial difficulties in addition to a lack of infrastructure and markets, leading to the takeover and concentration of many small settler plots by ranching interests. By the end of the 1990s the rate of plot abandonment and ongoing displacement and migration at the agricultural frontier ranged from 45 to 50 percent in state-subsidized frontier land distribution projects (MDA-INCRA, 2001). Many settlers were displaced by large-scale private agricultural development projects and ranches. In consequence, frontier land administration strategies, rather than shifting the relations of land and power in the countryside through land redistribution, actually further cemented land and political inequality while fostering capitalist development (Cardoso and Muller, 1977; Ianni, 1979; Oliveira, 1987).

To sum up, land reform and land distribution have been used as strategies in state resource administration in over 25 countries since 1900, but have largely failed to improve economic conditions or ensure political incorporation for rural residents (Prosterman, Temple, and Hanstad, 1990).[1] De Janvry and Sadoulet (1989) have argued decisively that these primarily state-led reforms failed to fundamentally shift power relations in Latin America largely because their focus on (and incentives for) agricultural modernization by large landowners consolidated the economic and political power of the rural oligarchy, thereby preventing agrarian reforms from redistributing large areas of productive land. Under the rubric of distribution, land concentration actually increased in some areas and local power relations continued to be structured in favor of large landholders, while the mobility of settlers leaving failed colonization schemes perpetuated landlessness and the easy appropriation of rural labor at the agricultural frontier.

Grassroots Demands for Land and Citizenship

By the 1980s, movements for agrarian reform in Brazil were demanding access to land as a material right linked to membership in the nation, associating the struggle for land to the struggle for social incorporation in a way that made sense based on the traditional relationship between land and power in Brazil. Over time, however, the struggle for land became more than about just access to land; it became a political starting point for "defining, deepening, and expanding alternative spaces aimed at pursuing effective forms of democratic citizenship" (Robles, 2002), in addition to the material aims of improving prospects for rural employment and food security. Politicizing the struggle for land began to challenge traditional territorial relationships between state and society, in which land access historically served as an enfranchisement mechanism.

Responding to grassroots mobilization as part of the return to democracy, the federal Brazilian government developed the first National Plan for Land Reform in 1985. The new policy included clear references to the grassroots demands for citizenship, illustrated by language that referenced the objectives of reform as not only a rural modernization strategy but also a chance to "create equal opportunities for all" through policies of land distribution and tenure regularization. In 1985, Nelson Ribeiro, Brazil's Minister of Agrarian Development, declared that the "great objective of agrarian reform is to incorporate millions of landless workers into the Brazilian citizenry" (Ribeiro, 1985). But land reform activists were careful to explain that they demanded rights to land as a function of citizenship, not as a prerequisite to it.

Their mobilization to counter the government co-optation of the grassroots citizenship discourse included gathering over a million signatures advocating for an agrarian reform clause in the 1988 Constitution. They saw in the 1988 Constituent Assembly the possibility to "install new equilibriums in benefit of a collectivity with territory as a backdrop" (Santos, 2002, p. 23). The movements were successful in instigating a public discussion of how the constitution would define the social function of land, resulting in its inclusion in the 1988 constitution as one of the fundamental rights and guarantees of citizenship. This added both discursive and legal weight to the demands of the rural land reform movements.

In Brazil, legislation linking land ownership to productive use has been an ongoing way to contest and control property. A social function clause had appeared previously in the 1934 Constitution, disappearing in the 1937 Constitution, and returning in the 1946 Constitution with reference to requiring land use to foster "social wellbeing" (Pereira, 2000, p. 109). Although liberal land legislation linking ownership to productivity dates back to Portuguese colonial law, in practice this legislation was widely ignored. By the mid-1980s, however, Brazilian rural worker's unions, the MST, and other rural social movements began to promote a concept of the social function of land that went beyond the criteria of economic production. They advocated legislation that required land use to be environmentally sustainable, economically productive, and foster equitable social relations. As related by a rural leader in Mato Grosso, these movements considered a wide spectrum of social rights to be associated with land, including:

> the right to participate, the right to leisure, schools, health, roads...all the public goods that citizens have a right to. [It is a land relation that] respects labor rights...a healthy environment preserved for future generations, and democratizes access to land. It is within this democratization that we go beyond the economic vision of productivity that the legislation talks about.... We ask "what productivity is of interest to society"? From the point of view of social gain and from the point of view of necessity, the public interest should be above purely economic interests.[2]

In response to grassroots pressure, Article 186 of the 1988 Brazilian constitution exhibits a conceptual advance in the content of the social function of land, with several specific legal criteria, including: rational and adequate use (based on legislated norms of economic productivity), preservation of the environment, and compliance with labor regulations. By legislating a land–society relation that considers community and environmental well-being (in the form of fair labor practices and environmental conservation) as equally important as individual use rights and economic productivity, the Brazilian constitutional assembly recognized that the interests of individuals do not exist separately from those of the community.

Transforming Citizenship Post-Settlement

An important component of rural struggles in Brazil is the changing perception by rural workers of land as a *condition* of citizenship to land as a *right* of an expanded citizenry. Between 1984 and 2004, the MST organized over 350,000 families in 2,200 land reform settlements in 23 of Brazil's 27 states, while since 2004 another 150,000 families have been organized in occupations and camps.[3] For MST leaders, land distribution is necessary to keep rural land in food production, and to provide jobs for the landless. But the MST also frames its struggle around "the social question" of agrarian reform, which not only involves lobbying the state for investment in programs designed to support rural livelihoods, protect the agricultural landscape, and foster local food security, but also seeks broader political incorporation.

In actions as diverse as developing a national plebiscite on the Free Trade Area of the Americas, participating in a nation-wide Popular Assembly to legislate an alternative form of popular sovereignty, and building networks of rural social movements across Latin America and globally, the members and leadership of the MST seek to enact a structure of citizenship that provides a space for all people to participate in constructing a national project while receiving the material benefits of membership in the nation. The formation of alternative ways of organizing at the local, regional, and national levels, rather than linkage to political parties or formal interaction with the legislative structure, is a key characteristic that differentiates the MST from traditional political parties and rural worker's unions in Brazil.

After acquiring land in a reform settlement, settlers are required by the Brazilian government to maintain membership in an agricultural service organization (e.g., MST or an agricultural association) to access material benefits, including agricultural credit payments, housing materials, seeds, or agricultural extension visits. Continued membership in the MST requires ongoing participation in political activities, meetings, and neighborhood groups associated with the movement. When some settlers, as a result of political differences with movement leaders, distance or formally disassociate themselves from the MST after obtaining land, they most often subsequently join one of several agricultural associations linked to Rural Worker's Unions, political parties, or Municipal Agricultural Offices.

An ethnographic examination of how citizenship action is negotiated post-settlement offers insights into how rural people characterize and contest forms of citizenship, political participation, and the rights and responsibilities associated with land. The reconfiguration of land–society relationships provides settlers with the opportunity to engage in debate and political practice over the different meanings and experiences attached to land, membership in the MST, and alternative organizations of civil society.

The Antonio Conselheiro Settlement

The following case is based on six months of participant observation in the Antonio Conselheiro land reform settlement in Mato Grosso in 2004 in addition to follow-up visits in 2005 and 2006.[4] Over 100 interviews were conducted within the settlement, half with those designated here as MST activists (settlers who have maintained active participation in the movement for more than 5 years after obtaining land in the settlement) and half with former members of the MST who remain in the settlement but no longer self-identify as members of the movement. The MST arrived in Mato Grosso in 1994, more than a decade after establishing a strong presence in southeast and northeast Brazil. The movement was in a phase of national expansion, and saw in Mato Grosso demand for rural organization combined with the highest land concentration in the country. Building on a national experience of grassroots organization based on the methods of popular education (Freire, 1970), the MST began to integrate land occupations in Mato Grosso with political education designed to foster a process of personal transformation linked to the construction of community well-being. The MST's method of organizing differed from the traditional model of rural organization in Mato Grosso, which historically had been based on political membership in rural workers' unions with strong links to political parties. One MST activist who participated in the earliest land occupations in Mato Grosso remembers:

> There were several movements here that had already organized the workers, but in a way very much about profit.... But [through the MST] they came to know and practice a new idea, a new discourse, something that was going to bring benefit for the families that organized themselves with us.[5]

Key to this statement are two important aspects of membership in the MST—a new organizational praxis, and "something that was going to bring benefit for the families." Many settlers joined the MST simply because they wanted land, and they had heard that the MST members were usually successful at obtaining it. But in the lengthy process of political mobilization leading to the legalization of a settlement, the MST delivers a program of political education about "the movement in theory." This process seeks to teach settlers how to negotiate bureaucracy through collective action to obtain the agricultural supports (land, credit, technical assistance) to which they

Exhibit 11.1 When negotiations stall with municipal authorities over release of agricultural credit and housing assistance already budgeted for the settlement, MST members organize a sit-in at city hall.

have rights as rural producers, but also situates their particular agricultural problems as small producers within the larger historical context of global political economy and the influence of neoliberal policies—including increasing government support for large-scale export agriculture and decreasing support for small farmers—on their agricultural futures.

In presettlement organizing meetings, the influence of neoliberalism on rural displacement, local food relations, and environmental degradation were key topics of discussion. By connecting the individual struggle for survival to a collective agrarian situation beyond local boundaries, this process of political education teaches the importance of a personal responsibility to act in support of the collective good, as an agrarian ideal. As an MST activist involved in organizing the Antonio Conselheiro settlement explains:

> We show the other side of the conquest of land, the social question. [Settlers] first have to learn the theory…politically who is the enemy, who isn't, to understand the political process of the whole society and how it functions. The movement goes through a process of the people conquering a space of their own, with their own force.[6]

As such, the MST activists highlight the significance of political education and conscious recognition of the roots of agricultural and social challenges as a basis for citizenship practice, rather than just the accomplishment of material objectives (land access and agricultural credit). For long term activists, the substantive transformation of agrarian citizenship goes beyond just conquering rural space, to involve a process of personal transformation that occurs through consciously informed strategic action challenging traditional power relations in the countryside that are based on land possession.

Land occupations are the most significant public acts asserting rights to rural land for members of the movement. MST activists identify a property that is deemed to not fulfill a social function—an unproductive estate, a land use that is damaging to the environment, or a plantation that uses coercive labor practices. The movement members "occupy" this land by setting up a temporary camp and school facilities and planting subsistence crops. This initial act of occupation requires the construction of a new form of social organization comprised of previously isolated individuals and families coming from different spheres of society. The structure of social organization in a land encampment challenges traditional land–society relations in rural Brazil. The Antonio Conselheiro families conducted an initial occupation of an idle ranch in 1996 and immediately formed about 40 "family groups" charged with the political and material organization of the settlement. Rather than electing one settlement leader, "nuclei" groups comprised of 25 to 30 families each elected two coordinators (one man and one woman) to sit on a settlement coordination council. The groups also elected representatives to each of the settlement-wide committees (production and environment, health, security, political formation, education, security). This organizational structure assigned each individual person a *tarefa*, a task or action that benefits the settlement as a whole, intended to foster processes of self-education and responsibility.

This way of organizing sought to ensure that political and other survival tasks "not be centered in the hands of few people."[7] It also functions as a model of decision making that breaks the history of patronage and dependency that characterized the political relationship of landless workers with the rural elites.

Antonio Conselheiro settlers remained camped for over two years waiting for the legalization of their land claim. Discussions took place among the settlers on strategies of settlement organization, models of production, and ongoing political issues facing agriculture in Brazil. The MST continued to offer courses and workshops on political education, livestock management, agro-forestry and agro-ecological systems, cooperative marketing, organic farming and reforestation, and other survival concerns, as well as organizing basic education, adult literacy classes, and improvised health clinics.

During the period of encampment families participated in intense discussions about both the political and social direction of the settlement, and divisions began to occur within the movement members that resulted in the withdrawal of over 300 families from the movement, while maintaining their physical stakes in the settlement and continuing to participate in land negotiations and camp management. Interviews with participants identified several factors in the split, including some settlers who distrusted the leadership, squabbles over organizational finances, and the influence of political outsiders offering alternative organizational options, in the form of traditional rural associations. The ongoing tensions and dialogue between these two sets of settlers over what constitutes participation, and how different forms of participation relate to the relationship between land access and responsibilities, explored in the subsequent sections, illustrates the ongoing dynamism of rural politics and the changing implications of agrarian citizenship in Brazil.

Forms of Political Participation

For MST activists, participation in monthly family group meetings was the minimum required to maintain affiliation with the movement. By planning the structure of community living in a way that integrated the physical space of settlement and daily practice of community participation, MST activists challenged a rural social structure that was traditionally based on vertical and individualized power relations. As explained by these representative quotes from the MST national newsletter and the MST-Mato Grosso workbook series used in the family discussion groups,

> In this way, democracy is no longer representative and comes to be participatory. This horizontal structure functions in circles and not from top to bottom. This thing of hierarchy doesn't have space within the MST. The participation of everyone is a way to raise the level of consciousness, to form leadership, and to exercise democracy.[8]

> No one should represent anyone else, each man and woman represents him or herself. We want to overcome the problem of representativity, of delegation of powers. It is in participating that everyone represents themselves.[9]

Group discussions centered around the political and agrarian conjuncture of Brazil and on particular questions having to do with the organization of the MST in Mato Grosso. *Cadernos de Núcleo,* or discussion guides prepared by the state organizing office, foster such questions as:

> What is the seed [origin] of our landless, camped, and settled families?
>
> What can our núcleo do to help the MST overcome its challenges?
>
> What concrete actions can the núcleo develop?
>
> What do you think of the organizational proposal of the MST?
>
> How do you evaluate the current MST State Coordinating Council?
>
> What are your criticisms of the current leadership and what are your suggestions for the next leaders?
>
> How does our núcleo act and think about a new model of agricultural development?
>
> What does our núcleo understand by resistance? What should we be resisting?[10]

These questions, also debated by all settlement members throughout the period of encampment, were intended to help settlers reconsider the way in which rural citizens take power, by consciously creating their own history. Rather than a hierarchical model in which rural workers take direction from a landed employer, the struggle for land has also created alternative political spaces in an autonomous rural settlement. In addition to núcleo meetings, day-to-day interactions toward the resolution of agricultural problems and response to political and physical threats to the settlement provided opportunity for collective discussions and action. Families also participated in occasional marches, municipal demonstrations, and in educational courses on alternative agricultural models. MST activists emphasized the need to keep collectively occupying political space after settlement. For example, at a 2004 MST workshop, an activist from the Antonio Conselheiro settlement explained:

> When I talk about our collective and organized actions, I'm talking about occupation, I'm talking about marches, I'm talking about public acts, I'm talking about the shared work (*multirão*) in the camp, the settlement, about all of the actions of struggle that we know. Through our collective and organized actions in the struggle to win land, we as landless workers rescue our right to have our own consciousness and to use it to participate in a different life. To the extent that we enter into the struggle…we begin to mark our right to be conscious of our rights. We also go on changing our role, as citizens, in conducting our own history. To the extent that we fight, we begin to occupy a geographic and political space in society.[11]

This statement emphasizes that the struggle for land is a vehicle for a broader social transformation that involves changing individual perspectives on both their roles and their rights as Brazilian citizens. In "conducting their own history" as rural citizens that not only produce food through the development of agro-ecological production models, but also come out as political participants on a national stage through "public acts," the new agrarian citizens challenge the historical conditions of the countryside in which small producers were marginalized and subjected to political patronage. Through the process of political education and political practice enacted in the social organization of the settlement and in regional organizations and movement networks, activists mark the change in their individual consciousness toward a recognition of their multiple productive (economic and political) roles within the collectivity.

By contrast, day-to-day political participation in the confrontational style of the MST was not a stated priority for association settlers, who highlighted the administrative, rather than political, function of their organizational structure. One settler explained that he moved away from the MST because the movement wasn't "doing anything for us," and thought he and his family would have a better chance of obtaining materials for their house through one of the associations.[12] Another remarked that participation in the MST wasn't "worth it," as he wasn't compensated for his political activities and needed time to cultivate his land, and that it was easier to "seek out benefits" through an association.[13] The initial dissenting association called itself "Tapirapuá," mimicking the name of the latifundio which had been expropriated for the settlement, in a sharp reminder of the political power the traditional landholding elite had over this population. The link to this name, which represented the traditional limits and boundaries of agrarian citizenship—land possession, wealth, and political power—highlighted the historical channels of power in the countryside in which progress and material assistance were most easily achieved through patronage. Rural associations involved the representation of one member of each family rather than the participation of all family members and required a monthly dues payment. Administrative meetings were held sporadically to discuss projects for credit, infrastructure, and government agricultural extension programs, and were often called to order by an urban-based politician. The associations, supported by local politicians, used material incentives (access to agricultural credit and inputs, cash payments, food, and clothing) to attract new membership away from the MST.

One president of an association, who identified himself as an MST activist before distancing himself from the movement to start his own association, sees this traditional organizational form as an effective way to achieve material gains, rather than a forum for broader political debate and discussion. For this settler, the purpose of land reform and rural enfranchisement was to provide agricultural work and economic gain, while staying politically informed through traditional channels. In the association model, the president controlled the flow of information and material resources to members from municipal political leaders in a historical form of vertical political relations. As other settlers transitioned from movement to association, they remarked upon the de-politicization of daily life and their narrowed focus on family survival and agricultural production. This mode of political participation falls more directly in line with the government-promoted rationale for agrarian reform: rural economic modernization as the centerpiece of both liberalism and developmentalism.

Agrarian Citizenship as Personal and Collective Transformation

Despite these differences in day-to-day political organization strategies and objectives, MST members and association settlers both exemplify the changing norms of agrarian citizenship in the Brazilian countryside. They do this by fundamentally challenging a land-based notion of citizenship by developing an autonomous, and sometimes internally contentious, set of settler organizations in the countryside. Now it is political organization and debate (whether via associations or MST), and autonomy in agricultural production that links settlers to their rural identity as citizens, not their exclusion from land. In this vein, a MST leader notes a fundamental difference in political work as a result of the transformative struggle for land.

> Before, it was easier for a single farmer to go and talk with the mayor, than for a worker's representative or leader. They isolated people who were struggling for the collective good. Now, collectively we put the greater good on the agenda, we pull [the mayor] out of that small circle that they have there.[14]

The ability of settler associations, whether linked to the MST or not, to engage with rural and urban policy makers stands in direct contrast to the traditional patronage system associated with property colonization in Brazilian history. This engagement stems from the learned forms of political practice and organizing strategies gained during the grassroots mobilization for land experienced by all members of the settlement. Several Antonio Conselheiro MST settlers suggested that an important factor mediating their ability to combine political activities with agricultural settlement practices and to survive as both small producers and political actors in the face of ongoing challenges to small-scale production in Brazil was the level of personal transformation that they had experienced as a result of the ongoing practical struggle to stay on the land. One activist explained: "if the body stops, the consciousness stops, it gets stagnant."[15] Another settler explained his view that some people leave the settlement altogether because of their inability to experience personal transformation:

> People who join the MST and then leave, and hang around defaming the movement, these people did not experience any social transformation. I think that people don't change because they don't want to. You have to have a lot of strength and courage and even sacrifice, because many times we have to leave things aside to enter into this struggle. If you can't do that, you will never be able to carry out a transformation of yourself.[16]

Association members within the settlement pointed out that they were more politically active than they had ever been before joining the settlement, but they were just using different strategies and tactics than currently practiced by the MST in the settlement. As each settlement member learned in the encampment and political education process, the MST's Freirian educational model seeks to engage each individual in a form of political awakening that allows him or her to recognize the historical foundations of the obstacles that have prevented previous political participation. This education is then used as a method of understanding how to overcome those obstacles. To the extent that the political awakening is incomplete, the individual remains isolated and not free, subject to continued manipulation. For settlers in the Antonio Conselheiro settlement, opportunities for this kind of informed transformation are continual: the daily opportunities to participate in settlement activities around agricultural production and negotiation of credit, the collective protection of environmental reserve areas, adult education, and literacy are all simultaneously opportunities to engage in political action. Even the occasional political or settlement management conflicts between sectors of the settlement were a new terrain upon which to settle differences, according to newly installed processes of autonomous political negotiation.

Another activist redefined activism as not just "going to the streets with flag and staff, but undergoing permanent changes in our daily life…with the objective not only immediate and material needs like land and credit but also permanent issues like citizenship and class struggle."[17] MST activists explained that settlers commonly focus first on material needs, and only later see the benefits of a transformative political model:

> In the beginning there was that strong resistance, like "No, I want my piece of land." It's that culture of property, right? Then you put a fence up…but with time you begin to realize that it's not like you thought. It's only later when you see that by yourself things just don't work, that they begin to reflect about coming together.[18]

In the case of the Antonio Conselheiro settlement, the process of personal transformation expressed by both MST and association settlers gave rise to the development of a collective consciousness, despite political differences, that is key in the reformulation of agrarian citizenship. Through collaboration between MST and association members to develop alternative agricultural practices, foster markets for local food production, and to protect a riverine reserve within the settlement, individual settlers become part of a collectivity. In MST workshops and internal debates, the idea of being "woken up" or "reborn" through political education is a common topic of discussion. But care is made to emphasize the collective nature of individual transformation. As one activist explained,

> Collective and individual reflection is one of the principles of struggle coming out of our 20 years of accumulated experience in political and methodological practice. The advancement of consciousness is done collectively, in community, as opposed to a process of individual reflection like that done in a monastery. It is done through a three-legged process of organization, political education, and struggle. Our ideas and our people are re-born every day as we move forward in the struggle that places new challenges before our conscious and permanent participation. We have the commitment to participate.[19]

Creating space for ongoing political organization and participation is a continual task in the process of reframing agrarian citizenship, and an important outcome of the process of personal transformation and the development of a collective rural consciousness. In the Antonio Conselheiro settlement in 2004, the MST undertook an active campaign to politically reorganize the settlement. Families from the settlement

Exhibit 11.2 While day to day decision making on settlement affairs takes place in family group (nucleus) or sectoral meetings, settlement members also participate in biannual general assemblies.

carried out door-to-door grassroots recruiting, recalling the initial urban work to bring people into the movement. Families who had drifted away from the movement toward association membership were encouraged to reformulate their *núcleo* groups and attend settlement assemblies to discuss material settlement needs and larger political issues. MST leaders sought to provide forums for collective debate and political action that could transcend the organizational divisions of previous years. They did so by reframing organizational goals in collective terms (e.g., accessing credit and agricultural development programs, improving settlement schools and infrastructure). In a follow-up visit to the settlement in 2006, a number of interviewed families indicated that they had reframed their daily political practices within the settlement organization as congruent with the objectives of the MST, and now considered themselves "back in the movement." What is interesting is that this seemed more a transition of discourse, rather than a change in practice. Both self-identified association members and self-identified MST members were speaking the same language of personal transformation and collective action.

In addition to issues of internal organization with the settlement and ongoing political engagement with the state and federal authorities on issues pertaining specifically to agrarian reform, settlement members have played an active role in fostering local and regional political and economic change, as part of the commitment to continued engagement in the public issues. Regular marches and demonstrations at the municipal and state level—organized by both the MST and association groups—have addressed urban worker's rights, legalization of transgenic seeds and foods, support for the local farmer's market, and improvements to rural schools and health services. Settlers have collaborated with the State University of Mato Grosso (UNEMAT) to organize an ongoing seminar on Agro-Ecology and Family Agriculture attended by over 800 local farmers and students, as well as new extension relationships with the UNEMAT Department of Agronomy. These programs foster agro-ecological production practices, the preservation of forest reserves, and the implementation of a community supported agriculture in a nearby city that supports the settler's commitment to increased local control over the food supply.

An MST activist from Antonio Conselheiro summarizes the importance of participation in a broader rural and national social transformation as follows:

> No change will exist in our country if the people don't participate. This power of mobilization is found in the willingness to struggle and in the consciousness and the organization of the people. Change requires the organization of work, it requires indignation. And we understand that this will, this desire for change by the people, needs to be woken up again and again. From the people we need to construct a new space (*terreno*), a critical consciousness, deepened within us, with our spirit of indignation. That spirit of indignation has many spaces and directions, leading to changes in reality, and changes in ourselves, as subjects of a historical process.[20]

As illustrated here, the concept of citizenship employed by members of rural social movements in Brazil is not derived from just access to land (or simply equating land possession with citizenship). Rather, it situates land-holding in a complex and changing set of social relations, rights, and responsibilities that are (re)produced through democratizing access to land, as one factor in creating space for political participation. It is a seemingly subtle but fundamental difference that begins with pre-settlement organization and continues with political education during the practice of land occupation. Rural politics in this sense moves from acquiescence to a state- or elite-directed territorial administration to, as one interviewee explained,

> to exercise participation from the smallest decisions, the small processes… in order for the small farmer to become the subject of his/her own history. The moment of conquering the right [to land] and to social rights in general, fundamental rights, leads to participation in the history of workers, the history of the settlement, the encampment, as a group and as part of society, in community and collective life and in political life…in the process of human and social development…as a citizen of society as a whole.[21]

These words illustrate the changing self-conception of rural workers and the emerging notion of agrarian citizenship. From a set of isolated individuals in rural areas, settlement members have become an organized collectivity that, despite internal political debates and differences, sees itself as part of society "as a whole." This self-conception emphasizes a strategic shift in the notion of agrarian citizenship: the implicit nature of rights and responsibilities associated with rural production and settlement becomes collective, rather than individual. This is further explained by this statement from another rural leader:

> Citizenship from an individual point of view is related to fundamental rights and guarantees of liberty, of the right to a name and title…[and other individual rights enumerated in the constitution]. But from the point of view of social advancement, of improvement in quality of life for small farmers and for the working class, for the earth and for the small ones of the earth, it is a collective project. Because from the individual point of view this confrontation [social change] is impossible."[22]

Conclusion

The preceding discussion from movement activists illustrates how changing visions and practices of citizenship enacted by contemporary grassroots actors directly contest the traditional marginalization of rural dwellers from political participation. Challenging liberal notions of the relation between property and citizenship, incorporation into the rural citizenry in Brazil is not accomplished solely through the individual acquisition of land, as demonstrated by the failure of the rural colonization projects implemented by the Brazilian government from the mid-20th century onwards to change social relations and patterns of political participation in the countryside. Instead, the grassroots vision of a particularly agrarian citizenship prioritizes the creation of new rural social relations, in which citizenship is not an assumed right but rather an accomplishment. For grassroots organizers in Brazil, this accomplishment includes using land in accordance with a social function perspective—providing food for the nation, respecting labor rights and the environment, and providing rural space for political action. Agrarian citizenship thus recognizes the agency of rural peoples in challenging the classical/liberal binaries of modernity/peasantry, landed/landless, and subject/citizen.

As shown in the contested organizational practices of settlers who acquire land through the struggle for agrarian reform, the day-to-day construction of this process of change is a complicated process. Many settlers had never accomplished political enfranchisement, with lives embedded in histories of patronage and clientelism as foundational to their perception of what is politically possible. The transformation of their personal self-vision and relation to a larger social network, through the collective struggle for land, alters the politics of the possible and broadens horizons for action. The decision to be a dissenter—even from the grassroots network that initiated that very dissent in the countryside—demonstrates that diversity is not only possible, but in itself is transformative. The ongoing debate between political and organizational strategies between MST and association members has, in the end, contributed to a vibrant rural political community characterized by debate and dissent.

This paper has paid attention to how citizenship is expressed and renegotiated around a struggle for land, reframing the meaning and practice of active citizenship in the Brazilian countryside. By unpacking the historical development of the relationship between land and power, and exploring how these relations are contested and reframed by members of land-based rural social movements, this analysis demonstrates the contours of a particularly "agrarian" citizenship. This is a form of citizenship in which rights are won and practiced not through simple presence in a rural locality but through transformative rural action, with implications for the basis of power beyond the rural spheres. As urban absentee landowners are forced to relinquish control or renegotiate relations with rural workers, the traditional land base of power erodes. Thus, a broadened conception of citizenship goes beyond a passive and hierarchical relationship between individual persons and the state, in which the state mediates the awarding of rights according to particular terms and subjectivities. These terms and subjectivities, in Brazil, have had a close historical relationship to the possession of land, as demonstrated by the long history of linking territorial adminis-tration and governing power to political enfranchisement. The new practices of active agrarian citizenship, as developed by grassroots actors through independent produc-tion and political activities, address and transform relationships within and between individuals, rural and urban communities, and the state in such a way as to challenge the assumption that access to land alone will lead to the development of new forms of citizenship and rights.

Notes

* Dedication: The author is grateful for helpful comments from Charles Geisler, Phil McMi-chael, Raj Patel, and Razack Karriem. Field research was funded by NSF Graduate Research Fellowship. An earlier version of this paper appeared in the *Journal of Rural Studies* (2009).
1. Examples of "successful" top-down land reforms include West Bengal, Japan, South Korea, and Taiwan. Successful revolutionary or bottom-up reforms include Kerala, pre-1992 Mexico, and Cuba.
2. Interview #231, CPT, Cuiabá 12/20/2004.
3. For additional information on MST land distribution figures, see www.mst.org.br and the DATALUTA Project recording land reform activity at the University of São Paulo, http://www4.fct.unesp.br/dataluta/
4. Multisited field research was conducted in Brazil during a period of 18 months between 2003 and 2006, including participant observation in nine land reform settlements, numerous meet-ings and political activities organized by settlement leaders, and over 200 interviews with set-tlers and social movement leaders. The bulk of interviews and observations were carried out in four settlements, two organized by the MST, one organized by a Rural Workers Union, and one organized by a municipal government.
5. Interview #30, 14 de Agosto settlement, 4/17/2003.
6. Interview #30, 14 de Agosto settlement, 4/17/2003.
7. MST-MT *Caderno do Núcleo* No. 9, Julho de 2002, Cuiabá—MT
8. *Jornal Sem Terra,* edicão especial May 2004.
9. MST-MT *Caderno do Núcleo* No. 9, Julho de 2002, Cuiabá—MT and *Caderno de Núcleo* no. 11, Outubro 2002.
10. Questions drawn from MST-MT *Cadernos de Núcleo* nos. 1, 9, 10. 11 (2001–2002).
11. MST activist, state workshop, Cuiabá, 12/9/2004.
12. Interview #144, Antonio Conselheiro settlement, 3/31/2004.
13. Interview #104, Antonio Conselheiro settlement, 1/29/2004.
14. Interview #30, 14 de Agosto settlement, 4/17/2003.
15. MST activist, interview #164, state workshop, Cuiabá, 12/9/2004.
16. Settler from Antonio Conselheiro, #202, MST state meeting Cuiabá, 12/9/2004.
17. MST meeting participant, Antonio Conselheiro settlement, 3/26/2004
18. interview #241, Dorcelina Foledor settlement, 6/25/2004.
19. Antonio Conselheiro leader, MST state meeting Cuiabá, 12/9/2004
20. Statement at MST Mato Grosso workshop, 12/10/2004.
21. Interview #231, CPT, Cuiabá 12/20/2004.
22. Interview #231, CPT, Cuiabá 12/20/2004.

12.
DEMILITARIZING SOVEREIGNTY
Self-Determination and Anti-Military Base Activism in Okinawa, Japan*

Kelly Dietz

Military occupation by US military forces is compounded by Japanese internal colonialism of the Okinawan people, whose self-determination struggle mirrors other autonomist and indigenous rights struggles in an age of global markets and resource competition. Struggle against internal colonial basing is simultaneously a struggle to reformulate the meaning of sovereignty and citizenship, beyond individual citizenship and toward collective rights.

Introduction

On a typically warm and humid Okinawan autumn afternoon in 1987, grocery store owner Chibana Shōichi gained instant notoriety throughout Japan and beyond when he was arrested for setting fire to Japan's Rising Sun flag at the opening ceremony of the country's National Athletic Meet. The annual event was being held for the first time in Okinawa, to commemorate the fifteenth anniversary of the end of the US military's formal occupation of the remote island territory and its reincorporation into the Japanese state. At the time Chibana said he considered the Japanese flag a "symbol of the militarism that drove many people in Okinawa to commit mass suicide." He was referring to a wartime practice by the Japanese Imperial Army, which had forced Okinawan civilians to commit collective suicide rather than face capture by Allied Forces.

A decade later, Chibana found another Japanese flag buried deep in a closet. This one was old and tattered. It was from his high school days, when he joined his fellow students in the popular movement to end the United States' postwar occupation of Okinawa. "In the 1960s, the teacher's union had a flag purchasing drive, so I bought one myself," he explained. When asked if he would burn this flag too, he shook his head. "No," Chibana replied. "I'm not going to burn it. It's different from the one raised at the Athletic Meet. This flag was intended to free me from American tyranny."[1]

The narratives above capture two historical moments of rule and militarization in Okinawa. The flag Chibana chose to keep, the flag from the 1960s, symbolized the hope he and other Okinawans had in the possibilities of citizenship during their struggle to end the US postwar occupation. Okinawans were a stateless people throughout America's twenty-seven-year rule over the islands. As a subjugated people striving for rights conferred by citizenship, theirs was an anti-imperialist struggle. What made it different from similar struggles taking place throughout the world during the same period was that Okinawans rallied under the Japanese flag in their effort to oust the US military. They sought membership in an *existing* state, Japan—the very state that had colonized their territory nearly a century earlier.

By the time of the National Athletic Meet in the late 1980s, the Rising Sun flag had come to symbolize a history of Japanese oppression for Chibana. It had become a symbol of Japan's betrayal of Okinawans in war *and* in peace. The Okinawan struggle successfully brought an end to America's post-war rule in 1972, but not its occupation. Today, 75% of all US bases in Japan remain in distant Okinawa Prefecture, which constitutes just 0.6% of Japan's total land mass. Fifty thousand US troops, their dependents, and US civilian employees maintain 37 installations on Okinawa Island alone (see map below).[2] Of its occupation-era installations that the United States forfeited, many were merely transferred to Japan's Self Defense Forces. Thus as new citizens of Japan, Okinawans became doubly occupied (see Exhibit 12.1).

Chibana's shifting interpretations of the Japanese flag and the Japanese state are important not only as expressions of his individual experience, but also for what they capture more generally. First, they embody a much broader political shift in the sixty-year long Okinawan resistance to the US military. Under US occupation Okinawans mobilized as *Japanese* nationals to force the United States to relinquish its control to "motherland Japan." More recently, however, an increasing number of Okinawans articulate a desire for greater freedom from Japan's control as well. A politicized *Okinawan* national identity animates demands for more local autonomy alongside citizens' demands for equal treatment by the state.

Exhibit 12.1 Map of U.S. military installations currently on Okinawa Island. Source: Okinawa Prefecture Military Base Affairs Division

Second, viewed in a global context, the politicization of Okinawan identity comes at a time when demands for greater ethnic autonomy are increasing around the world. Despite the apparent success of anti-imperialist movements and post-war decolonization, contemporary movements for self-determination are on the rise and span the globe: from Ogoniland in Nigeria to Nagaland in India; from Scotland and the Basque region of Spain to the Kurdish region that transverses Turkey and Iraq. Within Japan itself the ethnically distinct Ainu began making indigenous rights claims against the Japanese government in the 1980s.

Thus the kinds of claims emerging within the Okinawan anti-base movement—rooted in identities separate from the state but equally territorial—make this transitional moment within Okinawa more than just a window on the politics of US military basing in this one locale; it reminds us that the struggle over who and what would be the subject of sovereignty continues to unfold globally.

This chapter attempts to understand what links these challenges to state sovereignty to one another and to this historical moment. After sixty years of struggle against the US military, the emergence of collective rights claims in Okinawa compels us to ask: What is different about the current historical period that makes possible new ways of challenging US forces in Okinawa, and what is it about the Okinawan context that makes collective rights increasingly meaningful?

I argue that the political shift within Okinawa's struggle against US military presence sheds light on historically specific relations of rule and foreign military basing I conceptualize as *internal colonial basing*. This expresses the particular relations of coloniality that underpin America's continued occupation of the islands. Japan's fundamental relationship with its new citizens—that of colonizer and colonized—did not change, nor was it resolved through Okinawa's "reversion" to Japan in 1972. Instead this relationship of colonizer and colonized was subsumed within the Japanese state, taking the form of state and (second-class) citizenry. At that point America's occupation of Okinawa came to depend not only on Japan's compromised sovereignty vis-à-vis the United States but also Okinawa's status as an *internal* colony of Japan. US military presence in Okinawa came to rest on the categories used to legitimate military expansion within the post-war state system: state sovereignty and citizenship.

Rather than a relation through which Okinawans' rights are protected, however, their Japanese citizenship became the mechanism through which colonization and militarization shape and sustain one another. The extension of US–Japan security arrangements to Okinawa in 1972 provided a legal and discursive framework that renders the everyday effects of continued US military presence a "normal" experience of Okinawan citizenship, narrows the scope of resistance, deflects accountability away from both governments, and divides the Okinawan people. This has led to a sense of inevitability with regard to the bases. At the same time we also see profound disillusionment in the state as a rights-giving institution, and an emerging ethnic perspective on the formation of the Japanese state and its citizenship relations. New political identities, coalitions, and alternative visions of the state–citizen relation mark the increasing convergence of the Okinawan movement with contemporary self-determination movements elsewhere.

By contributing to this crisis of citizenship in Okinawa, the US military is in effect pulling the legitimating rug out from under its own presence there. Like other contemporary struggles for autonomy, the significance of the "ethnic turn" within the Okinawan anti-base movement lies in its facilitation of new kinds of claims that have the potential to re-work the state–citizen relation in Japan, and by extension the relations governing internal colonial basing.

Setting the Stage For (Re)Constructions of Okinawa

That US military presence has become a catalyst for nationalist sentiment in Okinawa is not surprising. Accounts of anti-US military base movements from Puerto Rico (Barreto 2002) to South Korea (Feffer 2001) and the Philippines (Garcia and Nemenzo 1988), to the United Kingdom (Enloe 2000) demonstrate that resistance to US military presence is often rooted in a concern over the impact of security arrangements on national sovereignty. In particular, it is rooted in concerns about basic rights and the extent to which elected representatives, or the average citizen, have any say regarding US military practices within their borders.

However, the politicization of Okinawan identity in the Okinawan de-militarization movement implies a different story and outcome from the nationalist sentiments animating anti-US military movements in, for example, South Korea, the Philippines, and even mainland Japan. In these places, nationalist sentiment is rooted in a notion of citizens' popular sovereignty and a desire to strengthen *state* capacities vis-à-vis the United States. In contrast, claims and efforts aimed at securing greater autonomy in Okinawa implicate Japanese practices of rule in ways far beyond a critique of particular administrations that bow to US pressure, or to pressures from domestic forces benefiting from the presence of US forces. Okinawan rights claims against US military presence increasingly challenge the legitimacy of the Japanese state itself; they call into question its very meaning within Okinawa's territorial and socio-political context.

Like other contested terrain where the United States has a military presence, dominant representations of Okinawans and their territory as inherently part of host nation Japan have been critical to the United States' ability to keep its military there. However, such representations obscure alternative versions of Okinawans' history as an independent people and ignore their colonial relationship with Japan.

Sixty years of postwar US military presence in Okinawa comes on the heels of and converges with a history of Japanese colonization of the once independent Ryūkyū Kingdom. The kingdom's invasion and formal annexation by a newly consolidated Japanese state in the 1870s made the Ryūkyūs one of Japan's first territorial conquests in its imperial expansion. Establishing a colonial administration in the kingdom's capital city of Naha, Tokyo imposed its education system, the Japanese language, and redirected economic outputs toward Japan (Kerr 1958).

Okinawans' colonization set the stage for their experience of the Pacific War and its aftermath. As imperial subjects of Japan, Okinawans endured dispossession of their lands, inadequate provisions, forced labor and conscription, and forced collective suicide by the Imperial Army. Toward the end Japanese leaders designated the

Ryūkyūs as a strategic buffer zone, to be sacrificed in order to protect the "mainland" (Ota 2000; Purves 2006). In the spring of 1945, the United States led the Allied invasion against Japanese forces amassed in the islands. Nearly 200,000 people, a third of Okinawa's population, perished in the bloodiest battle of the Pacific War.

By the time of Japan's surrender in September 1945, the US military had transformed Okinawa Island into a major site of operations, which it had every intention of keeping. Initially the islands were treated in the same way as Japan's other imperial conquests in the Pacific. Allied Commander General Douglas MacArthur formally separated the Ryūkyū Archipelago from the occupation's administering authority in Tokyo and placed it under US military rule. Long-term control came about through a deal with Japan's leaders. As negotiations to end the Allied occupation of Japan got under way, Japanese leaders faced ongoing US military presence in their country. They once again took a sacrificial approach to Okinawa. Emperor Hirohito and government leaders offered the United States long-term control over the Ryūkyū Archipelago in exchange for its independence and substantial US military drawdown (Purves 2006).

Having been "de-linked" from the Ryūkyūs after the war, however, the Japanese government's ability to lease its former colony to the United States depended on re-establishing Japan's claims over the islands. The Truman Administration accomplished this at the 1951 San Francisco peace talks. The United States recognized Japan's "residual sovereignty" over the Ryūkyūs while ensuring that the Peace Treaty named the United States the interim administering authority.

By the mid-1960s, US control over the Ryūkyūs became untenable in the face of widespread Okinawan resistance. But by then the United States no longer needed to wield direct control over Okinawa to maintain its bases. The already entrenched postwar institution of foreign basing provided America with a clear incentive to give up direct control over the islands: The burden of the legitimacy of US military presence in Okinawa would become Japan's, a country that had already demonstrated its willingness to sacrifice Okinawans for its own interests.

Thus what appeared to be altruistic responsiveness to local concerns is better understood as a shift in the way empire "works." America's long-term occupation of the Ryūkyūs depends not just on Japan's compromised sovereignty vis-à-vis the United States, but also on Okinawans' compromised sovereignty vis-à-vis Japan. The US bombing of Hiroshima and Nagasaki, together with its leading role in the Allied occupation and formal inclusion of Japan under its "security umbrella," contributed to America's particular post-war dominance over Japan (Dower 1993; McCormack 2007). But Japanese leaders were and are not without options, and so to portray US military presence in Okinawa as a result of US bullying of Japan is to disregard the hegemonic character of contemporary foreign military basing, particularly under the conditions of coloniality created by reincorporating the Ryūkyū Islands into the Japanese state.

Global Politics of Decolonization and the Creation of Internal Colonial Basing

Critical to an understanding of the broader conditions of sustained US military presence in Okinawa is that the official shoring-up of Japan's claims to the Ryūkyūs was part of a global process of "internalizing" colonial relations. The United Nations presided over the completion of the state system, but through a deliberately circumscribed de-colonization process. To diffuse the political momentum coalescing against colonialism at the time, the US government and other Western states involved in orchestrating post-war de-colonization under UN auspices insisted on a narrow reading of the UN Charter's central provision of the "right of all peoples and nations to self-determination." Maintaining that the entire populations of newly emerging states (at that time largely in Asia and Africa) would benefit from liberation from colonial oppression, they developed the "blue water thesis." This limited territories slated for statehood to *existing* colonized territories where political encroachment involved "organized colonization" by European powers of peoples on *distant* continents—over blue water.[3] In other words, colonization that involved crossing into adjacent territory or relatively proximate areas (e.g., nearby islands) did not count.

Efforts to limit de-colonization succeeded, and the effects were far-reaching. First, western powers effectively excluded nations situated within and across the borders of newly emerging states from participating in the expanding international community. Second, it excluded those peoples whose territories were unilaterally subsumed within settler nations[4]—North and South America, Australia and New Zealand—and other "older" established states like Japan, China, Russia, Turkey, and across Scandinavia.

Although this approach to de-colonization acknowledges and condemns the systematic way in which European powers ruled over other peoples, it dismisses the histories of invasion, colonization, and systematic discrimination of peoples within emerging and established nations. It also discounts the significance of ethnic difference, long exploited by colonial powers and now fixed within often arbitrary borders that cut across pre-colonial socio-political territories. Ultimately, a limited decolonization ignored the salience of the relationship between identity and place.

Today we see the consequences of these post-war politics of de-colonization. Emergence of autonomist claims around the globe reveals the extent to which post-war state making (and state-*preserving*) via a carefully limited de-colonization actually subsumed many colonial relationships rather than resolve them.

It is in this context that US military forces in Okinawa and other contested territories—and the popular struggles that emerge and connect under such conditions—must be viewed. By internalizing certain colonial relations, the twin processes of decolonization and state making also extended these relations into the post-war regime of military expansion, rendered legitimate through security arrangements between ostensibly sovereign states. This obscured internal colonial basing on a global scale. Japan's colonial regard for Okinawans and their territory did not change with Okinawa's "reversion"; it was merely subsumed within the state-citizen relationship. US occupation of the Ryūkyūs after reversion took the form of internal colonial basing.[5]

Hindsight offers, perhaps too easily, a critical lens on the Okinawan reversion movement, as the oppressive conditions they face today beg the question of why the Okinawan anti-US occupation movement of the 1950s and 60s overwhelmingly sought re-incorporation into Japan. The Okinawan struggle against the twenty-seven-year long US post-war occupation brought together individuals and groups from a diverse set of interests united behind two related convictions: First, that re-incorporation into the Japanese state meant protection under Japan's "peace constitution," in which Japan relinquished its right to wage war and maintain a regular standing military. Second, that re-incorporation was therefore the most expedient way to both guarantee Okinawans' basic rights and liberate their islands and lives from US imperialism. So like many other peoples who threw their lot in with a generalized "big-N" Nationalism during the anti-imperialist movements sweeping the globe at the time, the promises of protection and participation embodied in the state–citizen relation grew to have concrete, imaginable consequences for Okinawans during the formal US occupation.

Higa Yuriko, a 59-year-old anti-base organizer and peace activist explains her identification with Japan during the reversion movement in terms of the movement's political aims. Like Chibana Shōichi, she joined in the 1960s struggle to end the US occupation:

> It wasn't that I or most Uchinanchū[6] really felt we were Japanese instead of Uchinanchū during the reversion movement—though many certainly tried—especially given the way that Japan had treated us before and during the war. But Uchinanchū grew more and more willing to put those experiences behind us because more than anything we wanted the US military to leave. We wanted to be citizens…. Most of us spoke Japanese by then, and Japan was prospering…. It also had renounced war and military in its new constitution. I wanted to be a citizen of a country with a peace constitution.

For this veteran activist, "to be Japanese" did not mean to be ethnically Japanese; it meant to become a Japanese *citizen* and end America's military grip on Okinawa.

By all accounts, however, May 15, 1972—the day sovereign control over the Ryūkyūs reverted to Japan—was filled with anger and despair. Negotiations between the United States and Japanese governments stipulated that the US military would remain in the islands, bolstered by several US bases relocated from the Japanese mainland. As part of Japan, Okinawa Prefecture would also become host to Japanese forces.

Thus Okinawans' Japanese citizenship was negotiated and militarized as a *global* rather than a national relation, reflecting a particular form of compromised sovereignty. Citizenship is always both a negotiated and a militarized relation, but Okinawans' citizenship was and remains significantly constituted through interactions between the US and Japan governments and their intertwined military policies. The very terms of Okinawans' membership in the Japanese state were established bilaterally by the Nixon and Sato administrations in the course of the two countries' late-1960s "reversion talks" and negotiations over the pending renewal of the US–Japan Security Treaty in 1970. Okinawans' citizenship was predicated on continued US military presence, with their territory as the geographical cornerstone of the two countries' security arrangement.

Accomplishing Internal Colonial Basing

The intertwining of international basing arrangements and internal colonial relations creates new structures of oppression and forms of inequality through the relations of citizenship. Discursively and politically, the extension of Japanese citizenship to Okinawans facilitated what Timothy Mitchell refers to as a "new means of manufacturing the experience of the real" (1988: ix). Ideological representations of Okinawans' membership in the Japanese state justify and compel their "participation" in its security arrangements—it is their right and their duty as citizens—while simultaneously obscuring their compromised ability to seek protection from the effects of these arrangements as citizens.

Problems associated with routine US military operations and the actions of US servicemen and civilian contractors are a fact of everyday life in Okinawa. It is no exaggeration to say they are a permanent feature of local newscasts and the front pages of Okinawa's newspapers. The sheer regularity of such reports lends a peculiar mundaneness to the effects of US military presence: oil and chemical spills; destruction of habitat due to jungle warfare training and base construction; wildfires and cracks in buildings from bombing practice; stray bullets from live-fire machine gun training; installing an urban warfare training facility near a residential neighborhood; covert use of depleted uranium in bombing exercises; unexploded ordinance; pieces of aircraft and equipment dropping from the sky; an amphibious assault vehicle sinking onto a coral reef; a four-to-one ratio of water usage and garbage production by military base households compared with Okinawan households; not to mention muggings, burglary, and rape by US servicemen and contractors.

These same news reports originate from stories of Okinawan dissent. Like the incidents themselves, struggle against the bases is a part of everyday life in Okinawa. And while reincorporation into Japan did not alter Okinawans' experience of US military presence, it did change the terms through which US occupation would continue. With reversion to Japan, the representative claims of the state provided Okinawans with a new basis for claims making, and new yet circumscribed avenues for redress. The modes of struggle—demands aimed at public officials, litigation, elections, and public protest—ultimately reveal a depoliticizing effect of Okinawans' citizenship. Rather than facilitate the continuation of the pre-1972 movement to end US occupation, the provisions of citizenship served to narrow the focus of activists' claims, channeling the greater part of their energies into particular campaigns to end specific practices (e.g., bombing exercises that project ordinance across public roadways) or seek justice for specific acts (e.g., rape). While there have been countless successes in the thirty-five years since reversion, continued US military presence ensures a never-ending supply of targets for particularized claims and campaigns.

Moreover, intervening in and distorting Okinawans' efforts to seek redress is the deference both the US and Japanese governments demonstrate for their security arrangement in the Okinawan context, which makes accountability for base effects an elusive prospect. The approach both governments take to base issues is not geared toward lessening their impact as much as it is toward managing their impact so that military needs are not compromised. Providing the central framework for this is the US–Japan Security Treaty and its elaborate Status of Forces Agreement (SOFA).[7] The treaty codifies the terms in which basing matters are problematized, which in turn locates decision-making power and "solutions" at the national and international levels.

What this means in practice is most visible when high profile incidents threaten to jeopardize military operations. Such was the case in August 2004 when a large transport helicopter from the US Marine Corps' Futenma Air Station crashed in central Okinawa's urban Ginowan City. Spinning out of control before it exploded on the campus of Okinawa International University, the helicopter lost its tail assembly, a 36-foot-long rotor blade, and over thirty other pieces in the surrounding residential neighborhood.

Okinawans' anger stemmed as much from the US military's actions following the crash as from the incident itself. Without permission, military personnel immediately took control of the private campus, preventing Okinawan police, university authorities, and city officials from accessing the site. News footage showed US soldiers shouting at and using force against residents, blocking cameras and confiscating film, and entering private property without permission. Images of soldiers in full-body protective gear removing a large covered object and topsoil from the crash site fueled citizens' fears. Military officials refused Okinawan authorities' demands to investigate the wreckage. Resentment grew when, with the burned-out remains of the helicopter still on the ground and the military's own investigation of the crash ongoing, the Marines resumed flights from Futenma, citing "operational necessity" in the "Global War on Terror." Small protests occurred daily at the crash site and activists began a month-long sit-in at Futenma's main gate, culminating in a rally of 30,000 at the campus.

But Okinawans' anger was directed equally if not more so at the Japanese government's reaction. Then Prime Minister Koizumi refused to meet with Okinawan officials immediately because he was on summer vacation. Within days of the crash and before any formal investigation, Japan's Foreign Minister praised the pilots' "superior flying skills" and concluded that military actions in the wake of the crash had not violated the SOFA.

For the US Military, the crash was officially a "regrettable accident." But it also signaled more delays in the Pentagon's plans to modernize its military capabilities in Okinawa. Central to this objective is the two governments' plan to build a massive new offshore US air base in northern Okinawa's Henoko Bay, with related training sites nearby. The plan was the cornerstone of a 1996 agreement between the US and Japanese governments to "lessen the burden" of the US military on Okinawa by closing Futenma Air Station and other aging facilities. The joint agreement was hailed at the time as an altruistic response to widespread local anger after the 1995 gang-rape of a 12-year-old girl by three US servicemen. But the United States made its closure of Futenma base conditional on the completion of the state-of-the-art air base.

For Japanese leaders, the crash was officially a "horrendous accident," but also a major setback. Under pressure from the United States, the government had tried for eight years to convince or compel Okinawans to accept the new air base, which Japan was committed to funding and building for the US military.

For Okinawans, the crash and its aftermath were life under conditions of internal colonial basing. That Japanese leaders downplayed the crash and dismissed any notion of wrongdoing on the part of the United States was hardly surprising to Okinawans who long ago stopped viewing Tokyo as an advocate. "In the end, we didn't get a constitution, we got ANPŌ," explained 68-year-old Arakaki Gikei, referring to the US–Japan Security Treaty. Although the effects of US military occupation are experienced bodily and psychologically by Okinawans in their everyday lives, within the security framework "solutions" to base problems cannot be determined locally, but rather only through interstate negotiation and decision making.

In an Orwellian twist, officials from both governments cited the crash as evidence that progress on the construction of the Henoko air base is critical to the "safety of Okinawans." Although the crash confirmed the military's own acknowledgments of the dangers Futenma base poses to the residents of Ginowan—including that of Secretary of Defense Donald Rumsfeld (quoted in Takahashi 2004)—it did not lead the Pentagon to reconsider its decision to keep Futenma in operation until the new air base is complete. Nor did the crash lead to the question of whether Okinawans could or should "host" yet another massive military installation. The question remained how to accomplish it.

The Japanese government quickly set up an office near the crash site to distribute compensation for residents' property damage. The United States vowed to make its investigation public in a timely fashion. Both governments agreed to set up a joint committee to review handling of future accidents. All sides know it is only a matter of time before another incident happens. Most flights from Futenma are "touch and go" drills for combat operations. Helicopters take off, circle low over the city, touch down and take off again, repeating the drill. In other words, it is a matter of policy for helicopters to fly a few hundred feet above the OIU campus and Ginowan's urban neighborhoods (see Exhibit 12.2).

The everydayness of the effects of the bases normalizes their physical, psychological, and ecological toll as much as it normalizes the presence of the bases themselves—

Exhibit 12.2 Aerial view of U.S. Marine Corps Futenma Air Station, located in the center of Ginowan City. Source: City of Ginowan Military Affairs Division

and local resistance to them. The fact is, no Okinawan younger than 65 years old knows or remembers Okinawa without the massive US military presence and odd jumble of American cultural influences. Anti-base activist Toma Shisei evokes the bases' seemingly natural presence:

> *Uchinanchū* grow up with aircraft noise, looking at broad green lawns through chain-link fencing, going to the local A&W, and watching our aunties date US soldiers. The bases are just another part of the Okinawan landscape and Okinawan life.

In this context, six decades of foreign military occupation despite six decades of resistance has led to a palpable sense of resignation among the general public in Okinawa. Nakashima Yoshio, a 59-year-old owner of a used electronics shop near Futenma expresses his skepticism about the US military leaving:

> Will the bases go? No, I don't think so. People protest and protest. I myself protested for years, for a very long time, but I realized I could spend the rest of my life protesting and the bases would probably still be here. Of course I don't want the US military here, but now I just think, if it is going to be here, we might as well get at least some benefit from the bases.

Nakashima's sense of resignation and urge to derive "at least some benefit" from the bases speak to how little the massive US military force is perceived as a source of protection. They also suggest that the seeming inevitability of the bases has become tied psychologically to everyday needs and ambivalent ideas of how best to meet them.

Okinawans remain caught in a complicated structure of economic dependence as a result of US military presence (McCormack 2003). Direct revenue from American military presence has dropped to 5.5% of Okinawa's GDP, compared with 23% from tourism (Okinawa Prefecture 2001). However, very significant is the indirect flow of "host nation support" from Tokyo, in the form of lease payments to those whose land is occupied by the bases, payments for public works in municipalities adjacent to US bases, and capital for base construction and maintenance.[8] At the same time, US control of a significant amount of Okinawa's air, sea, and especially land distorts property values and makes impossible comprehensive development strategies. Although Okinawa was incorporated into Japan's booming post-industrial economy, its GDP and per capita income levels are lowest among Japan's 47 prefectures, and its rate of unemployment ranks highest.

The poor state of Okinawa's economy remains a key rhetorical weapon of conservative politicians and business leaders who support the Henoko plan and US military presence more generally. In particular, representations of Okinawa as dependent *on* US military presence rather than *because of* US military presence are powerful. They reinforce the lived experiences of Okinawans whose livelihood, or that of family members or friends, is somehow tied to the bases: shop and restaurant owners, car and used furniture dealers, real estate agents, employees of construction firms, employees on the bases, and so on. Although public opinion polls consistently show that the vast majority of Okinawans either want the US bases closed immediately or reduced steadily over time, Okinawans routinely elect "pro-base" officials to consequential municipal and prefectural offices.

Legitimation of US military presence is therefore not simply a state-driven process. It is also simultaneously socially experienced and reproduced by Okinawans themselves, borne of a desire to make life livable and shaped by living alongside the bases all one's life (c.f. Sayer 1994).[9] It was the promise of a ten-year, 100 billion yen ($40,000 per capita) "economic stimulus package" and the creation of jobs associated with the proposed new base that added to the ambivalence among residents in Okinawa's rural, impoverished northern region. Competing images of a re-energized, vibrant region on the one hand, and the continuation of a base-entrenched resource-siphoning stagnant economy on the other, amplified social divisions over the issue.

The US and Japanese governments count on this kind of ambivalence to continue to hold sway in prefectural elections and more generally. When the effects of the bases cannot be managed via everyday forms of accommodation, however, both governments know Tokyo has the option of exchanging carrot for stick. The politics surrounding the Henoko plan epitomize how US military presence is also maintained via a complicated arrangement of political coercion and exclusion, conditional economic inducements and the ability to create divisions within the Okinawan community.

Okinawan Governor Ota Masahide had been elected on an anti-base platform, and in the wake of the 1995 rape, he refused to act in his role as proxy signatory to renew leases on private land occupied by US bases. Tokyo sued Ota and pressured him into signing the leases the following year, but the central government ensured that such democratically inspired actions by Okinawa's future governors would be impossible. It pushed through a new law permanently transferring the renewal of Okinawans' land leases to the Office of the Prime Minister.

When Ota then rejected the Henoko air base project, the central government abruptly cut off all communications with the Okinawan government and postponed payment on the economic stimulus package it had promised Okinawa's northern region. Only after Okinawans elected as governor a Tokyo-backed Okinawan businessman who was more amenable to the new base was the economic package reinstated (Yonetani 2001).

By then a multi-pronged campaign to stop the construction of the Henoko base was under way in Okinawa, spurred on when Tokyo (and Washington) ignored the results of a 1997 local referendum on the new base, in which the majority rejected the proposal. The campaign has engendered litigation in Japan and the US, formal condemnation in international fora, and sustained non-violent civil disobedience at Henoko. If built, the installation would be the 38th US military base in Okinawa. It would stretch 2.5 km across the tip of Cape Henoko, involving massive land reclamation of the bays on either side. These waters are the primary habitat of Okinawa's critically endangered *dugong* (sea manatee) and several other endangered species (see Exhibit 12.3).

The US government's stance regarding the Henoko project is the same it takes in all conflicts regarding its bases in other countries, which is to distance itself officially

Exhibit 12.3 Protesters (in wet suits) occupy a drilling platform to stop workmen (with hardhats) from building drilling platforms that would be used to survey the bottom of Henoko Bay in preparation for building the new U.S. air base. Private security observe from a boat in the foreground. The campaign against the offshore air base has combined a decade of non-violent civil disobedience at Henoko with litigation and other forms of popular protest locally, nationally and internationally.

and especially legally from the base construction.[10] Portraying the new base as a Japanese government project may allow the US to evade legal responsibility for the impact of the construction, but it must rely on the Japanese government to push the project through. So far Tokyo has gone to great lengths to do so, which it justifies with reference to the US–Japan Security Treaty, including violation of its own environmental protection laws within Okinawa (see Yoshikawa 2009).

For over a decade activists have managed to prevent any real progress on the Henoko project. In an unprecedented development, sustained and widespread opposition to the air base and the delayed closure of Futenma Air Station forced the US and Japan back to the negotiating table in 2005. But instead of abandoning the project, the two governments unveiled new plans that provide not only for the initially proposed Marine air base but also a naval port that will extend into neighboring Oura Bay. However, this "new" plan, Okinawan activists were quick to point out, is in fact a very old one. A 1966 US military map reveals that the proposed expansion is nearly identical to a plan the US devised during its formal occupation of the islands. What the US was unable to do (or unwilling to fund) in the final years of its earlier occupation, it is attempting to accomplish via the relations of internal colonial basing.

And so Okinawans' struggle against US military presence continues, gradually exposing the contradictions in a post-war regime of foreign military expansion framed in terms of state sovereignty and citizenship but rooted in colonial relations. Challenges to state sovereignty that are emerging within the Okinawan anti-base movement reveal the unraveling of the assumptions and accommodations of the state–citizen relation under conditions of internal colonial basing. The struggle over the proposed Henoko air base is Okinawa's most significant single campaign in decades. If realized, it will be the first new major US military installation built in Okinawa in nearly fifty years. But this campaign is being waged alongside countless smaller campaigns, and drains immeasurable resources (time, money, energy, spirit) that would likely be channeled toward more comprehensive ends. This fact is not lost on Okinawan activists themselves. It is in their deliberate efforts to not lose sight of the larger struggle for an alternative future for Okinawa that we glimpse the more profound implications of foreign military presence in contested territories.

From Second-Class Citizens to Okinawan Subjects

The strongest tendency among Okinawan activists is still to seek redress via the institutions and rights associated with citizenship. However, Japan's complicity in Okinawans' experience of US military presence has become more central to their analysis, evoking an ethnic perspective on the Japanese state and US occupation. The politicization of Okinawan ethnicity is reflected in new political identities, new alliances, and novel rights claims that express alternative visions for Okinawa's future.

Politicizing their ethnic identity in the current conjuncture has provided Okinawan activists with a broader basis to interpret and challenge their political position vis-à-vis the United States and Japan. Specifically, it makes possible the emergence of claims rooted not in rights conferred by citizenship but by new political identities. Okinawan activists are variously interpreting Okinawans' experience under US military presence in terms of their collective identity as an *ethnic minority* politically and socially displaced within Japan; as a *nation/people* historically connected to the Ryūkyū Islands and ethnically and culturally distinct from the Japanese; and as an *indigenous people* denied their right to self-determination. Taken together these identities and claims imply a global analysis of local circumstances. While they can only emerge out of a strong attachment between a particular people and place, they rest fundamentally on an ability to locate Okinawans' particular history and circumstances within a world-historical context that exposes the imperial dimensions of the state system.

This global analysis is expressed in Okinawan anti-base activists' alliances. Although Okinawan activists' frequent exchanges with anti-US military activists in the region (e.g., South Korea, Guam, and the Philippines) would presumably center on the immediacies of base problems, interviews suggest that this is not the only or, for many, even the primary basis for their solidarity. Instead, these ties are informed as much by a sense of shared experience in relation to Japanese imperialism and its historical intertwining with US imperialism. Exchanges and actions with Ainu and Korean activists within Japan also rest on shared experiences of Japanese imperialism, ongoing ethnic marginalization, and (with the Ainu) a desire for greater autonomy.

Political identities like "indigenous peoples" and "minority" provide Okinawans not only with new political partners but also new venues which, if not concrete means of redress, allow them to create additional political space for telling an alternate version of the history and contemporary circumstances of the Ryūkyūs. Beginning in 1996, Okinawans joined Ainu and other self-identified indigenous activists from around the world to challenge internal colonial relations in venues like the UN and other international fora. Together with the Ainu, Okinawan activists are intervening in dominant representations of Japan as a mono-ethnic and historically and territorially coherent nation-state (Siddle 2003).

Although the international caché of the term "indigenous people" itself has been slow to catch on among Okinawa's broader activist community,[11] members of the Association of Indigenous Peoples in the Ryūkyūs (AIPR) see merit in the interventions it allows Okinawans to make outside Japan. AIPR member Oyakawa Yūko explains how the concept of indigenous peoples helps others "make sense" of the problems of US military presence in the Okinawan context:

> The US bases are the immediate cause of so many day-to-day problems in our society. So when we have an opportunity to speak to people outside Okinawa, we must let them know what is happening here. No one really knows. But we also must explain *why* it is happening here. No one knows that Okinawans are a different people or that Okinawa was once independent. Most think Okinawa is Japan, and Okinawans are Japanese. But a lot of people outside Japan know what "indigenous people" means. So when we talk about our situation and say, "This and this and this are happening in Okinawa because of the US military bases," people are always surprised. When we explain that Okinawans are not Japanese but an indigenous people in Japan, suddenly our situation makes sense to them. The term "indigenous peoples" is a kind of global code.

Another effort in recent years has brought together activists, policy makers, and scholars over a common recognition of Okinawa's ethnic and historical distinctiveness to lay out, concretely, a vision of what a self-governing Okinawa might look like (Okinawa jichi kenkyu kai 2002, 2005). Established as the Study Group on Okinawan Self-governance—*Okinawa jichi kenkyu kai*—the group is systematically considering different forms of "home rule" and self-governance, seeking inspiration from other "internalized" territories such the Äland Islands (under Finland's jurisdiction) and even Scotland. For Jichiken members, central to greater territorialized autonomy in Okinawa would be to reclaim Okinawa's right to negotiate its own diplomatic relations (*gaikōken*)—now only a right of states—in order to negotiate with the US government directly (*Okinawa jichi kenkyu kai* 2004).

The alternative future that most Okinawan anti-base activists seek does not, at least for now, involve independence. Most speak of a form of territorialized autonomy like that sought by Jichiken members, via which Okinawans would have greater political, cultural, and economic control over the islands than the central government.

What are the implications of such a vision and of emerging collective rights claims, both for the state–citizen relation and for the presence of US forces in Okinawa? The answer lies in the historical moment. Self-determination movements in the past challenged the relations of colonialism. Contemporary collective self-determination claims, however, have the state as their object of struggle. They challenge the exclusionary processes in the liberal project expressed in the modern state and, by extension, in the modern state system as governed by the relations of empire.

Although counter-intuitive, by seeking to re-work their relationship to the state rather than pushing for independence, Okinawans and their counterparts making similar challenges elsewhere present the greater challenge to state sovereignty. They seek to re-work the state–citizen relation, rather than reproduce it. To be sure, truly separatist movements pose a threat to the territorial and political integrity of states. However, because the resulting polity would most likely take the nation–state form (e.g., East Timor or Eritrea), this scenario merely re-inscribes the state form and hence the state system. In contrast, non-secessionist autonomist movements (e.g., Nunavut, Chiapas, or Okinawa), have the potential to fundamentally re-work the state–citizen relation. Rather than reproduce the state as such, the challenges animating the Okinawan anti-base movement reflect a desire to re-configure its imperial dimensions.

The Okinawan de-militarization struggle thus problematizes the very premises legitimating US military presence, namely, sovereignty and citizenship. By contributing to this crisis of citizenship and efforts to re-formulate sovereignty, the United States is jeopardizing the legitimating apparatus it has relied on for thirty-five years.

Conclusion

By articulating a form of territorialized collective autonomy within Japan, a growing number of Okinawan activists subvert the idea that individual liberal subjects are the building-blocks of the state. Called into question is the notion of the state as the only repository of sovereignty and guarantor of rights. Rather than rejecting citizenship altogether, however, Okinawans are challenging citizenship as governed by the relations of internal colonial basing. Furthermore, the struggle to demilitarize sovereignty in Okinawa resonates with movements elsewhere, reformulating citizenship rights in historically concrete terms that challenge the abstract rights of the liberal subject, and politicize the meaning of sovereignty.

As I have argued, such re-working proceeds on two related fronts: first, identifying the coloniality of power embedded in the process of state system completion under UN auspices, and second, exposing the articulation between coloniality and militarization of the state system under US hegemony. The latter relationship is the stimulus for a more fundamental post-colonial critique of the liberal narrative informing modern citizenship, a critique animating movements for collective rights to territory, culture, and resources.

Notes

*   Dedication: I am grateful to Gillian Hart, Philip McMichael, Jackie Smith, Alicia Swords, Sidney Tarrow, and Shelley Feldman for their helpful comments on earlier versions of this essay.
1. I thank Chibana Shōichi and Okinawan photographer Ishikawa Mao for sharing this story with me. Ishikawa highlights Chibana's shifting relationship to the Japanese flag in her series of photos, *What the Japanese Flag Means to Me* (1995–1999).
2. The US military also controls 29 maritime zones and 20 air spaces around the small island prefecture. Okinawa Island stretches just 70 miles (112 km) north to south, and is 13 km at its widest part.

3. For governments arguing for a limited de-colonization, particularly those from North, Central, and South America, a more open interpretation of the right to self-determination would have had implications for the sovereign peoples within their own respective borders.
4. The terms "settler state" and "settler nation" are used in scholarship and discourse on indigenous rights. It denotes those countries that were colonized through massive settlement of people from the colonizing country rather than ruled from afar via a cadre of colonizers and local elites.
5. Of course, for those who view themselves and their territory as sovereign in relation to the state within whose borders they reside, "foreign" military presence includes the military forces of the national government. In the case of Okinawa, Japan's Self-Defense Force (SDF) has a small presence in the prefecture relative to US forces. It is worth noting that Okinawan anti-US base activists, especially those who desire greater autonomy from Japan, are equally determined to oust the SDF.
6. *Unchinanchū* is the Okinawan term for a person and the people of *Uchinaa*, the largest and most populated island of the Ryūkyū Archipelago, Okinawa Island. Even though all but the oldest Okinawans primarily speak Japanese, everyday speech of most is peppered with the Okinawan language, and most use the term *Uchinanchū* rather than refer to themselves in the Japanese language. Although the rest of the Ryūkyū Islands are subsumed under the name "Okinawa Prefecture" and their inhabitants are "Okinawans" in Japanese and in English, the archipelago is multicultural and multilingual.
7. The treaty obliges both parties to resist armed attack and to assist each other in case of attack on Japanese territory. The treaty's "Status of Forces Agreement" governs the legal status and elaborates far-reaching rights of US military personnel within Japan.
8. Public works constitute 90% of Tokyo's funding to Okinawa (Mitsuyoshi 2000, cited in Yonetani 2001: 92). But spending figures can be misleading. One consequence of reversion was the gradual dominance of Okinawa's construction industry by large Japanese corporations. The biggest US contracts typically go to Japanese or multi-national defense firms, like Halliburton.
9. Sayer's insight draws on the notion that state power comes from the implicit threat of coercion, rather than overt coercion. Although citizens may not consent to a state project, to make their everyday lives bearable they routinely enact the practices that sustain the project. Through such collaboration, the individual and the society become disempowered in ways that state reliance on overt force may never accomplish.
10. A landmark 2005 ruling by a Ninth Circuit federal judge in the aptly named case *Dugong v. Rumsfeld* rejected the Pentagon's attempts to deny involvement in the Henoko plan. The trial is pending.
11. The problem appears to stem from preconceptions of the term as a descriptor of a particular way of life, rather than as a political position vis-à-vis states. AIPR member Toma Shisei suggests that "too many associate the term with hunter–gatherer traditions, which isn't compatible with Okinawans' understanding of our traditional lifestyle."

13.

DECOLONIZING KNOWLEDGE

Education, Inclusion, and the Afro-Brazilian
Anti-Racist Struggle

Alexandre Emboaba Da Costa

Examines Afro-Brazilian struggles to establish a municipal education project that re-values forms of knowledge, embodied learning, and values produced in and through Afro-descendant communities. In revaluing Afro-Brazilian cultures as sites of knowledge production, their efforts go beyond address-ing inequality through inclusion into an already defined system to develop alternative notions of citizenship. Rather, they challenge racial inequality by developing other ways of understanding history, progress, and collectivity. As such, their politics challenge unequal histories of power underlying the very meaning of knowledge that counts in understanding the making of moder-nity, race, and development.

All of you already know that I am a defender of inclusion in its most diverse manifested forms, whether it is the inclusion of handicapped individuals, or the inclusion of excluded people for whatever social reason. I am a fighter for the cause of education.

Riberião Preto's Education Secretary, Inauguration Ceremony of the Projecto Baboá[1]

Practice shows us that racist thought, even when it talks about integration, about the accep-tance of diversity, of accepting those who are different, in most cases colludes to eliminate those who are different, to exterminate black as black and accept them as an individual whose difference appears merely in the color of his skin or in his colorful clothing.

Paulo Oliveira, President, Orùnmilá Cultural Center

Introduction

Cultural diversity, multi-culturalism, inclusion, difference: Since the 1990s in Latin America, these words have entered vocabularies with newfound enthusiasm, ini-tiating constitutional reforms and social policies. Governments have responded to growing demands for racial and ethnic equality by Indigenous and Afro-descendant populations with efforts in relation to issues such as land claims, education, employ-ment, and health. The bases of Indigenous and Afro-descendant claims are often tied to cultural rights and a critical examination of the past, as these groups seek poli-cies to redress centuries of inequality, disadvantage, and cultural domination. In Brazil, Afro-descendant[2] movements have not only sought to address racial inequality through better access to and improvement in education. They have also targeted how, historically, the devaluing of their forms of knowledge and cultural practices underlie the exclusion of Afro-Brazilian history and culture from the school curriculum and classroom. These exclusions have, over time, contributed to the reproduction of racial hierarchies in the social, cultural, and economic spheres.

This chapter explores contemporary Afro-Brazilian anti-racist struggles in education over the terms of multi-cultural policies of inclusion and diversity in a neo-liberal development context. These struggles aim to reshape education and build substantive citizenship and racial equality. They concern the terms on which Afro-Brazilians are included, and how some power hierarchies may be challenged and others reproduced through anti-racist educational projects and associated actions. Exploration of these questions in the Brazilian context also considers their implications for the broader project of decolonizing education, knowledge, and development in other settings.

The focus of analysis is the anti-racist politics of the Afro-Brazilian Centro Cultural Orùnmilá (Orùnmilá Cultural Center) and their Projeto Baobá (Baobab Project). This project aims to include substantive African and Afro-Brazilian history and culture in the school curriculum and classroom. The philosophy and content of the Projeto Baobá engages with Afro-Brazilian ancestral knowledge in order to "decolonize" education in Brazil. To decolonize education is to question the dominant worldview, or knowledge, shaping conventional notions of societal progress and development, and to transform the content and practice of education. The goal of this struggle is to overcome the limits of a neo-liberal understanding of difference and inclusion via "multi-culturalism." This neo-liberal understanding facilitates more equal participation in market society for excluded "minorities," as opposed to more equal representation of their history and culture in the education system as a means to transform society.

Orùnmilá activists contest the limits of official conceptions of inclusion implied by a discourse of "multi-culturalism," proposing instead a *critical* multi-culturalism that would introduce themes that substantively draw upon Black culture and knowledge in educational curricula and establish respect for Afro-Brazilian history and culture. Rather than treat cultural diversity as an abstract good or inclusion as the superficial incorporation of marginalized groups, critical multi-culturalism engages hitherto devalued cultures and excluded forms of knowledge as building blocks for constructing new understandings of pedagogy and social collectivity. In this way, critical multi-culturalism both re-values the substance of excluded cultures and draws upon them to challenge institutionalized practices and values that reproduce hierarchy and inequality.

The Struggle for Substantive Inclusion

The opening quotes above express two contrasting perspectives on questions of diversity and inclusion held by state representatives on the one hand, and an Afro-Brazilian activist on the other. Their concern is with Brazilian Federal Law 10,639, passed in

2003, which mandates the teaching of African and Afro-Brazilian culture and history in the school curriculum. The Orùnmilá Cultural Center has struggled to implement this law in their home municipality of Ribeirão Preto, in the state of São Paulo. They designed the Projeto Baobá to accomplish this goal through transforming the school curriculum to include African and Afro-Brazilian history and teach Afro-Brazilian cultural practices as forms of knowledge and sites of knowledge creation and transmission.[3]

Despite the education secretary's enthusiasm and crucial support for the project, and his proactive approach to inclusion in education, at the Projeto Baobá's inauguration ceremony he acclaims its importance through an ambiguous, generalized discourse of inclusion and diversity. By placing Afro-descendants as one group among many types of excluded peoples, he generalizes exclusion and discounts the specific history and experience of Afro-descendants that warrants a law like Law 10,639. The vague language of such discourse discounts concrete discussion of racial inequalities and their impact on the educational system in which people are meant to be included. In contrast, the quote from Orùnmilá's *Sorò Dúdú* newspaper[4] questions the implications of inclusion for Afro-descendants into an education system structured around cultural and racial inequalities.

Paulo Oliveira, Orùnmilá's president, suggests that inclusion and integration of Afro-descendants into unequal power relations turns difference into something merely skin deep, ornamental (e.g., colorful clothing) or cosmetic, as opposed to engaging with the knowledge produced through experiences and cultural practices within Black communities. Cosmetic acceptance of difference and diversity reproduces rather than addresses racial inequality within Brazilian educational institutions and society more broadly. This perspective informs how the Orùnmilá Cultural Center redefines the meaning, content, and practice of education through their cultural work to reconstruct inclusion for Afro-descendants on substantive grounds.

Historically, Brazilian development patterns and formal education marginalized the multiple forms of knowledge, and corresponding values, practices, and understandings of community and development present among its diverse population. The struggle to teach African and Afro-Brazilian history and culture in the school curriculum aims to redress absences as well as deconstruct representations of Afro-descendants that devalue their culture as folklore and perpetuate a racial hierarchy that reinforces prejudice and inequality. These efforts reveal how dominant values displace other ways of being and learning, and underline how they narrow opportunity and welfare for minority communities. Diversifying both curriculum content and classroom pedagogies establishes the basis for multiple, alternative, or "other" possibilities for organizing knowledge, and thus reorganizing society to respect difference and promote opportunity.

Education researchers and Afro-Brazilian activists work on two fronts against racism in the formal education system and its exclusionary consequences. On the one hand, efforts target everyday racism in the school space (classroom, playground, etc.), the lack of positive representations of Africa and Afro-Brazilians in school textbooks, and the superficial treatment of the role of Afro-Brazilians in shaping the nation. At the same time, scholars and activists argue for incorporating Afro-Brazilian cultural practices into school curricula. These practices, they argue, affirm the diversity of knowledge production and transmission, or ways of learning and knowing.[5] In their view, drawing creatively on this excluded knowledge can both re-value Afro-descendant cultures and diversify the methods, epistemologies, and foci of the curriculum ("Centro Cultural Orùnmilá e a 10,639," 2006).[6] The overall aim is to redress negative, limited, or stereotyped representations of Afro-Brazilians and their historical contributions to the nation, at the same time revaluing Afro-Brazilian knowledge and culture. The purpose of this struggle is twofold: first, to reduce racial inequality inside and outside the classroom, and second, to assert that more than one form of knowledge is necessary for democratic social development.

Coloniality of Power, Knowledge, and Blackness in Brazil

Colonization and colonial projects of rule in the Americas involved a cultural classification of peoples and their incorporation into hierarchical capitalist relations (Mignolo, 2000; Quijano, 2000). Colonizing epistemologies organized the production of knowledge about places, peoples, and their cultures. The "colonial difference"—the classification of different cultures, peoples, and their corresponding geographies—was translated into values expressing levels of humanity, civilization, progress, and development (Mignolo, 2000). Together, forced subjugation and its legitimations shaped hierarchical systems of racial and cultural classification that attached roles and places within the division of labor to categories of people—Spanish or Portuguese, Indians, Blacks, or Mestizos. These designations shaped control over productive resources while also defining attributes associated with Whiteness—high status, education, development, modernity, and ownership of capital—and that associated with Blackness—slavery, inferiority, low status, cultural backwardness, and manual labor.

In this process, Afro-descendant cultures, symbolic universes, and models of community and meaning making were either assimilated, defined as inferior, or folklorized. Overall, the construction of modern/colonial Latin America involved,

> [1] the conversion of the knowledges of colonized peoples and of the diversity of their cultures and cosmologies to expressions of irrationality, of superstition, or, at best, to practical and local forms of knowledge whose relevance was dependent on their subordination to modern science, [which was] perceived as the sole source of true knowledge, or to religious conversion or acculturation; [2] the subordination of their customs to the law of the modern state and of their practices to the capitalist economy; and [3] the reduction of the variety of their forms of social organization to the state/civil society dichotomy (Santos, Nunes, & Meneses 2007, p. xxxiii).

The coloniality of power and knowledge produces and values certain cultures and understandings of the world, representing them as superior and desirable forms of social organization and progress. Integration into European colonialism and the imposed demands of Eurocentric development devalued the knowledges and practices of Afro-descendants because they did not produce wealth, status, or monetary value within the paradigm of capitalist development. Consequently, through coloniality, Blackness and Afro-descendant culture took on negative and static meanings.

In Brazil, these negative and static meanings associated with Blackness were shaped by ideologies of whitening (or *embranqueamento*) and racial democracy. Social classification and discrimination has been, and remains, highly correlated with color as individuals were historically classified based on phenotypic appearance and the "degree of cultural 'whiteness' (education, manners, wealth) he was able to attain" (Skidmore 1993, p. 40). Early twentieth century elite and governmental proposals to "whiten" the population reflected beliefs that the large Afro-descendant population (and their culture and Blackness) presented a problem for the nation's social, economic, and cultural development and modernization. European immigration, racial intermixing (where whiteness would eventually eliminate Blackness), and cultural uplift (hygiene, education, literacy, etc) shaped ideologies and practices of whitening that sought to eliminate traces of the "Black race" (Hanchard, 1999; Moura, 1988; Skidmore, 1993). This included Black cultural practices that did not fit the portrait of modernity.

In the 1930s, proposals for explicit whitening gave way to "racial democracy," the idea that racial and cultural mixture (*mestiçagem*) was a positive national trait for producing harmonious race relations and a modern civilization in the tropics. Together with scholars and intellectuals of the time, President Getúlio Vargas's regime (1930–1945) promoted an aggressive nationalism that embraced racial and cultural mixture as a means to integrate the Brazilian people and promote a vision for a racially tolerant nation (Davis, 1999; Telles, 2004).[7] On the one hand, "racial democracy" defied the bind that scientific racism's negative assessment of Blackness and race mixture placed on Brazil's future development. On the other hand, racial and cultural Blackness remained markers of inferiority because racial democracy fetishized the *form* of Afro-Brazilian difference, disregarding its *substantive content*. In other words, notions of racial mixture appropriated Blackness to produce the ideal, mixed-race Brazilian subject (the *mestiço*). Yet coloniality continued to articulate Blackness as a signifier of inferiority in the Brazilian imagination (Pravaz, 2008; D. Silva, 1998).

The whitening bias persisted. European cultural superiority remained presupposed and Blacks were relegated to "subjugated collaborators" as opposed to equal partners in constituting the ideal national subject (D. Silva, 1998, p. 221). Social development was associated with proximity to physical and cultural whiteness where assimilation and mobility for Afro-descendants required avoiding or masking racial and class appearance and cultural traits and practices constructed as negative[8] (Guimarães, 1995; Moura, 1988; Vargas, 2004). At the same time, the state increased its management of Afro-Brazilian culture, promoting particular forms like samba, capoeira, and Candomblé as "national culture."[9] The promotion of these forms stood as proof of Afro-Brazilian inclusion in the nation,[10] despite such a folklorization of Afro-Brazilian culture and the lack of substantive engagement with Afro-descendant community practices. At the same time, in comparison with Whites, Afro-Brazilians lacked access to educational and employment opportunities that provided a means to socio-economic betterment. Racism, discrimination, and unequal access in education and employment have played a large part in the ongoing reproduction of racial inequality. Consequently, despite positively revaluing racial and cultural mixture to emphasize unity and inclusion, the ideology of racial democracy enabled certain practices of racial exclusion and discrimination to persevere. Thus, the particular ways Afro-Brazilian inclusion was managed contributed to the maintenance of racial inequality.

Recently the turn to multi-culturalism continues to reproduce racial and ethnic inequalities, despite the recognition of cultural difference and rights. Government policies recognizing cultural rights do not fully address historical experiences of inequality. Like the delimited inclusion produced by racial democracy, the implementation of multi-cultural education policy may acknowledge Afro-Brazilians and their history and culture, but without actually questioning or transforming curriculum content and classroom pedagogies and thus the value given to historically marginalized knowledges and cultural practices. Multi-culturalism celebrates cultural difference and diversity, but often as supplementary elements existing within a broader societal structure defined by historically dominant ethnic or racial groups and their worldviews. In other words, the recognition of racial inequality and Afro-Brazilian cultural rights does not in itself legitimize Afro-descendant ways of being or viewing the world. Accordingly, states use multi-cultural policy in their struggle to accommodate growing demands for collective rights by formerly excluded populations (e.g., Afro-descendant and Indigenous) without undermining the neo-liberal project of development (Hale, 2002, 2005; Walsh, 2002; Žižek, 1997). In fact, in Latin America, multi-cultural constitutional reforms and discourses geared to strategies of inclusion reinforce neo-liberalism's emphasis on expanding market opportunity (Speed & Sierra, 2005; Hale, 2002, 2005). In this way, the neo-liberal form of multi-culturalism reinforces the social order by accommodating certain claims by oppressed populations for citizenship without addressing underlying historic racial, ethnic, gender, and class hierarchies.

As Paulo Oliveira's introductory quote indicates, neo-liberal-style multi-culturalism perpetuates a subjugated, rather than substantive form of inclusion of Black and Indigenous populations into national development projects.[11] Afro-Brazilian anti-racist struggles therefore ask: How can public policy work toward integrating Black Brazilians in substantive ways that recognize and incorporate historically different cultural experience to produce a more equal society? This is the task set by the Orùnmilá Center and its Projeto Baobá.

Reproducing Coloniality through Curriculum and Classroom

Curriculum content and students' everyday experiences in Brazilian schools legitimate cultural and racial prejudice in ways that reproduce the coloniality of power. Teachers' differential treatment of white and Afro-descendant students based on associations of skin color with behavior and academic ability reproduces the naturalized associations such treatment presupposes. Also, Afro-Brazilian children's schoolmates subject them to "nicknames, name calling, and mockery [*ironias*] [that] consolidate and perpetuate latent prejudices and discrimination" (Cavalleiro, 2005, p. 14). In relation to curriculum content, educational texts include deprecating representations of Afro-descendants as subservient or occupying demeaning social positions, and as passive subjects of national history[12] (Cavalleiro, 2001). Humanity and citizenship are represented by the middle class white male, while women, Blacks, and Indigenous people's existence are identified by their gender and skin color. At the same time, associations of Afro-Brazilians and Blackness with incompetence, dirt, and ugliness (e.g., Black hair as "bad hair"),[13] poverty, passivity, and slavery persist (A. Silva, 2005; Lima, 2005). These stigmatized representations and associations affect how both Black and White children learn dominant understandings of race and Blackness.

André, an Orùnmilá member and President of the NGO Memórias Vivas [Living Memories] articulates how one-dimensional curricular representations frame conceptions of Afro-descendants and naturalize the subaltern status of Afro-Brazilians. But he also reveals another element:

> Today in schools we see teachers say that Blacks were slaves, that Blacks were beaten and punished, that Blacks worked in the sugarcane fields. This is what we see. [The content] is very limited, you know? If they could, they would remove it [from the books]. They would even forget that the "Other" was enslaved. This is what they do to our kids in the schools.

The suggestion that educators would erase even these limited representations of Blacks alludes to the perceived unimportance of presenting a complex history. It reflects the naturalization of the subordinate position of Black history and the Black experience in Brazil. In addition, the desire to "forget that the 'Other' was enslaved" points to the avoidance of subject matter that goes against national narratives of racial harmony post-slavery. The historical processes formative of contemporary racial inequality are minimally addressed in school materials.

Afro-Brazilian cultural and religious forms are often portrayed in school curricula as cultish or folkloric legacies of the past (Fernandes, 2005). African-matrix religions, key sites for the transmission of cosmovisions, culture, and knowledge, are one example.[14] Negative portrayals of spirit possession and other rituals further entrench perceptions of these religions as backward, demonic, or as non-religions. Moreover, such representations risk (1) alienating and denigrating students whose families participate in these religious forms; (2) alienating Afro-descendant students through a stigmatized association with Blackness; and (3) reasserting notions of superiority for non-Afro-descendant pupils (Barros & Cavalcanti, 2006; Oliveira, 2006 ; M. Silva, 2001). These representations have the power to make Afro-descendants see and experience themselves as "Other," producing self-rejection and negative self-esteem that both stems from and reinforces dominant aesthetic, cultural, and civilizational values in society (e.g., Whiteness, European history and development, and European colonizers' contributions to the nation).

Silvany, Orùnmilá member and teacher appointed as advisor on Afro-descendant issues in Ribeirão Preto's education secretariat, sums up the situation:

A system of education like the Brazilian one, all based in the culture of Europe, a history that only credits heroes of European origin, that only addresses the science produced by Europe, is a history, a culture, a science that discriminates. So for our students, [as] they grow up in school, the idea of European superiority and African inferiority is reinforced.

By socializing Black and White children in this way, the education system realizes coloniality in reproducing cultural hierarchies and normalizing racial superiority and inferiority. Everyday racism is bolstered by the structure and transmission of knowledge, affecting Black children's identity and white children's sense of superiority and perceptions of Afro-Brazilians.[15]

Contesting Coloniality at the Orùnmilá Center: *Ancestralidade*, Knowledge, and Pedagogy

To address how the school curriculum and classroom pedagogies reproduce Brazilian racial exclusions, Orùnmilá advocates a serious effort to incorporate and engage with the epistemologies or ways of learning that are African and Afro-Brazilian in origin (cf. Botelho, 2006; Machado, 2003). This includes oral and embodied knowledge shared through dance, song, the plastic arts, percussion, and other forms that stimulate learning through the various senses and help students understand how different cultures produce and share knowledge in different ways. An Afro-Brazilian epistemology would encompass these values and worldviews stemming from African and Afro-Brazilian culture while also incorporating knowledge about society acquired through the subaltern experience of being Black and Brazilian. In this way, this epistemology involves an ancestral reservoir of cultural knowledge re-created and transmitted through generations of oral and physical practice as well as knowledge produced through the specific lived experience of being Black and Brazilian. This perspective can mobilize what is called *an-other thinking*, which originates within the Afro-Brazilian historical experience of the coloniality of power and knowledge. *An-other thinking* involves a critical, alternative way of understanding history and constructing collectivity that challenges hegemonic values and conceptions of society and development (Mignolo, 2000; Walsh and León, 2006).

In its broader anti-racist struggle, the Orùnmilá Center mobilizes Afro-Brazilian *ancestralidade*—ancestral wisdom/knowledge, cultural practices, and lived experience—to challenge racial inequalities. Founded as a *terreiro de Candomblé* (house of Candomblé worship) in the 1980s, the two founders Paulo and Neide converted the space into a community cultural center in the mid-1990s. While religious rituals and practices remain an important part of the Center, Orùnmilá primarily focuses on cultural and anti-racist work and policy advocacy in the city of Ribeirão Preto and the state of São Paulo more broadly. The Center organizes a range of activities, including African dance and percussion workshops, Capoeira classes, hip-hop workshops, college entrance exam courses, and seminars on African and Afro-Brazilian culture and politics. They also operate a website and a community radio station and call attention to Black cultural struggle and racial inequality through their participation in the annual municipal Carnaval.

Orùnmilá's activities integrate oral and written knowledge with lived experience and physical practice, or embodied knowledge, stressing the different ways these forms constitute learning. With Candomblé as an anchor, Paulo and Neide emphasize *ancestralidade* and how the transmission of knowledge occurs through cultural practices, historical memory, and orality (*oralidade*).[16] Value is placed on the oral and bodily transmission of *ancestralidade* through song, dance, and speech[17] with emphasis placed on how knowledge involves mind, body, spirit, and community.[18] *Ancestralidade* is taught, transmitted, and experienced as a lived and spiritual engagement with history.

For members of Orùnmilá, *ancestralidade* forms a cultural base built of knowledge/wisdom and historical experiences strongly linked to the formation of a cultural identity and present conceptions of collectivity. *Ancestralidade* involves four main aspects: First, it involves a *set of cultural values, knowledge, and cosmovision (worldview)* stemming from ancestral memory, philosophical teachings, and principles that order life and community relations and construct a way to understand and act in the world (see also Walsh and León, 2006). Second, *ancestralidade* involves the *historical processes and experiences* that over time shape individual and community identity and status. *Ancestralidade* is not static; it is cumulative and emergent. It draws on philosophical teachings and principles as its base while building on the articulation of values, meanings, and actions in new contexts. *Ancestralidade* ties present being to that of ancestors in ways that encompass historical experience and change over generations. Third, *ancestralidade* involves the *oral and expressive practices* that generate and transmit embodied knowledge and history as well as the *particular spaces* that enabled such transmission. Throughout the Americas, Afro-descendants re-created or created new institutions and forms of sociability that aided struggles for self-determination within contexts shaped by displacement, enslavement, and ongoing racial discrimination. Fourth, *ancestralidade* merges knowledge, spirituality, values, and cosmology with historical experience to construct an *Afro-diasporic political practice* that frames alternatives and future possibilities for the substantive achievement of Afro-descendant equality. *Ancestralidade* is, then, a multi-faceted and historicized means to cultural identity and collectivity. As such, it informs struggles against racial hierarchies and inequality.

During workshops, political action, and in day-to-day lived experience, Orùnmilá members cultivate practices like Candomblé, Capoeira, samba, and hip-hop as critical, alternative orientations to knowledge, community, and identity.[19] As Paulo and Silas[20] state in *Soró Dùdù*, "The historical characteristics [of Capoeira, Candomblé, Hip Hop, etc.] were and are constructed through political struggle, in the fight for the liberation and emancipation of a people."[21] Such practices were/are not only a means to construct identity, but they also can be mobilized to critique coloniality and its devaluing of Blackness and Afro-Brazilian culture. These practices reproduce time-honored African cosmo-visions and practices while also reflecting historical experiences of Blacks in Brazil. As such, they produce *an-other* perspective about history cultivated through Afro-Brazilian epistemologies and alternative personal and collective identities.

Paulo and Silas emphasize how this worldview and its philosophies and practices differ from "the conception developed in the West since Aristotle," and thus "permit the development of a sharp, clear critique of the limitations and wounds [*mazelas*] of Western culture."[22] In other words, lack of equal citizenship, the denigration of Blackness, and the constraints on Afro-Brazilian knowledge and culture *are* the limitations of Western culture to which Blacks have been subjected. Paulo and Silas's statement also identifies how Western culture and epistemological assertions (especially the values and institutions of market capitalism, as universal, as progress, and as development) has affected a majority of the planet through colonialism, inequality, poverty, racism, sexism, and environmental degradation.

In short, Orùnmilá's cultural work, drawing on perspectives of *an-other thinking*, opens new space for social change beyond the current form of social development, based as it is on the marginalization of Afro-descendant epistemologies, knowledge, and culture.

Shaping Affirmative Education Policy

Starting in the mid-1990s, the Brazilian government began undertaking initiatives in response to Black movement mobilizations and scholarly production about racial inequality. Former president Fernando Henrique Cardoso's administration (1995–2002) was the first to contemplate affirmative action and multi-cultural state policy to address racial inequality (Htun, 2004). His successor Luiz Ignácio "Lula" da Silva has also sought to address Afro-descendant rights through government initiatives. In March 2003, President Lula created a federal secretariat, the Secretaria Especial de Políticas de Promoção da Igualdade Racial, (Special Secretariat of Policy and Promotion of Racial Equality; SEPPIR). He also signed federal Law 10,639/2003, which makes obligatory the teaching of African and Afro-Brazilian history and culture in public and private schools. Law 10,639 determines that school curricula—especially the areas of art education, history, and literature—include the study and discussion of the struggle of Blacks in Brazil, teach about Afro-Brazilian culture and participation in the formation of national society, and redeem Black people's contributions in social, economic, and political spheres. The law also requires the academic calendar to include of November 20 as the National Day of Black Consciousness.[23]

The implementation of Law 10,639 necessitates that municipalities train administrators and teaching faculty and revise curricula and educational materials. These government initiatives have not guaranteed implementation, nor has federal policy created willingness among education secretariats, school administrators, and teachers to spend the time and money to realize projects related to Law 10,639. Discussion and implementation has depended on the advocacy and initiative of NGOs, scholars, and activists. In Ribeirão Preto, the Orùnmilá Cultural Center's advocacy prompted the mayor to sign a decree in November 2005 for policies to address Afro-Brazilian demands. This decree created an advisor in the education secretariat to coordinate and implement 10,639, including teacher and administrator training, school curriculum changes, and dealing with racism and discrimination in the municipal school system.[24]

To move toward implementing 10,639 in the municipality, Silvany and the Orùn-milá Center designed the Baobá Project, a teacher training project that incorporates lectures and assignments covering historical themes like colonialism and slavery in detail and with a critical lens. The project also engages Afro-Brazilian cultural production and forms of embodied knowledge like music, dance, drum making, percussion, and Capoeira through workshops and activities that incorporate the history, philosophy, and meaning behind these practices. The 120-hour course seeks to educate teachers about African and Afro-Brazilian history and culture by integrating formal educational practices, such as readings and lectures, with embodied/physical practice and lived experience.[25] The project also simultaneously targets the denigration of Blackness and Afro-Brazilian history and culture, which addresses questions of representation and self-esteem. Acknowledging 10,639's potential for decolonization through an-other thinking, Orùnmilá members write,

> Valorizing all the senses by using your whole body, movement, music, dance, experience, [physical] contact, by identifying a leaf or building a drum, valorizing memory and not just writing, valorizing nature and *ancestralidade* [can]…reformulate teaching methodologies that, in most cases, already reveal themselves as limited in reference to complete child development, particularly of Black children and adolescents (Centro Cultural Orùnmilá e a 10,639, 2006, p. 5).

Building on this sentiment, Silvany highlights what the shift to substantive inclusion for Afro-descendants really means:

> In our case, to include means more than guarantee our presence in schools. It means re-structuring education in Brazil based on values that this education always rejected [*negou*], to re-structure pedagogical theories and practices, the didactics of teaching…. It is not only guaranteeing that the student has matriculated, that he has a space, and that he remains in school. It's revolutionizing the national education system.

To "revolutionize" the implementation of a law like 10,639, we must evaluate how to educate and train teachers and administrators in a manner that challenges taken for granted knowledge, culture, and racial hierarchies and values inherent in the formal education system. This process targets world-historical narratives of Eurocentric colonialism and capitalist development, while also *decolonizing* discourses produced in Latin American societies (e.g., whitening, racial democracy, modernization/development). It challenges the given parameters of possibilities through historical reconstruction and engagement with other ways of constructing community.

Contested Histories, Contested Inclusions

The discourses of inclusion deployed by public officials reveal the subtle yet profound limitations on a substantive, critical multi-cultural inclusion. Administrators and public officials generalize remedies for Afro-descendant exclusion into universal discourses of equal opportunity, diversity, or inclusion. While open to multi-culturalism, officials' statements reflect an ahistorical and apolitical engagement with the issue. It was rare in Ribeirão Preto that any public official discussed Afro-descendant issues explicitly, even when inaugurating projects specific to that population. At the Baobá Project inauguration in March 2007, after Paulo and Silvany highlighted the specific importance of the project for Afro-descendants, the mayor stated,

> I think [the issue of inclusion] is extremely important. In my opinion, these victories [like the Baobá project] will only occur when those that govern implement free education and universal health care for *all classes*, for *all categories*... We have to give equal opportunity to all people and may *the best* and *most dedicated* be successful, be they white, black, sons and daughters of immigrants, or anyone else.

For Afro-Brazilians, the mayor's statement offers inclusion without dialogue, without addressing histories of power involving the hierarchical valuing of certain knowledges and cultures. Claiming a goal of universal education and health care *for all* invokes lofty liberal ideals without dealing with specific inequalities among classes and categories of citizens. Furthermore, notions of equal opportunity and success re-inscribe ideals of individualism and meritocracy into the substance of societal relations (e.g., we will provide benefits as long as it bolsters competition and self-gain). Such declarations mask the very racial and cultural inequalities that historically shape how factors besides being "the best" affect opportunities and possibilities. After presenting this limited view of inclusion, the mayor re-asserts a vision of success based on individual aspirations and achievement, leaving unaffected the market paradigm's unequal distribution of cultural value and economic resources. Such statements to an audience of Afro-Brazilians who have worked hard for the implementation of 10,639 ignore a claim to history and thus discount their struggle.[26]

Addressing the same audience, the recently appointed education secretary[27] also spoke of inclusion: "...I am a defender of inclusion in its most diverse manifested forms, whether it is inclusion of handicapped individuals, or the inclusion of the excluded for whatever social reason, I am a fighter for the cause of education." Like the mayor, the secretary omits the connection between biography and history, obscuring the political and historical significance of the implementation and content of the Baobá Project for Afro-descendants. Instead, the secretary prefers to claim his credentials as a champion of broad, abstract inclusion. The avoidances of "race" betray a lack of acknowledgment of the specifics of why or how Blacks must be included. Rather, officials see Blacks as simply one more element to be added into the mix. By not engaging with 10,639's transformative potential, they express a limited vision of such policies as a step toward bringing *more* people into the already established educational system.

The paucity of official attention and resources given to addressing racial inequality in Ribeirão Preto also diminishes the significance of Afro-descendant claims. Demonstrating an honest interest in dealing with questions of racial inequality, the new education secretary started his term by giving Silvany office space at the Education secretariat.[28] Yet, while he gave her a dedicated space, Silvany was expected to work on the secretariat's range of issues. The education secretary pointed this out at the Baobá inaugural event stating,

Silvany works at the Secretariat on a project that has the characteristic of inclusion. Yes! To diffuse and triumph over the barriers [in terms of] black culture, *but* she also participates on the whole body of educational projects. She is not a *marginalized* person, [like] "she can only do one thing." No! She works on all projects that represent inclusion, that represent actions of the secretariat *for all*. So, Silvany, I hope that you don't feel … *excluded at the Secretariat*.

While Silvany's participation in general inclusion projects and policies represents an interest in her input for diverse initiatives in the secretariat, her hiring was based on Black movement demands that her priorities sit with implementing Law 10,639.[29] Implementing Law 10,639 is already a tall order, considering the amount of work it would take to train four to five thousand municipal teachers, order educational materials, examine school curricula, and address racism and racist incidents in municipal schools. The idea that she would be marginalized by only working on Afro-descendant issues illustrates the underlying marginal status of such work and the fact that her position exposes the very need for (at least) one full-time employee working on such issues. His suggestion that she spread her time devalues her focused tasks, while his (and others') use of the term "inclusion" render it so banal that it loses its ability to address the specificity of historic forms of social exclusion. Historical guilt is publicly dulled and the hard work of constructing equality diminished through his speech.[30] Formulating inclusion so abstractly glosses over historic power relations in shaping opportunities and possibilities for Afro-Brazilians and their cultures and dampens the impact a critical, substantive multi-culturalism may have for transforming prevailing structures of power and knowledge.

Conclusion

The Baobá Project represents a nascent effort to implement Federal Law 10,639 in a substantive way, concerning questions of knowledge and development, and addressing racial inequality. While at this time the experience and outcome of implementation is under evaluation, the Baobá case indicates one framework Afro-Brazilians are developing for programs geared toward constructing a substantive form of inclusion and citizenship. Thus Orùnmilá's vision goes beyond pressing for inclusion into a pre-defined system and structure of education. Rather, they seek to shift the terms of the debate towards *an-other* decolonizing vision and modify the curriculum and classroom pedagogies accordingly. Cultural work by anti-racist groups like the Orùnmilá Cultural Center encourages vigilance over and critique of multi-cultural programs currently being implemented in places like Brazil.

These multi-cultural programs generally reinforce neo-liberal visions of individual aspirations for self-gain, ignoring individual and collective aspirations for realization of the promise of cultural diversity and respect. As such, they fail to reconstruct societal knowledge, social relations, and collectivity. Through discourse and policy, neo-liberal multi-culturalism claims to advance citizenship but without addressing how coloniality structures power and inequality. Orùnmilá's Baobá Project contests discourses and programs that re-create restricted citizenship for Afro-descendants for contemporary times, prefiguring how to construct a decolonizing knowledge and education that strives toward a more egalitarian collective through a critical, substantive multi-culturalism.

The recognition of epistemological diversity (values, practices, and forms of knowledge) and engagement with its collective possibilities anticipates a substantive multi-cultural transformation of the Brazilian school curriculum. Rather than the fetishized difference, cosmetic inclusion, or the simple valuing of diversity in and of itself, this critical multi-culturalism aims for a "cosmopolitan ecology of knowledges" that sets up "dialogues and alliances between diverse forms of knowledge, cultures, and cosmologies in response to different forms of oppression that enact the coloniality of knowledge and power" (Santos, Nunes, & Meneses 2007, p. xiv). The goal is to give students access to different forms of knowledge and learning present in Brazilian society and to re-value them as different ways of organizing and building development and collectivity. Reforming institutions along these lines better reflects the social and cultural reality of Brazil, educating Black and White students to value and learn through difference.

Because multi-culturalism has framed government policy and societal discourse since the 1990s in Latin America, Afro-descendants and Indigenous peoples must remain vigilant about the proposed nature of inclusion in various contexts—education, employment, state institutions, and the media. How projects take shape and to what extent they substantively engage with subaltern or minority knowledges and cultures will determine whether they transform institutions and pedagogical and political practices or simply provide more access to the "opportunity" of neo-liberal development that ultimately reproduces inequality.

Notes

* Acknowledgments I thank Philip McMichael for helpful editorial comments and suggestions on various versions of this chapter, including the final one. I also thank Dia Da Costa, Karuna Morarji, and the anonymous reviewers of the book for their helpful suggestions on previous versions of this chapter.
1. A project organized to implement the teaching of African and Afro-Brazilian history and culture in the municipal school curriculum according to Federal Law 10,639/03.
2. I use the terms *Afro-descendant, Black, non-White*, and *Afro-Brazilian* interchangeably, conforming to usage by those I interviewed and the academic literature demonstrating that, despite some advantages experienced by lighter-skinned Blacks, there is greater difference between non-White and White Brazilians than among Afro-Brazilians of different skin tones. The term *negro*, which directly translates to "Black," is used by many people, especially Black movement activists, as a method of claiming a politicized identity through a term that historically had negative connotations and associations. The terms *Afro-Brazilian* and *Afro-descendent* are seen as more encompassing, as they include those that may not identify politically as *negro*, but are of visible African ancestry.
3. The Baobá Project in Ribeirão Preto represents one of the first, if not the first, instance of a municipal-wide implementation of Law 10,639. Generally, the implementation of the law is the responsibility of municipal governments, who can turn to non-governmental organizations that design and run the implementation project. Organizations with the capacity to implement a project, which includes instructors, materials, lesson plans, and workshop designs, compete for a public contract and funds. While a handful of programs

have been created over the past few years, including state-level programs in São Paulo to sensitize high school teachers and municipal employees to issues of racial and ethnic discrimination and inequality, little research exists on project implementation. In creating their own project, the Orùnmilá Center aimed to avoid issues they saw emerging in other local and statewide projects, such as brevity, project staff inadequately prepared to deal with the racial theme, inconsistency in educational materials and teacher training, and lack of substantive engagement with knowledge, philosophies, and practices underlying Afro-Brazilian culture.

4. Periodically published, *Sorò Dúdú* contains editorials and articles covering current issues and debates relevant to Afro-Brazilian culture and politics locally and nationally.

5. See, for example, Cavalleiro (2001), Machado (2003), and Theodoro (2005).

6. See also Botelho (2006) and Xavier (2006).

7. See also Reichmann (1999) and Skidmore (1993).

8. Expressing a keen awareness of the implications of skin color and Blackness, Brazilians still selectively use color and racial terminology to distance themselves and others from the "darker end" of the color spectrum (cf. Burdick, 1998; Sansone, 2003; Sheriff, 2001).

9. Capoeira is an Afro-Brazilian martial art/dance. Candomblé is an Afro-Brazilian religious manifestation with origins in African spiritual and religious practices, in particular, those of the Yoruba, Ewe, Fon, and Bantu peoples.

10. For in-depth examinations of this process as well as the ideology of racial democracy, see Caldwell (2007), Davis (1999), Hanchard (1994), Ortiz (1985), Pravaz (2008), Santos (1998), Sheriff (2001), and D. Silva (1998).

11. Contemporary instances include valuing "local" knowledges/cultures without displacing dominant practices of economic and social development, using "culture-as-resource" and expedient within global development institutions and frameworks (cf. Yúdice, 2003), and commodifying "indigenous," "local," and Black cultures for tourism in ways that reify culture and ways of life as products for consumption by modern, developed (often foreign) people.

12. For more detailed description and discussion of this issue, see also Fernandes (2005), Munanga (1996), and A. Silva (2005).

13. The notion of (curly, Afro) hair being "bad hair" [*cabelo ruim*] and a marker of Blackness has remarkable effects on young children, especially girls, often causing negative self-esteem and attempts to change one's appearance to gain social acceptance (cf. Burdick, 1998; Caldwell, 2007).

14. African-matrix refers to religious or cultural practices in the African Diaspora that have cultural continuities with forms originating on the African continent.

15. Material effects are explicitly visible in Afro-Brazilian dropout rates and low self-esteem. They are also visible in how the value given to particular forms of culture, knowledge, and history inculcates the denigration of certain groups and appreciation and valuing of the contributions of others. Orùnmilá's project seeks to address the inclusion/valuing of Afro-Brazilian knowledge while also creating a welcoming school space that shares in the diverse history of all Brazilians.

16. One example involves the beliefs, practices, and conducts shaping behavior in Candomblé including humility, self-awareness, self-reflection, and self-development in complementarity with community (Merrell 2007).

17. A central element in Candomblé is *axé,* the energy that enables action, which is transmitted in various forms, including the spoken word. As such, orality transmits the power of realization (Santos 1976).

18. For more detailed examinations of these elements of Afro-Diasporic forms in Brazil, see Botelho (2006), Browning (1995), Daniel (2005), Harding (2006), Jones (2005), and Merrell (2007).

19. For more on these forms as alternative orientations, see, for example, Browning (1995), Harding (2000), Merrell (2007), Pardue (2008), and Sodré (2002 [1988]).

20. Professor of sociology and communications and senior member of Orùnmilá.
21. From *As Dimensões Inseparáveis de Política e Cultura e a Luta do C. C. Orùnmilá,*" [The Inseparable Dimensions of Politics and Culture in the Orùnmilá Cultural Center's Struggle], 2004, p. 2.
22. Ibid.
23. *Diretrizes Curriculares Nacionais para a Educação das Relações Étnico-Raciais e para o Ensino de História e Cultural Afro-Brasileira e Africana* [National Curricular Directives for the Education of Ethno-Racial Relations and for the Teaching of Afro-Brazilian and African History and Culture], Ministry of Education. http://www.publicacoes.inep.gov.br/arquivos/%7B2A0A514E-6C2A-4657-862F-CD4840586714%7D_AFRO-BRASILE-IRA.pdf (accessed May 7, 2009).
24. The decree also created an advisory position in the Culture Secretariat, which was eventually moved to the Casa Civil, or Mayor's cabinet. In May 2006, the mayor signed a decree creating the Commission for the Coordination and Accompaniment of Affirmative Action Policies for Afro-descendants, where representatives from civil society and from various municipal secretariats and local universities discuss the creation and implementation of initiatives.
25. Orùnmilá emphasizes the inclusion of practitioners of Afro-Brazilian cultural forms generally excluded as teachers due to formal education requirements, such as Capoeira masters, elder samba school directors, and musicians. This effort seeks to simultaneously legitimize cultural practices and the practitioners with the most experience, ability, and respect as holders [*detentores*] and teachers of such knowledge/wisdom. Despite being versed in cultural practices through years of experience, training, and a system of rules, such skills are illegible to municipal school systems focused requiring "formal" credentials.
26. The point here is not to neglect how the mayor was responsive to *some* Afro-Brazilian demands, implementing various initiatives. Rather, it is to highlight how generalized discourses of inclusion exist and avoid addressing certain issues explicitly, *despite* the fact that they engage with Afro-Brazilian demands. More generally, elected officials' and municipal leaders' knowledge and understanding of racial inequality was poor, thus reflected in their apolitical multi-cultural discourse.
27. This new education secretary took office in January 2007, and due to his support for the Projeto Baobá, made it possible for Silvany to implement the project and other actions related to Law 10,639. At the same time, as examined here, he also expressed a generalized discourse of "inclusion" and consistently avoided talking specifically about "race" and education.
28. The prior secretary ordered Silvany to work at a municipal school far from the center of town with minimal infrastructure and resources. Bringing her to the secretariat was an important moment for the Black movement in Ribeirão Preto and improved her ability to carry out education projects.
29. Just like Silvany in the Education Secretariat, the advisor to the mayor on ethnic and racial issues was also consistently asked to manage general mayoral affairs and serve the mayor rather than carry out Black movement demands and actions to address racial inequality.
30. Silvany explained to me that she used this demand to insert the racial theme into various other spaces in the secretariat, such as general pedagogical meetings and committee discussions. As Park and Richards (2007) show with Mapuche state employees in Chile, state workers actively subvert internal constraints placed on them by neo-liberal models of governance and multi-cultural policy through everyday practice as in Silvany's case.

14.

CHALLENGING MARKET AND RELIGIOUS FUNDAMENTALISMS

*The Emergence of "Ethics, Cosmovisions, and Spiritualities" in the World Social Forum**

Andreas Hernandez

This extraordinary initiative in the World Social Forum resists the abstract reductionism of both market and religious fundamentalisms, concretizing the spiritual dimension in human life as a global ethic of plural and ecumenical solidarity (social hope). It represents an embedding of a new religious subjectivity in social change movements, in opposition to the self-interest and individualism of neo-liberal subjectivity that identifies development with the spread of a market culture, and a "self-fashioning" subjectivity in contradistinction to an ethic of "global citizenship."

Introduction

The World Social Forum (WSF) has become one of the most sustainable forms of a global counter-movement to neo-liberal development. "Ethics, Cosmovisions, and Spiritualities" emerged as one of the eleven themes of the 2005 WSF held in Porto Alegre, Brazil. Whereas the initial 2001 Forum was conceived as a more professionalized meeting of NGO and social movement leaders, the expansion and increasingly participatory nature of the Forum and its organization was accompanied by a surge in the religio-spiritual dimensions of popular struggle within the WSF. Indeed, many of the most vital popular social movements from around the planet have profound religio-spiritual roots, from the Landless Movement of Brazil (MST) and the Zapatistas of Mexico, to the Chipko Movement of India. However, the spiritual grounding of social movement struggle is often overlooked, marginalized or ignored in social movement scholarship and analysis of social alternatives.

This essay situates the religio-spiritual dimensions of WSF politics as a significant part of the contemporary double movement, where neo-liberal market culture is contested by collective impulses for social protection. Religion is central to this double movement—as the base for conservative social mobilizations in coalition with free market economic forces, as well as a component of the counter-movement to regulate and democratize the market according to human values within everyday life. In this sense, religion is a critical terrain of contest in both the dis-embedding and social re-embedding of market relations. This proposition frames my analysis of the emergence of the "Ethics, Cosmovisions, and Spiritualities" thematic terrain in the WSF.

I argue that the religio-spiritual dimensions of social struggle reveal notions of market/self-interest and social protection/social power as embodying profoundly different processes of subjectification, which are manifested in the religious and spiritual dimensions of politics. Market fundamentalism is the hallmark of the neo-liberal movement, which abstracts human agency through the metaphor of the "invisible hand" of the free market, compounded by a fundamentalism of "other worldly" conceptions of the divine. Both of these realms are outside of human action and experience. The global counter-movement, as represented in the WSF, struggles to re-embed the market and the divine into human experience, democratizing and pluralizing human agency. This process of grounding religio-spiritual ways of imagining, perceiving, and experiencing in social movements—conceptualized in this essay as *embedded religious subjectivity*—challenges the reductionism of neo-liberalism, heralding more complex views of humanity's relationship to social, natural, and cosmological issues. In short, an ecumenical and plural vision of a shared humanity espoused by counter-movements rejects the religious and market fundamentalisms consolidated during the neo-liberal era, and offers an alternative basis for "global citizenship."

Religion as a Political Terrain of Contest

The following section examines the contemporary double movement through a religio-spiritual lens. I locate three historical coordinates which define the contemporary double movement: the revolutions of 1968 and the crises of Euro-American hegemony; the capitalist mobilization launched symbolically with the first meeting of the World Economic Forum in 1971, and the social counter-movement launched symbolically with the first meeting of the World Social Forum in 2001. This examination reveals religion as a crucial terrain of contest in the current conjuncture and historically contextualizes the emergence of the religio-spiritual dimensions of the WSF.

1968: The Crisis of Euro-American Hegemony

The revolutions of 1968 may be understood as a crisis moment in the erosion of Euro-American hegemony in both historically liberal regions, as well as in subordinated regions across the globe. These were at once crises of the political, economic, and subjective structures of liberalism. Politically, the revolts challenged not only conservative powers, but also the anti-capitalist potency of the traditional Left, now entrenched in modern political systems (Wallerstein, 2002). Economically, the late 1960s experienced an accumulation crisis, resulting in rising unemployment as the post-World War II era of national development lost momentum (Arrighi & Silver, 1999). Liberal ideologies of self-interest and individual gain were challenged by eruptions of new forms of social power and subjectivity: from Euro-communism in Prague, to Black Consciousness in South Africa, to the cultural revolutions and student revolts of core liberal countries. Religio-spiritual currents were integral to many of the uprisings across the world—such as anti-colonial struggles, civil rights movements, the contemporary ecological movement, peasant movements across Latin America, and second wave feminism (West, 1999; Kurtz, 2005).

WEF: Market and Religious Fundamentalism

Arguably, the neo-liberal project was symbolically, and to some extent concretely, launched with the 1971 meeting of the first World Economic Forum (WEF) in Davos, Switzerland (Wallerstein, 2002). The neo-liberal project marked the worldwide politicization of the liberal economic project, in response to the crises of 1968. The state has been central to this project of expanding global capital networks, in coalition with corporations and multi-national lending agencies. The annual WEF meetings brought together not only heads of state but also heads of the corporate world, academicians and intellectuals, and media industry leaders. These gatherings affirmed the project of deregulation of the global economy, and deployment of public resources, to serve a corporate mobilization against both the crisis-ridden post-World War II welfare/development system as well as the new social mobilizations.

At the same time, conservative social forces mobilized in defense of what was perceived as an attack on traditional values and ways of life (Guattari & Rolnik, 1986). Fundamentalist religions often became touchstones in this process. For example, the rise of the Christian Right in the United States was a key popular force for bringing in the Reagan era. Hindu nationalism has provided the popular bedrock on which rapid economic liberalization was pushed through in India. Conservative wings of the Catholic Church were important pillars in Pinochet's regime in Chile, where the first large-scale experiments of structural adjustment policies were implemented in the 1970s. Elsewhere, religious forces have been less direct in processes of deregulation, but religious and moral undertones may be seen as playing important roles—such as in Canada in the 1980s or Brazil in the 1990s. The unsteady and contradictory coalitions between conservative social mobilizations (particularly religious-based) and corporate mobilizations have provided the substance and power base of the neo-liberal project.

WSF: Resistance in the Current Conjuncture

The implementation of the neo-liberal project since the late 1970s has led to the systematic dismantling of social protections and increased commodification of socio-ecological processes, challenging livelihoods, ecologies, social systems, and ways of life. Numerous movements have been called forth across the planet since the late 1970s in projects of social protection, development, and the constitution of social power. The connections among movements as diverse as labor, feminist, peasant, ecological, gay, church-based, youth, ethnic minority, artistic, indigenous, and local governance organizations are growing in intensity and extent; they share an increasing sensibility of a strategic diversity against a common world historic condition of neo-liberalism and market rule, in a movement to democratize processes of globalization

(McMichael, 2005). These networks embody "cosmopolitan localism" in a plural globalization "from below" (Sachs, 1993). The WSF has emerged as the symbolic launching of a global counter-movement to neo-liberalism increasingly interconnected in its rejection of neo-liberalism (B. d. S. Santos, 2005b).

Many of the most vital popular movements struggling against the neo-liberal project have deep religious roots and motivations. For example, the Indian Narmada Bachao Andolan movement actively draws from and reformulates diverse religio-spiritual forms, such as the Gandhian notion of satyagraha (The Hindu, 2004). In Chiapas, rebellion has been rooted in the co-mingling of indigenous cosmovisions with liberation theology (Clarke & Ross, 2000). In the Brazilian Landless Movement, the ecumenical *mistica,* or mysticism, is central to organizing, utopia, and struggle (Sampaio, 2002). Rahmena (1997, p. 170), in speaking of the Gandhian, Chipko, Lokayan, and Swadhyana movements of India, argues that,

> As a rule, the necessity for a spiritual dimension, and for the revival of the sacred in one's everyday relationships with the world, seems to be rediscovered as a basic factor for the regeneration of people's space. Wherever this spiritual dimension has been present, it has, indeed, produced a staggering contagion of intelligence and creativity, much more conducive to people's collective "efficiency" than other conventional forms of mass mobilizationÖthis dimension has served as a most powerful instrument in reviving the old ideals of a livelihood based on love, conviviality and simplicity, and also helping people resist the disruptive effects of economization.

This examination of the religio-spiritual dimensions of the contemporary double movement outlines the contradictory and uneasy coalition of religious and market fundamentalisms of the neo-liberal project. It also brings forth the religio-spiritual dimensions integral to the mobilization of global counter-movements, offering an alternative view of religion as a touchstone for grounding economic relations into human values of everyday life. Religion is revealed as an important terrain of contest in dis-embedding and re-embedding economic relations.

The World Social Forums

The first World Social Forum held in Porto Alegre, Brazil in 2001 was conceived by a coalition of French and Brazilian NGOs and social movements to be a counter-weight to the World Economic Forums. Initially held in parallel to the WEF, the WSF quickly emerged as a process in its own right, becoming one of the most sustainable and wide-reaching manifestations for progressive and counter-hegemonic globalization, and an emergent counter-hegemonic civil society. In its widest definition, the WSF is the set of initiatives and exchanges among social movements, NGOs, religious groups, academics, and other organizations, articulating local, national, continental, and global struggles against all the forms of oppression brought about or made possible by neo-liberal globalization. At its core, the WSF is a struggle for inclusion and recognition, in that the neo-liberal project is accomplished through numerous forms of oppression that affect, among others women, ethnic minorities, indigenous peoples, peasants, the unemployed, informal sector workers, legal and illegal immigrants, ghetto sub-classes, gays and lesbians, and children and the young. Whitaker (2005), a member of the Forum's first organizing committee, argues that the WSF has opened a space for the emergence and consolidation of civil society as the central political agency at all levels, including the planetary level. B. d. S. Santos (2005b) argues that the WSF is a powerful reference in the re-emergence of a critical utopia, or the radical critique of contemporary reality and the aspiration for a better society. This utopian dimension is explicitly plural in its claim that alternatives be grounded, simultaneous, and diverse, and is affirmed with the possibility of a counter-hegemonic globalization. In this way, the notion of utopia through the WSF process is radically democratic.

The organization of the Forum is both an expression of emergent forms of politics as well as the catalyst for these emergent forms. The Forum is self-organizing, in that events (workshops, seminars, testimonials, organizing meetings, etc.) are proposed and run by participating groups. The Charter of Principles prevents the WSF from organizing collective actions in its name. However, the innumerable local, national, continental, and global actions carried out by the networks of groups, movements, and organizations that are part of the Forum may be considered as part of the WSF process.

Porto Alegre, a city known for social mobilization and creatively radical gover-nance, became the Forum's base, with new editions in 2002, 2003, and 2005—growing from 10,000 participants in 2001 to 180,000 participants in 2003. In order to increase possibilities for participation in the WSF for groups outside of Latin America, the Forum became itinerant in 2004, moving to Mumbai, India. The WSF was decentral-ized in 2006, held simultaneously in Venezuela, Pakistan, and Mali. In 2007 the WSF convened in Kenya. The 2009 Forum gathered in the Amazonian city of Belem, Brazil, with a particular focus on socio-ecological questions.

The Emergence of the "Ethics, Cosmovisions, and Spiritualities" Thematic

An organizer for the Global Ecumenical Coalition reported that the organization had one representative in the first 2001 WSF, and by the 2005 Forum there were 2000 Coalition representatives. The involvement of groups and movements bringing spiri-tual and religious concerns to the Forum has exploded from an almost clandestine beginning to having one of the eleven thematic spaces of the 2005 WSF dedicated to "Ethics, Cosmovisions, and Spiritualities." This expansion of religio-spiritual dynam-ics has been a result of increasing democratization and popular participation in the Forum.

Each successive Forum has had greater degrees of participatory structure and programming, in that each edition has had more extensive input and collaboration by the groups and movements taking part. The 2005 WSF was positioned by the Organiz-ing Committee to be more popular and propositive. The Porto Alegre Forums were widely held to excel in discussion and debate, while the 2004 Mumbai Forum brought forth cultural and religious dimensions of struggle. The organizers of the 2005 Forum worked to bridge the strengths of the Porto Alegre and Mumbai Forums through a participatory programming methodology, which sought to amplify convergence, multiply dialogues, and avoid unarticulated repetition of activities of the same theme. A WSF organizer reported: "We conducted a broad public study of entities and individuals from around the world, using the Internet and also forms that we sent out to those who don't have this technology, to arrive at 11 thematic spaces in which to hold the 2,000 activities proposed by 5,700 organizations from more than 100 countries" (Queiroz, 2005, ¶ 9). Through this process, "Ethics, Cosmovisions, and Spiritualities: Resistances and Challenges for a New World" emerged as one of the eleven "thematic terrains" that constituted the 2005 Forum. Further, five "transversal themes" were established that were seen to cross every thematic terrain.

Thematic Terrains
- Assuring and Defending the Earth and People's Common Goods—As an Alternative to Commodification and Transnational Control
- Arts and Creation: Weaving and Building People's Resistance Culture
- Communication: Counter—Hegemonic Practices, Rights and Alternatives
- Defending Diversity, Plurality, and Identities
- Human Rights and Dignity for a Just and Egalitarian World
- Sovereign Economies for and of People—Against Neo-Liberal Capitalism
- Ethics, Cosmovisions and Spiritualities—Resistances and Challenges for a New World
- Social Struggles and Democratic Alternatives—Against Neo-Liberal Domination
- Peace, Demilitarization and Struggle against War, Free Trade, and Debt
- Autonomous Thought, Reappropriation and Socialization of Knowledge and Technologies
- Towards Construction of an International Democratic Order and People's Integration

Transversal Themes
- Social Emancipation and Political Dimensions of Struggles
- Struggle against Patriarchal Capitalism
- Struggle against Racism and Other Types of Exclusion Based on Ancestry
- Gender
- Diversities

The first edition of the WSF was set forth as a more professionalized gathering of progressive and Left social movement, NGO, and academic leaders. Cultural, religious, and artistic dimensions of struggle were virtually not present in the first meeting of the WSF. The expansion of religio-spiritual concerns in the WSF reflects the expansion of popular participation in the Forum process. Contributing to the "Ethics, Cosmovisions, and Spiritualities" thematic terrain were representatives from groups, movements, churches, temples, universities and other organizations from around the globe. The following is a partial listing of groups which participated in the organization of the theme:

- Ananda Marga
- Brazilian Association of Biodynamic Agriculture
- Catholics for the Right to Decide
- Falun Dafa
- Global Ecovillage Network
- Indigenous Environmental Network
- Kairos
- Latin American Council of Churches
- M.K. Gandhi Institute for Nonviolence
- Pax Christi
- Via Campesina
- World Council of Churches
- Zendo Brazil
- Waldorf School Federation
- 50 Years is Enough Network
- Brahma Kumaris
- Brazilian Landless Movement
- Caritas Internationalis
- Coordinating Body for Indigenous Organizations of the Amazon Basin
- Franciscan Service of Solidarity
- Global Ecumenical Coalition
- Institute for Research on the Non-violent Resolution of Conflicts
- Lama Gangchen World Peace Foundation
- Lutheran World Foundation
- Pastoral Land Commission
- Sojourners
- World Vision

Themes of Debate and Discussion

The Ethics, Cosmovisions, and Spiritualities thematic terrain was comprised of hundreds of official and unofficial workshops, debates, and discussions. Following the self-organization of the WSF, these gatherings were organized by the groups participating in them. The thematic terrain was spread over several acres filled with large tents, temporary structures, forested glens, and grassy common areas. At most moments throughout the day there were ten or more formal activities happening simultaneously, and hundreds of informal conversations in small groups. Through analysis of these gatherings, I have identified seven emergent and interrelated themes constituting the thematic terrain. Taken together, these themes elaborate the substance of the religio-spiritual resistances at the WSF and suggest that they are mobilized against both market logic and religious fundamentalisms.

Human Complexity

One of the central theses of the thematic terrain was that the neo-liberal reductionism of societies to self-interest and markets does not offer an adequate view of the human being. The neo-liberal project was frequently seen in this thematic as a coalition between market logic and religious fundamentalisms. Many workshops dealt with the notion that another world cannot be constructed through market values or the values of reductionist religions. It was widely discussed how religion and spirituality may offer more complex and ecological understandings of the human being in relation to the cosmos, against the market and religious reductionisms. A core point of consensus running through much of thematic terrain was that more relational views of the human being are necessary to construct alternatives to the neo-liberal project. Ulrich Duchrow, a theologian and organizer of the Global Ecumenical Coalition argued, "We won't survive with an ethics that is considered as individual private value judgment." He continued, "If we consider ethics as a condition for life, we mustn't see each other as atomic individuals or as rivals but as closely connected beings. A future ethics must be relational, it must be an ethics of solidarity." He further argued that, "A voice consisting of churches and social movements is required to confront the fundamentalism of the market."

Radical Ecumenicalism

Radical Ecumenicalism was a core theme traversing the great majority of workshops and other gatherings. The German theologian Hans Kung was widely cited for his notion that world peace requires peace between religions. Radical ecumenicalism was generally agreed to refer not only to tolerance between religious traditions, but to the recognition of diverse traditions as different expressions of the same truths and mysteries. One participant expressed that ecumenicalism is "the recognition of the common humanity within all religions." It was widely held across the thematic terrain that dialogue and listening around the issues of ethics, cosmovisions, and spiritualities with the widest range of social actors possible, are urgently needed at this moment of intensive globalization as a precondition for openness between religions, the development of ethics that embrace a common humanity, and the deep questioning of the meanings of human fulfillment. Many groups situated the Forum historically as an important moment in the history of ecumenicalism. José Luiz Del Roio, from the coordination of the World Forum for Alternatives observed, "The Forum exists to create dialogues that are apparently impossible, like the hug between a Muslim and a native Brazilian Shaman. It's a space of meeting of religiosities, visions and sensitivities of the human being, it does not matter the culture or the geographical area." Beyond historical gatherings of ecumenicalism, this thematic terrain was explicitly political, and gathered a much wider and deeper range of social actors who are actively constituting new forms of ecumenical religiosity as political praxis. In this way, this WSF ecumenicalism was grounded in the praxis of social change. These themes were addressed in workshops such as: "Religious Pluralism in the Gestation of Another Possible World"; "Strengthening Inter-Religious Dialogue"; "Fighting Religious Fundamentalism" and "Interreligiosity, Politics, and Peace."

Spiritual Experience

The "Ethics, Cosmovisions, and Spiritualities" thematic terrain was filled with discussions and workshops on spiritual practices, from "Zen and Social Transformation," to "The Contemporary Use of Ayahuasca [an Amazonian psychoactive]," to various forms of group prayer. Most of these practices emphasized spiritual experience over religious belief. Workshops tended to posit a trans-religious spirituality, often in relation to the natural world. For example, Siddhartha, the founder of a democratically run activist ashram in India, promoted a "transformative spirituality" that "transcends religious limits." An important aspect of this emergent spirituality, he argued, is the dialogue between religious and secular groups. These workshops on spiritual practices in great part expressed that these practices are critical for the lived experience of interrelation between people, Nature, and the Cosmos. Many of the spiritual practices in the thematic terrain included the conception and experience of some sense of a cosmic energy, defined in various ways, such as the workshop "Group Energy Channeling." In a spectrum of workshops and gatherings throughout the entire Forum was the theme of the nurturing of an ethic, consciousness, and culture of non-violence. A number of groups positioned spiritual practices as particularly helpful for developing a mind and culture that reduces violence, hate, and anger to a minimum. There was significant debate with groups expressing diverse notions about how much attention should be concentrated on personal growth and how much on social and ecological change, and whether these two poles can be usefully considered separately.

Democratization of Religion

The democratization of religion was a significant theme of workshops of the "Ethics, Cosmovisions, and Spiritualities" thematic terrain. It was widely held that popular movements must appropriate and reformulate theologies in order to embed them into local and particular lived realities and ways of perceiving and being. These workshops, such as "Can Religion Be Democratized," challenged both the totalizing theological concepts of many fundamentalisms which seek to establish absolute truths, as well as their often hierarchical structures. The constitution of liberation theologies emerging from popular movements was seen as integral to movement political praxis. Many groups expressed that the construction of liberatory theologies should be radically inclusive, particularly in the context of social movements. There were also numerous calls on the importance of including youth in the creation and renewal of liberation theologies. Several workshops brought together participants from popular movements, theologians, academics, and others to work together in the construction and elaboration of liberation theologies, which took advantage of the rare gathering of, and diverse groups in, the Forum. One workshop entitled "Liberating Theologies in Social Movements" engaged Freirian techniques of popular education to construct ecumenical and hybrid forms of liberation theology—with the proposal to reinvigorate and broaden this historical legacy of social movements stemming from Catholic and Lutheran sources. Other workshops dealt with specific traditions such as the gathering entitled "Progressive Islam and Liberation Theology." The democratization and grounding of religion was often seen to be a process of hybridization, bringing together theological tools as required for local situations making plural and interrelated theologies. This is clearly evident in the religious forms of the Brazilian Landless Movement (MST). The *Mistica* of the MST, a kind of religiously and spiritually oriented popular theater, brings together catholic, Afro-Brazilian, indigenous, spiritualist, and other influences in a hybrid form that embraces and contains a fluid multiplicity of religious expressions around the common notion of "mystery." The mistica of the MST was held numerous times throughout the 2005 WSF.

Democratization of Prophecy

The powers and potentialities of prophetic thought were discussed and engaged in various workshops throughout the thematic terrain. In particular, the abilities of popular movements to embody and democratize the prophetic voice was put forth as imperative for challenging market logic and totalizing fundamentalisms. Religion was posited as possessing alternative human values to set against economic reductionism, through which to constitute other social possibilities. Additionally, the capacity of religious thought to question and confront established power relations was set against the notion in many fundamentalisms of reward after death for suffering, patience, and hard work during life. Debates ensued on how to renew the prophetic dimensions of religions and spiritualities, to amplify their ethical, non-violent, and utopic potentials. It was widely asserted that many popular movements have deep religious dynamics which inform their actions; this was reflected in the participation by members of diverse popular movements. Korean theologian Huyn Kyung positioned feminist and ecological movements as the privileged places for utopic action. She argued that feminist movements go beyond the dualisms of public-private and body-spirit, and promote smaller utopias in the everyday. Ecological movements, she argued, call forth a "green organic-orgasmic Earth that is a living organism. Kyung claimed that the interreligious movements call the world to "love and save the Earth" and to "look deeply into life." With this, she suggested that it is necessary to create many incorporated and possible utopias, here and now, to constitute "a marvelous life and a life of plentitude."

Religious Exclusions and Inclusions

The thematic terrain also highlighted many of the ways in which reductionisms and exclusions function in religious fundamentalisms. For example, fundamentalisms reduce social, ecological, and cosmological complexities to specific interpretations of texts, and exclude people who do not subscribe to the same interpretations of those texts. These reductions and exclusions foreclose ways of imagining, perceiving, and being, and thus social possibilities. It was maintained that the religious inclusion and intervention by feminists, gays, and other marginalized groups, opens theological possibilities for not only social justice, but for expanded and deepened modes of being. Beyond excluded social groups, there was much debate on the exclusion of categories and facets of human life set aside as "profane." For example, a number of workshops in the "Ethics, Cosmovisions, and Spiritualities" thematic terrain addressed how the body is marginalized within many religious traditions. In the workshop "Feminist Spirituality of Life and Dignity" it was widely agreed upon that emergent liberating theologies must incorporate the experience and divinity of the human body as part of effective political praxis. The embrace of sensuality within religious spheres was also addressed in the workshop, challenging the idea that the senses and pleasure are hindrances to, or outside of, divinity. This workshop may be seen as part of a larger theme of making concrete human life sacred.

The possibilities for hopeful alternatives emerged as the reductionisms of fundamentalisms were challenged and broadened in the discussions that embraced the divinity of the Earth itself. There was wide agreement that the Earth could emerge as a shared reference for divinity across religious and spiritual traditions. In a series of workshops on ecumenicalism facilitated by the Global Ecumenical Coalition, the conception of Earth as divinity was a point of convergence in debate and discussion. One of the organizers of this series spoke, "Tragically, for many people in the world today, she [the Earth] has been reduced to nothing more than 'real estate, wealth, mineral or resource.' We seem to have forgotten that the Earth is the source of all life, and that we have evolved from her. We are children of the Earth, and if we treat her with respect, she will continue to nourish us physically, psychologically, and spiritually." This mode of thought was echoed in many ecologically based workshops of the thematic terrain, such as "Biodynamic Agriculture—Constructing New Paths," and "Experiential Learning for a Sustainable World." Notions of the divinity of the Earth were a central reference to the Puxirum Indigenous Arts and Knowledge space which was a component of the "Ethics, Cosmovisions, and Spiritualities" thematic terrain. It was particularly in the Puxirum space that discussions centered on the possibilities of multiple and simultaneous cosmovisions—that differing cosmovisions do not necessarily negate each other, but may address differing aspects of human life. Again the Earth was brought in as a common reference for this. As one Puxirum participant expressed, "Indigenous people have much to offer the world right now, like ecology, like spirituality, but we must also engage with science, with technology."

Religion, Spirituality, and Social Power

Locating the religio-spiritual dimensions of the WSF in terms of the contemporary double movement reveals notions of market/self interest and social protection/social power as embodying profoundly different processes of subjectification, which are manifested through the religious and spiritual dimensions of politics. Guattari and Rolnik (1986) argue that subjectivity is the "raw material" of any social system: they position subjectivity as integral to social and productive infrastructure. Subjectivity, the mode of being and perceiving, is produced through complexes of social, economic, symbolic, and cultural structuring forces, such as the state, science, ideology, and religion. Processes of subjectification model: perception, behavior, sensibility, sexual relations, worldview, sense of self, emotions, identities, desire, gestures, and other dimensions of being and perceiving. Rooted in the rational, emotional, kinesthetic, and intuitive dimensions of social actors, subjectivity before being individual, is collective, social, and historical.

The history of the expansion of Euro-American capitalism is also the history of the production of capitalist subjectivities—what Guattari and Rolnik (1986) have termed "the colonization of subjectivity." This is the production of subjectivities mediated by market relations. Where subjectivities not compatible with market relations (such as wage relations) were encountered, genocide or colonization were deployed to destroy, enslave, or otherwise forcibly subdue and order populations. This process began within Europe itself through the violence of events such as the enclosures in Britain and is at the heart of neo-liberal development currently underway across the globe.

The hallmark of neo-liberal development is market fundamentalism—a decontextualized interpretation of market behavior and subjectivity as the basis of social reality. The idea of the market as the ultimate form of social organization abstracts human agency through the metaphor of the "invisible hand." The very concept of the invisible hand carries a pseudo-religious sense to it of an unseen force acting upon human relations. Thus, in neo-liberalism, social and political decisions of how to organize human life are largely surrendered to a transcendent notion of power, one which is outside of human agency. However, this is actually the disembedding of social power to groups and institutions which structure market relations, such as multi-national banks, state agencies, corporations, and the ideological apparati of these actors including think tanks and corporate-owned media. From this perspective, neo-liberal political and economic restructuring is the restructuring of subjectivity. Through the production of worldview, desire, ideology, sense of self, time, and other dynamics, human agency is disembedded from social relations and placed in the market.

At the core of neo-liberal subjectification is the idea of the human being as rational, self-interested, and calculating. The neo-liberal self is understood as individual in the absolute sense, the unit to which all social processes may be reduced. This notion of being and perceiving is a radicalization of the model of economic behavior posited by eighteenth and nineteenth century theorists of the free market. These economic and political theorists put forth a simplified model of the human being as an economic actor seeking to rationally maximize his or her own gain. However, these theorists distinguished between behavior in markets and behavior in other social and political spheres of life. Markets were generally understood in the context of a social contract which bound communities together through mutual responsibilities. Adam Smith, the theorist of the "invisible hand," viewed "moral sentiments" in social and political life, such as "sympathy" and "understanding for others," as equally important to economic self-interest in the ordering of society. Neo-liberal subjectification has been the transformation of a model of economic behavior in markets into a general idea of human nature. Motivation is channeled to consumption and preferences for private goods; neo-liberal theory terms this "rational choice," the logical endpoint of which is the consumer society, in which the market, not politics, is the organizing force of societies. For this extreme version of liberal subjectivity, participation in groups is a means for individual ends. Public space is privatized and becomes the medium for mass processes of seduction and the production of subjectivity through the images, sounds, and texts of advertising. What comes to attention is not the making of strong individual agents, but indeed the disempowering of collective agency, producing systems of atomized individuals mediated through market relations. Perhaps the vision of neo-liberal subjectivity was best expressed by Margaret Thatcher who claimed "There is no society, only individuals." The mass subjectification of this kind of market being is a new chapter in the capitalist colonization of subjectivity.

Above, I argued that religion has been a key terrain of contest in the dis-embedding of markets and re-embedding of markets from their context of social relationships. Religion is a core process of subjectification across the planet, structuring worldview, desire, sense of self, time, ideology, and other dynamics of being and perceiving. Fundamentalisms within religions tend to posit an "other worldly" divine placing agency outside human realms, surrendering the organization of human life to a transcendent notion of power. In effect this is a consolidation of power by placing agency with groups that control religious ideas and interpretations. Thus, where religious forces have been articulated with market forces it has been in a shared conservative project against the crisis of 1968, attempting to reassert a social order in crisis and reinforce crumbling ways of being and perceiving. Perhaps nowhere has this been stronger than in the contemporary hegemonic epicenter of the United States where the Religious Right has been in coalition with conservative political and economic forces. The Religious Right is associated with a radical individualism of self-help and self-salvation, under the idea of an other worldly, all powerful God—a construction of atomized individuals surrendering social power to a transcendent idea of the divine.

Embedded Religious Subjectivity

The religio-spiritual contentions of the WSF, through their criticism of neo-liberal social forms, values, and ethics, challenge neo-liberal subjectivity as being inadequate to address the complexity and richness of human and ecological life and empty in its promise of self-realization. Interrelation between humans, nature, and the cosmos are asserted over atomistic separateness and mediation by "other-worldly" transcendent forces, be they market or religious. Siddhartha, a participant in the "Ethics, Cosmovisions, and Spiritualities" thematic terrain remarked that individualism, as promoted by market fundamentalism views the "other" as a constant threat or competitor, and "with this it is impossible to construct true community, and also impossible to continue living in an environment of constant insecurity and competition." As the hegemonic structures of subjectification are eroded with the ongoing crisis of Euro-American capitalist expansion, social movements function as collective processes of subjectification, capturing and democratizing subjectivity. The re-engagement with religio-spiritual concerns in the WSF signals emergent and expanded terms of resistance to the abstract reductionism of market and religious fundamentalisms. These religio-spiritual reformulations of subjectification, which are integral to larger processes of the democratization of subjectivity in the WSF, herald more complex views of humanity's relationship to social, natural, and cosmological issues.

Examination of the debates, workshops, and discussions of the "Ethics, Cosmovisions, and Spiritualities" thematic terrain shows popular movements as active agents constructing religious forms—grounding, democratizing, and hybridizing religio-spiritual conceptions and experience into the social and ecological realities of counter-movements. Through this process of embedding the divine into human and natural worlds, popular movements are transforming and restructuring religious ways of imagining, perceiving, and being as components of their collective agency; movements are appropriating and transforming theologies and democratizing religious conceptions and subjectivities. In this pluralization of theologies is also the building of connections through the ethic of ecumenicalism and the vision of the earth as a shared reference of divinity. The struggle between the dis-embedding and re-embedding of the divine into socio-ecological relationships in the contemporary double movement is clearly revealed here. I conceptualize this key process of the production of counter-hegemonic subjectivities in social movement struggle as embedded religious subjectivity. From this perspective, social struggle is then intimately intertwined with theological struggle; social movements become also theological agents, restructuring and grounding the critical process of religio-spiritual subjectification into their struggle, constructing emergent forms of social power.

One of the most vivid examples of embedded religious subjectivity is found in the many global iterations of liberation theologies, which place social and natural systems as integral to the divine. In the Christian versions of liberation theology, Christ is held as the liberator of the oppressed. The Vatican's censuring of liberation theologians has formally been based around the argument that these theologies are "material" and "temporal" and the oppressed are best served through salvation, ensuring a trajectory to an other-worldly Paradise.

The "Discovery of Society"

The embedding of religious subjectivity in the WSF and global counter-movement is the making of ecumenical, hybrid, and relational subjectivities and reflects a wider desire for individuals and collectivities to appropriate the processes of subjectification. Against the imposition of market and religious fundamentalist subjectivities, these emergent counter-hegemonic subjectivities are increasingly relational and systemic. The experiences of these transforming subjectivities are then more encompassing of social, material, and cosmic flows—the lived experience of being an integral component of wider systems. One presenter in the workshop "Can Religions be Democratized" captured this well saying, "if we acknowledge it or not, we are all intimately connected with trees, birds, animals and all other human beings—we are not merely beings, we are inter-beings." In religio-spiritual language, these emergent forms are spiritual, but as Siddhartha (cited above) explains, in ways not confined to religion—spirituality that goes beyond the secular and the religious. While termed spiritual in the "Ethics, Cosmovisions, and Spiritualities" thematic terrain, this may also be comprehended as *ecological subjectivity* in the most experiential and profound senses—the subjectivity of being an integral and interdependent mode of human, ecological, and cosmic ecologies. The emergence of ecological subjectivities may be understood as a basis of social cohesion and emergent social power.

Polanyi theorized the "discovery of society" in the historical double movement arising from the crises of the late nineteenth century and early twentieth century English Free Market. He understood this new social power emerging in opposition to wholesale commodification of land, labor, and money to create state systems of social protection. Polanyi later wrote that this "Great Transformation" did not come to be as he had predicted in 1943—however, he brought to light the slow rise of social power through the twentieth century. The conception of "civil society" as social power has perhaps come to maturity in the contemporary double movement with the WSF's emergent conceptions of civil society as the privileged political agency.

The "discovery of society" is then not a resurgence of an already existing primordial social form as suggested by Polanyi. It is instead the trajectory of individual and collective capture of processes of subjectification and the constitution of subjectivities, which concretely challenge the atomistic self-interest of market culture and the "other worldly" absolutism of factional religious fundamentalisms. The continuing discovery of society, or perhaps more aptly, active construction of plural society, is rooted in the democratization and construction of inter-relational subjectivities. Embodied in the metaphor of social power is the transformation of human subjectivities to ecological modes of perceiving and being. These processes of counter-hegemonic subjectification are simultaneously preserving and producing difference across geographies and histories, while constructing interdependent social webs through a shared ethics of ecumenicalism and ecology and recognition of mutual struggle.

Conclusion

In summary, the "Ethics, Cosmovisions, and Spiritualities" thematic terrain in the WSF represents an integral part of the global countermovement struggling to substitute an ecumenical and plural vision of a shared humanity for the market and religious fundamentalisms consolidated during the neoliberal era. In the place of fractured religious differences, and societies and development models driven by self-interest, this plural and ecumenical vision of humanity emerging from the WSF may be a necessary basis for the making of "global citizenship" and a plural, democratic global order.

Note

* Acknowledgments I wish to thank Phil McMichael, Thomas Hirschl, Sudeshna Mitra, Dia Mohan, Razack Karriem, Karuna Morarji, and Chad Futrell for their feedback and comments on multiple drafts of this essay.

CONCLUSION

15.
DEVELOPMENT AND ITS DISCONTENTS
Philip McMichael and Karuna Morarji

Struggles of the disempowered offer perspective on development claims, and new ways of thinking about social change, approaches that question the development narrative and the market episteme, advocating for the right to represent and realize different ways of living in this world, and transcending the development impasse.

Introduction: The Paradox of Development

"Development" is a concept with a long lineage, deriving from the European experience of urban-industrialization and colonial domination. As such it performs a self-referential function, canonized in classical political economy. It categorizes European endeavors and accomplishments as the touchstone of "modernity": a liberal ideal whereby modern societies are governed by states characterized by political pluralism, universal citizenship, and equal opportunity in the marketplace. Development is the process of achieving this condition via statehood and economic growth. Through colonization, Europe affirmed its development credentials, representing itself as a civilizing force in the non-European world, which force eventually generated independence struggles across Europe's empire. Through decolonization, and the extension of statehood to the post-colonial world, development came to be seen as the natural, universal destiny of all peoples.[1]

The legacy of this passage from European colonialism to universal development is significant for the social struggles depicted here. Not only was colonialism once considered necessary to the civilizing project, but also colonial subjects were once considered incapable of self-organization. The rupture of the colonial relationship revealed the limiting assumptions of colonial rule, founded on an elemental racism that portrayed subjects as backward, passive, and uncivilized. It took a monumental and historic struggle to unsettle the categories through which Europe perceived the world (in its own image).[2]

Consider the impact on Enlightenment discourse of the late eighteenth century slave revolt in Haiti, a turning point that, for Michel-Rolph Trouillot, revealed the "unthinkable even as it happened." In this revolt the category of "slave" was limiting because European categorical and philosophical discourse could not account for slave self-organization. Trouillot chronicles the silences that forbade Europeans, and slaves, from recognizing the significance of the revolution as it unfolded. Thus, a French colonist in Saint-Domingue wrote to his wife in France, in 1790: "there is no move-ment among our Negroes.... They don't even think of it. They are very tranquil and obedient. A revolt among them is impossible." In this way, self-referential discourse simply "othered" the slave: "the more European merchants and mercenaries bought and conquered other men and women, the more European philosophers wrote and talked about Man" (Trouillot, 1995, pp. 72, 75).

Ultimately, Trouillot's point regarding the shock of the Haitian revolution is that the European "contention that enslaved Africans and their descendants could not envision freedom—let alone formulate strategies for gaining and securing such freedom—was based not so much on empirical evidence as on an ontology, an implicit organization of the world and its inhabitants" (p. 73). In other words, systems of domi-nation tend to proclaim their own normalcy, silencing their internal contradictions, and the possibility that the terms of reference can be contested and turned against those who construct these terms. Thus C.L.R. James suggests the Haitian slave revolt was carried out in the liberatory terms of the French Revolution, as the slaves held up a mirror to their French masters, demanding equivalence. In addition, the slave revolt affected the course of the French revolt. The masses supported abolition: "Servants, peasants, workers, the labourers by the day in the fields all over France were filled with a virulent hatred against the 'aristocracy of the skin'. There were so many so moved by the sufferings of the slaves that they had long ceased to drink coffee, thinking of it as drenched with the blood and sweat of men turned into brutes" (in this they anticipated the anti-sweatshop consumer today). And: "The blacks were taking their part in the destruction of European feudalism begun by the French Revolution, and liberty and equality, the slogans of the revolution, meant far more to them than to any French-man" (James, 1963, pp. 139, 198).

At the time, while the slaves of Haiti conceived their struggle in (their) terms of liberty and equality, their struggle was not recognized as such, but dismissed by their masters as insurgent resistance. What we can take from this is that the mean-ing of "social change" is bounded by a set of self-referential categories, reproducing an ontology (a way of being) specific to a political order. Unruliness is regarded as (negative) resistance because of the unthinkability of (positive) self-organization by its subjects. And yet, precisely because colonial ontology underestimated slave revolt as unthinkable, once begun it ignited a long struggle for decolonization. At the point at which empire became too costly, non-European claims for development were given legitimacy as "self-determination," but within an extended European state-system.[3] That which was once unthinkable was now thinkable, within a reformulated power structure.

The struggles documented in this volume perhaps are analogous, in the sense that within the current development frame they represent the unthinkable. Individually and together, their challenge is to reformulate power relations, opening new spaces of social possibility.

The struggles are united by their epistemic critique of development claims in par-ticular settings. These include spatial settings (urban, rural, frontier, interstitial), edu-cational institutions, electoral processes, indigenous territories, and the World Social

Forum. The encroachment of market culture on schooling, identity, gender relations, biodiversity, land use, elections, governance, the social contract, and more, presents itself as a moral agenda[4] in a variety of locations—from pasturelands in northern Pakistan through electoral politics in the Nigerian delta to civic education in urban Brazil. Market rule brings an economic calculus to cultural and social relationships, in the name of democratization (individual choice) and market efficiency (individual maximization). These cultural ideals are deeply embedded in the development episteme, which views the market as a vehicle of universal progress. By normalizing market rule, challenges to it appear either "unthinkable" or "negative resistance," and are marginalized by definition. Our ethnographic encounters with these struggles contextualize marginalization, in its intent as well as its impact. They reveal the reductionism of conceptions of normality, opening up future possibilities.

Development and Its Material and Epistemic Exclusions

The reductionism of development discourse and practice is exclusionary. People are not just excluded because they lack the means to participate in the market. They may be excluded because their aspirations and practices do not fit with the market culture, or because the market culture itself consigns them to redundancy. Through the lens of the market calculus they may be excluded, and classified as "undeveloped," "residual," or even "have-nots." The social struggles here contest such classification—not to be academic, but to claim their own definition. These struggles remind us of two things: first, development, particularly in its neoliberal garb, is increasingly exclusionary, and second, there is more than one way to give meaning to social existence. In other words, these are struggles against exclusion, *and* to reclaim multiple meanings of social existence.

Our ethnographic fieldwork has sought to access these other meanings, or claims, as they engage the dominant claims of the market culture. Our concern is with how such engagement challenges the market calculus via an "epistemic critique" of development's failure of imagination (in addition to its failure to deliver). It is also with how people rearticulate meaning and therefore possibility in the struggle against processes of exclusion and disempowerment. That is, their engagement is interactive, and their struggles are effective to the extent that they are able to subvert and appropriate dominant meanings to their own cause. Thus we capture how these struggles generate new formulations of "citizenship," "property," "conservation," "education," "democracy," and "sovereignty," in framing alternative conceptions and practices of development.

More than one in six humans now live in slums, over one billion in a world of jobless growth, or no growth, and in which the link between urbanization and industrialization has been irrevocably undone (Davis, 2006). Symptomatic of a world in which the promise of "development" appears as a receding horizon to its majority, poverty and marginality suggest redundancy. Arguably, it is a modern problem for which there is no modern solution (B. d. S. Santos, 2002, p. 1). Indeed, modern solutions are often the source of the problem, as development continues to generate new inequalities. To the extent that this is so, solutions must come from practices and movements that engage critically with development and its assumptions, and prefigure alternative practices. Thus these struggles challenge the "epistemic privilege" through which powerful institutions and discourses construct particular visions of the world as natural, and as the universal and inevitable path of human progress.

Epistemic privilege is etched into the narrative of development because the terms of human development are power-laden in their origin and their import. Through colonization European elites set the stage for modern capitalist development that has defined a uniform standard and goal institutionalized in the modern state system. Defined as a universal ladder (Sachs, 2005), development is essentially a self-referential metaphor that justifies a particular ordering of the world. While the people at the base of the ladder are presumed to be "developmentally challenged," this definition excludes their self-definition. It assumes their challenge is to develop. But the struggles in this volume suggest that their challenge is *with* development. While they may acknowledge the existence of some kind of "ladder" the meaning they give to it is not necessarily the meaning imparted from those at the top of the "development ladder." Their struggle is precisely to define the terms through which their lives find meaning, and this in turn imparts a different meaning and substantive content to development.

Struggles over meaning or resources raise questions about "development"—questions that focus on both its paradoxical assumptions of equal worth in a diverse world, and its paradoxical outcomes in promoting accumulation of material wealth through inequality and dispossession. At a time when limits to economic growth are becoming apparent in the face of energy, climate, food, and financial crises, these struggles draw attention to new ways of thinking about development from the perspective of its subordinates—approaches that question the consumer ethic and the psychology of self-interest, and, in self-organizing, demand the power of self-representation as a condition of emancipation. This volume has sought to clarify and re-envision development by representing the claims of the disenfranchised.

Clarity comes from recognizing that those who struggle are not necessarily struggling to realize what is valued in the development narrative. Marketplace participation is not always the solution for those with other cultural terms of reference. Survival comes first, and that often implicates protection of life-worlds. Retaining access to resources, most of which are common resources (public lands, forests, pastures, waterways, seeds, knowledges, social networks, public services), is central to survival. It is commonplace for developers (including governments) to proclaim that the route to "inclusion" lies through market mechanisms,[5] ignoring the social resources and resourcefulness of the disenfranchised as foundations for their own life-worlds, however impoverished they seem to those with a development ladder vision of the world. Furthermore, to developers (e.g., governments, banks, corporations, NGOs, the World Bank) the occupation and use of resources in common retards their conversion to private property and inclusion in the marketplace, thereby providing a "development obstacle."[6] But privatizing social resources is precisely the mechanism whereby development can actively undermine durable forms of social reproduction—through sometimes violent processes of imposing a singular and simplifying calculus of market value on complex cultural and ecological relations.

Through the struggles represented here it becomes obvious that people mobilizing against exclusion are not necessarily or simply demanding inclusion, but are questioning familiar binaries with which we work, such as inclusion/exclusion, modern/backward, and developed/undeveloped. In other words they are questioning how their condition is viewed, and what is considered the appropriate "solution" to their condition. They may not see the world through the same lens, or impart the same meaning to their condition. And as their own lens comes into focus, as this collection allows, it is possible to see the limiting assumptions of the development lens. What is understood as normal (epistemic), they view as problematic.

Thus when peasants mobilize to protect and sustain their life-world, they are not just claiming rights, but also questioning the epistemic assumption that in a modern world they are supposed to disappear.[7] The coincidence of the mass production of slums with an epistemic assumption of peasant obsolescence underscores the limits of "modern solutions." And yet a recent World Bank *World Development Report* argues for more of the same, on the assumption that absorbing peasants into agro-industrial "value chains" will increase their productivity—producing food mostly for export, however, rather than for local food security—deepening fossil fuel dependence, reducing biodiversity, and increasing carbon emissions. The epistemic challenge asserts that smallholders have rights to produce in the modern world, in a sustainable way.[8] But conventional development categories ("economic efficiency," "specialization," and "comparative advantage") legitimize, in this instance, soil mining and the devaluation and displacement of a substantial portion of humanity. These categories belong to an economic calculus. But the people subjected to these terms do not necessarily live by such a calculus. Why should they be held to such an abstract standard, for what purpose, and in whose interest?

These struggles, then, are *diagnostic* insofar as the terms of reference of "development" are held up to examination by those who experience redundancy, in material and epistemic ways. Not only do they lose resources (land, knowledge, networks as peasants), or experience exclusion from social resources (civil and social rights as slum-dwellers), but also they may forfeit a distinctive value calculus forged *in situ*, rather than in an economics textbook. Certainly their calculus is not immune to the objectifying pressures of the global marketplace, but long-standing adaptations draw on values rooted in cultural or ecological attachments. Thus Karuna Morarji's chapter 4 depicts the contradictory epistemic experiences of rural students and their families as they struggle to make sense of the ambiguities of modern education in northern India. Promising individual and social mobility ("progress") through education for a commercialized urban existence, such schooling forecloses the inter-generational securities of agrarian livelihoods, and yet does not guarantee urban employment. The assumed link between education and development (a UN Millennium Development Goal) is not so seamless after all. Insecure villagers from Jaunpur must reconcile the individualizing values of development with the customary collective values and moral codes of the rural culture they are supposed to leave behind. Struggling between two worlds represents what it means to be modern in Jaunpur, underlining the complexity of development as a process across time and space. Across the world, the Afro-Brazilians depicted in Alex Da Costa's chapter 13 struggle to incorporate into municipal education their cultural heritage as a legitimate form of knowledge, complicating the meaning of "inclusion" and recalibrating development assumptions regarding the status of minority cultures.

These struggles do not necessarily reject development ideals or principles (equality, rights, citizenship, education, social contract); rather, they challenge the content of these ideas and suggest different grounds for, or terms of realization of, those ideals. As Hannah Wittman shows in chapter 11, landless workers in Brazil challenge the normalizing association of civilization with urbanization. Instead, they advocate an "agrarian citizenship" that values the social function of smallholding in stabilizing rural populations, providing new opportunities for *favela* inhabitants to resettle the land, and developing agro-ecological methods of food production.

In short, the chapters in this collection describe, with ethnographic detail, social struggles by people *doubly marginalized* by development and its narrowing lens. What is at stake is not just the lives and livelihoods of the people concerned, but development itself, which has become synonymous with a combination of crises (food, environmental, energy, financial, and climate). The single-minded pursuit of an economic calculus in the name of development is marked by violent appropriations and devaluations of material resources, by redundancy of certain categories of people, and by a foreclosure of social visions and possibilities. Yet these dynamics also generate struggles that contest and rework the terms of crisis—struggles incubated within the neoliberal development project[9] but dedicated to transcending its answers by reformulating the questions. New questions bring the unthinkable into play, creating new horizons of possibility, as anticipated in the birth pangs of development during the colonial era.

Development Struggles

Neither a global ethnography concerned to link the "local" to the "global,"[10] nor a conventional analysis of social movements concerned to theorize the political efficacy of mobilization, this collection has addressed a different question: how do social struggles around the world expose the material and epistemic shortcomings of "development"? By questioning the normalizing claims of development, struggles from a variety of settings serve to politicize, and historicize, the current global order. In particular, they uncover the "normative foreclosure" implicit in market rule, namely, the way it reduces culture and development to an economic calculus, erasing history, and rendering alternatives invisible or unthinkable. Thus these struggles potentially alter the conditions of possibility for a paradigm, and world, in crisis.

In this regard, as claimed in chapter 1, the struggles represented here reach beyond the conventions of the "social movement" paradigm: namely, that "development" realizes liberal modernity through statehood and economic growth. Social movements enact (or retard) this process through demands for social justice, democratic representation, equal rights, economic opportunity, and so on. In other words, development is the implicit narrative through which social movements are typically examined. As Della Porta and Tarrow note, although "social movements have often pushed for a conception of 'direct' democracy, the institutions and actors of representative democracy have long structured movements, political opportunities and constraints within the boundaries of institutional politics" (2005, pp. 1–2).

Our struggles, however, work against this grain: they are not constrained or inclined to work to realize the development vision of liberal modernity. Well, all but one, but this is the exception that proves the rule. In Emelie Peine's chapter 9, soy farmers on the Brazilian frontier misconstrue the state as the problem in a market collapse because they have internalized the norm of "market neutrality," which serves agribusiness interests. Their demand for the state to correct the market contradicts their identification as "free market" producers in a global market of highly subsidized U.S. and European farmers. Such self-identification obscures their utter dependence on the real masters of the market, the corporate grain traders, who in turn organize the (neoliberal) state. This seemingly anomalous critical struggle is the proof of the pudding, so to speak, where accommodation by soy farmers affirms the hegemony of the market paradigm, its naturalization of the state as politically neutral, and its appeal to self-gain and the current development ideal.

What distinguishes the other struggles is their reflexivity, in questioning assumptions about their needs or destiny. "Development" implies uniform direction ("stages of growth"), uniform means (market resources), and uniform meanings (self-interest, self-improvement). Instead of simply reforming political structures to manage or regulate development, these struggles refocus on the shortcomings of the development episteme through their own particular experiences. They bear witness to its limitations, not just in material failure, but also in subjective misrepresentations. They self-organize, and, as Gayatri Menon's chapter 10 on pavement dwellers challenging Mumbai's code of citizenship shows, they encroach on and reformulate the terms of their subjection to the development narrative.

In challenging normalized expectations these struggles contest and reveal "that what does not exist is in fact actively produced as non-existent, that is, as a non credible alternative to what exists."[11] That is, they transgress silences that underwrite the *status quo*—thus in Alex Da Costa's chapter 13, Afro-Brazilians assert recognition of their cultural heritage as indispensable to an equitable notion of "civil rights." In doing so, these struggles challenge premature categorical closure, through which existing power relations are normalized. Land markets, for example, may appear as a neutral approach to equitable or efficient distribution of resources, until landless peoples or peasants struggle against land *concentration* for the right to land to make their own contribution to society. The new religious struggles in the World Social Forum, as depicted in Andreas Hernandez's chapter 14, collapse the religious/secular dichotomy (and its configuring of power) in order to realize a plural and ecumenical form of spirituality anchored in a collective human ethic. Through self-organization, these critical struggles realize the unthinkable.

Expressing a formative politics of the "margins," generated by the deepening development crisis, these struggles articulate central political questions of our times. Whether women demanding public accountability for the disabling impact of liquor licensing as a government revenue shortcut, peasants invoking food sovereignty, religious subjectivity movements reformulating spiritual experience beyond doctrinal boundaries and individualist faith, or indigenous people making claims for autonomy—such struggles are viewed as anomalies through the self-referential lens of development. Yet these struggles, far from being anomalous, test development norms that presume their protagonists' non-existence. Whether the subjects of these struggles create emancipatory movements or critique social orderings, they point toward alternative, emergent futures of an equitable and sustainable form of development.

Emancipation is not simply about access to resources, but also about the terms of access. Thus, reformulating "citizenship" to include claims of shack-dwellers, peasants, indigenous peoples, and Afro-Brazilians, for example, is a twofold accomplishment. It seeks accommodation of people written out of existence in the development narrative. And in seeking accommodation in their terms it transforms the categories through which we understand modern history. Struggles for indigenous rights and knowledges contest the "monoculture of linear time" presumed by liberal modernity, through which history is presented "as having a unique and known direction" leading to "the Western way of life, its knowledge, its institutions and its social organization" (Agostino, 2008, p. 232). Such struggles reveal the *partial* efficacy and truth of ruling ideas and categories, which serve as a tool of power and dispossession *and* as a tool of struggle and repossession.

Conclusion: The Development Lens in Perspective

While early (Enlightenment) modernity advocated the *desirability* of progress, or human self-improvement, subsequent European state-building and colonial ventures universalized the goal of progress as *inevitable,* spawning "development" as a master concept of the social sciences.[12] Development provided commonsense meanings of social change, consolidated in the era of decolonization. But as master concept, development legitimizes authoritative representations of social change through social scientific knowledge—by which a European self-referential concept has come to frame possibility and how it can unfold. Thus, "[i]f modernity is the figure to which social theory unavoidably refers itself, development is the prime index we use to assess efforts toward modernization," and this ontological construction involves "a public appropriation of societal transformation in the name of development" (Sivaramakrishnan and Agrawal, 2003, pp. 2, 3). As development is naturalized as both process and aspiration, it represents a set of values through which people come to organize their everyday actions.[13]

Yet while development "works" in a sense as a "lodestar" (Wallerstein, 2001), "there is more to the idea of development in its historical context: like other concepts, this one can be seized, turned around from a structure of depoliticization into a claim for entitlements" (Stoler and Cooper, 1997, p. 35). This is our point—struggles problematize the claims and scope of development. To illustrate, the chapters by Alicia Swords and Dia Da Costa highlight struggles in Chiapas, Mexico and West Bengal, India, respectively that transform "private" problems into legitimate subjects of public concern. They reveal how liberal developmentalism limits the domain of rights (and citizenship) to the marketplace, invisibilizing gender exploitation within households and communities. In each case, networks of learning and protest activate community struggles to offset assumptions that the market is the sole appropriate (and neutral) medium of development. In so doing they express the shared goal of this collection: to politicize development, and unsettle its claims to define social change by re-opening possibilities.

Notes

1. For various accounts of this phenomenon, see Escobar (1995), Cowan and Shenton (1996), Rist (1997), Cooper and Packard (1997).
2. Even so, Immanuel Wallerstein notes: "All these categories are now so deep in our subconscious that we can scarcely talk about the world without using them. World-systems analysis argues that the categories that inform our history were historically formed (and for the most part only a century or so ago). It is time that they were re-opened for examination" (1987, p. 322).
3. As Gilbert Rist has noted: "Their right to self-determination had been acquired in exchange for the right to self-definition" (1997, p. 79). See also Saldaña-Portillo (2003).
4. Cf. Corrigan and Sayer's concept of "moral regulation" as central to the process of state formation (1985).
5. Cf. the new industry to develop the two billion at the "bottom of the pyramid" (Prahalad, 2006; Collier, 2007). Julia Elyachar's research (2005) suggests micro-credit "empowerment" exploits and dispossesses cultural resources shared among myriad workshops, owners, and customers in Cairo.
6. Thus Hernando de Soto (1990) pioneered the notion of alleviating urban poverty by converting the "dead" assets of the poor (their shacks) into "live" capital by incorporating shacks "inside the capitalist economy" as loan collateral.
7. Paul Nicholson, representing the international peasant movement, remarks: "To date, in all the global debates on agrarian policy, the peasant movement has been absent: we have not had a voice. The main reason for the very existence of Vía Campesina is to be that voice and to speak out for the creation of a more just society" (quoted in Desmarais, 2002, p. 96).
8. For a critical review of the Bank's Report, see McMichael (2009), and for an elaboration of the epistemic critique embodied in the international peasant movement, see McMichael (2008b).
9. The "neoliberal development project" is a cultural specification of the political-economic restructuring associated with "globalization," and its privatizing neoliberal creed (cf. McMichael, 2008a). The financial crisis notwithstanding, privatization of resources, and displacement of populations, will intensify as energy, food, climate, and security concerns intensify.
10. Cf. Burawoy et al. (2000).
11. Santos, quoted in Agostino (2008, p. 232).
12. For elaboration, see Araghi and McMichael (2006).
13. See, for example, Pigg (1992), Klenk (2004), and Baviskar (2005).

REFERENCES

Abrams, P. (1982). *Historical sociology*. Ithaca, NY: Cornell University Press.

Abrams, P. (1988[1977]). Notes on the difficulty of studying the state. *Journal of Historical Sociology, 1*, 58–89.

Adesina, A. (2006, September 13). *Building input supply systems to improve access for farmers*. Paper presented at the high level technical session of the Africa Fertilizer Summit, Abuja, Nigeria.

Agamben, G. (2003). Beyond human rights. In A. Levy & E. Cadava (Eds.), *Cities without citizens* (pp. 3–12). Philadelphia: Slought Foundation.

Agostino, A. (2008). Going beyond development monoculture: Critical reflections on the MDGs. *Development, 51*, 228–235.

Agrawal, A. (2001a). State formation in community spaces? Decentralization of control over forests in the Kumaon Himalya, India. *Journal of Asian Studies, 60*(1), 9–40.

Agrawal, A. (2001b). Common property institutions and sustainable development. *World Development, 29*(10), 649–672.

Ake, C. (1994). *Democratization and disempowerment in Africa* (CASS occasional monograph No. 1). Port Harcourt, Nigeria: Malthouse Press.

Ali, I., & Butz, D. (2003). The Shimshal governance model: A community conserved area, a sense of cultural identity, a way of life. *Policy Matters, 12*, 111–120.

Almond, M. 2006). 'People power' is a global brand owned by America. *The Guardian*, August 15. Retrieved August 25, 2009, from http://www.guardian.co.uk/comment/story/0,,1844573,00.html

Andreasson, S. (2003). Economic reforms and "virtual democracy" in South Africa and Zimbabwe: The incompatibility of liberalisation, inclusion and development. *Journal of Contemporary African Studies, 21*(3), 383.

Appadurai, A. (1996). *Modernity at large: Cultural dimensions of globalization*. Minneapolis: University of Minnesota Press.

Appadurai, A. (2002). Deep democracy: Urban governmentality and the horizon of politics. *Public Culture, 14*(1), 21–47.

Appadurai, A. (2004). The capacity to aspire: Culture and the terms of recognition. In V. Rao & M. Walton (Eds.), *Culture and public action* (pp. 59–84). Stanford, CA: Stanford Social Sciences.

Applebaum, R. P., & Robison, W. I. (Eds.). (2005). *Critical globalization studies*. New York: Routledge.

Araghi, F. (1995). Global de-peasantization: 1945–1990. *Sociological Quarterly, 36*(2), 337–368.

Araghi, F., & McMichael, P. (2006). Regresando a lo históric-mudial: Una crítica del retroceso postmoderno en los estudios agrarios [Returning to the world-historical approach: a critique of the retreat into postmodernism in agrarian studies]. *Revista* (ALASRU), 3, 1–47.

Arendt, H. (1943). We refugees. *Menorah Journal, 1*, 77.

Arrighi, G., & Silver, B. (1999). *Chaos and governance in the modern world system*. Minneapolis: Minnesota University Press.

As Dimensões Inseparáveis de Política e Cultura e a Luta do C. C. Orùnmilá [The inseparable dimensions of politics and Cclture in the Orùnmulá Cultural Center's struggle]. (2004, May). *Sorò Dúdú: Fala Negro*, p. 2.

Ashby, J., Garcia, M., Guerrero, D. P., Patino, C. A., Quiros, C. A., & Roa, J. I. (1997). Supporting local farmer research committees. In L. van Veldhuizen, A. Waters-Bayer, R. Ramirez, D. A. Johnson, & J. Thompson (Eds.), *Farmers' research in practice: Lessons from the field* (pp. 245–261). London: IT Publications.

Ashby, T. (2007). Yar'Adua takes helm of crisis-ridden Nigeria. Reuters. Retrieved May 29, 2007, from http://www.reuters.com/article/worldNews/idUSL2963095620070529

Atvater, A., & Mahnkopf, B. (1997). The world unbound. *Review of International Political Economy, 4*(3), 448–471.

Avery, A., & Avery, D. (2003). High-yield conservation: More food and environmental quality through intensive agriculture. In R. E. Meiners & B. Yandle (Eds.), *Agricultural policy and the environment: Problems, prospects, and prosperity* (pp. 135–150). Lanham, MD: Rowman & Littlefield.

Badiou, A. (2001). *Ethics: A essay on the understanding of evil* (P. Hallward, Trans.). London: Verso.

Badiou, A. (2005a). *Being and event*. London: Continuum.

Badiou, A. (2005b). *Metapolitics* (J. Barker, Trans.). London: Verso.

Bandy, J., & Smith, J. (Eds.). (2005). *Coalitions across borders: Transnational protest and the neoliberal order*. Lanham, MD: Rowman & Littlefield.

Bannerjee, M. (2007, April 28). Sacred elections. *Economic and Political Weekly, 42*, 1556–1562.

Barreto, A. A. (2002). *Vieques, the navy, and Puerto Rican politics*. Gainesville: University of Florida Press.

Barros, R. R., & Cavalcanti, C. (2006). Os afro-brasileiros e o espaço escolar—por uma pedagogia do lúdico e do informal. In M. L. S. Braga, E. P. Souza, & A. F. M. Pinto (Eds.), *Dimensões da Inclusão no Ensino Médio: Mercado de trabalho, religiosidade e educação quilombola* (pp. 161–178). Brasilia: SECAD.

Barta, A. (2004). Rebellious cornfields: Toward food and labor self-sufficiency. In G. stero (Ed.), *Mexico in transition: Neoliberal globalism, the state and civil society* (pp. 18–36). London: Zed.

Baviskar, A. (2005). The dream machine: The model development project and the remaking of the state. In A. Bakiskar (Ed.), *Waterscapes: The cultural politics of a natural resource* (pp. 281–313). Delhi: Permanent Black.

Bayat, A. (2000). From "dangerous classes" to "quiet rebels": Politics of the urban subaltern in the global south. *International Sociology, 15*(3), 533–557.

Beinhart, W. (1984). Soil erosion, conservationism and ideas about development: A southern African exploration, 1900–1960. *Journal of Southern African Studies, 11*, 52–83.

Belenky, M. F., Bond, L. A., & Weinstock, J. S. (1997). *A tradition that has not name: Nurturing the development of people, families and communities*. New York: Basic Books.

Bellinghausen, H. (2006 July 7). Estúpido culpar al EZLN por no apoyar a López Obrador: Marcus (Marcos: It is stupid to blame the EZLN for not supporting López Obrador). *La Jornada*.

Beverley, J. (2004). Subaltern resistance in Latin America: A reply to Tom Brass. *The Journal of Peasant Studies, 31*(2), 261–275.

Bezner Kerr, R. (2005a). Food security in northern Malawi: Historical context and the significance of gender, kinship relations and entitlements. *Journal of Southern African Studies, 31*, 53–74.

Bezner Kerr, R. (2005b). Informal labor and social relations in northern Malawi: The theoretical challenges and implications of ganyu labor for food security. *Rural Sociology, 70*, 167–187.

Bezner Kerr, R. (2006). *Contested knowledge and disputed practice: Maize and groundnut seeds and child feeding in northern Malawi*. Ithaca, NY: Cornell University, Department of Development Sociology.

Bezner Kerr, R., Snapp, S., Chirwa, M., Shumba, L., & Msachi, R. (2007). Participatory research on legume diversification with Malawian smallholder farmers for improved human nutrition and soil fertility. *Experimental Agriculture, 43*, 1–17.

Bhaduri, A. (2007). Alternatives in industrialisation. *Economic and Political Weekly, 42*(18), 1597–1601.

Bhattacharya, B. (2001). School teachers in rural West Begal. *Economic and Political Weekly, 36*(8), 673–683.

Bhattacharya, B. (2007, January 21). We cannot fail people's expectations. *People's Democracy*, 31 (weekly organ of the communist party of India [Marxist]). XXX1(3). Retrieved January 21, 2007, from http://pd.cpim.org/2007/0121/01212007_buddhadeb's%20letter.htm

Bonatsos, C., Bezner Kerr, R., & Shumba, L. (2008). *SFHC food security status and crop diversification 2007/2008 survey report*. Ekwendeni, Malawi: Ekwendeni Hospital SFHC Project.

Bond, P., & Dada, R. (Eds.). (2005). *Trouble in the air: Global warming and the privatised atmosphere*. Durban, South Africa: Centre for Civil Society, School of Development Studies, University of KwaZula-Natal.

Bose, S. (1997). Instruments and idioms of colonial and national development: India's historical experience in comparative perspective. In F. Cooper & R. Packard (Eds.), *International development and the social sciences* (pp. 45–63). Berkeley: University of California Press.

Botelho, D. (2006). Orixás/Inquices/Voduns e perspectivas educacionais. *Ìrohìn, 11*(18), 16–17.

Brazil, Ministério de Desenvolvimento Agrário/Instituto Nacional de Colonização e Reforma Agrária (MDA-INCRA). (2001). *Percentuais e causas das evasões nos assentamentos rurais* . Brasília: MDA-INCRA.

Brazil, Ministry of Education. (2004). Diretrizes Curriculares Nacionais para a Educação das Relações Étnico-Raciais e para o Ensino de História e Cultural Afro-Brasileira e Africana [National curricular directives for the education of ethno-racial relations and for the teaching of Afro-Brazilian and African history and culture]. Retrieved January 8, 2009, from http://www.publicacoes.inep.gov.br/arquivos/%7B2A0A514E-6C2A-4657-862F-CD4840586714%7D_AFRO-BRASILEIRA.pdf

Breunig, L. A. (2006). *Conservation in context; Establishing natural protected areas during Mexico's neoliberal reformation*. Doctoral dissertation, University of Arizona.

Brockington, D., & Homewood, K. (2001). Degradation debates and data deficiencies: The Mkomazi Game Reserve, Tanzania. *African Affairs, 71*(3), 449–480.

Brown, S. (2001). Authoritarian leaders and multiparty elections in Africa: How foreign donors help to keep Kenya's Daniel arap Moi in power. *Third World Quarterly, 22*(5), 725–739.

Browning, B. (1995). *Samba: Resistance in motion.* Bloomington: Indiana University Press.

Bruno, R. (2003). Nova república: A violência patronal rural como prática de classe. *Sociologias, 5*(10), 284–310.

Bryceson, D. F., & Fonseca, J. (2006). Risking death for survival: Peasant responses to hunger and HIV/AIDS in Malawi. *World Development, 34,* 1654–1666.

Brysk, A., & Shafir, G. (2004). Introduction: Globalization and the citizenship gap. In *People out of place: Globalization, human rights, and the citizenship gap* (pp. 3–10). London: Routledge.

Burawoy, M., Blum, J., George, S., Gille, Z., Thayer, M., et al. (2000). *Global ethnography: Forces, connections and imaginations in a postmodern world.* Berkeley: University of California Press.

Burdick, J. (1998). *Blessed Anastácia: Women, race, and popular christianity in Brazil.* New York: Routledge.

Butz, D. (1996). Sustaining indigeous communities: Symbolic and instrumental dimensions of pastoral resource use in Shimshal, Northern Pakistan. *The Canadian Geographer, 40,* 36–53.

Butz, D. (1998). Orientalist representations of resource use in Shamshal, Pakistan, and their extra-discursive effects. In I. Stellrecht (Ed.), *Karakoram—Hindukush—Himalays: Dynamics of change* (part 1), (pp. 357–386). Cologne: Rüdiger Köppe Verlag.

Butz, D. (2002). Resistance, representation, and third space in Shimshal village, Northern Pakistan. *ACME: An International Journal of Critical Geographies, 1,* 15–34.

Caldwell, K. L. (2007). *Negras in Brazil: Re-envisioning black women, citizenship, and the politics of identity.* New Brunswick, NJ: Rutgers University Press.

Cameron, A., & Palan, R. (2004). *The imagined economies of globalization.* London: Sage.

Cape Argus. (2005, October 13). 66 cops injured in illegal service delivery protests. *Cape Argus.* Retrieved November 2, 2006, from http://www.abahlali.org/node/173

Caraway, N. (1991). Crossover dreams: Towards a multicultural feminist politics of solidarity. In N. Caraway (Ed.), *Segregated sisterhood: Racism and the politics of American feminism* (pp. 171–203). Knoxville: University of Tennessee Press.

Cardoso, F. H., & Muller, G. (1977). *Amazônia: expansão do capitalismo.* São Paulo, Brazil: Editora Brasiliense.

Carothers, M. (2007). How democracies emerge: The sequencing fallacy. *Journal of Democracy, 18*(1), 12–27.

Castaneda, J., & Morales, M. (2007). The Mexican standoff: Looking to the future. *Journal of Democracy, 18*(1), 102–112.

Cavalleiro, E. (Ed.). (2001). *Racismo e Anti-Racismo na Educação [Racism and anti-racism in education].* São Paulo: Selo Negro.

Cavalleiro, E. (2005). Introdução [Introduction]. In *Educação anti-racista: Caminhos abertos pela Lei Federal nº 10.639/03 [Anti-racist education: Paths opened by federal law 10,639/2003]* (pp. 11–18). Brasilia: MEC, SECAD.

Cederlof, G., & Sivaramakrishnan, K. (Eds.). (2006). *Ecological nationalisms: Nature, livelihoods, and identities in South Asia.* Seattle: University of Washington Press.

Centro Cultural Orùnmilá e a 10,639 [The Orùnmilá Cultural Center and 10,639]. (2006, November). Sorò Dúdú: Fala Negro, pp. 4–5.

Centro de Derechos Humanos Fray Bartolomé de las Casas. (2005). *Balance annual 2005 sobre la situación de los derechos humanos en Chiapas [2005 Annual evaluation of human rights In Chiapas].* CDHFB: San Cristóbal de Las Casas, Chiapas.

Chang, H.-J. (2002). Kicking away the ladder. In *Development strategy in historical perspective.* London: Anthem Press.

Chatterjee, P. (1993). *The nation and its fragments.* Princeton, NJ: Princeton University Press.

Clarke, B., & Ross, C. (2000). *Voices of fire: Communiques and interviews from the Zapatista national liberation army.* San Francisco: Freedom Voices.

Collier, G. A., & Quaratiello, E. L. (1999). *Basta! Land and the Zapatista rebellion* (Rev. ed.). Oakland, CA: Institute for Food & Development Policy.

Collier, P. (2007). *The bottom billion: Why the poorest countries are failing and what can be done about it.* Oxford, UK: Oxford University Press.

Cooper, F., & Packard, R. (Eds.). (1997). *International development and the social sciences.* Berkeley: University of California Press.

Cornwall, A., Harrison, E., & Whitehead, A. (2007). *Feminisms in development: Contradictions, contestations and challenges.* London: Zed Books.

Corrigan, P., & Sayer, D. (1985). *The great arch: English state formation as cultural revolution.* London: Blackwell.

Courson, E. (2007). *The burden of oil: Social deprivation and political militancy in Gbaramatu Clan, Warri South West LGA Delta State, Nigeria.* Berkeley: Economies of Violence Project, University of California Press.

Cowan, M. P., & Shenton, R. W. (1996). *Doctrines of development.* London: Routledge.

Crawford, E., Jayne, T. S., & Kelley, V. (2006). *Alternative approaches to promoting fertilizer us in Africa.* Washington, DC: World Bank.

Cronon, W. (1995). The trouble with wilderness; or, getting back to the wrong nature. In W. Cronon (Ed.), *Uncommon ground: Rethinking the human place in nature* (pp. 69–90). New York: W. W. Norton.

Cutler, A. C. (2002). Private regimes and inter-firm cooperation. In R. B. Walker & T. J. B. Hall (Eds.), *The emergence of private authority in global governance* (pp. 23–42). Cambridge, UK: Cambridge University Press.

Da Costa, D. (2007). Tensions of neo-liberal development: State discourse and dramatic oppositions in West Bengal. *Contributions to Indian Sociology, 41*(3), 287–320.

Da Costa, D. (2008). Spoiled sons and sincere daughters: Schooling, security, and empowerment in rural West Bengal, India. *Signs: Journal of Women and Culture, 33*(2), 283–308.

Da Costa, D., & McMichael, P. (2007). The poverty of the global order. *Globalizations, 4*(4), 593–607.

Da Costa, E. V. (2000). *The Brazilian empire: Myths and histories* (Rev. ed.). Chapel Hill: University of North Carolina Press.

Daniel, Y. (2005). *Dancing wisdom: Embodied knowledge in Haitian Vodou, Cuban Yoruba, and Bahian Candomblé.* Springfield: University of Illinois Press.

Davis, D. J. (1999). *Avoiding the dark: Race and the forging of national culture in modern Brazil* (Research in migration and ethnic relations series). Aldershot, UK: Ashgate.

Davis, M. (2004). Planet of slums: Urban involution and the informal proletariat. *New Left Review, 26*, 5–34.

Davis, M. (2006). *Planet of slums.* London: Verso.

De Certeau, M. (1984). *The practice of everyday life* (S. Rendall, Trans.). Berkeley: University of California Press.

de Janvry, A., & Sadoulet, E. (1989). A study in resistance to institutional change: The lost game of Latin American land reform. *World Development, 17*(9), 1397–1407.

Della Porta, D., & Tarrow, S. (Eds.). (2005). *Transnational protest and global activism.* Lanham, MD: Rowman & Littlefield.

Desmarais, A. (2007). *La Vía Campesina: Globalization and the power of peasants.* Ontario, Canada: Fernwood.

Desmarais, A. A. (2002). The vía campesina: Consolidating and international peasant and farm movements. *The Journal of Peasant Studies, 29*(2), 91–124.

De Soto, H. (1990). *The other path: The invisible revolution in the third world.* New York: Harper & Row.

de Souza, M. L. (2006). Together with the state, despite the state, against the state: Social movements as "critical urban planning" agents. *City, 10*(3), 327–342.

Devereux, S. (2002). The Malawi famine of 2002: Causes, consequences and policy lessons. *IDS Bulletin, 33*, 70–78.

Dietz, M. (1992). Context is all: Feminism and theories of citizenship. In C. Mouffe (Ed.), *Dimensions of radical democracy: Pluralism, citizenship, community* (pp. 63–88). London: Verso.

Dower, J. (1993). *Japan in war and peace: Selected essays.* New York: New Press.

Dreze, J., & Sen, A. (1995). *India: Economic development and social opportunity.* Delhi: Oxford University Press.

Eatwell, J. (1999). From cooperation to coordination to control? *New Political Economy, 4*(3), 410–415.

The Economist. (2007, March 29). Cities without limits. Retrieved March 29, 2007, from: http://www.lexisnexis.com.proxy.library.cornell.edu/us/lnacademic/results/docview/docview.do?docLinkInd=true&risb=21_T7165271496&format=GNBFI&sort=RELEVANCE&startDocNo=1&resultsUrlKey=29_T7165271499&cisb=22_T7165271498&treeMax=true&treeWidth=0&csi=7955&docNo=1

Edelman, M. (1999). *Peasants against globalization: Rural social movements in Costa Rica.* Stanford, CA: Stanford University Press.

Eisenstadt, T., & Poire, A. (2007). *Explaining the credibility gap in Mexico's 2006 presidential election, despite strong (albeit perfectable) electoral institutions.* (Working Paper). Washington, DC: Center for North American Studies, American University.

Elson, D., & Pearson, R. (1981). The subordination of women and the internationalization of factory production. In K. Young, C. Wolkowitz, & R. McCullagh (Eds.), *Of marriage and the market* (pp. 18–40). London: CSE.

Elyachar, J. (2005). *Markets of dispossession: NGOs, economic development, and the state in Cariro.* Durham, NC: Duke University Press.

Englund, H. (2006). *Prisoners of freedom: Human rights and the African poor.* Berkeley: University of California Press.

Enloe, C. (2000). *Maneuvers: The international politics of militarizing women's lives.* Berkeley: University of California Press.

Environmental Rights Action (ERA). (2003, May 13). *Armed struggle as election. Lagos, Guardian,* p. 17.

Escobar, A. (1995). *Encountering development: The making and unmaking of the third world.* Princeton, NJ: Princeton University Press.

Escobar, A. (2008). *Territories of difference: Place, movements, life, redes.* Durham, NC: Duke University Press.

European Union. (2007, April). *Statement of preliminary findings and conclusions: Elections fail to meet hopes and expectations of the Nigerian people and fall far short of basic international standards.* Abuja, European Union Election Observation Mission.

Fanon, F. (1965). *The wretched of the earth* (C. Farrington, Trans.). London: Penguin.

Faulty policies hurt liquor trade in state. (2002). *The Times of India.* Retrieved January 1, 2008, from http://timesofindia.indiatimes.com/articleshow/23898459.cms

Feffer, J. (2001). Korea: Liberation and self-determination. *Foreign Policy in Focus.* Retrieved May 1, 2009, from http://www.fpif.org/selfdetermination/crisiswatch/0108Korea.html

Femia, J. V. (1981). *Gramsci's political thought.* Oxford, UK: Clarendon Press.

Ferguson, J. (1999). *Expectations of modernity: Myths and meanings of urban life on the Zambian copperbelt.* Berkeley: University of California Press.

Fernandes, J. R. O. (2005). Ensino de História e Diversidade Cultural: Desafios e Possibilidades [Teaching history and cultural diversity: Challenges and possibilities]. *Caderno Cedes, 25*(67), 378–388.

Fernandes, L. (2006). *India's new middle class: Democratic politics in an era of economic reform.* Minneapolis: University of Minnesota Press.

Fernandes, L., & Heller, P. (2006). Hegemonic aspirations: New middle class politics and India's democracy in comparative perspective. *Critical Asian Studies, 38*(4), 495–522.

Forbis, M. M. (2003). Hacia la Autonomía: Zapatista women developing a new world. In C. Eber & C. Kovic (Eds.), *Women of Chaipas: Making history in times of struggle and hope* (pp. 231–252). London: Routledge.

Foucault, M. (1980a). *Power/knowledge: Selected interviews and other writings 1972–1977.* New York: Pantheon.

Foucault, M. (1980b). Truth and power. In C. Gordon (Ed.), *Knowledge/power: Selected interviews and other writings 1972–1977* (pp. 109–133). New York: Pantheon Press.

Franco, J. (1989). *Plotting women: Gender and representation in Mexico.* New York: Columbia University Press.

Freire, P. (1970). *Pedagogy of the oppressed.* New York: Continuum.

Friedmann, H. (2005). From colonialism to green capitalism: Social movements and the emergence of food regimes. In F. H. Buttel & P. McMichael (Eds.), *New directions in the sociology of global development: Vol. 11. Research in rural sociology and development* (pp. 229–267). Oxford, UK: Elsevier.

Fukuyama, F. (1992). *The end of history and the last man.* Free Press: New York.

Fukuyama, F. (2007). Liberalism versus state building. *Journal of Democracy, 18*(3), 10–13.

Garcia, E., & Nemenzo, F. (1988). The sovereign quest: Freedom from foreign military bases. *Journal of Peace Research, 25*(4), 450.

Gardner, G., Assadourian, E., & Sarin, P. (2004). The state of consumption today. In *State of the world 2004,* (pp. 3–23). Washington, DC: Worldwatch Institute.

Gareau, B. J. (2007). Ecological values amid local interests: Natural resource conservation, social differentiation, and human survival in Honduras. *Rural Sociology, 72*(2), pp. 244–268.

Geisler, C. (2003). A new kind of trouble: Evictions in Eden. *International Social Science Journal, 55*(175), 69–78.

Gibson-Graham, J. K. (2006). *A postcapitalist politics.* Minneapolis: University of Minnesota Press.

Gotz, G., & Simone, A. (2003). On belonging and becoming in African cities. In R. Tomlinson, R. A. Beauregard, L. Bremner, & X. Mangcu (Eds.), *Emerging Johannesburg: Perspectives on the postapartheid city* (pp. 123–147). New York: Routledge.

Gramsci, A. (1971). Selections from the prison notebooks of Antonio Gramsci, Q. Hoare, & G. N. Smith (Eds.). New York: International.

Gramsci, A., & Buttigieg, J. A. (1992). *Prison notebooks.* New York: Columbia University Press.

Grellier, B. (2006). A transhumant shepherd on Mount Aigoual: Sheep transhumance and the shepherd's knowledge. *International Social Science Journal, 58*(187), 161–164.

Guattari, F., & Rolnik, S. (1986). *Micropolitica: Cartografias do desejo.* Petrópolis, Brazil: Vozes.

Guha, R. (1989). *The unquiet woods: Ecological change and peasant resistance in the Indian Himalaya.* Delhi: Oxford University Press.

Guimarães, A. S. A. (1995). Racism and anti-racism in Brazil: A post-modern perspective. In B. P. Bowser (Ed.), *Racism and anti-racism in world perspective* (pp. 208–226). Thousand Oaks, CA: Sage.

Gupta, A. (1998). *Postcolonial developments: Agriculture in the making of modern India.* Durham, NC: Duke University Press.

Gupta, A. (2003). The transmission of development: Problems of scale and socialization. In K. Sivaramakrishnan & A. Agrawal (Eds.), *Regional modernities: The cultural politics of development in India* (pp. 65–74). New Delhi: Oxford University Press.

Gupta, D. (2005). Whither the Indian village. *Economic and Political Weekly, 40*(8), 751–758.

Haggblade, S., & Tembo, G. (2003). *Conservation farming in Zambia.* Washington, DC: IFPRI.

Hale, C. R. (2002). Does multiculturalism menace? Governance, cultural rights and the politics of identity in Guatemala. *Journal of Latin American Studies, 34,* 485–524.

Hale, C. R. (2005). Neoliberal multiculturalism: The remaking of cultural rights and racial dominance in Central America. *POLAR: Political and Legal Anthropology Review, 28*(1), 10–28.

Hall, S. (1990). Cultural identity and diaspora. In *Identity: Community, culture, difference* (pp. 222–237). London: Lawrence & Wishart.

Hall, S., & Held, D. (1990). Cities and citizenship. In S. Hall & M. Jacques (Eds.), *New times: The changing face of politics in the 1990s* (pp. 173–188). London: Verso.

Hallowell, A. I. (1943). The nature and function of property as a social institution. *Journal of Legal and Political Sociology, 1*(3-4), 115–138.

Hallward, P. (2003). *Badiou: A subject to truth.* Minneapolis: University of Minnesota Press.

Hamilton, C. (2003). *Growth fetish.* Sydney, Australia: Allen & Unwin.

Hanchard, M. G. (1994). *Orpheus and power: The movimento negro of Rio De Janeiro and São Paulo, Brazil, 1945–1988.* Princeton, NJ: Princeton University Press.

Hanchard, M. G. (1999). *Racial politics in contemporary Brazil.* Durham, NC: Duke University Press.

Hansen, T. B. (2001). *Wages of violence: Naming and identity in postcolonial Bombay.* Princeton, NJ: Princeton University Press.

Harding, R. E. (2000). *A refuge in thunder: Candomblé and alternatives spaces of blackness: Blacks in the diaspora.* Bloomington: Indiana University Press.

Harding, R. E. (2006). É a Senzala: Slavery, women, and embodied knowledge in Afro-Brazilian Candomblé. In R. M. Griffith & B. D. Savage (Eds.), *Women and religion in the African Diaspora: Knowledge, power, and performance* (pp. 3–18). Baltimore, MD: Johns Hopkins University Press.

Harvey, D. (1997). Contested cities: Social process and spatial form. In N. Jewson & S. McGregor (Eds.), *Transforming cities: Contested governance and new spatial divisions* (pp. 19–27). London: Routledge.

Harvey, D. (2003). *The new imperialism.* New York: Oxford University Press.

Harvey, D. (2005). *A brief history of neoliberalism.* Oxford, UK: Oxford University Press.

Harvey, N. (1998). *The Chiapas rebellion: The struggle for land and democracy.* Durham, NC: Duke University Press.

Held, D. (2000). Regulating globalization: The reinvention of politics. *International Sociology, 15*(2), 394–408.

Heller, P. (2001). Moving the state: The politics of democratic decentralization in Kerala, South Africa, and Porto Alegre. *Politics & Society, 29*(1), 131–163.

Hernandez, A. (2006). Etica, cosmovisoes, e espirtualidades. In M. Sauquet (Ed.), *100 propostas do forum social mundial* (pp. 233–253). Petropolis, Brazil: Vozes.

Hernandez Castillo, R. A. (1995). Reinventing tradition: The women's law. *Cultural Survival Quarterly, 19*(1), 24–25.

Hidalgo, O. (2006). *Tras los pasos de una guerra inconclusa: Doce años de militarización en Chiapas [Through the steps of an unconcluded war: Twelve years of militarization in Chiapas].* San Cristóbal de las Casas: Centro de Investigaciones Económicas y Políticas de Acción Comunitaria.

Hindu. (2004, July 13). Medha patkar launches satyagraha. Retrieved from http://www.hinduonnet.com

Hodge, J. M. (2007). *Triumph of the expert: Agrarian doctrines of development and the legacies of British colonialism.* Athens, OH: Ohio University Press.

Holston, J. (2008). *Insurgent citizenship: Disjunctions of democracy and modernity in Brazil.* Princeton, NJ: Princeton University Press.

hooks, b. (1990). *Yearning: Race, gender, and cultural politics.* Boston: South End Press.

Hopkins, T. K. (1978). World-system analysis: Methodological issues. In B. H. Kaplan (Ed.), *Social change in the capitalist world-economy* (pp. 119–218). Beverly Hills, CA: Sage.

Htun, M. (2004). From "racial democracy" to affirmative action: Changing state policy on race in Brazil. *Latin American Research Review, 39*(1), 60–89.

Human Rights Watch. (2007). Election or "Selection"? Human rights abuse and threats to free and fair elections in Nigeria. Retrieved from http://www.hrw.org/en/reports/2007/04/04/election-or-selection

Ianni, O. (1979). *Colonização e contra reforma agrária na Amazônia*. Petropolis, Brazil: Vozes.

Ibeanu, O. (2006). Simulating landslides: primitive accumulation of votes and the popular mandate in Nigeria. In *conflict tracking dossier toward the 2007 elections: Perspectives on the 2003 elections in Nigeria* (pp. 40–51). Abuja, Nigeria: Idasa Nigeria.

Icaza-Herrera, M. (2006, March). *Signos Inequivocos de Manipulacion en el PREP. Queretaro UNAM* (Africa Report No. 123). Centro de Física Aplicada y Tecnología Avanzada. Unpublished manuscript.

Igoe, J., & Brockington, D. (2007). Neoliberal conservation: A brief introduction. *Conservation and Society, 5*(4), 432–449.

International Assessment of Agricultural Science, Technology and Development (IAASTD). (2008). Executive summary of the synthesis report. Retrieved from http://www.agassessment.org/docs/SR_Exec_Sum_280508_English.pdf

International Business Times. (2006). Produtor de soja vai fechar rodovias em 3 Estados. April. Retrieved April 30, 2006, from http://www.ibtimes.com.br/articles/20060429/agricultor-produtor_2.htm

International Union for Conservation of Nature (IUCN). (1994). *Guidelines for protected area management categories*. Gland, Switzerland: IUCN.

International Union for Conservation of Nature (IUCN). (1999). *Central Karakoram National Park: Draft management plan*. Gland, Switzerland: IUCN.

International Union for Conservation of Nature (IUCN). (2003). *Customary laws: Governing natural resource management in the Northern Areas*. Karachi, Pakistan: IUCN.

Isin, E. F. (Ed.). (2000). *Democracy, citizenship and global city*. London: Routledge.

Isin, E. F., & Turner, B. (Eds.). (2002). *Handbook of citizenship studies*. London: Sage.

Ito, M., Matsumoto, T., & Wuinones, M. A. (2007). Conservation tillage practice in Sub-Saharan Africa: The experience of Sasakawa Global 2000. *Crop Protection, 26*, 417–423.

Jackson, C. (1999). Men's work, masculinities and gender division of labour. *The Journal of Development Studies, 36*(1), 89–108.

Jagarnath, V. (2006). *Sydenham: A social historical study of the impact of apartheid race legislation*. Durban, South Africa: University of KwaZulu-Natal.

James, C. L. R. (1963). *The black jacobins: Toussaint l'Ouverture and the San Domingo revolution*. New York: Vintage Books.

Jeffrey, C., Jeffery, P., & Jeffery, R. (2008). *Degrees with freedom? Education, masculinities and unemployment in North India*. Stanford, CA: Stanford University Press.

Jenkins, J. C., & Form, W. (2005). Social movement organizations and strategies. In T. Janoski, R. Alford, A. Hicks, & M. Schwartz (Eds.), *The handbook of political sociology: States, civil societies, and globalization,* (pp. 331–349). Cambridge, UK: Cambridge University Press.

Jones, J. L. (2005). Yoruba diasporic performance: The case for a spiritually-and-aesthetically-based diaspora. In T. Falola & A. Genova (Eds.), *Orisa: Yoruba gods and spiritual identity in Africa and the diaspora* (pp. 321–331). Trenton, NJ: Africa World Press.

Joseph, R., Kew, D., Lewis, S., Morrison, S., & Paden, J. (2007). *Joint statement on Nigerian elections*. Chicago: Center for African Studies, Northwestern University.

Kalinga, O. E. (1993). The master farmers' scheme in Nyasaland 1950–1962: A study of a failed attempt to create a "yeoman" class. *African Affairs, 92*, 356–387.

Kalonde, Pk. (2000). *Okongola Sanyada*. Lilongwe: Sunrise Publications.

Kaplan, R. A. (1994). The coming anarchy. *Atlantic Monthly*. Retrieved from http://www.TheAtlantic.com/atlantic/election/connection/foreign/anarcf.htm

Keeley, J., & Scoones, I. (2000). Knowledge, power and politics: The environmental policy-making process in Ethiopia. *Journal of Modern African Studies, 38*, 89–120.

Kerr, G. (1958). *Okinawa: History of an island people*. Boston: Tuttle Books.

Kettlewell, R. W. (1965). *Agricultural change in Nyasaland: 1945–1960*. Palo Alto, CA: Stanford University Food Research Institute.

Klenk, R. (2003). Difficult work: Becoming developed. In K. Sivaramakrishnan & A. Agrawal (Eds.), *Regional modernities: The cultural politics of development in India* (pp. 99–121). New Delhi: Oxford University Press.

Klenk, R. (2004). Who is the developed woman? Women as a category of development discourse, Kumaon, India. *Development and Change, 35*(1), 57–78.

Klesner, J. (1994). The 1994 Mexican elections: Manifestation of a divided society? *Mexican Studies, 11*(1), 137–149.

Knudsen, A. (1999). Conservation and controversy in the Karakoram: Khunjerab National Park, Pakistan. *Journal of Political Ecology, 56*, 1–29.

Kreutzmann, H. (2006). High mountain agriculture and its transformation in a changing socio-economic environment. In H. Kreutzmann (Ed.), *Karakoram in transition: Culture, development, and ecology in the Hunza Valley*. Karachi, Pakistan: Oxford University Press.

Kristeva, J. (1982). *Powers of horror: An essay on abjection* (L. S. Roudiez, Trans.). New York: Columbia University Press.

Kurtz, L. (1995). *Gods in the global village: The world's religions in sociological perspective*. Thousand Oaks, CA: Pine Forge Press.

Kydd, J. G., & Christiansen, R. E. (1982). Structural change in Malawi since independence: Consequences of a development strategy based on large-scale agriculture. *World Development, 10*, 377–396.

Laclau, E., & Mouffe, C. (1985). *Hegemony and socialist strategy: Towards a radical democratic politics* (W. Moore & P. Cammack, Trans.). London: Verso.

Lamb, S. (2000). *White saris and sweet mangoes: Aging, gender and body in North India*. Berkeley: University of California Press.

Langanparsad, M. (2006, March 2). Shack dwellers boycott the ballot. *Daily News*, p. 6.

LaTouche, S. (1993). *In the wake of the affluent society: An exploration of post-development*. London: Zed.

Leal, V. N. (1977 [1949]). *Coronelismo: The municipality and representative government in Brazil* [Coronelismo, enxada e voto]. (J. Henfrey, Trans.). Cambridge, UK: Cambridge University Press.

Lefebvre, H. (1996[1968]). *Writings on cities* (E. Kofman & E. Lebas, Trans.). Oxford, UK: Blackwell.

Lewis, P. (2003). Elections in a fragile regime. *Journal of Democracy, 14*(3), 131–144.

Leyva-Solano, X. (2002). Catequistas, Misioneros y Tradiciones en las Cañadas[Catechists, missionaries and traditions in the Canyons]. In J. P. Viqueira & M. Humberto Ruz (Eds.), *Chiapas: Los rumbos de otra historia* [*Chiapas: The paths of another history*], (pp. 375–402). México, D.F.: Centro de Estudios Mayas del Institúto de Investigaciones Filológicas, Centro de Investigaciones y Estudios Superiores en Antropología Social.

Li, T. (2002). Engaging simplifications: Community-based resource management, market processes, and state agendas in upland Southeast Asia. *World Development, 30*(2), 265–283.

Li, T. M. (1999). Compromising power: Development, culture, and rule in Indonesia. *Cultural Anthropology, 14*(3), 295–322.

Liechty, M. (2003). *Suitably modern: Making middle-class culture in a new consumer society*. Princeton, NJ: Princeton University Press.

Lima, H. P. (2005). Personagens negros: Um breve perfil na literatura infanto-juvenil. In K. Munanga (Ed.), *Superando o Racismo na Educação* (2nd ed., pp. 101–116). Brasília: Ministério da Educação.

Lodge, T. (1983). *Black politics in South Africa since 1945*. London: Longman.

Lopez Obrador, A. M. (1995). *Entre La Historia y la Esperanza: Corrupcion y Lucha Democratica en Tabasco*. Mexico, D.F.: Grijalbo.

Lopez Obrador, A. M. (2008). *La gran tentacion: El petroleo de Mexico*. Mexico: Grijalbo.

Lwanda, J. (1996). *Promise, power, politics and poverty: The democratic transition in Malawi 1961–1999*. Glasgow: Dudu Nsomba.

MacDonald, K. (2005). Global hunting grounds: Power, scale, and ecology in the negotiation of conservation. *Cultural Geographies, 12*, 259–291.

Machado, V. (2003). Por uma pedagogia nagô. In D. P. R. D. Fonseca (Ed.), *Resistência e inclusão: história, cultura, educação e cidadania afro-descendentes no Brasil e nos Estados Unidos* (Vol. 1, pp. 119–137). Rio de Janeiro: Pontifícia Universidade Catolica.

Mafongoya, P. L., Bationo, A., Kihara, E. J., & Waswa, B. S. (2006). Appropriate technologies to replenish soil fertility in Southern Africa. *Nutrient Cycling in Agroecosystems, 76*, 137–151.

Mapanje, J. (2002). Afterword: The morality of dictatorship: In defense of my country. In H. Englund (Ed.), *A democracy of chameleons: Politics and culture in the new Malawi* (pp. 178–187). Stockholm: Nordic Africa Institute.

Mariola, M. J. (2005). Losing ground: Farmland preservation, economic utilitarianism, and the erosion of the agrarian ideal. *Agriculture and Human Values, 22*(2), 209–223.

Marshall, T. H. (1964). *Class, citizenship and social development: Essays*. Garden City, NY: Anchor.

Marshall, T. H., & Bottomore, T. (1992). *Citizenship and social class*. London: Pluto Press.

Martinez-Alier, J. (2002). *The environmentalism of the poor: A study of ecological conflicts and valuation*. Cheltenham, UK: Edward Elgar.

Marx, K. (1967). *Capital* (Vol. 1). Moscow: Progress.

Marx, K. (1979). *Capital* (Vol. 1). London: Penguin Books.

Marx, K., & Bender, F. L. (1988). *The communist manifesto: Annotated text*. New York, London: W. W. Norton.

Masson, S. (2001). *La lucha de las mujeres indigenas en Chiapas y sus implicaciones personales, politas y teóricas para una feminista occidental blanca* [The struggle of indigenous women in Chiapas and its personal, political and theoretical implications for a white, western feminist]. CIESAS Sureste. Unpublished manuscript.

Maylam, P., & Edwards, I. (1996). *The people's city: African life in twentieth-century Durban*. Pietermaritzburg, South Africa: University of Natal Press.

Mazzarella, W. (2003). *Shoveling smoke: Advertising and globalization in contemporary India*. Durham, NC: Duke University Press.

Mbeki, T. (2005, May 13–19). Mbeki, speaking at the municipal imbizo in Rustenburg. *Mail and Guardian*, p. 17.

McAfee, K. (1999). Selling nature to save it? Biodiversity and the rise of green developmentalism. *Environment and Planning D: Society and Space, 17*(2), 133–154.

McCormack, G. (2003). Okinawa and the structure of dependence. In G. Hook & R. Siddle (Eds.), *Japan and Okinawa: Structure and subjectivity* (pp. 93–132). New York and London: Routledge/Curzon.

McCormack, G. (2007). *Client state: Japan in the American embrace*. London: Verso.

McCracken, J. (1986). Coercion and control in Nyasaland: Aspects of the history of a colonial police force. *Journal of African History, 27*, 127–147.

McMichael, P. (1990). Incorporated comparison within a world historical perspective: An alternative comparative method. *American Sociological Review, 55*, 384–397.

McMichael, P. (2005). Globalization. In T. Janoski, R. Alford, A. Hicks, & M. Schwartz (Eds.), *The handbook of political sociology: States, civil societies and globalization* (pp. 587–606). Cambridge, UK: Cambridge University Press.

McMichael, P. (2006). Peasant Prospects in a neo-liberal age. *New Political Economy, 11*(3), 407–418.

McMichael, P. (2007). Globalization and the agrarian world. In G. Ritzer (Ed.), *The Blackwell companion to globalization* (pp. 216–238). Oxford, UK: Blackwell.

McMichael, P. (2008a). *Development and social change. A global perspective*. Thousand Oaks, CA: Pine Forge Press.

McMichael, P. (2008b). Peasants make their own history, but not just as they please. *Journal of Agrarian Change, 8*(23), 205–228.

McMichael, P. (2008c). The peasant as "canary"? Not too early warnings of global catastrophe. *Development, 51*(4), 504–511.

McMichael, P. (2009). Banking on agriculture: A review of the world development report. *Journal of Agrarian Change, 9*(2), 235–246.

McMurtry, J. (2002). *Value wars: The global market versus the life economy*. London: Pluto.

McNeely, J. A. (Ed.). (1993). *Parks for life: Report of the IVth world congress on national parks and protected areas*. Gland, Switzerland: IUCN.

Menegheti, G. (2005). E. Agora, Valcir? *Produtor Rural, 149*, 19–28.

Merrell, F. (2007). *Capoeira and Candomblé: Conformity and resistance through Afro-Brazilian experience*. Princeton, NJ: Markus Wiener.

Meyer, L. (2007, August 16). "Y crecieron los enaos" Mexico. *La Reforma*. Retrieved August 25, 2009, from http://www.elsiglodetorreon.com.mx/noticia/291959.y-crecieron-los-enanos-agenda-ciudadana.html

Metz, O., Wadley, R. L., Nielsen, U., Bruun, T. H., Colfer, C. J. P., de Neergaard, A., et al. (2008). A fresh look at shifting cultivation: Fallow length an uncertain indicator of productivity. *Agricultural Systems, 96*, 75–84.

Mignolo, W. (2000). *Local histories/global designs: Coloniality, subaltern knowledges, and border thinking*. Princeton, NJ: Princeton University Press.

Ministerio de Desenvolvimento Agricola (MDA). (2003). *Plano nacional de reforma agrária, proposta: Paz, produção e qualidade de vida no meio rural*. Brasília: Ministério de Desenvolvimento Agrícola.

Mitchell, D. (2003). *The right to the city: Social justice and the fight for public space*. New York: Guilford Press.

Mitchell, T. (1988). *Colonizing Egypt*. Berkeley, CA: University of California Press.

Mitchell, T. (2002). *Rule of experts: Egypt, techno-politics, modernity*. Berkeley: University of California Press.

Mngxitama, A., Alexander, A., & Gibson, N. C. (2008). Steve Biko's paradise lost: Extract from *Biko Lives. The Sunday Independent* .

Mohan, D. (2003). *Scripting power and changing the subject: Jana Sanskriti's political theatre in rural North India*. Ithaca, NY: Department of Development Sociology, Cornell University.

Moore, D. (1993). Contesting terrain in Zimbabwe's eastern highlands: Political ecology, ethnography, and peasant resource struggles. *Economic Geography, 69*(4), 380–401.

Moore, H., & Vaughan, M. (1993). *Cutting down trees: Gender, nutrition, and agricultural change in the northern province of Zambia, 1890-1990*. London: James Currey.

Mosse, D. (2004). Is good policy unimplementable? Reflections on the ethnography of aid policy and practice. *Development and Change, 35*(4), 639–671.

Moura, C. (1988). *Sociologia Do Negro Brasileiro* [The sociology of Brazilian Blacks]. São Paulo: Editora Atica.

Mulwafu, W. O. (2002). Soil erosion and state intervention in estate production in the Shire Highlands economy of colonial Malawi, 1891-1964. *Journal of Southern African Studies, 28*, 25–43.

Munanga, K. (Ed.). (1996). *Estratégias e Políticas De Combate à Discriminação Racial* [Policies and strategies to combat racial discrimination]. São Paulo: Estação Ciência, Universidade de São Paulo.

Mustapha, A. R. (2007, June 28). Nigeria after the April 2007 elections: What next? *Pambazuka News.*

Nascimento, A. D. (1989[1979]). *Brazil, mixture or massacre? Essays in the genocide of a black people.* Dover, MA: Majority Press.

Nash, J. C. (2001). *Mayan visions: The quest for autonomy in an age of globalization.* New York: Routledge.

Nasser, A. M. (1998). *Fundacão Mt Um caso de ação coletiva no agribusiness .* Paper presented at the VIII seminário internacional pensa de agribusiness. Program de estudos dos negócios do sistema agroiroindustrial (PENSA), Sao Paulo, Brazil.

National Council of Applied Economic Research. (2006). Uttaranchal development report (draft). New Delhi: Author.

Neumann, R. (2001). Disciplining peasants in Tanzania: From state violence to self-surveillance in wildlife conservation. In N. Peluso & M. Watts (Eds.), *Violent environments* (pp. 305–326). Ithaca, NY: Cornell University Press.

Neumann, R. (2004). Nature-state Territory: Toward a critical theorization of conservation enclosures. In R. Peet & M. Watts (Eds.), *Liberation ecologies,* (pp. 195–217). New York: Routledge.

Neuwirth, R. (2005). *Shadow cities: A billion squatters, a new urban world.* New York: Routledge.

Nsirimovu, A., & Niger Delta Civil Society Coalition. (2007). Niger Delta civil society support mass action statement. *Port Harcourt News.*

Nyasaland Protectorate. (1910). *Annual report on the agriculture and forestry department for the year ended March 31, 1909.* Zomba, Malawi: Nyasaland Protectorate.

Nyasaland Protectorate. (1927). *Annual report on the department of agriculture for the calendar year 1926.* Zomba, Malawi: Nyasaland Government Printer.

O'Connor, M. (1994). On The Misadventures of Capitalist Nature. In M. O'Connor (Ed.), *Is capitalism sustainable?* (pp. 125–151). Guilford: New York.

Offe, C. (1999). Democracy and trust. Collegium, Budapest: Institute for Advanced Study. Retrieved August 25, 2009, from http://www.colbud.hu/honesty-trust/offe/pub02.PDF

Okinawa J. K. K. (2002). *Atarashii Jichi to kore kara no machizukuri: Kenkyu Kaigiroku* [New self-governance and the future of community development research proceedings]. Ginowan, Japan: Ryukyu Daigaku Gakushu Kyoiku Kenkyu Sentaa.

Okinawa J. K. K. (2004). *Okinawa ni jichi wa dour suru?* [How might Okinawa self-govern?]. Ginowan, Japan: Ryukyu Daigaku Gakushu Kyoiku Kenkyu Sentaa.

Okinawa J. K. K. (2005). *Okinawa jichi shu: Anata wa dou kangaeru?* [Okinawa as a self-governing region: What do you think?]. Naha, Japan: Deigo Insatsu.

Okinawa Prefecture. (2001). *Beigun teikyô shisetsu kuiki no nayô* [Facilities and areas provided to the U.S. military]. Naha, Okinawa: Okinawa Prefecture.

Okonta, I. (March 26, 2007). Nigeria—Danger signs on democracy road. *Pambazuka News.* Retrieved August 25, 2009, from http://www.pambazuka.org/en/category/features/40717

Olivera, M. (1998). Acteal: Los Efectos de la Guerra de Baja Intensidad. [Acteal: The effects of the low-intensity war]. In R. A. Herandez Castillo (Ed.), *La Otra Palabra: Mujeres y violencia en Chiapas, Antes y Despúe Acteal* [The other word: women and violence in Chiapas] (pp. 114–124). Mexico: CIESAS.

Olivera, M. (2006). Violencia Femicida: Violence against women and Mexico's structural crisis. *Latin American Perspectives, 33*(2), 104–114.

Oliveira, A. U. D. (1987). *Amazônia: Monopólio, expropriação e conflitos. Campinas,* SP: Papirus.

Oliveira, J. M. (2006). Matrizes religiosas afro-brasileiras e educação [Afro-Brazilian Matrix Religions and Education]. In M. L. S. Braga, E. P. Souza, & A. F. M. Pinto (Eds.), *Dimensões da Inclusão no Ensino Médio: Mercado de trabalho, religiosidade e educação quilombola* [Dimensions of inclusion in secondary education: The labor market, religiosity, and quilombola education] (pp. 203–236). Brasília: SECAD.

Olivera, M. (1998). Acteal: Los Efectos de la Guerra de Baja Intensidad. (Acteal: the effects of the low-intensity war). In R. A. Hernandez Castillo (Ed.), *La Otra Palabra: Mujeres y violencia en Chiapas, Antes y Despué de Acteal* [The other word: women and violence in Chiapas] (pp. 114-124). Mexico: CIESAS

Orùnmilá, C. C. (2004, May). As Dimensões Inseparáveis de Política e Cultura e a Luta do Sorò Dúdú: Fala, 2.

Osuoka, I. (2007). Nigeria: Oil, Elections and the International Community, ZNET. Retrieved from http://www.zmag.org/znet/viewArticle/15547

Ota, M. (2000). Re-examining the history of the battle of Okinawa. In *Essays on Okinawa problems .* Gushikawa, Okinawa, Japan: Yui.

Otero, G. (1999). Farewell to the peasantry? Political class formation in rural Mexico. Boulder, CO: Westview Press.

Otero, G. (2007). *Mexico's crisis of hegemony: Challenges for the social and the political left.* Paper presented at the Latin American Studies Association Meetings, Montreal.

Palmer, R. (1985). White farmers in Malawi: Before and after the depression. *African Affairs, 84*, 211–245.

Pardue, D. (2008). *Ideologies of marginality in Brazilian hip hop.* New York: Palgrave Macmillan.

Parker, G. (2006). The country code and the ordering of countryside citizenship. *Journal of Rural Studies, 22*(1), 1–16.

Pastor, R. (2006). *A full recount to achieve closure: Comment on the Eisenstadt Poire working paper.* Washington, DC: Center for North American Studies, American University.

Patel, R. (2007). *Stuffed and starved: Markets, power and the hidden battle for the world food system.* London: Portobello.

Patel, R. (forthcoming). Fairytale violence or Sondheim on solidarity, from Karnataka to Kennedy Road. In S. Essof & D. Moshenberg (Eds.), *Searching for South Africa.* Pretoria: UNISA Press.

Patel, R., & McMichael, P. (2004). Third worldism and the lineages of global fascism: The regrouping of the global south in the neo-liberal era. *Third World Quarterly, 25*(1), 231–254.

Patel, R., & Pithouse, R. (2005, May 20–26). An epidemic of rational behavior. *Mail and Guardian.*

Pedersen, J. D. (2001). India's industrial dilemmas in West Bengal. *Asian Survey, 41*(4), 646–668.

Pereira, R. P. C. R. (2000). A teoria da função social da propriedade rural e seus reflexos na acepção clássica de propriedade. In J. J. Strozake (Ed.), *A questão agrária e a justiça* (pp. 88–129). São Paulo: Editora Revista dos Tribunais.

Peterside, S. (2007). On the militarization of Nigeria's Niger Delta: The genesis of ethnic militia in Rivers State, Nigeria. In *Economies of violence project* (working paper). Berkeley: University of California Press. Retrieved August 25, 2009, from http://geography.berkeley.edu/ProjectsResources/ND%20Website/NigerDelta/WP/21-Joab-Peterside.pdf

Peterside, S., & Zalik, A. (2008). *The commodification of violence in the Niger Delta.* New York: Monthly Review Press.

Phimister, I. (1986). Discourse and the discipline of historical context: Conservationism and ideas about development in Southern Rhodesia. *Journal of Southern African Studies, 12*, 263–275.

Pickard, M. (2003). Grassroots protests force the Mexican government to search for a new PPP strategy. Retrieved January 22, 2003, from http://www.ciepac.org/bulletins

Pigg, S. L. (1992). Constructing social category through place: Social representations and development in Nepal. *Comparative Studies in Society and History, 34*, 491–513.

Pigg, S. L. (1997). Found in most traditional societies: Traditional medical practitioners between culture and development. In F. Cooper & R. Packard (Eds.), *International development and the social sciences: Essays on the history and politics of knowledge* (pp. 259–290). Berkeley: University of California Press.

Pieterse, J. N. (1998). My paradigm or yours: alternative development, post-development or reflexive development. *Development and Change, 29*(2), 343–373.

Pithouse, R. (2005). *The left in the slum: The rise of a shack dwellers movement in Durban, South Africa.* Unpublished manuscript.

Pithouse, R. (2006). *Our struggle is thought, on the ground running.* Center for Civil Society, Research Reports, 40. University of Abahlali base Mjondolo.

Pithouse, R. (2007). Shack dwellers on the move in Durban. *Radical Philosophy, 141.* Retrieved March 3, 2007, from http://www.radicalphilosophy.com/default.asp?channel_id=2187&editorial_id=23275

Pithouse, R., & Butler, M. (2007). *Lessons from eThekwini: Priahs hold their ground against a state that is both criminal and democratic.* Pietermaritzburg, South Africa: Association for Rural Advancement.

Polanyi, K. (1957[1944]). *The great transformation: The political and economic origins of our times.* Boston: Beacon Press.

Portilla Bobadillo, M. (2006). Estudio de las Incongruencias Numericas en el Conteo Distrital al comparar los Votos de las Urnas de Presidente, Senadores y Diputados. UNAM, Instituto de Matematicas. [Study of the numericalInconsistencies in the district counts as compared to the votes in presidential, senatorial and congressperson elections]. Unpublished manuscript.

Pralahad, C. K. (2006). *The fortune at the bottom of the pyramid: Eradicating poverty through profits.* Philadelphia: Wharton School.

Pratt, M. L. (1999). Apocalypse in the Andes. *Americas, 51*(4), 38–47.

Pravaz, N. (2008). Hybridity Brazilian style: Samba, carnaval, and the myth of "racial democracy" in Rio De Janeiro. *Identities: Global Studies in Culture and Power, 15*(1), 80–102.

Prosterman, R. L., Temple, M. N., & Hanstad, T. M. (1990). *Agrarian reform and grassroots development: Ten case studies.* Boulder, CO: Lynne Rienner.

Puplampu, K. P., & Tettey, W. J. (2000). State-NGO relations in an era of globalisation: The implications for agricultural development in Africa. *Review of African Political Economy, 27*, 251–272.

Purves, J. (2006). The battle Okinawa: A strategic overview: The contemporary Okinawan website. Retrieved from http://niraikanai.wwma.net/pages/modern_Okinawa/8.okin_senso.html

Queiroz, M. (27 January, 2005). Original venue, new and improved methodology for GIAT meet. Inter Press Service. Retrieved from http://www.commondreams.org

Quijano, A. (2000). Coloniality of power and Eurocentrism in Latin America. *International Sociology, 15*(2), 215–232.

Rahmena, M. (1997). Poverty. In W. Sachs (Ed.), *The development dictionary* (pp. 158–176). Hyderabad, India: Orient Blackswan.

Rancière, J. (1998). *Disagreement: Politics and philosophy.* Minneapolis: University of Minnesota Press.

Rangarajan, M. (2006). Battles for nature: Contesting wildlife conservation in 20th century India. In C. Mauch, N. Stoltzfus, & D. Weiner (Eds.), *Shades of green: Environmental activism around the globe* (pp. 161–182). New York: Rowman & Littlefield.

Ray, D. (2006a). In the agricultural whodunit, subsidies may not be the prime suspect. *Weekly Agricultural Policy Columns.* A. P. A. Center, Knoxville, University of Tennessee. Retrieved from http://www.agpolicy.org/weekcol/287.html

Ray, D. (2006b). WTO panel identifies problem, but will their implied solution work? *Weekly Agricultural Policy Columns.* A. P. A. Center, Knoxville, University of Tennessee. Retrieved from http://www.agpolicy.org/weekcol/284.html

Reddy, W. M. (1987). *Money and liberty in modern Europe: A critique of historical understanding.* Cambridge, UK: Cambridge University Press.

Reichmann, R. (Ed.). (1999). *Race in contemporary Brazil: From indifference to inequality.* University Park: Pennsylvania State University Press.

Resendiz, F., & Silva, A. (2009, May 28). Cupula perredista denuncia sesgo politico en operativos. *El Universal.*

Ribeiro, N. D. F. (1985). *O estatuto da terra e o problema fundiário.* Brasília: MIRAD, Coordenadoria de Comunicação Social.

Rist, G. (1997). *The history of development: From western origins to global faith.* London: Zed Books.

Roberts, J. T., & Hite, A. B. (Eds.). (2007). *The globalization and development reader: Perspectives on development and global change.* Oxford, UK: Blackwell.

Robles, W. (2002). Review: Breaking ground: Development aid for land reform. *Canadian Review of Development Studies, 23*(1), 159–161.

Rodriguez Castaneda, R. Jesus Esquivel, J., &Delgado, A. (2008, October 26). Elecciones 2006: En defensa de la libertad (text of Proceso Director's intervention in the Interamerican Centre for Human Rights, October 23, 2008) and commentary. *Proceso No. 1669,* 6–19.

Roe, E. (1994). *Narrative policy analysis.* Durham, NC: Duke University Press.

Rojas, R. (1999). *Chiapas: ¿Y las mujeres qué?* [Chiapas: And what about the women?]. México, D.F.: Centro de Investigación y Capacitación de la Mujer.

Roman, R., & Velasco Arregui, E. (2007). Mexico's Oaxaca Commune. In L. Panitch & C. Leys (Eds.), *Global flashpoints, socialist register* (pp. 248–264). New York: Monthly Review Press.

Rose, C. M. (1994). *Property and persuasion: Essays on the history, theory, and rhetoric of ownership.* Boulder, CO: Westview Press.

Rostow, W.W. (1960). *The stages of economic growth: a non-communist manifesto.* Cambridge, UK: Cambridge University Press.

Rovira, G. (1997). *Mujeres de maiz* [Women of corn]. México, D.F.: Ediciones Era.

Ruggie, J. G. (1982). International regimes, transactions, and change: Embedded liberalism in the postwar economic order. *International organization, 36,* 397–415.

Saberwal, V. K. (1999). *Pastoral politics: Shepherds, bureaucrats, and conservation in the Western Himalayas.* Delhi, India: Oxford University Press.

Sachs, J. (2005). *The end of poverty: Economic possibilities for our time.* New York: Penguin.

Sachs, W. (1992). (Ed.). *The development dictionary: A guide to knowledge as power.* London: Zed Books.

Sachs, W. (1993). One world. In W. Sachs (Ed.), *Global ecology* (pp. 102–115). London: Zed Books.

Sagardoa, J. (2006). *El verdadero resultado.* Unpublished doctoral dissertation, Mexico Instituto Technologico Suizo.

Sahn, D., & Arulpragasam, J. (1991). The stagnation of smallholder agriculture in Malawi: A decade of structural adjustment. *Food Policy,* 219–234.

Said, E. (1978). *Orientalism.* New York: Pantheon.

Saldaña-Portillo, M. J. (2003). *The revolutionary imagination in the Americas in the age of development.* Durham, NC: Duke University Press.

Sampaio, P. (2002). Mistica in the MST: The movement's use of culture and hope. Retrieved from http://www.mstbrazil.org/20020824_268.html

Sansone, L. (2003). *Blackness without ethnicity: Constructing race in Brazil.* New York: Palgrave Macmillan.

Santos, B. d. S. (2002). *Towards a new legal common sense.* London: Butterworth.

Santos, B. d. S. (2005a). *Democratizing democracy: Beyond the liberal democratic canon.* London and New York: Verso.

Santos, B. d. S.(2005b). Beyond neoliberal governance: The world social forum as subaltern cosmopolitan politics and legality. In B. Santos & C. Rodriguez-Garavito (Eds.), *Law and globalization from below: Towards a cosmopolitan legality* (pp. 29–63). Cambridge, UK: Cambridge University Press.

Santos, B. d. S., J. A. Nunes, & M. P. Meneses. (2007). Opening up the canon of knowledge and recognition of difference. In B. d. S. Santos (Ed.), *Another knowledge is possible* (pp. xvix–lxii). London: Verso.

Santos, B. d. S., & Rodriguez-Garavito, C. A. (2005). Law, politics, and the subaltern in counter-hegemonic globalization. In B. d. S. Santos & C. A. Rodriguez-Garavito (Eds.), *Law and globalization from below: Towards a cosmopolitan legality* (pp. 1–26). New York: Cambridge University Press.

Santos, J. E. (1976). *Os Nagô e a Morte.* Petropolis: Vozes.

Santos, J. E. (1998). A mixed-race nation: Afro-Brazilians and cultural policy in Bahia, 1970–1990. In H. Kraay (Ed.), *Afro-Brazilian culture and politics, Bahia, 1790–1990s* (pp. 117–133). Armonk, NY: M. E. Sharpe.

Santos, M. (2002). *O Brasil, a globalização e a cidadania.* São Paulo: Publifolha.

Sarkar, T. (1984). Politics and women in Bengal: The conditions and meaning of participation. *Indian Economic and Social History Review, 21*(1), 91–101.

Sassen, S. (1996). *Losing control? Sovereignty in an age of globalization.* New York: Columbia University Press.

Saul, J. S. (2004). Globalization, imperialism, development: False binaries and radical resolutions. In L. Panitch & C. Leys (Eds.), *The new imperial challenge: Socialist register* (pp. 220–244). London: Merlin.

Sayer, D. (1994). Everyday forms of state formation: Dissident remarks on hegemony. In D. Nugent (Ed.), *Everyday forms of state formation: Revolution and the negotiation of rule in modern Mexico* (pp. 367–378). Durham, NC: Duke University Press.

Schedler, A. (2007). The mobilization of distrust. *Journal of Democracy, 18*(1), 88–102.

Schlecht, E., Buerkert, A., Tielkes, E., & Bationo, A. (2006). A critical analysis of challenges and opportunities for soil fertility restoration in Sudano-Sahelian West Africa. *Nutrient Cycling in Agroecosystems, 76,* 109–136.

Sen, A. (2000). *Development as freedom.* New Delhi: Oxford University Press.

Shaxson, L., & Tauer, L. W. (1992). Intercropping and diversity: An economic analysis of cropping patterns on smallholder farms in Malawi. *Experimental Agriculture, 28,* 221–228.

Sheriff, R. E. (2001). *Dreaming equality: Color, race, and racism in urban Brazil.* Brunswick, NJ: Rutgers University Press.

Shimshal Nature Trust. (1999). Fifteen year vision and management plan. Retrieved from http://www.brocku.ca/geography/people/dbutz/shimshal.html

Shivji, I. G. (1975). *Class struggles in Tanzania.* London: Heinemann.

Siddle, R. (2003). Return to Uchinaa: The politics of identity in contemporary Okinawa. In G. Hook & R. Siddle (Eds.), *Japan and Okinawa: Structure and subjectivity* (pp. 133–147). London: Routledge.

Silva, A. C. d. (2005). A Desconstrução da Discriminação no Livro Didático [Deconstructing racism in school textbooks]. In K. Munanga (Ed.), *Superando o Racismo na Educação* [Overcoming racism in education] (2nd ed, pp. 21–38). Brasília: Ministério da Educação.

Silva, D. F. (1998). Facts of blackness: Brazil is not (quite) the United States…and racial politics in Brazil. *Social Identities, 4*(2), 201–234.

Silva, L. O. (1996). *Terras devolutas e latifúndio: Efeitos da lei de 1850.* Campinas, SP, Brazil: Editora da UNICAMP.

Silva, M. A. d. (2001). Formação de educadores/as para o combate ao racismo: mais uma tarefa essencial [Training educators to combat racism: one more essential task]. In E. Cavalliero (Ed.), *Racismo e Anti-Racismo na Educação* [Racism and anti-racism in education] (pp. 65–82). São Paulo: Selo Negro.

Singer, J. W. (2000). Property and social relations: From title to entitlement. In C. Geisler & G. Daneker (Eds.), *Property and values: Alternatives to public and private ownership* (pp. 3–20). Washington, DC: Island Press.

Sivaramakrishnan, K., & Agrawal, A. (2003). Regional modernities in stories and practices of development. In K. Sivaramakrishnan & A. Agrawal (Eds.), *Regional modernities: The cultural politics of development in India* (pp. 1–61). New Delhi: Oxford University Press.

Skidmore, T. E. (1993). *Black into white: Race and nationality in Brazilian thought.* Durham, NC: Duke University Press.

Smith, N. (2002). New globalism, new urbanism: Gentrification as global urban strategy. *Antipode, 34*(3), 427–450.

Snapp, S. S. (2008). Designing for the long term: Sustainable agriculture. In S. Snapp & B. Pound (Eds.), *Agricultural systems: Agroecology and rural innovation for development* (pp. 89–127). San Diego, CA: Academic Press.

Snapp, S. S., Mafongoya, P. L., & Waddington, S. (1998). Organic matter technologies for integrated nutrient management in smallholder cropping systems of Southern Africa. *Agriculture Ecosystems & Environment, 71*, 185–200.

Snow, D. A. (2004). Social movements as challenges to authority: Resistance to an emerging conceptual hegemony. *Research in social movements, conflicts and change, 25*, 3–25.

Society for Integrated Development of Habitat (SIDH). (2002). *Child and the family: A study of the impact of family structure upon children in rural Uttarakhand*. Mussoori, India: SIDH.

Society for the Promotion of Area Resource Centres (SPARC). (1985). *We, the invisible: A census of pavement dwellers*. Bombay, India: SPARC.

Sodré, M. (2002 [1988]). *O Terreiro e a Cidade: A Forma Social Negro-Brasileira [The terreiro and the city: The form of Black Brazilian sociality]*. Salvador: Secretaria da Cultura e Turismo.

South African Press Association (SAPA). (October 29, 2004). Mbeki like PW on Tutu issue. *SAPA*. Retrieved December 12, 2005, from http://www.news24.com/News24/South_Africa/Politics/0,2-7-12_1628547,00. html

Speed, S., & Forbis, M. (2005). Embodying alternative logics: Everyday leaders and the diffusion of power in Zapatista autonomous regions. *LASA Forum, 36*(1), 19–21

Stahler-Sholk, R. (2000). *A world in which many worlds fit: Zapatista responses to globalization*. Latin American Studies Association, Miami, Florida. Retrieved August 15, 2004, from http://lasa.international/pitt.edu/ Lasa2000/Stahler-Sholk.pdf

Starr, A. (2005). *Global revolt: A guide to the movements against globalization*. London: Zed Books.

Stephen, L. (1992). Women in Mexico's popular movements: Survival strategies against ecological and economic impoverishment. *Latin American Perspectives, 19*(1), 73–96.

Stephen, L. (2000). The construction of indigenous suspects: Militarization and the gendered and ethnic dynamics of human rights abuses in southern Mexico. *American Ethnologist, 26*(4), 822–842.

Steward, C. (2007). From colonization to "environmental soy": A case study of environmental and socio-economic valuation in the Amazon frontier. *Agriculture and Human Values, 40*, 107–122.

Stoler, A. L., & Cooper, F. (1997). Between metropole and colony: Rethinking a research agenda. In F. Cooper & A. L. Stoler (Eds.), *Tensions of empire: Colonial cultures in a bourgeois world* (pp. 1–56). Berkeley: University of California Press.

Sunday Hindustan Times. (2007, January 21). Gaon goes global. Retrieved from http://www.itcportal.com/ newsroom/press22jan07b.htm

Takahashi, K. (2004). On Okinawa, trouble at home base. *Asia Times Online*. Retrieved September 9, 2004, from http://www.atimes.com/atimes/Japan/FI09Dh05.html

Tarrow, S. (1998). *Power in movement: Social movements and contentious politics* (2nd ed.). New York: Cambridge University Press.

Tax reintroduced: Liquor licensing liberalized. (2003). *Hindu Business Line*. Retrieved January 1, 2008, from http://www.blonnet.com/2003/03/21/stories/2003032101681700.htm

Telles, E. E. (2004). *Race in another America: The significance of skin color in Brazil*. Princeton, NJ: Princeton University Press.

Theodoro, H. (2005). Buscando Caminhos nas Tradições [Searching for paths within traditions]. In K. Munanga (Ed.), *Superando o Racismo na Educação [Overcoming racism in education]* (2nd ed., pp. 83–100). Brasília: Ministério da Educação.

Theoharis, J., & Woodard, K. (2005). *Groundwork: Local black freedom movements in America*. New York and London: New York University Press.

Tilly, C. (2004). *Social Movements, 1768–2004*. Boulder, CO: Paradigm.

The Sunday Express. (2007, January 28). P. Chidambaram at the Express, p. 8.

Toledo Tello, S. (2002). Fincas, poder y cultura en Simojovel, Chiapas [Plantations, power and culture in Simojovel, Chiapas] (Vol. 4). *Programa de Investigaciones Multidisciplinarias sobre mesoamérica y el Sureste [Program for multidisciplinary research about Mesoamerican and the southeast]*. San Cristp de las Casas, Chiapas: UNAM & Instituto de Estudios Indigenas, UNASCH.

Trouillot, M. (1995). *Silencing the past: Power and the production of history*. Boston: Beacon.

Tsing, A. L. (2004). *Friction: An ethnography of global connection*. Princeton, NJ: Princeton University Press.

Turner, B. (Ed.). (1993). *Citizenship and social theory*. London: Sage.

Tutu, D. (2004). Look to the rock from which you were hewn: The second Nelson Mandela foundation lecture. Retrieved from http://www.africanreviewofbooks.com/Reviews/essays/tutu1104.html

Ukiwo, U. (2003). Charity begins abroad. *Polis, RCSP 11*, 113–140. Retrieved August 25, 2009, from http://www. polis.sciencespobordeaux.fr/vol11ns/ukiwo.pdf

Uribe Iniesta, R. (2008). *Privatización que no se dice tal, Reforma Energética que no lo es: la Cuestión de la Superficie Petrolera*. Cuernavaca, Mexico: CRIM/UNAM. (Centro Regional de Investigaciones Multidisciplinarias/Universidad Nacional Autónoma de México). Unpublished manuscript.

Vaaler, P., Schragge, B., & Block, S. (2006). Elections, opportunism, partisanship and sovereign ratings in developing countries. *Review of Development Economics, 10*(1), 154–170.

Vail, L. (1983). The political economy of East-Central Africa. In D. Birmingham & P. M. Martin (Eds.), *History of Central Africa* (Vol. 2, pp. 200–250). London: Longman.

Vargas, J. H. C. (2004). Hyperconsciousness of race and its negation: The dialectic of white supremacy in Brazil. *Identities: Global Studies in Culture and Power, 11*(4), 443–470.

Vasavi, A. R. (2006). An emergent new reality? Some reflections from schools. In M. E. John, P. K. Jha, & S. C. Jodhka (Eds.), *Contested transformations: Changing economies and identities in contemporary India* (pp. 95–112). New Delhi: Tulika Books.

Vaughan, M. (1987). *The story of an African famine: Gender and famine in twentieth-century Malawi*. Cambridge, UK: Cambridge University Press.

Volman, D. (2008). Africom: From Bush to Obama. *Pambazuka News.* Retrieved from http://www.pambazuka.org/en/category/comment/52409

Wallerstein, I. (1974). *The modern world-system*. (Vols. 1, 2). New York: Academic Press.

Wallerstein, I. (1987). World-systems analysis. In A. Giddens & J. Turner (Eds.), *Social theory today*. Stanford, CA: Stanford University Press.

Wallerstein, I. (2001). Development: Lodestar, or illusion? In I. Wallerstein (Ed.), *Unthinking social science: The limits of nineteenth-century paradigms* (pp. 104–123). Philadelphia: Temple University Press.

Wallerstein, I. (2002). Porto alegre 2002. Retrieved from http://fbc.binghamton.edu

Walsh, C. E. (2002). The (re)articulation of political subjectivities and colonial difference in Ecuador: Reflections on capitalism and the geopolitics of knowledge. *Nepantla, 3*(1), 61–97.

Walsh, C. E., & León, E. (2006). Afro-Andean thought and diasporic ancestrality. In P. Banchetti-Robino & C. R. Headley (Eds.), *Shifting the geography of reason: Gender, science, religion* (pp. 211–224). Newcastle-upon-Tyne, UK: Cambridge Scholars Press.

Waring, M. (1988). *If women counted: A new feminist economics*. San Francisco: Harper & Row.

Warnken, P. F. (1999). *The development and growth of the soybean industry in Brazil*. Ames: Iowa State University Press.

Watts, M. (2004). Resource Curse? Governmentality, oil and power in the Niger Delta, Nigeria. *Geopolitics, 9*(1), 50–80.

Weis, A. (2007). *The global food economy: The battle for the future of farming*. London: Zed Books.

Weiss, B. (2004). Contentious futures: Past and present. In B. Weiss (Ed.), *Producing African futures: Ritual and reproduction in a neoliberal age* (pp. 1–20). Leiden, The Netherlands: Brill.

West, C. (1999). *The Cornel West reader*. New York: Basic Civitas Books.

Whitaker, C. (2005). *O desafio do fórum social mundial: um modo de ver*. São Paulo, Brazil: Editora Fundação Perseu Abramo.

Whitehead, L. (2007). The challenge of closely fought elections. *Journal of Democracy, 8*(1), 14–28.

Whiteside, M. (2000). Ganyu labour in Malawi and its implications for livelihood security interventions: An analysis of recent literature and implications for poverty alleviation. *Agricultural Research and Extension Network Paper, 99,* 1–10.

Williams, R. (1977). *Marxism and literature*. Oxford, UK: Oxford University Press.

Woods, M. (2006). Political articulation: The modalities of new critical politics of rural citizenship. In P. Cloke, T. Marsden, & P. Mooney (Eds.), *Handbook of rural studies* (pp. 457–471). London: Sage.

Woods, M. (2008). Social movements and rural politics. *Journal of Rural Studies, 24,* 129–137.

World Bank (2007). *World development report 2008: Agriculture for development*. Washington, DC: The World Bank.

World Wildlife Fund (WWF). (1996). *Management plan: Khunjerab National Park*. Gilgit, Pakistan: WWF.

Xavier, J. (2006). O papel decisivo das pesquisas para o conhecimento dos valores ancestrais afrodescendentes [The decisive role of the research to understand afrodescendant ancestral values]. In M. L. S. Braga, E. P. Souza, & A. F. M. Pinto (Eds.), *Dimensões da Inclusão no Ensino Médio: Mercado de trabalho, religiosidade e educação quilombola* [*Dimensions of inclusion in secondary education: The labor market, religiosity, and quilombola education*] (pp. 131–138). Brasilia: SECAD.

Yashar, D. J. (2005). *Contesting citizenship in Latin America: The rise of indigenous movements and the postliberal challenge*. New York: Cambridge University Press.

Yonetani, J. (2001). Playing base politics in a global strategic theater: Futenma relocation, the G-8 summit, and Okinawa. *Critical Asian Studies, 33*(1), 70–94.

Yoshikawa H. (2009), Dugong swimming in uncharted waters: US judicial intervention to protect Okinawa's natural monuments and halt base construction, *The Asia-Pacific Journal*. Retrieved June 4, 2009, from http://www.japanfocus.org/-Hideki-YOSHIKAWA/3044

Young, I. M. (1990). *Justice and the politics of difference*. Princeton, NJ: Princeton University Press.

Yúdice, G. (2003). *Expediency of culture: Uses of culture in the Global era*. Durham, NC: Duke University Press.

Zakaria, F. (1997). The rise of illiberal democracy. *Foreign Affairs, 76*(6), 22–43.

Zalik, A. (2009). Zones of exclusion: Offshore extraction, the contestation of space and physical displacement in the Nigerian Delta and the Mexican Gulf. *Antipode, 41*(3), 557–582.

Zancopé. G. J. (2005). *O Brasil Que Deu Certo: A saga da soja brasileira* . Curitiba, Brazil: Triade Editoria.

Zermeno, S. (1996). *La Sociedad Derrotada: El Desorden Mexicano del Fin de Siglo.* Mexico: Siglo Veintiuno Editores.

Zikode, S. (2005). The third force. Retrieved November 26, 2005, from http://www.ukzn.ac.za/ccs/default.asp?2,40,5,886

Žižek, S. (1997). Multiculturalism, or, the cultural logic of late capitalism. *New Left Review, 225,* 28–51.

CONTRIBUTORS

Nosheen Ali is a postdoctoral researcher affiliated with Stanford University. A recipient of the ACLS/Mellon Early Career Fellowship, she is working on a book illuminating how progressive struggles for political and environmental rights in Northern Pakistan provide new ways of envisioning the meaning of citizenship and development.

Alexandre Emboaba Da Costa received his PhD from the Department of Development Sociology at Cornell University. His research focuses on black cultural struggle and anti-racism in Brazil. He is an Instructor in the Department of Global Development Studies at Queen's University in Kingston, Canada.

Dia Da Costa is an assistant professor at Queens University at Kingston. Her forthcoming book is titled Development Dramas. Her current research is on a community in western India using theater to overcome the stigma of being historically labeled "born criminals" reinforced through involvement in liquor production and thieving for survival.

Kelly Dietz is an assistant professor in the Department of Politics at Ithaca College. Her research and teaching focuses on militarization, colonialism, and East Asian politics.

Andreas Hernandez is a lecturer at Ithaca College and has taught at the Elmira Maximum Security Penitentiary through Bard College's prison initiative. He directed and produced a film on the World Social Forums titled Hope Will Win Over Fear.

Rachel Bezner Kerr is an assistant professor in the Department of Geography at the University of Western Ontario. She began working with farmers in Malawi a decade ago. She loves gardening and spending time with her family. She has published in Rural Sociology, Experimental Agriculture, and Social Science and Medicine, among others.

Philip McMichael is professor of Development Sociology at Cornell University. His research focuses on the politics of globalization, agrarian struggles, and climate change. Author of Development and Social Change, he recently prepared a report for UNRISD on the food crisis, and works with La Vía Campesina and the food sovereignty movement.

Gayatri A. Menon is a postdoctoral associate at Cornell University, collaborating on a project on security and insecurity in the contemporary world. Her research focuses on urbanization and the politics of homelessness, and is inspired by the struggles of the alliance of SPARC, Mahila Milan, and NSDF and other activist organizations with whom she is affiliated.

Karuna Morarji is a PhD candidate in the Department of Development Sociology at Cornell University. She is on the faculty of the Gap Year College, an alternative learning space in India.

Raj Patel is a visiting scholar at the UC Berkeley Center for African Studies and an honorary research fellow at the University of KwaZulu-Natal's School of Development Studies. He has degrees from Oxford University, the London School of Economics, and Cornell University, and continues to work with shackdwellers in South Africa. He is the author of *Stuffed and Starved: The Hidden Battle for the World Food System* and *The Value of Nothing*.

Emelie Kaye Peine earned her PhD in development sociology from Cornell University in 2009. She is currently assistant professor of international political economy at the University of Puget Sound in Tacoma, Washington where she teaches classes on the political economy of food and hunger.

Alicia Swords is assistant professor of sociology at Ithaca College and a member of the Tompkins County Workers Center and the Poverty Initiative. In teaching and research, she draws on and contributes to learning among social and economic justice movements. She has published in *Latin American Perspectives*, and has coauthored a book with Ron Mize, *Mexican Labor for North American Consumptions: From Braceros to NAFTA, 1992–2009*.

Hannah Wittman is assistant professor of sociology and Latin American studies at Simon Fraser University in Vancouver, BC. She has worked for many years with alternative peasant and small farmer movements in Paraguay, Brazil, Guatamala, and British Columbia, and recently co-edited *Food Sovereignty: International Perspectives on Theory and Practice* with Annette Desmarais and Nettie Wiebe.

Anna Zalik is an assistant professor in the Faculty of Environmental Studies at York University where she teaches global enviornmental politics and critical development studies. She has conducted extensive field research in Nigeria and Mexico, on the politics of oil, including social justice struggles and electoral in particular during Nigeria's 2003 and 20007 election periods and the lead-up to the 2006 election in Mexico.

INDEX